我的心灵藏书馆

The Heart Is a Lonely Hunter
心是孤独的猎手

著：［美］卡森·麦卡勒斯
Carson McCullers
丛书主编：彭萍
丛书副主编：（按姓氏拼音排序）
沈忆文 吴樯 徐阳 周玮
注释：张美珍

中国宇航出版社
·北京·

图书在版编目（CIP）数据

心是孤独的猎手 = The Heart Is a Lonely Hunter : 汉文、英文 / (美) 卡森·麦卡勒斯 (Carson McCullers) 著 ; 张美珍注释. -- 北京 : 中国宇航出版社, 2025. 1

（我的心灵藏书馆 / 彭萍主编）

ISBN 978-7-5159-2216-4

Ⅰ. ①心… Ⅱ. ①卡… ②张… Ⅲ. ①英语—语言读物②长篇小说—美国—现代 Ⅳ. ①H319.4：I

中国国家版本馆CIP数据核字（2023）第075926号

策划编辑	陈　伟	装帧设计	李彦生
责任编辑	冯佳佳　张芸哲	责任校对	刘　杰

出　版 发　行	中国宇航出版社		
社　址	北京市阜成路8号 （010）68768548	邮　编	100830
网　址	www.caphbook.com		
经　销	新华书店		
发行部	（010）68767386 （010）68767382		（010）68371900 （010）88100613（传真）
零售店	读者服务部		（010）68371105
承　印	北京中科印刷有限公司		
版　次	2025年1月第1版		2025年1月第1次印刷
规　格	880×1230	开　本	1/32
印　张	14	字　数	436千字
书　号	ISBN 978-7-5159-2216-4		
定　价	59.80元		

本书如有印装质量问题，可与发行部联系调换

丛书总序一

那是一个春寒料峭的日子，中国宇航出版社的策划编辑战颖找到我，要我负责主编一套世界经典名著的导读和注释丛书，想请我邀北外的一些老师加入到这一工作中来。我看了她给我的书单后，心中不由地一动，多么熟悉的书名啊，这些经典名著的英文版和中文版是伴我度过大学时期的重要精神食粮之一。因为在我的大学时代，校园里不像现在这样充斥着浮躁的气氛，而是一种宁静的读书氛围，我们读古诗词、现代抒情诗、三毛的散文、席慕蓉的散文和诗歌、罗兰的小品文等，而我们这些英语专业的学生当然还要阅读英文经典名著，不是老师布置的作业，而是主动为之。时至今日，这些经典中的主人公形象依然留在自己的脑海中，这些经典中的故事情节依然让人心潮澎湃。所以，我禁不住想答应下来。可是，经验告诉我，为英语读物作注释，尤其是为英文原版小说作注释，看起来或听起来是一件简单的事情，而真正做起来却是耗时、费力的工作，因为文学著作的注释不是简单的单词注释，还有很多地名、人名、历史事件、文化典故等诸多百科全书式的东西要为读者解释出来。作长篇巨著的注释更是很多人望而却步的事情，所以对能否邀请到一些同事从事这一工作我有些不敢确定。虽然我本人愿意为经典的传播、为读者的阅读提供自己的一点见解和帮助，可个人的力量毕竟是有限的。因此，当时我犹豫了，但对经典名著的情结又让我对这一工作难以割舍。于是，我跟战颖编辑说，我先询问一下看有多少人愿意去做这件事。让我欣慰的是，我找到了几个如我一样热爱文学的同事，他（她）们表示愿意承担这样的工作。于是，“我的心灵藏书馆”丛书的导读和注释工作从此拉开序幕。而现在，就在我写这篇总序的时候，北京正由深秋迈向寒冬，外面刚刚下过一场秋雨，天还是阴阴的，冷冷的，可面对完成的一本本书稿，我心里依然是春天般的温暖。

文学是人性和社会的一面镜子，又是滋养人心灵的沃土，优秀的文学作品亦给人以思想的启迪和审美的愉悦。无论哪个年代，阅读文学的人都不会孤独，不会空虚。具体说来，文学首先具有审美价值。阅读一部文学作品，读者首先是通过各种风格的语言、曲折的情节和人物的艺术形象等获得一种审美体验。读者可以融自己的想象于阅读过程当中，从而使自己的体验得到美的升华。其次，文学具有社会现实价值。任何文学作品的创作都离不开其所在的时代和社会，是时代和社会现实的重要体现。通过阅读文学作品，读者从其中的人物性格、命运及家庭、社会环境的发展脉络可以窥见人的本质和社会现实。第三，文学具有文化意义。通过阅读经典名著，可以领略到作品透射的文化背景，从而丰富历史、地理、宗教、风俗等百科全书式的知识。尤其是一些经典名著，无论从上述哪个方面讲，都是人类不可或缺的精神食粮。

中国宇航出版社之所以选择《简·爱》《呼啸山庄》《飘》《傲慢与偏见》《老人与海》《欧·亨利短篇小说精选》《鲁滨逊漂流记》《瓦尔登湖》《理智与情感》《了不起的盖茨比》等作为“我的心灵藏书馆”系列的第一批入选书目，是基于这些经典不朽的主题和魅力。可以说，以上名著是对世界各国读者影响最为深远和最为广泛的经典作品，其形象塑造、语言艺术、情节设计、思想意义等从著作诞生那时起至今日，已经影响和启迪了一代又一代的读者，这些著作的情节和人物塑造在中国读者群中享有很高的赞誉，给中国读者留下了深刻的印象。《简·爱》通过简·爱与罗切斯特的爱情故事，塑造了简·爱这样一个追求个性自由、主张男女平等的独立女性形象；《呼啸山庄》使用现实主义、浪漫主义、象征主义等表现手法讲述了希刺克厉夫和凯瑟琳的真挚而最终走向悲剧的爱情故事，塑造出希刺克厉夫这样一位由爱生恨、具有极度反叛精神的人物形象；《飘》以美国南北战争前后的南方佐治亚州为背景，以一个种植园主的女儿郝思嘉为核心人物，通过几个家族的兴衰变化反映了美国南方各州在这一重要历史时期的社会现实；《傲慢与偏见》通过伊丽莎白和达西的故事以及其他几个人的爱情故事，揭示出傲慢与偏见是生活中常见的弱点，只有加深了解，才能有更客观的认识，以及婚姻应以爱情为基础这样看似平凡却又非常深刻的道理；《老人与海》用简约的风格塑造出一个真正的硬汉形象，告诉人们“人可以被毁灭，但不能被打败”的人生哲学；欧·亨利的短篇小说亦庄亦谐，很多故事从小处着眼，却塑造出不同阶层的人物形象，尤其是下层人民的形象，读来不免发人深思；《鲁滨逊漂流记》通过写实的手法塑造出鲁滨逊这样一位理想的资产阶级英雄形象；《瓦尔登湖》用幽默、睿智、优美的语言揭示出深刻的人生和社会哲理；《理智与情感》通过两位女主角的婚事波折揭示了当时英国社会中以婚配作为女子寻求经济保障和提高社会地位，却不重视女子情感和权利的陋习；《了不起的盖茨比》描写了主人公盖茨比与黛西的爱情悲剧，揭示了“美国梦”的破灭。当然，这些经典名著的意义不是一两句话就能概括出来的，只有真正走进去，沉浸其中，才能真正感受到文学的魅力。

通过阅读英语名著学英语一直以来被公认为行之有效的学习方法，也是经过了数代人的实践得出来的真理。因为名著的语言一般比较规范和地道，即人们经常说的“原汁原味的英语”。因此，阅读这些著作对形成英语的语感大有裨益。同时，阅读名著可以扩大词汇量，丰富百科知识，有助于增进对英语国家的了解。而本套丛书可谓“精华中的精华”，阅读这些书籍，读者一方面会沉浸于文学的殿堂中，感受书中的情节美、人物形象塑造美以及语言艺术美，提高文学的素养，同时又不知不觉浸染在“原汁原味”的英语当中，提高英语的表达能力，丰富英语文化知识。当然，对有些读者来说，阅读名著很多时候会存在一定的难度，比如遇到一些词汇、句法或背景知识等障碍，这时读者不免会产生一种“受挫感”。而本套丛书的注释正是为了帮助读者克服这样的“受挫感”，使读者不必阅读简易读物就能直接进入到原著气势恢宏的“殿堂”当中，定会愉快地将文学欣赏与英语学习有效地结合在一起。

本套丛书的原文大部分参考美国企鹅出版集团出版的“企鹅经典丛书”（Penguin Classics）和英国华兹华斯出版公司出版的世界名著系列（Wordsworth Classics）两种版本进行校对。本套导读与注释丛书的目的是想帮助读者更好地阅读和理解原版英文名著。具体说来，一方面可以使读者在阅读原著的过程中提高自己的英文语言水平，另一方面可以拉近读者与英文原著的距离，使读者更好地体会英文原著所传达出的各种信息，从而更好地欣赏原著。注释的原则和内容如下：（1）生词。本套丛书注释的单词基本为大学英语四级以上的词汇，同时各位注释作者也会根据自己的教学经验适当地进行取舍，但总体原则是注释的单词“宜多不宜少”。同时为一些常用单词提供一个短语或句子做例子，并给出了这个短语或句子的翻译，从而更好地说明单词的用法。考虑到读者第二次遇到一个生词后，可能会忘记前面已有的注释，所以一些单词有重复注释的现象。(2) 短语。英语短语的掌握对应用这门语言起着非常重要的作用，因此本套丛书的注释中没有忽视短语的注释，有些短语是读者熟悉的，有些是不熟悉的，读者通过这些短语的注释能够做到“温故知新”。重要和常见的短语后面一般均提供例句及其翻译，便于读者进一步巩固和学习这些短语的用法。(3) 专有名词。由于丛书所包含的著作涉及不同国家（尤其是英美国家）的不同历史时期和不同地点，因此注释也考虑到了其中的地名、人名、历史事件名等（个别虚构的地名和人名除外），对这些名称一般提供简短的说明。可以说，这一部分对丰富读者的地理和历史知识很有帮助，同时能帮助他们更好地把握著作的内容和写作背景。(4) 文化知识。这部分主要包括成语典故、宗教知识、引用等，对这些文化知识一般先注明其来源，然后提供简短的说明，从而使读者在阅读名著的过程中对英语的成语典故、宗教知识、名言警句等有一定的了解。(5) 复杂句。本套丛书中的著作有的风格简约，句式比较简单，有的则包含很多长句或复杂句。注释者根据自己的经验，对一些可能会让读者费解的句子首先稍作分析，然后提供译文。为有效利用已有的名著翻译成果，这些长句的译文大多数参考了现成的权威译文，标明出处；有些译文由注释者进行了改动，以使其更加忠实和通顺。(6) 黑人英语和非标准英语。名著中必然会出现一些对话，为了刻画人物的形象，一些作者会根据人物的身份或阶层使用非标准英语或黑人英语。注释中原则上提供这些非标准英语或黑人英语的标准表达法，个别地方给出了中文。除以上几点外，注释中还对一些精彩句和话语的隐含意义进行了注释，提供了汉语译文，同时还有个别地方注释了与上下文的联系。

值得一提的是，本套丛书导读和注释的团队成员均来自北京外国语大学，是教学经验极其丰富的一线骨干教师，长期从事英语精读、泛读（其中很重要的一部分就是指导学生阅读英语名著）、文学、翻译、语言学等教学和研究工作，均有着深厚的文学和语言功底。可以说，团队的每个成员都是读着这些以及更多英语名著成长的过来人，而且不少还都在继续研读这些经典著作。正如我在开篇所说，为名著作导读和注释是一件听起来容易、做起来相当耗神和耗时的工作，但是各位同仁本着对文学的热忱和对读者负责的态度，按预期的速度高质量地完成了这项工作，在此对他（她）们谨致谢意！

在本套丛书完稿之际，北京外国语大学陈德彰教授欣然提笔，为本套丛书撰写了寄语，这是对我们这个团队莫大的鼓励。同时，感谢中国宇航出版社为我们提供了这样一个为读者服务的机会，感谢策划编辑战颖女士提供的各项协助工作！

希望本套丛书提供的导读和注释能给广大的英语爱好者、英语学习者、英语文学爱好者和英语文学学习者提供一定的帮助，使读者朋友更轻松、更有信心地穿越时空，与经典名著进行心灵的对话和沟通。当然，由于时间紧迫，任务繁重，导读和注释中难免出现纰漏或疏忽之处，敬请广大读者予以谅解，并不吝赐教！

彭萍
2010年深秋
于北京海淀世纪城平心斋

丛书总序二

“我的心灵藏书馆”导读和注释丛书第一批10本面世以来，受到了读者的热烈欢迎。读者普遍反映，这套丛书不仅汇集了真正的经典名著，更重要的是降低了中国学生阅读国外原版名著的门槛。每当阅读到困惑之处时，这个版本都给出了恰到好处的注释，就好像一个耐心的老师随时等待亲爱的读者提出疑问并作出回答。而且，整套丛书无论是封面设计还是装帧工艺都堪称一流。可以说，本套丛书不仅具有帮助读者学习英语、提高文学修养的实用价值，还具有特别的文学收藏价值。在这个人人谈论和阅读电子书的时代，“我的心灵藏书馆”是一套真正可以带给读者阅读享受的好书，是世界名著纸本书的经典呈现，是值得收藏的珍贵版本。每当在网络上或者书店中看到、听到读者对该套丛书的青睐与好评，我们这一导读和注释团队就会感到读者的巨大热情与信任。为了让广大读者能走进更多的名著，熟悉更多的作品，后续多部英文经典名著经过10余名老师多年的努力，已陆续出版。希望这些英语经典名著及其导读和注释能一如既往地给予读者阅读上的愉悦和学习上的帮助。

此刻，我审阅着一本本的书稿，回忆着这些经典名著的情节，一个个鲜活的人物形象在我的脑海中逐渐清晰起来，向我展示着不同时代、不同背景下的人性及社会生活。优美的语言，错综复杂的故事情节，注释者细致的注释和讲解，使我在心中油然升起一种美的享受，犹如窗外的秋叶、湛蓝的天空和午后的暖阳，让我的心变得越来越温暖……

这批丛书包括《名利场》《莎士比亚故事集》《一九八四》《查泰莱夫人的情人》《小妇人》《马克·吐温短篇小说精选》《杰克·伦敦

小说精选》《嘉莉妹妹》《红字》《泰戈尔作品集》《茶花女》《苔丝》《格列佛游记》《永别了，武器》《夜色温柔》《哈姆雷特》《奥赛罗》《李尔王》《麦克白》《威尼斯商人》《仲夏夜之梦》《第十二夜》等。这些著作都是脍炙人口的作品，在世界文学中占据着重要地位。其主题分别可以概述如下：《名利场》通过蓓基·夏泼的钻营史和爱米丽亚与乔治的罗曼史，真实地描绘了1810—1820年摄政王时期，英国上流社会没落贵族和资产阶级暴发户等各色人物的丑恶嘴脸及弱肉强食、尔虞我诈的人际关系。《莎士比亚故事集》是英国散文家查尔斯·兰姆和姐姐玛丽·安妮·兰姆两人用叙事体散文编写的20个莎士比亚戏剧故事，希望读者通过这20个故事对原著产生兴趣，从而走进莎士比亚的戏剧世界，领略其中独一无二的丰富宝藏。《一九八四》通过对大洋国一名英格兰社会主义党的普通外围党员温斯顿·史密斯个人生活的细致入微、栩栩如生的刻画，向世人展示了一个令人感到窒息和恐怖、以追逐权力为最终目标的假想未来社会的景象。《查泰莱夫人的情人》讲述了贵族阶级的康斯坦斯·查泰莱夫人和在她丈夫领地上的守林员麦勒斯之间的爱情故事，反映出劳伦斯对阶级、人性和情感关系的思考。《小妇人》以美国南北战争期间马奇一家及其四姐妹的生活为描写对象，讲述了她们对自强自立精神的追求、对于家庭的眷顾和对爱情的忠诚。《马克·吐温短篇小说精选》汇集了美国讽刺小说家马克·吐温优秀的短篇小说，读者可以从作品轻松嬉笑的外表下，窥见作者对社会和人性的严肃批判。《杰克·伦敦小说精选》描述了人与自然之间的严酷搏斗，以及人与人之间错综复杂的社会关系，体现了杰克·伦敦对达尔文的“适者生存”，以及斯宾塞的社会达尔文主义的推崇。《嘉莉妹妹》通过农村姑娘嘉莉在大城市的经历，揭露了20世纪初美国人狂热追求美国之梦的悲剧事实，说明在以金钱为中心的资本主义社会里人们不可能有真正的幸福。《红字》一书以17世纪中叶的新英格兰为背景，通过对三个主要人物的思想矛盾和生活悲剧的描写，揭示了人性、社会、宗教压迫等各方面的图景。《泰戈尔作品集》共包括六个诗集：《飞鸟集》《新月集》《园丁集》《采果集》《吉檀迦利》和《流萤集》。这些诗集或讴歌灵魂，或赞颂生命，或描叙爱情，或充满宗教和哲学的精神，或表达赤子之情，其文字清澈隽永，描写细腻深刻，意象奇崛美妙，对20世纪世界文坛产生过深远而广泛的影响。《茶花女》通过阿尔芒和玛格丽特的爱情故事，使读者看到了浪漫主义的背后是现实的冷酷无情。《苔丝》通过农村姑娘苔丝曲折多变的命运和连连受挫的爱情，揭露了资产阶级虚伪的社会道德，强烈谴责了19世纪末资本入侵农村给农民带来的毁灭性打击。《格列佛游记》假托主人公格列佛医生自述他数次航海遇险，漂流到小人国、大人国、飞岛国和慧骃国几个童话式国家的遭遇和见闻，全面讽刺、揶揄了英国的社会现实。《永别了，武器》通过一个美国青年和一个英国女护士在一战中的恋爱悲剧，真实地描绘了战争的残酷和罪恶，以及战争给人造成的难以愈合的心理创伤。《夜色温柔》描写的是一位出身寒微但才华出众的青年对富有梦幻色彩的理想的追求，但他最终遭到失败，从而变得颓废消沉，暗示了“美国梦”的破灭。《哈姆雷特》的主要情节是：叔叔克劳狄斯谋害了哈姆雷特的父亲，篡取了王位，并娶了国王的遗孀乔特鲁德，而哈姆雷特王子因此为父王向克劳狄斯复仇。《奥赛罗》的主要故事情节是：威尼斯的勇将奥赛罗与元老的女儿苔丝狄梦娜相爱，在婚事受阻的情况下两人只好私下成婚，奥赛罗手下阴险的旗官伊阿古一心想除掉奥赛罗，便向元老告密，却不料促成了两人的婚事，但伊阿古又挑拨说另一名副将凯西奥与苔丝狄梦娜关系不同寻常，并伪造了所谓定情信物等，这让奥赛罗信以为真，在愤怒中掐死了自己的妻子，可后来他得知真相，便悔恨自刎，倒在了苔丝狄梦娜身边。《李尔王》讲述了年事已高的国王李尔王退位后，被大女儿和二女儿赶到荒郊野外，成为法兰西皇后的三女儿率军救父，却被杀死，李尔王伤心地死在她身旁。《麦克白》的主要情节是：麦克白在夫人的怂恿下谋杀国王邓肯之后做了国王，为掩人耳目和防止他人夺位，他又杀害了邓肯的侍卫以及有关的一些人物，可是恐惧和猜疑使麦克白心里越来越有鬼，也越来越冷酷，这时麦克白夫人因精神失常而自杀。在众叛亲离的情况下，麦克白面对邓肯之子和他请来的英格兰援军的围攻，落得被杀头的下场。在《威尼斯商人》中，威尼斯商人安东尼奥为朋友巴萨尼奥的婚事凑钱，便向犹太高利贷者夏洛克借钱，于是二人之间围绕割一磅肉的诉讼产生冲突，最后由巴萨尼奥的未婚夫鲍西亚女扮男装英明地判决了这一诉讼案件，夏洛克害人不成反而失去了财产，还被迫改变宗教信仰。《仲夏夜之梦》的故事发生在仲夏夜晚，两对恋人为了对抗一道荒谬无比的律法而出逃，当他们逃往林子后，精灵的介入使彼此爱的对象混淆，但一阵混乱之后，众人终于恢复理智与和谐。《第十二夜》中，伊利里亚公爵奥西诺向奥丽维娅小姐求爱屡遭拒绝，一对孪生兄妹航海到伊利里亚时在附近海上遇难，妹妹薇奥拉改扮男装，到奥西诺公爵家中做侍童，并充当了代奥西诺向奥丽维娅小姐求爱的使者，奥丽维娅对女扮男装的薇奥拉一见钟情，而薇奥拉却偷偷爱上了公爵。后来，奥丽维娅碰巧遇上薇奥拉的孪生兄长西巴斯辛，两人将错就错地结为夫妇，而公爵和薇奥拉也终成眷属。《罗密欧与朱丽叶》的故事对我国很多读者来说都是非常熟悉的，讲述的是罗密欧与朱丽叶因家庭矛盾而遭遇的爱情悲剧，最后双方殉情而死。《无事生非》的主要故事情节是：克劳狄奥向希罗求婚，得到希罗父亲的认可，但在婚礼上，阿拉贡亲王的庶弟约翰由于嫉妒和无聊捏造谗言，致使克劳狄奥上当受骗，以为希罗是不贞洁的女子而当面侮辱希罗，差点致希罗于死地。希罗的堂姐贝特丽丝想出计谋，让希罗假死然后查出真相，后来骗局被揭穿，克劳狄奥与希罗重归于好。

以上经典名著的导读和注释一如从前，其主要目的就在于帮助读者更好地阅读和理解英文原版名著。同时，我们在第一批书重印、再版时又进行过认真审读，也经常关注网络上读者对这批书的评论。在编写后续书时，将已获得的实践经验和读者的宝贵意见融入编写过程，达到更好服务读者的效果。时刻想着读者，让广大英语文学爱好者能够从我们的注释版名著读物中真正学到实用的知识，轻松读懂大部头文学佳作，是我们衷心的希望。

本次导读和注释的团队成员均来自北京外国语大学，在第一批丛书导读和注释队伍的基础上增加了四名教师，和原有的队伍一样，她们都是北外的骨干教师，有着极其丰富的教学经验，长期从事英语精读、泛读（其中很重要的一部分就是指导学生阅读英语名著）、文学、翻译、语言学等教学和研究工作。可以说，团队的每个成员都是读着这些著作以及更多英语名著成长的过来人，而且不少还都在继续研读这些经典著作。当然，为名著做导读和注释是一件听起来容易、做起来相当耗神和耗时的工作，但是各位同仁本着对文学的热忱和对读者负责的态度，按预期的速度高质量地完成了这项工作，在此本人对他们谨致谢意！

希望本套丛书提供的导读和注释能一如既往地为广大的英语爱好者、英语学习者、英语文学爱好者和英语文学学习者提供一定的帮助，使读者朋友更轻松、更有信心地穿越时空，与经典名著进行心灵的对话和沟通。当然，由于时间紧迫，任务繁重，导读和注释中难免出现纰漏或疏忽之处，敬请广大读者予以谅解，并不吝赐教！

彭萍

2024 年仲秋

于北京海淀世纪城平心斋

导 读

卡森·麦卡勒斯（Carson McCullers，1917—1967），20世纪北美最重要的作家之一。1940年，麦卡勒斯第一部长篇小说《心是孤独的猎手》出版，并迅速轰动美国文坛。卡森·麦卡勒斯的作品多以孤独为主题，这一主题始终贯穿在她的所有作品中，其代表作品有长篇小说《心是孤独的猎手》《黄金眼睛的映像》和短篇小说集《伤心咖啡馆之歌》等。

《心是孤独的猎手》讲述了一个在美国南方小镇发生的故事。

镇上有两个哑巴，辛格和安东纳普勒斯，他们一起生活了10年。直到辛格32岁时，安东纳普勒斯生病了，而这场病使安东纳普勒斯性情大变，成了一个暴躁的疯子。为了处理他鲁莽行事闯下的麻烦，辛格几乎花光了自己的所有积蓄。就在这时，安东纳普勒斯被表哥强制送进了疯人院。自此，辛格开始了独居生活，他无法忍受朋友的离开，于是搬了新家，同时认识了一群新的朋友，展开了在这个小镇上与另外四个主人公的故事。

咖啡店老板比夫总是通宵开店，只为了招待那些孤独的客人，也正因此，咖啡店这个小镇的一角便能映射整个小镇乃至社会的形态。比夫总是沉默地看着店里来往的人们，偶尔记起年幼时母亲作为支柱的存在。这仿佛是一种俄狄浦斯情结，事实上并非如此，他只是寂寞了。妻子生前，夫妻二人诸多不和，可是等到妻子突发急病死去了，却又有了念想，将妻子用剩下的花露水洒在肩头，定期使用妻子没用完的洗发水。

少女米克是个有趣的女孩，虽然才13岁，但个头足足有一米七高。她渴望成为一名音乐家，渴望拥有一架钢琴，却因为家庭境遇困顿无法实现。米克与父亲无法达成有效的沟通，姐妹们也嘲笑她假小子的装扮，她觉得自己始终孤独。就在这时，辛格成了她家的租客，她找到了懂得聆听她的“知音”。

激进工人杰克，热衷于政治话题，比如他觉得社会应该按劳分配。因此他一直在呼吁人们要团结起来对抗资本家，以获得更高的报酬，最好能达到共产主义。然而他前卫的观点非但无人响应，反而被别人称作“傻子”，只能借酒消愁。

黑人医生科普兰，则痛心于黑人群体的麻木与懒惰，致力于改变黑人的精神状态，从而提高黑人群体的地位。他不讲耶稣却讲马克思，到处宣扬平等与自由。从观点来说黑人医生与工人杰克有些相似，但两人的交谈却不欢而散，唯一相同的就是科普兰也没有得到众人的认同。

这四人原本生活在各自的世界中，辛格的到来打破了他们在这个小镇看似平淡的生活状态。他们对着辛格倾诉心中的秘密。而辛格只是微笑着点头，耐心地注视，这一切在四个人眼中却像一个先知一样充满了智慧与神圣。

尽管辛格的周围尽是热闹，可没有了安东纳普勒斯依旧是孤独的，于是他总会抽空去看望老友。安东纳普勒斯的身体越来越差，当辛格第三次去看望时，却得到了安东纳普勒斯已经去世的消息。听到这个消息，辛格的精神支柱彻底崩塌，他排解孤独的门永远地关闭了。最后，绝望的辛格选择饮弹自杀，永远告别了孤独。

这个时候，小镇上四个孤独人的心灵寄托也终结了，他们每个人在葬礼上表现着不同的情状：米克痛哭；杰克愤怒，他不明白辛格为什么要寻死；比夫沉默，他在几天之前想起这个被当成上帝的哑巴的真实情况——一年前，他是胖哑巴安东纳普勒斯影子一般的存在；科普兰低声啜泣。但是，辛格的死对他人产生的影响并不像安东纳普勒斯的死那般沉重。一个月之后，米克去上班了，她还是按点吃饭，按点睡觉；杰克离开小镇，却发誓坚决不离开南方；科普兰终于随着家人离开旧房子，回到了乡下农庄；而老比夫依旧守着他的咖啡厅，等待并观察着形形色色的客人。平淡的日子又继续了。

本书讲述了辛格与安东纳普勒斯的故事以及辛格眼中看到的小镇四人。从贯穿全书的字眼“孤独”(lonely)来说，其主题是一元的；同时从辛格身边的线索向外探索，其主题又是多元的。

在“孤独”主题中，作者利用平行叙事技巧，通过安东纳普勒斯看辛格的孤独，通过辛格的眼睛看到小镇上四个人的孤独，又通过这四个人的眼睛看所有的人。每个人之间都有些许关系，但每个人之间从未互相真正理解，就像一条条平行线。当四名角色都带着孤独与渴望被理解的心向辛格倾诉时，殊不知辛格的心所渴望靠近的是胖哑巴安东纳普勒斯。而同时，安东纳普勒斯也不是辛格的猎物。所有人都以为辛格能听懂他们的语言，辛格则一直以为安东纳普勒斯是唯一理解他的人，而事实上，只有安东纳普勒斯这个疯子是真正自由且不依赖他人的理解而生存的，没有人真正懂谁。

就在工人杰克与黑人医生大谈按劳分配和马克思主义时，欧洲正处于二战的水深火热之中，美国南部的小镇正如背后有力的推手，将每个人的人生推入绝境。通过四个角色的倾诉，作者卡森看到南方的变化，看到民权运动的到来，看到工人运动的起伏，也看到了法西斯的兴亡盛衰。

从语言来看，作者的语言是平实简洁的，正如她写孤独时直指人类心灵一般，没有太多费解的表达，却让人看完总能记得主人公们倾诉时的神情：比夫的忧郁，米克的渴望，杰克的愤慨以及科普兰的痛心。从表现手法来看，作者对小说叙事手法的运用是那么自然娴熟，多样化的手法让读者沉浸在故事中，放下书籍时久久难忘；平行叙事的手法让读者看到了多元化的世界和当时社会的发展形态；倾诉视角又让读者对前文存在的困惑恍然大悟，如辛格对好友安东纳普勒斯说的话："安东纳普勒斯，"辛格飞快地打着手势，"那个西班牙人说着我听不懂的语言，我甚至不能理解人的舌头如何能弯曲成那样的形状。"那个做商贩的西班牙人一直以为辛格是他在巴塞罗那的友人。至此，读者确定，辛格并不像众人眼中那样像上帝一般存在，读懂所有人的倾诉；更有甚者，作者还原人物角色，为表现美国南方小镇黑人英语的特点，大量的表达偏差和单词错误拼写，也是一种特别的表现手法，正是有了受教育程度不够的语言表达，才更进一步表现黑人白人不平等问题导致的社会分化。

合上书页，回想本书的五位主人公，他们都有着独立于作者之外的自我意识，而正是通过作品中人物之间的平等对话，小说的主题得到了充分的呈现与升华。米克认为，即使是个聋哑人，辛格也能理解她所说的话。她向辛格倾诉自己的感受，并且希望得到辛格一个表情或一个微笑的回应，这样的孤独体验在平等的对话中也被作者升华和释放，小说本身的结构和空间也有了多元的特点，其主题也得到了更好的升华：社会中每个人都想逃离困境，摆脱一切孤独的体验，但就在每个人挣扎的过程中，总有一种无形的力量在更大的空间里注视自己，人类无处可逃，只能陷入无尽的轮回中；而只有真正懂得孤独所在，接受了孤独本身，才能超然物外，在孤独中寻找自由。

《心是孤独的猎手》是麦卡勒斯一举成名、最具震撼力的代表作，首次出版于1940年，美国现代文库“20世纪百佳英文小说”位列第17位，被译为多种文字在世界范围内流传。目前，国内关于该作品的中文译本不多，主要包括以下几个版本：其中一个译本是由陈笑黎翻译，并由上海三联书店于2005年出版；还有一个译本是上海译文出版社于2018年出版的宋玲译本；2018年人民文学出版社出版了由秦传安翻译的版本，同年译林出版社出版了王金娥的译本。本书注释中的译文主要参考了译林出版社出版的王金娥译本。

本书在对词语进行注释时，主要给出了该词在上下文中的意思，一些重要短语和词语还给出了例句。由于读者的英文水平各不相同，因此对注释的要求也不尽相同。在注释本书时，以大学英语四级的水平为参考，主要对超过大学英语四级水平的词汇进行注释，同时兼顾一些不太常用的词语。由于时间和经验有限，尽管注释者尽了很大的努力，但在翻译和注释中难免会出现一些纰漏或错误，敬请读者批评指正。

张美珍

Contents

目录

Part Three

Part One

1

IN THE Town there were two mutes[①], and they were always together. Early every morning they would come out from the house where they lived and walk arm in arm down the street to work.[②] The two friends were very different. The one who always steered the way was an obese and dreamy Greek.[③] In the summer he would come out wearing a yellow or green polo shirt stuffed[④] sloppily[⑤] into his trousers in front and hanging loose behind. When it was colder he wore over this a shapeless[⑥] gray sweater. His face was round and oily, with half-closed eyelids and lips that curved in a gentle, stupid smile.[⑦] The other mute was tall. His eyes had a quick, intelligent expression. He was always immaculate[⑧] and very soberly[⑨] dressed.

Every morning the two friends walked silently together until they reached the main street of the town. Then when they came to a certain fruit and candy store they paused for a moment on the

---

① mute：哑巴

② 参考译文：每天一大早，他俩便离开住处，手挽手地走过大街去上班。（王金娥译，本书译文如无特别说明，均引自王金娥译本。）本句为 where 引导的定语从句，修饰 house。

③ 参考译文：每次领路的那个是希腊人，大腹便便，总是神情恍惚。本句用定语从句 who always steered the way 修饰主语 the one。（steer the way：带路，领路，例：He steered the way and showed us around his garden. 他领路带我们参观他的花园。dreamy：恍惚的。）

④ stuffed：塞满的

⑤ sloppily：凌乱地

⑥ shapeless：不成形的，不像样的

⑦ 参考译文：他的脸圆圆的，泛着油光，眼睛半闭着，唇边带着一丝温和而又傻气的笑容。本句 with 作伴随状语用于补充说明希腊人的形态特征。

⑧ immaculate：特别整洁的

⑨ soberly：朴素地

sidewalk outside. The Greek, Spiros Antonapoulos, worked for his cousin, who owned this fruit store. His job was to make candies and sweets, uncrate① the fruits, and to keep the place clean. The thin mute, John Singer, nearly always put his hand on his friend's arm and looked for a second into his face before leaving him. Then after this goodbye Singer crossed the street and walked on alone to the jewelry store where he worked as a silverware engraver②.

In the late afternoon the friends would meet again. Singer came back to the fruit store and waited until Antonapoulos was ready to go home. The Greek would be lazily unpacking a case of peaches or melons, or perhaps looking at the funny paper in the kitchen behind the store where he cooked. Before their departure Antonapoulos always opened a paper sack③ he kept hidden during the day on one of the kitchen shelves. Inside were stored various bits of food he had collected—a piece of fruit, samples of candy, or the butt-end of a liverwurst④. Usually before leaving Antonapoulos waddled gently to the glassed case in the front of the store where some meats and cheeses were kept.⑤ He glided⑥ open the back of the case and his fat hand groped⑦ lovingly for some particular dainty⑧ inside which he had wanted. Sometimes his cousin who owned the place did not see him. But if he noticed he stared at his cousin with a warning in his tight, pale face. Sadly Antonapoulos would shuffle⑨ the morsel⑩ from one corner of the case to the other. During these times Singer stood very straight with his hands in his pockets and looked in another

---

① uncrate：打开……的包装

② engraver：雕刻师

③ paper sack：纸袋

④ liverwurst：肝泥香肠

⑤ 参考译文：通常在离开之前，安东纳普勒斯会摇摇摆摆、慢慢悠悠地走到商店前的玻璃柜边上，那里面装着肉和奶酪。（waddle：蹒跚行走，摇摆地走，也可作名词使用，意为“摇摆的步伐，蹒跚的步态”。）

⑥ glide：滑移

⑦ grope：摸索，探索

⑧ dainty：美味

⑨ shuffle：把……变换位置

⑩ morsel：少量，一块（食物），例：a delicious morsel of food 一点可口的食物。

direction[1]. He did not like to watch this little scene between the two Greeks. For, excepting drinking and a certain solitary[2] secret pleasure, Antonapoulos loved to eat more than anything else in the world.

In the dusk[3] the two mutes walked slowly home together. At home Singer was always talking to Antonapoulos. His hands shaped the words in a swift series of designs.[4] His face was eager and his gray-green eyes sparkled[5] brightly. With his thin, strong hands he told Antonapoulos all that had happened during the day.

Antonapoulos sat back lazily and looked at Singer. It was seldom that he ever moved his hands to speak at all—and then it was to say that he wanted to eat or to sleep or to drink.[6] These three things he always said with the same vague, fumbling[7] signs. At night, if he were not too drunk, he would kneel down before his bed and pray a while. Then his plump[8] hands shaped the words 'Holy Jesus,' or 'God,' or 'Darling Mary. 'These were the only words Antonapoulos ever said. Singer never knew just how much his friend understood of all the things he told him. But it did not matter.

They shared the upstairs of a small house near the business section of the town. There were two rooms. On the oil stove[9] in the kitchen Antonapoulos cooked all of their meals. There were straight, plain kitchen chairs for Singer and an overstuffed[10] sofa for Antonapoulos. The bedroom was furnished mainly with[11] a large double bed covered

---

① in another direction：朝着另一个方向。in...direction：朝着……方向。

② solitary：独自完成的

③ dusk：黄昏；暮色

④ 参考译文：他的两只手用一系列快速手势表达着想说的词。此处 in 介宾短语作方式状语。(designs：此处应为 signs，指手势。)

⑤ sparkled：闪耀的，作后置定语。

⑥ 参考译文：他（安东纳普勒斯）几乎从不动手说话，即便动，也只是说他想吃饭、睡觉，或者喝酒。本句较长，使用 It was seldom that ... 状语从句说明“很少发生……的情况”，破折号解释说明动手说话一般是为了表达什么内容。

⑦ fumbling：支支吾吾的

⑧ plump：饱满的，胖乎乎的

⑨ oil stove：油炉

⑩ overstuffed：垫得又软又厚的

⑪ be furnished with：布置了……家具（furnished：布置家具）

with an eiderdown[①] comforter[②] for the big Greek and a narrow iron cot[③] for Singer.

Dinner always took a long time, because Antonapoulos loved food and he was very slow. After they had eaten, the big Greek would lie back on his sofa and slowly lick over each one of his teeth with his tongue, either from a certain delicacy or because he did not wish to lose the savor of the meal—while Singer washed the dishes.[④]

Sometimes in the evening the mutes would play chess[⑤]. Singer had always greatly enjoyed this game, and years before[⑥] he had tried to teach it to Antonapoulos. At first his friend could not be interested in the reasons for moving the various pieces about on the board. Then Singer began to keep a bottle of something good under the table to be taken out after each lesson. The Greek never got on to[⑦] the erratic[⑧] movements of the knights and the sweeping mobility of the queens, but he learned to make a few set, opening moves. He preferred the white pieces and would not play if the black men were given him. After the first moves Singer worked out the game by himself while his friend looked on drowsily[⑨]. If Singer made brilliant attacks on his own men so that in the end the black king was killed, Antonapoulos was always very proud and pleased.[⑩]

The two mutes had no other friends, and except when they worked they were alone together. Each day was very much like

---

① eiderdown：鸭绒

② comforter：被子

③ cot：简易床

④ 参考译文：吃完饭，大块头希腊人会躺倒在沙发上，用舌头慢慢挨个舔舐着每一颗牙齿，要么是因为刚吃完某种美食，要么是因为他不想就此告别这顿饭的味道，这时候辛格则在洗碗。本句中 either...or... 连接两个原因状语，用于表示希腊人舔舌头的原因；while 表示转折，辛格与希腊人饭后的状态形成对比。（lick：舔；delicacy：美味；savor：滋味）

⑤ play chess：下象棋。play+ 棋类名词：下……棋；play+the+ 乐器类名词：弹奏……乐器。

⑥ years before：多年以前，例：He still remembered her as the lively teenager he´d known years before. 他记忆中的她依然是他多年以前认识的那个活泼的少女。

⑦ get on to：意识到，例：People more and more get on to the importance of the environment protection to the earth. 人们越来越意识到环境保护对于地球的重要性。

⑧ erratic：不规则的，古怪的

⑨ drowsily：昏昏欲睡地（drowsy 的副词形式）

⑩ 参考译文：如果辛格漂亮地攻击了自己的棋子，最后吃掉了黑子的国王，安东纳普勒斯便得意扬扬、兴高采烈。（make attacks on：攻击……）

any other day, because they were alone so much that nothing ever disturbed[①] them. Once a week they would go to the library for Singer to withdraw a mystery book[②] and on Friday night they attended a movie. Then on payday they always went to the ten-cent photograph shop above the Army and Navy Store so that Antonapoulos could have his picture taken. These were the only places where they made customary[③] visits. There were many parts in the town that they had never even seen.

The town was in the middle of the deep South. The summers were long and the months of winter cold were very few. Nearly always the sky was a glassy[④], brilliant azure[⑤] and the sun burned down riotously[⑥] bright. Then the light, chill rains of November would come, and perhaps later there would be frost and some short months of cold. The winters were changeable, but the summers always were burning hot. The town was a fairly[⑦] large one. On the main street there were several blocks of two- and three-story shops and business offices. But the largest buildings in the town were the factories, which employed a large percentage of the population. These cotton mills were big and flourishing[⑧] and most of the workers in the town were very poor. Often in the faces along the streets there was the desperate look of hunger and of loneliness.[⑨]

But the two mutes were not lonely at all. At home they were content to eat and drink, and Singer would talk with his hands eagerly to his friend about all that was in his mind. So the years passed in this quiet way until Singer reached the age of thirty-two and had been in

---

① disturb：打扰，扰乱

② mystery book：悬疑小说

③ customary：通常的，习惯性的

④ glassy：像玻璃的；光亮透明的

⑤ azure：蔚蓝色

⑥ riotously：非常，极其

⑦ fairly：相当地

⑧ flourishing：繁荣的，兴旺的，此处形容棉纺厂生意兴隆。

⑨ 参考译文：走在大街上的那些人，脸上经常是一副饥饿和孤独的绝望表情。本句虽然未提及“人”这一主语，但实为借代，faces along the streets 指的就是走在大街上的人们的面部表情。

the town with Antonapoulos for ten years.[①]

Then one day the Greek became ill. He sat up in bed with his hands on his fat stomach and big, oily tears rolled down his cheeks. Singer went to see his friend's cousin who owned the fruit store, and also he arranged for leave from his own work.[②] The doctor made out a diet for Antonapoulos and said that he could drink no more wine. Singer rigidly[③] enforced the doctor's orders. All day he sat by his friend's bed and did what he could to make the time pass quickly, but Antonapoulos only looked at him angrily from the corners of his eyes and would not be amused.

The Greek was very fretful[④], and kept finding fault with[⑤] the fruit drinks and food that Singer prepared for him. Constantly he made his friend help him out of bed so that he could pray[⑥]. His huge buttocks[⑦] would sag[⑧] down over his plump little feet when he kneeled. He fumbled[⑨] with his hands to say 'Darling Mary' and then held to the small brass cross tied to his neck with a dirty string.[⑩] His big eyes would wall up to the ceiling with a look of fear in them, and afterward he was very sulky[⑪] and would not let his friend speak to him.

Singer was patient and did all that he could. He drew little pictures, and once he made a sketch of his friend to amuse him. This picture hurt the big Greek's feelings, and he refused to be reconciled

---

① 参考译文：岁月便这样静静地流逝。辛格三十二岁了，他已经跟安东纳普勒斯在镇上生活了整整十年。

② 参考译文：辛格去找好友的那位当水果店老板的表兄，而他自己也请了假不去上班。（arrange for leave from：请假不去做什么事）

③ rigidly：严格地

④ fretful：烦躁的

⑤ find fault with：挑剔，找茬，例：Nobody likes one who loves to find fault with others. 没人喜欢和爱挑剔别人的人在一起。

⑥ pray：祈祷

⑦ buttock：臀部

⑧ sag：（中间部分）下垂；下陷。此处指希腊人跪着祈祷时，其巨大的臀部压在小脚上从两边垂下去。

⑨ fumble：笨嘴笨舌地说

⑩ 参考译文：用手笨拙地比划着“亲爱的玛利亚”，然后握住脖子上用脏兮兮的绳子系着的黄铜十字架。句中 tied to his neck with a dirty string 为过去分词短语作后置定语。

⑪ sulky：阴沉的，生气的

until Singer had made his face very young and handsome and colored his hair bright yellow and his eyes china blue. And then he tried not to show his pleasure.①

Singer nursed② his friend so carefully that after a week Antonapoulos was able to return to his work. But from that time on there was a difference in their way of life. Trouble came to the two friends.

Antonapoulos was not ill any more, but a change had come in him. He was irritable③ and no longer content to spend the evenings quietly in their home. When he would wish to go out Singer followed along close behind him. Antonapoulos would go into a restaurant, and while they sat at the table he slyly put lumps of sugar, or a pepper-shaker, or pieces of silverware in his pocket.④ Singer always paid for what he took and there was no disturbance⑤. At home he scolded⑥ Antonapoulos, but the big Greek only looked at him with a bland⑦ smile.

The months went on and these habits of Antonapoulos grew worse. One day at noon he walked calmly out of the fruit store of his cousin and urinated⑧ in public against the wall of the First National Bank Building across the street. At times he would meet people on the sidewalk whose faces did not please him, and he would bump into these persons and push at them with his elbows and stomach.⑨

---

① 参考译文：这幅画伤害了希腊人的感情，他拒绝和好。直到辛格把他的脸画得又年轻又帅气，把头发画成亮黄色，眼睛画成瓷蓝色，他才作罢，却又竭力掩饰着自己的喜悦之情。until... 表示“直到……才”，描写了希腊人对自己画像的在意和辛格对希腊人的细微照顾。（reconcile：和解；china：瓷器）

② nurse：看护，照料；细心打理。也可作名词使用，意为“护士”。

③ irritable：急躁易怒的

④ 参考译文：安东纳普勒斯会到一家饭店去，坐下后便偷偷把糖块、胡椒瓶或者银制餐具塞进口袋。这里坐下的主体为 they，指辛格每次都陪伴安东纳普勒斯出去，随时准备善后工作。（slyly：秘密地；pepper-shaker：胡椒粉瓶）

⑤ disturbance：骚乱

⑥ scold：斥责

⑦ bland：无动于衷的；平淡的

⑧ urinate：排尿，小便

⑨ 参考译文：有时候，他走在街上，如果觉得哪个路人的长相让他不痛快，便会硬撞人家，还用胳膊肘和肚子推人家。本句含 whose 引导的定语从句，whose 在从句中也作定语，表示“路人的”。

He walked into a store one day and hauled out a floor lamp without paying for it, and another time he tried to take an electric train he had seen in a showcase.①

For Singer this was a time of great distress. He was continually marching Antonapoulos down to the courthouse during lunch hour to settle these infringements of the law.② Singer became very familiar with the procedure of the courts and he was in a constant state of agitation③. The money he had saved in the bank was spent for bail④ and fines⑤. All of his efforts and money were used to keep his friend out of jail because of such charges as theft, committing public indecencies, and assault and battery.⑥

The Greek cousin for whom Antonapoulos worked did not enter into these troubles at all. Charles Parker (for that was the name this cousin had taken) let Antonapoulos stay on at the store, but he watched him always with his pale, tight face and he made no effort to help him. Singer had a strange feeling about Charles Parker. He began to dislike him.

Singer lived in continual turmoil⑦ and worry. But Antonapoulos was always bland, and no matter what happened the gentle, flaccid⑧ smile was still on his face. In all the years before it had seemed to Singer that there was something very subtle and wise in this smile of his friend. He had never known just how much Antonapoulos understood and what he was thinking. Now in the big Greek's

---

① 参考译文：有一天，他走进一家商店，没付钱便将一盏地灯拖了出来。还有一次，他在橱窗里看见一列电动火车，硬要拿走。此处再次举例说明安东纳普勒斯行为之离谱，作者将例子描述得稀松平常，表现这类行为的频繁。

② 参考译文：他经常趁午餐时间，把安东纳普勒斯拉到法院去处理这些违法行为。本句用过去进行时表现一类持续性行为，可见这段时间辛格为安东纳普勒斯善后的次数之多。（infringement：侵犯，违反）

③ agitation：烦乱，焦虑不安

④ bail：保释金

⑤ fine：罚金，罚款

⑥ 参考译文：他花费了所有的精力和财力把好友弄出监狱。好友所犯的罪通常包括偷窃、公然猥亵、袭击和殴打他人。本句译文将原文的原因状语 because of... 另起一句翻译，使译文更加通畅简洁。

⑦ turmoil：骚乱，不安，焦虑

⑧ flaccid：无活力的

expression Singer thought that he could detect something sly and joking.[①] He would shake his friend by the shoulders until he was very tired and explain things over and over[②] with his hands. But nothing did any good.

All of Singer's money was gone and he had to borrow from the jeweler for whom he worked. On one occasion[③] he was unable to pay bail for his friend and Antonapoulos spent the night in jail. When Singer came to get him out the next day he was very sulky[④]. He did not want to leave. He had enjoyed his dinner of sowbelly[⑤] and cornbread with syrup[⑥] poured over it. And the new sleeping arrangements and his cellmates pleased him.

They had lived so much alone that Singer had no one to help him in his distress. Antonapoulos let nothing disturb him or cure him of his habits. At home he sometimes cooked the new dish he had eaten in the jail, and on the streets there was never any knowing just what he would do.

And then the final trouble came to Singer.

One afternoon he had come to meet Antonapoulos at the fruit store when Charles Parker handed him a letter. The letter explained that Charles Parker had made arrangements for his cousin to be taken to the state insane asylum two hundred miles away.[⑦] Charles Parker had used his influence in the town and the details were already settled. Antonapoulos was to leave and to be admitted into[⑧] the asylum the

---

① 参考译文：现在辛格觉得，他从大块头的表情里可以察觉到一种狡黠和戏谑。本句原文将状语前置，起强调作用。（detect：察觉，发现；sly：狡猾的；joking：戏谑的）

② over and over：反复，再三

③ on one occasion：曾经有一次，在某个特定的时刻或事件中发生过一次，例：On one occasion, she called me in the middle of the night. 有一次她深更半夜打电话给我。

④ sulky：生闷气的，愠怒的

⑤ sowbelly：腌猪肉

⑥ syrup：糖浆

⑦ 参考译文：信上说，查尔斯·帕克已经做好了安排，要把表弟送到两百英里之外的州立精神病院去。本句 to be taken 不定式做宾语 cousin 的补语，补充说明查尔斯·帕克给表弟做的具体安排。（make...arrangement for：为……做好安排。）

⑧ be admitted to：获准进入。此处有讽刺含义，安东纳普勒斯在自己没有决定权的情况下被“批准进入”了精神病院。

next week.

Singer read the letter several times, and for a while he could not think. Charles Parker was talking to him across the counter[①], but he did not even try to read his lips and understand. At last Singer wrote on the little pad[②] he always carried in his pocket:

You cannot do this. Antonapoulos must stay with me.

Charles Parker shook his head excitedly. He did not know much American. 'None of your business,' he kept saying over and over.

Singer knew that everything was finished. The Greek was afraid that some day he might be responsible for his cousin. Charles Parker did not know much about the American language—but he understood the American dollar very well, and he had used his money and influence to admit his cousin to the asylum without delay.[③]

There was nothing Singer could do.

The next week was full of feverish[④] activity. He talked and talked. And although his hands never paused to rest[⑤] he could not tell all that he had to say. He wanted to talk to Antonapoulos of all the thoughts that had ever been in his mind and heart, but there was not time. His gray eyes glittered[⑥] and his quick, intelligent face expressed great strain[⑦]. Antonapoulos watched him drowsily[⑧], and his friend did not know just what he really understood.

Then came the day when Antonapoulos must leave. Singer

---

① counter：柜台

② pad：便笺簿

③ 参考译文：查尔斯·帕克不太懂美国人的语言，但对美国的钱，他却懂得透彻，而且他正是利用自己的钱和关系，才让精神病医院立刻接收了自己的表弟。句中 admit sb/sth (to/into sth)，即为 to allow sb/sth to enter a place 意为“准许……进入（某处）”，例：The boy did not admit us to the theatre after the performance has started. 演出开始后，门外工作的男孩不允许我们进入剧场。

④ feverish：狂热的

⑤ pause to rest：停下来去休息

⑥ glitter：闪烁，闪光

⑦ strain：担忧，焦虑

⑧ drowsily：昏昏欲睡地（drowsy：昏昏欲睡的）

brought out his own suitcase and very carefully packed the best of their joint possessions. Antonapoulos made himself a lunch to eat during the journey. In the late afternoon they walked arm in arm down the street for the last time together. It was a chilly① afternoon in late November, and little huffs② of breath showed in the air before them.

Charles Parker was to travel with his cousin, but he stood apart from③ them at the station. Antonapoulos crowded into the bus and settled himself with elaborate preparations on one of the front seats.④ Singer watched him from the window and his hands began desperately to talk for the last time with his friend. But Antonapoulos was so busy checking over the various items in his lunch box that for a while he paid no attention. Just before the bus pulled away from the curb he turned to Singer and his smile was very bland and remote—as though already they were many miles apart.⑤

The weeks that followed didn't seem real at all. All day Singer worked over his bench in the back of the jewelry store, and then at night he returned to the house alone. More than anything he wanted to sleep. As soon as he came home from work he would lie on his cot and try to doze⑥ awhile. Dreams came to him when he lay there half-asleep. And in all of them Antonapoulos was there. His hands would jerk⑦ nervously, for⑧ in his dreams he was talking to his friend and Antonapoulos was watching him.

Singer tried to think of the time before he had ever known

---

① chilly：阴冷的，寒冷的

② huff：此处指吹出的气。

③ stand apart from：站得保持距离

④ 参考译文：安东纳普勒斯挤进了公交车，费了一番功夫后，终于在前排的一个座位上坐定。(elaborate：煞费苦心的)

⑤ 参考译文：车子就要驶离路边的时候，他才转身看看辛格，脸上的笑容如此温和和疏远，好像他们早已隔了好几英里似的。(just before...：就在……之前，例：Just before I left home, I called him. 就在我离开家之前，我给他打了个电话。)

⑥ doze：打瞌睡

⑦ jerk：猛然一动，指抽搐。

⑧ for：因为，由于，例：We listened eagerly, for he brought news of our families. 我们急不可待地听着，因为他带来了我们家人的消息。

his friend. He tried to recount to himself[①] certain things that had happened when he was young. But none of these things he tried to remember seemed real.

There was one particular fact that he remembered, but it was not at all important to him. Singer recalled that, although he had been deaf since he was an infant, he had not always been a real mute. He was left an orphan very young and placed in an institution for the deaf.[②] He had learned to talk with his hands and to read. Before he was nine years old he could talk with one hand in the American way—and also could employ both of his hands after the method of[③] Europeans. He had learned to follow the movements of people's lips and to understand what they said. Then finally he had been taught to speak.

At the school he was thought very intelligent. He learned the lessons before the rest of[④] the pupils. But he could never become used to[⑤] speaking with his lips. It was not natural to him, and his tongue felt like a whale in his mouth. From the blank expression on people's faces to whom he talked in this way he felt that his voice must be like the sound of some animal or that there was something disgusting in his speech.[⑥] It was painful for him to try to talk with his mouth, but his hands were always ready to shape the words he wished to say. When he was twenty-two he had come South to this town from Chicago and he met Antonapoulos immediately. Since that time he had never spoken with his mouth again, because with his friend there was no need for this.

Nothing seemed real except the ten years with Antonapoulos. In his half-dreams he saw his friend very vividly, and when he awakened

---

① recount...to oneself：使自己回想起……

② 参考译文：很小的时候，他便成为孤儿，被送到一所聋儿学校。

③ after the method of：用……的方式

④ the rest of：剩余的，其他的

⑤ become used to doing：习惯于做某事

⑥ 参考译文：用嘴巴说话时，对方怔怔的表情让他觉得，自己的声音一定听上去像某种动物，或者他说的话让人厌烦。本句较长，主干为 he felt that...，表达辛格通过别人表情感受到的他人对自己声音的看法。

a great aching loneliness would be in him.① Occasionally he would pack up a box for Antonapoulos, but he never received any reply. And so the months passed in this empty, dreaming way.

In the spring a change came over Singer. He could not sleep and his body was very restless②. At evening he would walk monotonously③ around the room, unable to work off④ a new feeling of energy. If he rested at all it was only during a few hours before dawn—then he would drop bluntly into a sleep that lasted until the morning light struck suddenly beneath his opening eyelids like a scimitar.⑤

He began spending his evenings walking around the town. He could no longer stand the rooms where Antonapoulos had lived, and he rented a place in a shambling boarding-house not far from the center of the town.⑥

He ate his meals at a restaurant only two blocks away. This restaurant was at the very end of the long main street and the name of the place was the New York Cafe. The first day he glanced over⑦ the menu quickly and wrote a short note and handed it to the proprietor⑧.

Each morning for breakfast I want an egg, toast, and coffee—$0.15

For lunch I want soup (any kind), a meat sandwich, and milk—$0.25

Please bring me at dinner three vegetables (any kind but cabbage),

---

① 参考译文：在半梦半醒之间，他看见了好友，那么真切。醒来时，一种巨大的孤独感涌上来，让他心痛。本句将并列句拆译成两句，后半句将形容词 aching 翻译为小分句，使译文通顺流畅。

② restless：坐立不安的；得不到休息的（词根为 rest，-less 为否定后缀）

③ monotonously：单调地，无聊地（monotonous 的副词形式）

④ work off：发泄，消除，例：Doing sports works off my anger if I've had a quarrel with someone. 与人争吵后，运动使我消除愤怒。

⑤ 参考译文：只有在破晓之前的几个小时里，他才能真正安歇下来，沉沉睡去，直到清晨的阳光猛然照射进来，像弯刀一样刺入他的眼睛。本句前半句用条件状语从句表达辛格入睡之困难，后半句用时间状语从句表现辛格醒来之易，前后对比，说明辛格睡眠变得很浅，体现了安东纳普勒斯走后对辛格造成的影响。（scimitar：短弯刀）

⑥ 参考译文：安东纳普勒斯曾经住的那个房间，他开始觉得无法忍受，于是他在镇中心附近找了一处死气沉沉的公寓，租住下来。（no longer：不再；shambling：呆滞的，此处指死气沉沉的；boarding-house：公寓）

⑦ glance over：浏览

⑧ proprietor：业主，老板

fish or meat, and a glass of beer—$0.35

Thank you.

The proprietor read the note and gave him an alert, tactful glance.① He was a hard man of middle height, with a beard so dark and heavy that the lower part of his face looked as though it were molded of iron.② He usually stood in the corner by the cash register③, his arms folded over his chest, quietly observing all that went on around him. Singer came to know this man's face very well, for he ate at one of his tables three times a day.

Each evening the mute walked alone for hours in the street. Sometimes the nights were cold with the sharp, wet winds of March and it would be raining heavily. But to him this did not matter. His gait was agitated and he always kept his hands stuffed tight into the pockets of his trousers.④ Then as the weeks passed the days grew warm and languorous⑤. His agitation gave way gradually to exhaustion and there was a look about him of deep calm.⑥ In his face there came to be a brooding⑦ peace that is seen most often in the faces of the very sorrowful or the very wise. But still he wandered through the streets of the town, always silent and alone.⑧

---

① 参考译文：老板读完便条，警觉而又克制地扫了他一眼。（give sb. a...glance：给了某人一个……的眼神，例：My mother gave me a doubtful glance when she heard my sad voice. 我的妈妈听见我悲伤的声音时，犹疑地看了我一眼。）

② 参考译文：老板体格健壮，中等身材，胡子又黑又密，让他的下半截脸看上去像铁铸的一样。（mold：mould的美式拼法，意为“浇铸”。）

③ cash register：现金出纳机，收银机

④ 参考译文：他总是把双手紧紧插在裤子口袋里，步伐中透露着焦虑不安。本句可以发现，中文译文将原文前后半句顺序对调，这是中英文表达方式的体现，英文倾向于先动后静，而中文总是先描述静态再将视角转向动态。（gait：步法，步态；agitated：焦虑的）

⑤ languorous：怠惰的，慵懒的

⑥ 参考译文：他的焦虑不安慢慢变成疲惫不堪，身上总透出一种深沉的平静。（give way to：变成，让位于，例：Small changes will give way to broader shifts. 微小的变化将会让位于更为广泛的变化。）

⑦ brooding：沉思的

⑧ 参考译文：然而，他依然在小镇的大街小巷徘徊，总是一个人，一言不发。still放在句首用于强调辛格的状态一直在持续，always silent and alone为形容词短语作主语状语修饰强调。

2

ON A black, sultry[①] night in early summer Biff Brannon stood behind the cash register[②] of the New York Cafe. It was twelve o'clock. Outside the street lights had already been turned off, so that the light from the café made a sharp, yellow rectangle on the sidewalk.[③] The street was deserted[④], but inside the café there were half a dozen customers drinking beer or Santa Lucia wine or whiskey. Biff waited stolidly[⑤], his elbow resting on the counter and his thumb mashing[⑥] the tip of his long nose. His eyes were intent[⑦]. He watched especially a short, squat man in overalls who had become drunk and boisterous.[⑧] Now and then his gaze passed on to the mute who sat by himself at one of the middle tables, or to others of the customers before the counter. But he always turned back to the drunk in overalls.[⑨] The

---

① sultry：闷热的

② cash register：收银机

③ 参考译文：外面，街灯早已熄灭，咖啡馆透出的灯光在人行道上投下一个鲜明的黄色长方形。（outside：位置状语，表示在外面；so that：此处连接结果状语从句，表示"以至于"；sharp：清晰的，鲜明的）

④ deserted：空无一人的

⑤ stolidly：神经麻木地，冷淡地

⑥ mashing：（mash 的动名词形式）原意为"捣碎，磨碎"，此处宾语为鼻尖，意为"使劲揉捏"。

⑦ intent：专注的

⑧ 参考译文：他正盯着一个穿工装的矮胖男人，这个男人喝得烂醉，吵嚷个不停。本句为定语从句 who... 修饰 man。（squat：矮胖的；in+ 服饰：穿着……衣服，in overalls：穿着工装的；boisterous：喧闹的）

⑨ 参考译文：比夫的目光又不时挪到那个哑巴身上，哑巴独自坐在中间的一张桌子前。他的目光也会落到柜台前其他顾客身上，但最后总会把目光转回到穿工装的醉鬼身上。（now and then：偶尔，时不时地；pass on to：传递，转移到；in overalls：穿工装裤，此处作后置定语。）

hour grew later and Biff continued to wait silently behind the counter. Then at last he gave the restaurant a final survey and went toward the door at the back which led upstairs.

Quietly he entered the room at the top of the stairs. It was dark inside and he walked with caution①. After he had gone a few paces his toe struck something hard and he reached down and felt for the handle of a suitcase on the floor. He had only been in the room a few seconds and was about to leave when the light was turned on.

Alice sat up in the rumpled② bed and looked at him. 'What you doing with that suitcase?' she asked. 'Can't you get rid of that lunatic without giving him back what he's already drunk up?③'

'Wake up and go down yourself. Call the cop and let him get soused on the chain gang with cornbread and peas. Go to it, Misses Brannon.④'

'I will all right if he's down there tomorrow. But you leave that bag alone. It don't belong to that sponger⑤ any more.'

'I know spongers, and Blount's not one,' Biff said. 'Myself—I don't know so well. But I'm not that kind of a thief.'

Calmly Biff put down the suitcase on the steps outside. The air was not so stale⑥ and sultry in the room as it was downstairs. He decided to stay for a short while and douse⑦ his face with cold water before going back.

'I told you already what I'll do if you don't get rid of that fellow for good tonight. In the daytime he takes them naps at the back, and

---

① with caution：小心地

② rumpled：凌乱的

③ 参考译文：你难道不能赶紧把那个疯子打发掉吗？干吗还要把他已经喝光了的东西还给他？本句译文将一句问句拆分为两句，首先缩短句型，同时更强调了爱丽丝此时的反感情绪。（get rid of：摆脱；lunatic：疯子；drunk up：完成时态，表示已经喝完。）

④ 参考译文：叫警察来，把他用铁链锁了去当苦力。到那儿就着玉米面包和豆子再去喝。去啊，布兰农太太。chain gang 指（过去在美国）用铁链锁在一起做工的囚犯们。此处 get soused on（沉醉在……）指让他在做苦工当囚犯的处境中去喝醉酒，是比夫故意说来刺激爱丽丝的话。

⑤ sponger：寄生虫

⑥ stale：（空气）不新鲜的，污浊的

⑦ douse：往……上泼水

then at night you feed him dinners and beer. For a week now he hasn't paid one cent. And all his wild talking and carrying-on will ruin any decent trade.[①]'

'You don't know people and you don't know real business,' Biff said. 'The fellow in question[②] first came in here twelve days ago and he was a stranger in the town. The first week he gave us twenty dollars' worth of trade. Twenty at the minimum.'

'And since then on credit[③],' Alice said. 'Five days on credit, and so drunk it's a disgrace to the business. And besides, he's nothing but a bum and a freak.[④]'

'I like freaks,' Biff said.

'I reckon you do! I just reckon you certainly ought to, Mister Brannon—being as you're one yourself.'

He rubbed his bluish chin and paid her no attention. For the first fifteen years of their married life they had called each other just plain Biff and Alice. Then in one of their quarrels they had begun calling each other Mister and Misses, and since then they had never made it up enough to change it.

'I'm just warning you he'd better not be there when I come down tomorrow.'

Biff went into the bathroom, and after he had bathed his face he decided that he would have time for a shave[⑤]. His beard was black and heavy as though it had grown for three days. He stood before the mirror and rubbed his cheek meditatively[⑥]. He was sorry he had talked

---

① 参考译文：我早就告诉过你，如果你今晚不把那个家伙彻底解决掉，看我怎么治他。白天，他在后面打瞌睡；晚上，你又好吃好喝地伺候他。现在都一个星期了，他一分钱没交过。他的胡言乱语，还有随身带的这些东西，会搅了我们的好买卖。本句 take them naps 为方言，可译为“睡他的大头觉”，take naps，译为“打瞌睡”。（for good：永久地，即彻底地；carrying-on：carry-on 意为“可以随身携带的”，此处 carrying-on 意为“随身携带的东西”，但更多时候 carrying-on 用来指“轻佻不当的行为”；decent：相当好的）

② in question：讨论中的

③ on credit：赊账

④ 参考译文：而且，他不过是个流浪汉加怪物。（besides：况且，而且；nothing...but：只不过，仅仅，例：He is nothing but a little boy. 他不过是个小男孩。）

⑤ shave：剃须

⑥ meditatively：沉思地，若有所思地

to Alice. With her, silence was better. Being around that woman always made him different from his real self. It made him tough and small and common as she was. Biff's eyes were cold and staring, half-concealed by the cynical droop of his eyelids.① On the fifth finger of his calloused② hand there was a woman's wedding ring. The door was open behind him, and in the mirror he could see Alice lying in the bed.

'Listen,' he said. 'The trouble with you is that you don't have any real kindness. Not but one woman I've ever known had this real kindness I'm talking about.③'

'Well, I've known you to do things no man in this world would be proud of. I've known you to—'

'Or maybe it's curiosity I mean. You don't ever see or notice anything important that goes on. You never watch and think and try to figure anything out. Maybe that's the biggest difference between you and me, after all.'

Alice was almost asleep again, and through the mirror he watched her with detachment④. There was no distinctive point about her on which he could fasten his attention, and his gaze glided from her pale brown hair to the stumpy outline of her feet beneath the cover. The soft curves of her face led to the roundness of her hips and thighs.⑤ When he was away from her there was no one feature that stood out in his mind and he remembered her as a complete, unbroken figure.

---

① 参考译文：比夫眼神冰冷，直愣愣的，眼皮玩世不恭地耷拉着，把眼睛遮住了一半。本句后半句为过去分词做主补，译文化被动为主动。（cynical：愤世嫉俗的，此处修饰眼皮耷拉的样子译为“玩世不恭地”；droop：下垂）

② calloused：起老茧的，粗糙的

③ 参考译文：我认识的女人当中，只有一个人有我说的这种善心。（not but one：只有一个，相当于 only one，例：Not but one of his family agrees with him. 他的家人中只有一个人同意他的做法。）

④ detachment：冷漠

⑤ 参考译文：她身上没有什么特别的地方能够牢牢吸引住他的注意力。他的目光从她淡褐色的头发滑到被子下面那双脚的粗短轮廓，从她柔和的面部曲线滑到她浑圆的屁股和大腿。本句译文灵活进行拆译及合译，使译文更符合中文表达。（fasten one's attention on：集中注意力在……；stumpy：粗短的；thigh：大腿）

'The enjoyment of a spectacle[①] is something you have never known,' he said.

Her voice was tired. 'That fellow downstairs is a spectacle, all right, and a circus[②] too. But I'm through putting up with him.[③]'

'Hell, the man don't mean anything to me. He's no relative or buddy of mine. But you don't know what it is to store up a whole lot of details and then come upon something real.[④]' He turned on the hot water and quickly began to shave.

It was the morning of May 15, yes, that Jake Blount had come in. He had noticed him immediately and watched. The man was short, with heavy shoulders like beams. He had a small, ragged mustache, and beneath this his lower lip looked as though it had been stung by a wasp.[⑤] There were many things about the fellow that seemed contrary[⑥]. His head was very large and well-shaped, but his neck was soft and slender[⑦] as a boy's. The mustache looked false, as if it had been stuck on for a costume party and would fall off if he talked too fast. It made him seem almost middle-aged, although his face with its high, smooth forehead and wide-open eyes was young. His hands were huge, stained, and calloused, and he was dressed in a cheap white-linen suit. There was something very funny about the man, yet at the same time another feeling would not let you laugh.

He ordered a pint of liquor and drank it straight in half an hour. Then he sat at one of the booths[⑧] and ate a big chicken dinner. Later

---

① spectacle：奇观

② circus：马戏团

③ 参考译文：但是，我已经受够他了。（be through：指结束某件事；put up with：忍受。结束忍受，即"受够了，受不了了"。）

④ 参考译文：但是，一个人留意了许多细节，然后突然真相大白，你根本就不懂这是种什么感觉。（store up：存储，"存储很多细节"，也就是"留意很多细节"；come upon：偶遇，邂逅，"邂逅真相"，即"发现真相"。）

⑤ 参考译文：这个男人个头不高，肩膀宽厚，像房梁一样，有撇小胡子，参差不齐，下嘴唇看上去像被黄蜂蛰了一样。本句描写男子外貌，故采取两句合译的方式将表达一体化。（beam：房梁；ragged：参差不齐的；wasp：黄蜂）

⑥ contrary：相反的，此处用在形容人身上指"不协调的"。

⑦ slender：细长的，苗条的

⑧ booth：隔开的用餐区（固定的长座围绕着餐桌）

he read a book and drank beer. That was the beginning. And although Biff had noticed Blount carefully he would never have guessed about the crazy things that happened later. Never had he seen a man change so many times in twelve days. Never had he seen a fellow drink so much, stay drunk so long.

Biff pushed up the end of his nose with his thumb and shaved his upper lip. He was finished and his face seemed cooler. Alice was asleep when he went through the bedroom on the way downstairs.

The suitcase was heavy. He carried it to the front of the restaurant, behind the cash register, where he usually stood each evening. Methodically[①] he glanced around the place. A few customers had left and the room was not so crowded, but the set-up[②] was the same. The deaf-mute still drank coffee by himself at one of the middle tables. The drunk had not stopped talking. He was not addressing anyone around him in particular, nor was anyone listening. When he had come into the place that evening he wore those blue overalls instead of the filthy linen suit he had been wearing the twelve days.[③] His socks were gone and his ankles were scratched[④] and caked with mud.

Alertly Biff picked up fragments of his monologue.[⑤] The fellow seemed to be talking some queer kind of politics again. Last night he had been talking about places he had been—about Texas and Oklahoma and the Carolinas. Once he had got on the subject of cat-houses, and afterward his jokes got so raw he had to be hushed

---

① methodically：有条不紊地

② set-up：（指设备的）组织（设计，布置）。去掉短破折号（set up）为动词词组，意为“设置，布置”。

③ 参考译文：那天晚上，他来到餐馆时，穿着一套蓝色工装，并没有穿先前那十二天里一直穿着的那件脏兮兮的亚麻布西装。本句较长，句首由 when 引导的时间状语从句表示讲述的那天晚上，句末由省略 that 的定语从句修饰表示“酒鬼”先前十二天一直穿着的亚麻布西装。（filthy：十分肮脏的，脏兮兮的）

④ scratched：划破的，有刮痕的

⑤ 参考译文：比夫很警觉地听着他独白的只言片语。（alertly：提高警觉地；fragment：片段或不完整的部分；monologue：独白）

up with beer.[①] But most of the time nobody was sure just what he was saying. Talk-talk-talk. The words came out of his throat like a cataract[②]. And the thing was that the accent he used was always changing, the kinds of words he used. Sometimes he talked like a linthead and sometimes like a professor. He would use words a foot long and then slip up[③] on his grammar. It was hard to tell what kind of folks he had or what part of the country he was from. He was always changing. Thoughtfully Biff fondled the tip of his nose. There was no connection. Yet connection usually went with brains.[④] This man had a good mind, all right, but he went from one thing to another without any reason behind it at all. He was like a man thrown off his track by something.[⑤]

Biff leaned his weight on the counter and began to peruse[⑥] the evening newspaper. The headlines told of a decision by the Board of Aldermen, after four months' deliberation, that the local budget could not afford traffic lights at certain dangerous intersections of the town.[⑦] The left column reported on the war in the Orient. Biff read them both with equal attention. As his eyes followed the print the rest of his senses were on the alert to the various commotions that went on around him.[⑧] When he had finished the articles he still stared down at the newspaper with his eyes half-closed. He felt nervous. The fellow was a problem, and before morning he would have to make some

---

① 参考译文：有一次，他还谈到妓院；后来，他的笑话实在太露骨，别人便用啤酒堵上了他的嘴。（cat-house：妓院；raw：粗俗的；hushed up：被掩盖的）

② cataract：大瀑布

③ slip up：疏忽；出差错，例：Even though I'm careful I still slip up . 尽管我很小心，但还是会有疏忽。

④ 参考译文：但只要动动脑子，就一定会找到关联。

⑤ 参考译文：他像一个被某种东西弄得偏离轨道的人。（throw off the track：脱离正轨，迷失方向）

⑥ peruse：细读，精读

⑦ 参考译文：大标题说，市议员委员会经过历时四个月的深思熟虑，终于做出决议：地方预算无法支付在镇上某些危险路口安装红绿灯的费用。本句 decision 后跟着一个 that 同位语从句，补充说明委员会做出的决议。（deliberation：审议，考虑；intersection：交集，交叉点，十字路口）

⑧ 参考译文：他的眼睛读着报纸，其他的感官则随时警惕着周围各种各样的动静。（commotion：骚动）

sort of settlement with him. Also, he felt without knowing why that something of importance would happen tonight. The fellow could not keep on forever.

Biff sensed that someone was standing in the entrance and he raised his eyes quickly. A gangling①, towheaded② youngster, a girl of about twelve, stood looking in the doorway. She was dressed in khaki shorts, a blue shirt, and tennis shoes—so that at first glance she was like a very young boy. Biff pushed aside the paper when he saw her, and smiled when she came up to him.

'Hello, Mick. Been to the Girl Scouts?'

'No,' she said. 'I don't belong to them.'

From the corner of his eye he noticed that the drunk slammed his fist down on a table and turned away from the men to whom he had been talking.③ Biff's voice roughened④ as he spoke to the youngster before him.

'Your folks know you're out after midnight?'

'It's O.K. There's a gang of⑤ kids playing out late on our block tonight.'

He had never seen her come into the place with anyone her own age. Several years ago she had always tagged behind⑥ her older brother. The Kellys were a good-sized family in numbers. Later she would come in pulling a couple of snotty⑦ babies in a wagon⑧. But if she wasn't nursing or trying to keep up with the bigger ones, she was by herself. Now the kid stood there seeming not to be able to make up her mind what she wanted. She kept pushing back her damp,

---

① gangling：瘦高且行动笨拙的

② towheaded：毛发带淡黄色的

③ 参考译文：他用眼角的余光注意到，那个醉鬼正用拳头砸桌子，并且转身背对着刚才的那些谈话对象。（slam：猛击，碰撞；fist：拳头；turn away from：转身背对某人，也可指厌恶某人。）

④ roughen：（声音）变粗

⑤ a gang of：一伙，一群

⑥ tag behind：紧紧地跟在后面

⑦ snotty：流鼻涕的

⑧ wagon：四轮小车

whitish hair with the palm of her hand.[①]

'I'd like a pack of cigarettes, please. The cheapest kind.'

Biff started to speak, hesitated, and then reached his hand inside the counter. Mick brought out a handkerchief and began untying the knot in the corner where she kept her money. As she gave the knot a jerk the change clattered to the floor and rolled toward Blount, who stood muttering to himself. For a moment he stared in a daze at the coins, but before the kid could go after them he squatted down with concentration and picked up the money.[②] He walked heavily to the counter and stood jiggling[③] the two pennies, the nickel, and the dime[④] in his palm.

'Seventeen cents for cigarettes now?'

Biff waited, and Mick looked from one of them to the other. The drunk stacked[⑤] the money into a little pile on the counter, still protecting it with his big, dirty hand. Slowly he picked up one penny and flipped[⑥] it down.

'Five mills for the crackers[⑦] who grew the weed and five for the dupes[⑧] who rolled it,' he said. 'A cent for you, Biff.' Then he tried to focus his eyes so that he could read the mottoes on the nickel and dime. He kept fingering the two coins and moving them around in a circle. At last he pushed them away. 'And that's a humble homage to liberty. To democracy and tyranny. To freedom and piracy.'

Calmly Biff picked up the money and rang it into the till. Mick

---

① 参考译文：她不停地用手掌把湿乎乎且有点发白的头发向后拢。（keep doing sth. 表示一直做某事；whitish：发白的）

② 参考译文：她猛地拽了一下结扣，里面的零钱哗啦掉到了地上，滚到布朗特旁边。布朗特正站在那里自言自语，他迷迷糊糊地盯着那几枚硬币看了一会儿，还没等那个孩子追过来，他便专注地蹲下身子，把钱捡了起来。本句 Blount 后"who stood muttering to himself"为非限定性定语从句，补充说明 Blount 当时的状态。（jerk：猛拉；change：零钱；mutter to oneself：自言自语；in a daze：在恍惚中；squat down：蹲下；pick up：捡起）

③ jiggling：抖动；轻摇（jiggle 的现在分词形式）

④ penny, nickel, dime：货币单位，分别指一分、五分、十分（即一角）。

⑤ stack：堆放，摞在一起

⑥ flip：掷，弹

⑦ cracker：（对几乎未受过教育的美国南方贫苦白人的轻蔑语）车把式

⑧ dupe：受骗者，上当者（尤指受骗参与违法之事的人）

looked as though she wanted to hang around awhile. She took in the drunk with one long gaze, and then she turned her eyes to the middle of the room where the mute sat at his table alone. After a moment Blount also glanced now and then in the same direction. The mute sat silently over his glass of beer, idly drawing on the table with the end of a burnt matchstick.①

Jake Blount was the first to speak. 'It's funny, but I been seeing that fellow in my sleep for the past three or four nights.② He won't leave me alone. If you ever noticed, he never seems to say anything.'

It was seldom that Biff ever discussed one customer with another. 'No, he don't,' he answered noncommittally③.

'It's funny.'

Mick shifted her weight from one foot to the other and fitted the package of cigarettes into the pocket of her shorts. 'It's not funny if you know anything about him,' she said. 'Mister Singer lives with us. He rooms in our house.'

'Is that so?' Biff asked. 'I declare—I didn't know that'

Mick walked toward the door and answered him without looking around. 'Sure. He's been with us three months now.'

Biff unrolled his shirt-sleeves and then folded them up carefully again. He did not take his eyes from Mick as she left the restaurant. And even after she had been gone several minutes he still fumbled④ with his shirt-sleeves and stared at the empty doorway. Then he locked his arms across his chest and turned back to the drunk again.⑤

Blount leaned heavily on the counter. His brown eyes were wet-

---

① 参考译文：哑巴默默地坐在那里，喝着一杯啤酒，用一根用过的火柴棒在桌子上无所事事地画着什么。本句为动名词短语作状语。（over his glass of beer：边喝着酒，over 相当于 during；idly：懒散地，无所事事地）

② 本句应为 "I've been seeing that fellow in my sleep for the past three or four nights." 现在完成时。

③ noncommittally：不明确地，含糊地

④ fumble：摸索

⑤ 参考译文：然后，他把双臂抱在胸前，又转头看着醉鬼。the + adj. 表示某一类人，如 the drunk 意为 "喝醉的人"，即 "醉鬼"。（lock：紧抱）

looking and wide open with a dazed[①] expression. He needed a bath so badly that he stank like a goat.[②] There were dirt beads on his sweaty neck and an oil stain[③] on his face. His lips were thick and red and his brown hair was matted on his forehead. His overalls were too short in the body and he kept pulling at the crotch[④] of them.

'Man, you ought to know better,' Biff said finally. 'You can't go around like this. Why, I'm surprised you haven't been picked up for vagrancy[⑤]. You ought to sober up[⑥]. You need washing and your hair needs cutting. Motherogod! You're not fit to walk around amongst people.'

Blount scowled[⑦] and bit his lower lip.

'Now, don't take offense[⑧] and get your dander up. Do what I tell you. Go back in the kitchen and tell the colored boy to give you a big pan of hot water. Tell Willie to give you a towel and plenty of soap and wash yourself good. Then eat you some milk toast and open up your suitcase and put you on a clean shirt and a pair of britches[⑨] that fit you. Then tomorrow you can start doing whatever you're going to do and working wherever you mean to work and get straightened out[⑩].'

'You know what you can do,' Blount said drunkenly. 'You can just—'

'All right,' Biff said very quietly. 'No, I can't. Now you just behave yourself.'

---

① dazed：茫然的

② 参考译文：他很久没洗过澡了，身上有股山羊的臭味。so...that：如此……，以至于……，故此处是先有布朗特急需洗澡，后有发臭的结果，也就是布朗特因很久没有洗澡导致身上发臭，翻译时需注意逻辑关系。

③ oil stain：油渍

④ crotch：裤裆

⑤ vagrancy：流浪

⑥ sober up：清醒，例：This event to me is a shock, but then I sober up. 这件事对我来说是个震撼，但随即我又清醒了过来。

⑦ scowl：作怒容；绷着脸

⑧ take offense：生气，介意

⑨ britches：（复数形式）裤子；马裤（长及膝盖的裤子）

⑩ get straightened out：改正，修正。主动格式为 straighten... out，意为“纠正错误”。

Biff went to the end of the counter and returned with two glasses of draught beer[①]. The drunk picked up his glass so clumsily that beer slopped down on his hands and messed the counter. Biff sipped his portion with careful relish. He regarded Blount steadily with half-closed eyes. Blount was not a freak, although when you first saw him he gave you that impression. It was like something was deformed[②] about him—but when you looked at him closely each part of him was normal and as it ought to be. Therefore if this difference was not in the body it was probably in the mind. He was like a man who had served a term in prison or had been to Harvard College or had lived for a long time with foreigners in South America.[③] He was like a person who had been somewhere that other people are not likely to go or had done something that others are not apt to do[④].

Biff cocked[⑤] his head to one side and said, 'Where are you from?'

'Nowhere.'

'Now, you have to be born somewhere. North Carolina—Tennessee—Alabama—some place.'

Blount's eyes were dreamy and unfocused. 'Carolina,' he said.

'I can tell you've been around,' Biff hinted delicately[⑥].

But the drunk was not listening. He had turned from the counter and was staring out at the dark, empty street. After a moment he walked to the door with loose, uncertain steps.

'Adios[⑦],' he called back.

Biff was alone again and he gave the restaurant one of his quick,

---

① draught beer：生啤酒，指桶装啤酒。

② deformed：畸形的

③ 参考译文：他这个人，像是曾经蹲过监狱，或者上过哈佛，或者在南美跟外国人混了很长时间。本句用三种不同的可能履历表现布朗特身上体现的多重特性。（serve a term：服刑）

④ be apt to do sth：易于、倾向于做某事，例：I am apt to cry when moved. 我被感动的时候容易哭。

⑤ cock：将（身体的一部分）转向一边

⑥ delicately：微妙地，巧妙地

⑦ adios：（西班牙语）再见

thorough surveys.[①] It was past one in the morning, and there were only four or five customers in the room. The mute still sat by himself at the middle table. Biff stared at him idly and shook the few remaining drops of beer around in the bottom of his glass. Then he finished his drink in one slow swallow[②] and went back to the newspaper spread out on the counter.

This time he could not keep his mind on the words before him. He remembered Mick. He wondered if he should have sold her the pack of cigarettes and if it were really harmful for kids to smoke. He thought of the way Mick narrowed her eyes and pushed back the bangs[③] of her hair with the palm of her hand. He thought of her hoarse, boyish voice and of her habit of hitching up her khaki shorts and swaggering like a cowboy in the picture show. A feeling of tenderness came in him. He was uneasy.

Restlessly Biff turned his attention to Singer. The mute sat with his hands in his pockets and the half-finished glass of beer before him had become warm and stagnant[④]. He would offer to treat[⑤] Singer to a slug of whiskey before he left. What he had said to Alice was true—he did like freaks. He had a special friendly feeling for sick people and cripples[⑥]. Whenever somebody with a harelip or T.B.[⑦] came into the place he would set him up to beer. Or if the customer were a hunchback or a bad cripple, then it would be whiskey on the house. There was one fellow who had had his peter and his left leg blown off in a boiler explosion, and whenever he came to town there was a

---

① 参考译文：又剩下比夫一个人，他快速而仔细地查看了一遍餐馆。(thorough：周密的，详细的；survey：审视，纵览)

② swallow：吞咽

③ bang：刘海

④ stagnant：(水或空气)不流动而污浊的

⑤ treat：款待(treat sb to sth 用某物款待某人)

⑥ cripple：残疾人

⑦ T.B.：肺结核(tuberculosis)

free pint waiting for him.[①] And if Singer were a drinking kind of man he could get liquor at half price any time he wanted it. Biff nodded to himself. Then neatly he folded his newspaper and put it under the counter along with several others. At the end of the week he would take them all back to the storeroom behind the kitchen, where he kept a complete file of the evening newspapers that dated back[②] without a break[③] for twenty-one years.

At two o'clock Blount entered the restaurant again. He brought in with him a tall Negro man carrying a black bag. The drunk tried to bring him up to the counter for a drink, but the Negro left as soon as he realized why he had been led inside. Biff recognized him as[④] a Negro doctor who had practiced in the town ever since he could remember. He was related in some way to young Willie back in the kitchen. Before he left Biff saw him turn on[⑤] Blount with a look of quivering hatred.

The drunk just stood there.

'Don't you know you can't bring no nigger in a place where white men drink?' someone asked him.[⑥]

Biff watched this happening from a distance. Blount was very angry, and now it could easily be seen how drunk he was.

'I'm part nigger myself,' he called out as a challenge.[⑦]

Biff watched him alertly[⑧] and the place was quiet. With his thick nostrils[⑨] and the rolling whites of his eyes it looked a little as though

---

① 参考译文：曾经有个家伙在一次锅炉爆炸中炸飞了下体和左腿，无论他什么时候来镇上，都有一品脱免费威士忌在这里等着他。（boiler explosion：锅炉爆炸；peter：［非正式］阴茎，下体）

② date back：追溯，指某事物的历史或起源可以追溯到过去的某个时期，例：The issue is not a new one. It dates back to the 1930s at least. 这杂志不是新的，它至少可以追溯到 20 世纪 30 年代。

③ break：暂停；间歇

④ recognize sb. as：认出某人是……

⑤ turn on：突然袭击，突然斥责，此处指黑人突然恶狠狠对布朗特。

⑥ 参考译文："你难道不知道，白人喝酒的地方，不能带黑鬼进来吗？" 有人问他。此处为反问句，表达中双重否定有误，实际应为：Don't you know you can't bring nigger......?

⑦ challenge：挑战，挑衅

⑧ alertly：留意地；提高警觉地

⑨ nostril：鼻孔

he might be telling the truth.

'I'm part nigger and wop[①] and bohunk[②] and chink[③]. All of those.'

There was laughter.

'And I'm Dutch and Turkish and Japanese and American.' He walked in zigzags[④] around the table where the mute drank his coffee. His voice was loud and cracked[⑤]. 'I'm one who knows. I'm a stranger in a strange land.'

'Quiet down,' Biff said to him.

Blount paid no attention to anyone in the place except the mute. They were both looking at each other. The mute's eyes were cold and gentle as a cat's and all his body seemed to listen. The drunk man was in a frenzy[⑥].

'You're the only one in this town who catches what I mean[⑦],' Blount said. 'For two days now I been talking to you in my mind because I know you understand the things I want to mean.'

Some people in a booth were laughing because without knowing it the drunk had picked out a deaf-mute to try to talk with. Biff watched the two men with little darting glances and listened attentively[⑧].

Blount sat down to the table and leaned over close to Singer. There are those who know and those who don't know. And for every ten thousand who don't know there's only one who knows. That's the miracle of all time—the fact that these millions know so much but don't know this. It's like in the fifteenth century when

① wop：意大利人，南欧人；移居美国的南欧黑肤人（尤指意大利人）

② bohunk：东欧人；从东欧来的低层无技术工人

③ chink：官方解释为窄眼、小缝隙，是英文中种族性的侮辱性用语，对象是华人或东亚人，指代性非常明确。

④ zigzag：之字形

⑤ cracked：（嗓音）嘶哑的

⑥ frenzy：狂怒，暴怒，狂暴

⑦ 布朗特在这里提出辛格是这个小镇上唯一懂他在说什么的人，同时是本书中第一次明写小镇上的人把辛格当做知己。而恰恰辛格是个哑巴，为后文故事埋下伏笔。

⑧ attentively：注意地；聚精会神地

everybody believed the world was flat and only Columbus and a few other fellows knew the truth.[①] But it's different in that it took talent to figure that the earth is round. While this truth is so obvious[②] it's a miracle of all history that people don't know. You savvy.'

Biff rested his elbows on the counter and looked at Blount with curiosity[③]. 'Know what?' he asked.

'Don't listen to him,' Blount said. 'Don't mind that flat-footed, blue-jowled, nosy[④] bastard. For you see, when us people who know run into each other mat's an event. It almost never happens. Sometimes we meet each other and neither guesses that the other is one who knows. That's a bad thing. It's happened to me a lot of times. But you see there are so few of us.'

'Masons[⑤]?' Biff asked.

'Shut up, you! Else I'll snatch[⑥] your arm off and beat you black with it,' Blount bawled. He hunched over close to the mute and his voice dropped to a drunken whisper. 'And how come? Why has this miracle of ignorance endured? Because of one thing. A conspiracy. A vast and insidious[⑦] conspiracy. Obscurantism[⑧].'

The men in the booth were still laughing at the drunk who was trying to hold a conversation with the mute. Only Biff was serious. He wanted to ascertain[⑨] if the mute really understood what was said to him. The fellow nodded frequently and his face seemed contemplative[⑩]. He was only slow—that was all. Blount began to crack a few jokes along with this talk about knowing. The mute

---

① 参考译文：正如 15 世纪，人人都觉得地球是平的，只有哥伦布和其他几个人知道真理。（Columbus：哥伦布，意大利航海家）

② obvious：明显的；显著的；平淡无奇的

③ curiosity：好奇，好奇心

④ nosy：好管闲事的；大鼻子的（此处首先指“大鼻子的”，同时隐讽为“好管闲事的”。）

⑤ mason：（相当于 freemason）共济会成员

⑥ snatch：一把抓起；夺去，此处指“把你的胳膊扯下来当棍子打你。”

⑦ insidious：阴险的；狡猾的

⑧ obscurantism：（尤指为避免人们发现真相的）故弄玄虚；蒙骗主义

⑨ ascertain：确定；查明；探知

⑩ contemplative：沉思的；冥想的

never smiled until several seconds after the funny remark had been made; then when the talk was gloomy again the smile still hung on his face a little too long. The fellow was downright[①] uncanny[②]. People felt themselves watching him even before they knew that there was anything different about him. His eyes made a person think that he heard things nobody else had ever heard, that he knew things no one had ever guessed before. He did not seem quite human.

Jake Blount leaned across[③] the table and the words came out as though a dam inside him had broken. Biff could not understand him any more. Blount's tongue was so heavy with drink and he talked at such a violent pace that the sounds were all shaken up together. Biff wondered where he would go when Alice turned him out of the place. And in the morning she would do it, too—like she said.

Biff yawned wanly[④], patting his open mouth with his fingertips until his jaw had relaxed. It was almost three o'clock, thc most stagnant[⑤] hour in the day or night.

The mute was patient. He had been listening to Blount for almost an hour. Now he began to look at the clock occasionally[⑥]. Blount did not notice this and went on without a pause. At last he stopped to roll a cigarette, and then the mute nodded his head in the direction of the clock, smiled in that hidden way of his, and got up from the table. His hands stayed stuffed in his pockets as always. He went out quickly.

Blount was so drunk that he did not know what had happened. He had never even caught on to the fact that the mute made no answers. He began to look around the place with his mouth open and his eyes rolling and fuddled[⑦]. A red vein stood out on his forehead

---

① downright：（强调反面的或令人不快的事物）彻头彻尾地，十足地
② uncanny：神秘的；离奇的
③ lean across：倾身越过，指将身体向前或向一侧倾斜，以便越过某物或接近某物。
④ wanly：苍白地；衰弱地（词根 wan：无血色的，苍白的）
⑤ stagnant：停滞不前的，死气沉沉的
⑥ occasionally：偶尔；间或
⑦ fuddled：糊涂的，口齿不清的

and he began to hit the table angrily with his fists. His bout[①] could not last much longer now.

'Come on over,' Biff said kindly. 'Your friend has gone.'

The fellow was still hunting for Singer. He had never seemed really drunk like that before. He had an ugly look.

'I have something for you over here and I want to speak with you a minute,' Biff coaxed.

Blount pulled himself up from the table and walked with big, loose steps toward the street again.

Biff leaned against the wall. In and out-in and out. After all, it was none of his business. The room was very empty and quiet. The minutes lingered[②]. Wearily he let his head sag forward. All motion seemed slowly to be leaving the room.[③] The counter, faces, the booths and tables, the radio in the corner, whirring[④] fans on the ceiling—all seemed to become very faint[⑤] and still.

He must have dozed. A hand was shaking his elbow. His wits came back to him slowly and he looked up to see what was wanted. Willie, the colored boy in the kitchen, stood before him dressed in his cap and his long white apron[⑥]. Willie stammered[⑦] because he was excited about whatever he was trying to say.

'And so he were l-l-lamming his fist against this here brick w-w-wall.'

'What's that? '

'Right down one of them alleys two d-d-doors away.'

Biff straightened his slumped shoulders and arranged his tie. 'What?'

---

① bout：发作，发病期

② linger：缓慢度过

③ 参考译文：屋子似乎慢慢凝固起来。（motion：运动，移动，此处说似乎所有的动态都离开了这个屋子，表示整个屋子似乎都不动了，即“凝固”了。）

④ whir：作呼呼声，呼呼作声地飞

⑤ faint：模糊的；微弱的

⑥ apron：围裙

⑦ stammer：口吃；结结巴巴地说

'And they means to bring him in here and they liable to pile in any minute—'

'Willie,' Biff said patiently. 'Start at the beginning and let me get this straight.'

'It this here short white man with the m-m-mustache.'

'Mr. Blount. Yes.'

'Well—I didn't see how it commenced[①]. I were standing in the back door when I heard this here commotion. Sound like a big fight in the alley. So I r-r-run to see. And this here white man had just gone hog wild. He were butting[②] his head against the side of this brick wall and hitting with his fists. He were cussing[③] and fighting like I never seen a white man fight before. With just this here wall. He liable to broken his own head the way he were carrying on. Then two white mens who had heard the commotion[④] come up and stand around and look—'

'So what happened?'

'Well—you know this here dumb gentleman—hands in pockets—this here—'

'Mr. Singer.'

'And he come along and just stood looking around to see what it were all about. And Mr. B- B-Blount seen him and commenced to talk and holler. And then all of a sudden he fallen down on the ground. Maybe he done really busted[⑤] his head open. A p-p-p-police come up and somebody done told him Mr. Blount been staying here.'

Biff bowed his head and organized the story he had just heard into a neat pattern. He rubbed his nose and thought for a minute.

'They liable[⑥] to pile in here any minute.' Willie went to the

---

① commence：开始发生
② butt：对接；冲撞
③ cuss：咒骂
④ commotion：骚动；暴乱
⑤ bust：使爆裂
⑥ liable：有责任的，有义务的

door and looked down the street 'Here they all come now. They having to drag him.'

A dozen onlookers and a policeman all tried to crowd into the restaurant. Outside a couple of whores[①] stood looking in through the front window. It was always funny how many people could crowd in from nowhere when anything out of the ordinary[②] happened.

'No use creating any more disturbance than necessary[③],' Biff said. He looked at the policeman who supported the drunk. 'The rest of them might as well clear out.'

The policeman put the drunk in a chair and hustled[④] the little crowd into the street again. Then he turned to Biff: 'Somebody said he was staying here with you.'

'No. But he might as well be,' Biff said.

'Want me to take him with me?'

Biff considered. 'He won't get into any more trouble tonight. Of course I can't be responsible—but I think this will calm him down.'

'O.K. I'll drop back in again before I knock off[⑤].'

Biff, Singer, and Jake Blount were left alone. For the first time since he had been brought in, Biff turned his attention to the drunk man. It seemed that Blount had hurt his jaw very badly. He was slumped down on the table with his big hand over his mouth, swaying backward and forward. There was a gash[⑥] in his head and the blood ran from his temple[⑦]. His knuckles[⑧] were skinned raw, and he was so filthy that he looked as if he had been pulled by the scruff[⑨] of the

---

① whore：娼妓，妓女

② out of the ordinary：不寻常的，非凡的，超出一般水平或标准的事物或情况。例：I don't see anything out of the ordinary. 我没看到什么异常状况。

③ 参考译文：别再制造不必要的麻烦了，没什么好处。No use doing sth. 意为"做某事没有用处"。

④ hustle：推搡；强力将（某人往特定方向）赶

⑤ knock off：歇工，下班，例：If I finish this report, I will knock off early. 如果我能完成这个报告，我会早点下班。

⑥ gash：很深的裂缝；砍得很深的伤口

⑦ temple：太阳穴，鬓角（此处指太阳穴、鬓角）；庙宇，寺院

⑧ knuckle：指关节

⑨ scruff：颈背，后颈

neck from a sewer[①]. All the juice had spurted[②] out of him and he was completely collapsed. The mute sat at the table across from him, taking it all in with his gray eyes.

Then Biff saw that Blount had not hurt his jaw, but he was holding his hand over his mouth because his lips were trembling. The tears began to roll down his grimy face. Now and then he glanced sideways at Biff and Singer, angry that they should see him cry. It was embarrassing. Biff shrugged his shoulders at the mute and raised his eyebrows with a 'what-to-do'? expression. Singer cocked his head on one side.[③]

Biff was in a quandary[④]. Musingly he wondered just how he should manage the situation. He was still trying to decide when the mute turned over the menu and began to write.

If you cannot think of any place for him to go he can go home with me. First some soup and coffee would be good for him.

With relief Biff nodded vigorously.

On the table he placed three special plates of the last evening meal, two bowls of soup, coffee, and dessert. But Blount would not eat. He would not take his hand away from his mouth, and it was as though his lips were some very secret part of himself which was being exposed. His breath came in ragged sobs and his big shoulders jerked[⑤] nervously. Singer pointed to one dish after the other, but Blount just sat with his hand over his mouth and shook his head.

Biff enunciated[⑥] slowly so that the mute could see. 'The

---

① sewer：下水道

② spurt：喷射，喷出；冲刺，迸发

③ 参考译文：辛格歪了一下脑袋。（cock：竖起，歪着；cock one's head on one side：把头歪向一边）

④ in a quandary：处于困境，处于无法确定如何解决问题或做出决策的困境。

⑤ jerk：痉挛；急拉

⑥ enunciate：清晰地发音

jitters[①]—' he said conversationally.

The steam from the soup kept floating[②] up into Blount's face, and after a little while he reached shakily for his spoon. He drank the soup and ate part of his dessert. His thick, heavy lips still trembled and he bowed his head far down over his plate.

Biff noted this. He was thinking that in nearly every person there was some special physical part kept always guarded[③]. With the mute his hands. The kid Mick picked at the front of her blouse to keep the cloth from rubbing the new, tender nipples beginning to come out on her breast.[④] With Alice it was her hair; she used never to let him sleep with her when he rubbed oil in his scalp. And with himself?

Lingeringly Biff turned the ring on his little finger. Anyway he knew what it was not. Not. Any more. A sharp line cut into his forehead. His hand in his pocket moved nervously toward his genitals. He began whistling a song and got up from the table. Funny to spot it in other people, though.

They helped Blount to his feet. He teetered[⑤] weakly. He was not crying any more, but he seemed to be brooding on something shameful[⑥] and sullen. He walked in the direction he was led. Biff brought out the suitcase from behind the counter and explained to the mute about it. Singer looked as though he could not be surprised at anything.

Biff went with them to the entrance. 'Buck up and keep your nose clean[⑦],' he said to Blount.

The black night sky was beginning to lighten and turn a deep

---

① jitter：紧张不安；神经过敏；激动（常用复数）

② floating：漂浮（float 的动名词形式）

③ guard：保卫，看守

④ 参考译文：那个叫米克的孩子用手拉扯上衣的前襟，是为了不让衣服摩擦到胸前刚刚开始发育的柔嫩乳头。（keep...from：保护……以避免；beginning to come out on her breast 为后置定语修饰 nipples）

⑤ teeter：摇晃，摇摇欲坠

⑥ shameful：可耻的；不体面的；不道德的；猥亵的

⑦ 参考译文：振作起来，别干犯法的事。（buck up：打起精神，振作；keep your nose clean：不卷入是非，做事规矩）

blue with the new morning. There were but a few weak, silvery stars. The street was empty, silent, almost cool. Singer carried the suitcase with his left hand, and with his free hand he supported Blount. He nodded goodbye to Biff and they started off together down the sidewalk. Biff stood watching them. After they had gone half a block away only their black forms showed in the blue darkness—the mute straight and firm and the broad-shouldered, stumbling Blount holding on to him. When he could see them no longer, Biff waited for a moment and examined the sky. The vast depth of it fascinated① and oppressed him. He rubbed his forehead and went back into the sharply② lighted restaurant.

He stood behind the cash register, and his face contracted and hardened as he tried to recall the things that had happened during the night. He had the feeling that he wanted to explain something to himself. He recalled the incidents in tedious detail and was still puzzled.

The door opened and closed several times as a sudden spurt of customers began to come in. The night was over. Willie stacked③ some of the chairs up on the tables and mopped at the floor. He was ready to go home and was singing. Willie was lazy. In the kitchen he was always stopping to play for a while on the harmonica④ he carried around with him. Now he mopped the floor with sleepy strokes and hummed his lonesome Negro music steadily.⑤

The place was still not crowded—it was the hour when men who have been up all night meet those who are freshly wakened and ready

---

① fascinated：着迷的，被深深吸引的

② sharply：强烈地

③ stack：堆放

④ harmonica：口琴

⑤ 参考译文：这会儿，他正昏昏欲睡地一下下地拖着地，一直哼着那首孤独的黑人歌曲。本句看似平实的描写，恰恰描述了小镇上人们百无聊赖的孤独感。（steadily：稳定地）

to start a new day.[①] The sleepy waitress was serving both beer and coffee. There was no noise or conversation, for each person seemed to be alone. The mutual distrust between the men who were just awakened and those who were ending a long night gave everyone a feeling of estrangement[②].

The bank building across the street was very pale in the dawn. Then gradually its white brick walls grew more distinct. When at last the first shafts[③] of the rising sun began to brighten the street, Biff gave the place one last survey and went upstairs.

Noisily he rattled the doorknob as he entered so that Alice would be disturbed.'Motherogod!' he said. 'What a night!'

Alice awoke with caution[④]. She lay on the rumpled bed like a sulky cat and stretched herself. The room was drab in the fresh, hot morning sun, and a pair of silk stockings hung limp and withered from the cord of the windowshade.

'Is that drunk fool still hanging around downstairs?' she demanded.

Biff took off his shirt and examined the collar to see if it were clean enough to be worn again. 'Go down and see for yourself.' I told you nobody will hinder you from kicking[⑤] him out.'

Sleepily Alice reached down and picked up a Bible, the blank side of a menu, and a Sunday-School book from the floor beside the bed. She rustled through the tissue pages of the Bible until she reached a certain passage and began reading, pronouncing[⑥] the words aloud with painful concentration. It was Sunday, and she was preparing the weekly lesson for her class of boys in the Junior Department of her

---

① 参考译文：店里并没有多少客人——这个时候，熬夜的男人们和刚睡醒准备投入新一天工作的男人们碰到了一起。本句较长，用破折号解释店里没有多少客人的具体情形，同时 it was the hour 后用 when 引导的同位语从句说明具体是什么样的时间段；同时 men 和 those（men）后跟 who 引导的定语从句修饰。

② estrangement：疏远；失和

③ shaft：（光、闪电等的）一道，一束

④ caution：小心，谨慎

⑤ hinder sb. from doing：阻碍某人做某事

⑥ pronouncing：发音（pronounce 的动名词）

church. 'Now as he walked by the sea of Galilee, he saw Simon and Andrew his brother casting a net into the sea: for they were fishers. And Jesus said unto them, "Come ye after me, and I will make you to become fishers of men." And straightway they forsook[①] their nets, and followed him.'

Biff went into the bathroom to wash himself. The silky murmuring continued as Alice studied aloud. He listened '... and in the morning, rising up a great while before day, He went out, and departed into a solitary place, and there prayed. And Simon and they that were with Him followed after Him. And when they had found Him, they said unto Him, "All men seek for Thee." '

She had finished. Biff let the words revolve again gently inside him. He tried to separate the actual words from the sound of Alice's voice as she had spoken them. He wanted to remember the passage as his mother used to read it when he was a boy. With nostalgia[②] he glanced down at the wedding ring on his fifth finger that had once been hers. He wondered again how she would have felt about his giving up church and religion.

'The lesson for today is about the gathering of the disciples,' Alice said to herself in preparation. 'And the text is, "All men seek for Thee." '

Abruptly Biff roused himself from meditation and turned on the water spigot at full force.[③] He stripped off his undervest and began to wash himself. Always he was scrupulously[④] clean from the belt upward. Every morning he soaped his chest and arms and neck and feet—and about twice during the season he got into the bathtub and cleaned all of his parts.

Biff stood by the bed, waiting impatiently for Alice to get up.

---

① forsake：抛弃；放弃

② nostalgia：怀旧之情

③ 参考译文：比夫猛地一下从思绪中清醒了，将水龙头拧到最大。（rouse oneself from meditation：从沉思中清醒过来；spigot：龙头，栓；at full force：最大挡）

④ scrupulously：一丝不苟地

From the window he saw that the day would be windless and burning hot. Alice had finished reading the lesson. She still lay lazily across the bed, although she knew that he was waiting. A calm, sullen[①] anger rose in him. He chuckled ironically[②]. Then he said with bitterness: 'If you like I can sit and read the paper awhile. But I wish you would let me sleep now.'

Alice began dressing herself and Biff made up the bed. Deftly he reversed the sheets in all possible ways, putting the top one on the bottom, and turning them over and upside down.[③] When the bed was smoothly made he waited until Alice had left the room before he slipped off his trousers and crawled[④] inside. His feet jutted[⑤] out from beneath the cover and his wiry-haired chest was very dark against the pillow. He was glad he had not told Alice about what had happened to the drunk. He had wanted to talk to somebody about it, because maybe if he told all the facts out loud he could put his finger on[⑥] the thing that puzzled him. The poor son-of-a-bitch talking and talking and not ever getting anybody to understand what he meant. Not knowing himself, most likely. And the way he gravitated[⑦] around the deaf-mute and picked him out and tried to make him a free present of everything in him.

Why?

Because in some men it is in them to give up everything personal at some time, before it ferments and poisons—throw it to some human being or some human idea.[⑧] They have to. In some men it is in them—The text is 'All men seek for Thee.' Maybe that was why—

---

① sullen：愠怒的，不高兴的

② ironically：讽刺地；说反话地

③ 参考译文：他娴熟地来回颠倒着床单，把上面一层放到下面，把它们翻过来，又首尾调了顺序。本句形容比夫和爱丽丝睡觉的习惯，用床单都要各睡各的来刻画二人的疏离。

④ crawl：爬行；匍匐行进

⑤ jut：突出；伸出

⑥ put his finger on：指出，确定，用于表示找到问题的关键点或确定某事的具体原因。

⑦ gravitate：被吸引

⑧ 参考译文：因为对有些人而言，他们会在某个时刻放弃一切个人的东西，趁着东西发酵、放毒之前——把它扔给某个人或某种想法。（ferment：发酵）

maybe—He was a Chinaman, the fellow had said. And a nigger and a wop and a Jew. And if he believed it hard enough maybe it was so. Every person and every thing he said he was—

Biff stretched both of his arms outward and crossed his naked feet. His face was older in the morning light, with the closed, shrunken eyelids and the heavy, iron-like beard on his cheeks and jaw. Gradually his mouth softened and relaxed. The hard, yellow rays of the sun came in through the window so that the room was hot and bright. Biff turned wearily and covered his eyes with his hands. And he was nobody but—Bartholomew—old Biff with two fists and a quick tongue—Mister Brannon—by himself.

3

THE SUN woke Mick early, although she had stayed out mighty late the night before. It was too hot even to drink coffee for breakfast, so she had ice water with syrup① in it and cold biscuits. She messed around the kitchen for a while and then went out on the front porch② to read the funnies. She had thought maybe Mister Singer would be reading the paper on the porch like he did most Sunday mornings. But Mister Singer was not there, and later on her Dad said he came in very late the night before and had company in his room. She waited for Mister Singer a long time. All the other boarders came down except him. Finally she went back in the kitchen and took Ralph out of his high chair and put a clean dress on him and wiped off his face. Then when Bubber got home from Sunday School she was ready to take the kids out. She let Bubber ride in the wagon with Ralph because he was barefooted③ and the hot sidewalk burned his feet. She pulled the wagon for about eight blocks until they came to the big, new house that was being built. The ladder was still propped④ against the edge of the roof, and she screwed up nerve⑤ and began to climb.

'You mind Ralph,' she called back to Bubber. 'Mind the gnats⑥

---

① syrup：糖浆
② porch：门廊
③ barefooted：赤着脚的
④ prop：支撑，倚靠（propped 为过去分词）
⑤ screw up nerve：绷紧（神经）
⑥ gnat：小昆虫

don't sit on his eyelids.'

Five minutes later Mick stood up and held herself very straight. She spread out her arms like wings. This was the place where everybody wanted to stand. The very top. But not many kids could do it. Most of them were scared, for if you lost your grip and rolled off the edge it would kill you. All around were the roofs of other houses and the green tops of trees. On the other side of town were the church steeples[①] and the smokestacks from the mills. The sky was bright blue and hot as fire. The sun made everything on the ground either dizzy[②] white or black.

She wanted to sing. All the songs she knew pushed up toward her throat, but there was no sound. One big boy who had got to the highest part of the roof last week let out a yell and then started hollering out a speech he had learned at High School—'Friends, Romans, Countrymen, Lend me your ears!' There was something about getting to the very top that gave you a wild feeling and made you want to yell or sing or raise up your arms and fly.[③]

She felt the soles[④] of her tennis shoes slipping, and eased herself down so that she straddled[⑤] the peak of the roof. The house was almost finished. It would be one of the largest buildings in the neighborhood—two stories, with very high ceilings and the steepest roof of any house she had ever seen. But soon the work would all be finished. The carpenters[⑥] would leave and the kids would have to find another place to play.

She was by herself. No one was around and it was quiet and she

---

① steeple：（教堂的）尖塔

② dizzy：头晕目眩的；使人眩晕的（dizzy white 意味“白得晃眼”）

③ 参考译文：上个星期，有个大男孩爬到了屋顶最高的地方，大喊一声，便开始大声发表在高中学过的一篇演说——“各位朋友，各位罗马人，各位同胞，请你们听我说！”爬到最高处，会让你有一种狂野的感觉，让你想要大喊、唱歌，或者抬起胳膊飞起来。本句包含两个定语从句，分别由 who 和 that 引导，并分别修饰 boy 和 something。文中提到的演说出自莎士比亚戏剧《裘力斯・凯撒》。

④ sole：脚底；鞋底

⑤ straddle：叉开腿；跨坐

⑥ carpenter：木匠

could think for a while. She took from the pocket of her shorts the package of cigarettes she had bought the night before. She breathed in the smoke slowly. The cigarette① gave her a drunk feeling so that her head seemed heavy and loose on her shoulders, but she had to finish it.

M.K.—That was what she would have written on everything when she was seventeen years old and very famous. She would ride back home in a red-and-white Packard automobile with her initials② on the doors. She would have M.K. written in red on her handkerchiefs and underclothes. Maybe she would be a great inventor. She would invent little tiny radios the size of a green pea that people could carry around and stick in their ears. Also flying machines people could fasten on their backs like knapsacks③ and go zipping④ all over the world. After that she would be the first one to make a large tunnel through the world to China, and people could go down in big balloons. Those were the first things she would invent. They were already planned.

When Mick had finished half of the cigarette she smashed⑤ it dead and flipped⑥ the butt down the slant⑦ of the roof. Then she leaned forward so that her head rested on her arms and began to hum to herself.

It was a funny thing—but nearly all the time there was some kind of piano piece or other music going on in the back of her mind. No matter what she was doing or thinking it was nearly always there. Miss Brown, who boarded with them, had a radio in her room, and all last winter she would sit on the steps every Sunday afternoon and listen in on the programs. Those were probably classical pieces, but they were

---

① cigarette：香烟
② initial：姓名中的大写字母
③ knapsack：背包
④ go zipping：此处指快速移动。
⑤ smash：捻熄（烟头）
⑥ flip：快速翻动
⑦ slant：斜面

the ones she remembered best. There was one special fellow's music that made her heart shrink up[①] every time she heard it. Sometimes this fellow's music was like little colored pieces of crystal candy, and other times it was the softest, saddest thing she had ever imagined about.

There was the sudden sound of crying. Mick sat up straight and listened the wind ruffled[②] the fringe of hair on her forehead and the bright sun made her face white and damp. The whimpering[③] continued, and Mick moved slowly along the sharp-pointed roof on her hands and knees. When she reached the end she leaned forward and lay on her stomach so that her head jutted over the edge and she could see the ground below.[④]

The kids were where she had left them. Bubber was squatting over something on the ground and beside him was a little black, dwarf shadow. Ralph was still tied in the wagon. He was just old enough to sit up, and he held on to the sides of the wagon, with his cap crooked on his head, crying.[⑤]

'Bubber!' Mick called down. 'Find out what that Ralph wants and give it to him.'

Bubber stood up and looked hard into the baby's face. 'He don't want nothing.'

'Well, give him a good shake, then.'

Mick climbed back to the place where she had been sitting before. She wanted to think for a long time about two or three certain people, to sing to herself, and to make plans. But that Ralph was still hollering and there wouldn't be any peace for her at all.

Boldly she began to climb down toward the ladder propped against the edge of the roof. The slant was very steep and there were

---

① shrink up：缩小

② ruffle：弄皱，弄乱

③ whimpering：呜咽

④ 参考译文：当她挪到屋顶的尽头时，便俯身向前，趴在屋脊上，把头探出边缘，这样就可以看见地面了。so that 引导目的状语从句，表示“以便”。

⑤ 参考译文：他还太小，只能勉强坐起身来。他抓着车子两边，帽子外带在头上，正在大哭。just...enough to do sth. 指刚好可以做某事，用于表示满足条件的临界点。（sit up：坐起身来）

only a few blocks of wood nailed down[①], very far apart from each other, that the workmen used for footholds[②]. She was dizzy, and her heart beat so hard it made her tremble. Commandingly she talked out loud to herself: 'Hold on here with your hands tight and then slide down until your right toe gets a grip there and then stay close and wiggle over to the left. Nerve, Mick, you've got to keep nerve.'

Coming down was the hardest part of any climbing. It took her a long time to reach the ladder and to feel safe again. When she stood on the ground at last she seemed much shorter and smaller and her legs felt for a minute like they would crumple up with her. She hitched her shorts and jerked the belt a notch tighter. Ralph was still crying, but she paid the sound no attention and went into the new, empty house.

Last month they had put a sign out in front saying that no children were allowed on the lot. A gang of kids had been scuffling[③] around inside the rooms one night, and a girl who couldn't see in the dark had run into a room that hadn't been floored and fallen through and broken her leg. She was still at the hospital in a plaster[④] parish cast. Also, another time some tough boys wee-weed all over one of the walls and wrote some pretty bad words. But no matter how many Keep Out signs were put up, they couldn't run kids away until the house had been painted and finished and people had moved in.

The rooms smelled of new wood, and when she walked the soles of her tennis shoes made a flopping sound that echoed through all the house. The air was hot and quiet. She stood still in the middle of the front room for a while, and then she suddenly thought of something. She fished in her pocket and brought out two stubs of chalk[⑤]—one green and the other red.

---

① nail down：用钉子钉住
② foothold：立足处（攀登时脚踩的地方）
③ scuffle：混战；扭打
④ plaster：石膏
⑤ chalk：粉笔

Mick drew the big block letters very slowly. At the top she wrote EDISON, and under that she drew the names of DICK TRACY and MUSSOLINI. Then in each corner with the largest letters of all, made with green and outlined in red, she wrote her initials—M.K. When that was done she crossed over to the opposite[①] wall and wrote a very bad word—PUSSY, and beneath[②] that she put her initials, too.

She stood in the middle of the empty room and stared at what she had done. The chalk was still in her hands and she did not feel really satisfied. She was trying to think of the name of this fellow who had written this music she heard over the radio last winter. She had asked a girl at school who owned a piano and took music lessons about him, and the girl asked her teacher.[③] It seemed this fellow was just a kid who had lived in some country in Europe a good while ago. But even if he was just a young kid he had made up all these beautiful pieces for the piano and for the violin and for a band or orchestra too. In her mind she could remember about six different tunes from the pieces of his she had heard. A few of them were kind of quick and tinkling[④], and another was like that smell in the springtime after a rain. But they all made her somehow sad and excited at the same time.

She hummed[⑤] one of the tunes[⑥], and after a while in the hot, empty house by herself she felt the tears come in her eyes. Her throat got tight and rough and she couldn't sing any more. Quickly she wrote the fellow's name at the very top of the list—MOTSART.

Ralph was tied in the wagon[⑦] just as she had left him. He sat up quiet and still and his fat little hands held on to the sides. Ralph looked

---

① opposite：对面的

② beneath：在……之下

③ 参考译文：关于这个人，她向学校里的一个女孩打听过。这个女孩家里有钢琴，而且上过关于他的音乐课。后来，这个女孩又去问自己的老师。本句为定语从句修饰“女孩”，并且出于句子拆分的考虑，参考译文将后半句拆译。

④ tinkling：发出清脆响声的（tinkle 的现在分词形式作形容词使用）

⑤ hum：发低哼声；哼（曲子）

⑥ tune：曲调；调子

⑦ wagon：四轮运货车

like a little Chinese baby with his square[1] black bangs and his black eyes. The sun was in his face, and that was why he had been hollering. Bubber was nowhere around. When Ralph saw her coming he began tuning up[2] to cry again. She pulled the wagon into the shade by the side of the new house and took from her shirt pocket a blue-colored jelly bean. She stuck the candy in the baby's warm, soft mouth.

'Put that in your pipe and smoke it,' she said to him. In a way it was a waste, because Ralph was still too little to get the real good flavor[3] out of candy. A clean rock would be about the same to him, only the little fool would swallow it. He didn't understand any more about taste than he did about talking. When you said you were so sick and tired of dragging him around you had a good mind to throw him in the river, it was the same to him as if you had been loving him. Nothing much made any difference to him. That was why it was such an awful bore to haul him around.

Mick cupped[4] her hands, clamped them tight together, and blew through the crack between her thumbs. Her cheeks puffed out and at first there was only the sound of air rushing through her fists. Then a high, shrill whistle sounded, and after a few seconds Bubber came out from around the corner of the house.

She rumpled the sawdust out of Bubber's hair and straightened Ralph's cap. This cap was the finest thing Ralph had. It was made out of lace and all embroidered[5]. The ribbon under his chin was blue on one side and white on the other, and over each ear there were big rosettes. His head had got too big for the cap and the embroidery scratched[6], but she always put it on him when she took him out. Ralph didn't have any real baby carriage like most folks' babies did, or

---

① square：正方形的
② tune up：调整到……的状态
③ flavor：味道
④ cup：使成杯状
⑤ embroidered：绣花的
⑥ scratched：有刮痕的

any summer bootees[①]. He had to be dragged around in a tacky[②] old wagon she had got for Christmas three years before. But the fine cap gave him face.

There was nobody on the street, for it was late Sunday morning and very hot. The wagon screeched[③] and rattled. Bubber was barefooted and the sidewalk was so hot it burned his feet. The green oak trees made cool-looking black shadows on the ground, but that was not shade enough.

'Get up in the wagon,' she told Bubber. 'And let Ralph sit in your lap.'

'I can walk all right.'

The long summer-time always gave Bubber the colic[④]. He didn't have on a shirt and his ribs were sharp and white. The sun made him pale[⑤] instead of brown, and his little titties[⑥] were like blue raisins[⑦] on his chest.

'I don't mind pulling you,' Mick said. 'Get on in.'

'O.K.'

Mick dragged the wagon slowly because she was not in any hurry to get home. She began talking to the kids. But it was really more like saying things to herself than words said to them.

'This is a funny thing—the dreams I've been having lately. It's like I'm swimming. But instead of water I'm pushing out my arms and swimming through great big crowds of people. The crowd is a hundred times bigger than in Kresses' store on Saturday afternoon. The biggest crowd in the world. And sometimes I'm yelling and swimming through people, knocking them all down wherever I go—and other times I'm on the ground and people are trompling all over

① bootee：毛线鞋；女人的短靴
② tacky：俗气的，劣质的
③ screech：发出尖锐刺耳的声音
④ colic：（尤见于婴儿的）腹绞痛
⑤ pale：苍白的；灰白的
⑥ titty：乳房，乳头（等于 teat）
⑦ raisin：葡萄干

me and my insides are oozing out on the sidewalk.[①] I guess it's more like a nightmare[②] than a plain dream—'

On Sundays the house was always full of folks because the boarders had visitors. Newspapers rustled and there was cigar smoke, and footsteps always on the stairs.

'Some things you just naturally want to keep private. Not because they are bad, but because you just want them secret. There are two or three I wouldn't want even you to know about.'

Bubber got out when they came to the corner and helped her lift the wagon down the curb[③] and get it up on the next sidewalk.

'But there's one thing I would give anything for. And that's a piano. If we had a piano I'd practice every single night and learn every piece in the world. That's the thing I want more than anything else.'

They had come to their own home block now. Their house was only a few doors away. It was one of the biggest houses on the whole north side of town—three stories high. But then there were fourteen people in the family. There weren't that many in the real, blood Kelly family—but they ate there and slept there at five dollars a head and you might as well count them on in. Mr. Singer wasn't counted in that because he only rented[④] a room and kept it straightened up himself.

The house was narrow and had not been painted for many years. It did not seem to be built strong enough for its three stories of height. It sagged on one side.

Mick untied Ralph and lifted him from the wagon. She darted[⑤] quickly through the hall, and from the corner of her eye she saw that

---

① 参考译文：有时候，我一边大喊，一边在人群里游，不管游到哪儿，都会把他们撞倒在地——还有时候，我躺在地上，人们纷纷从我身上踩踏过去，我的内脏流出来，淌到人行道上。本句用并列的几个动词进行时表示同时发生的几个动作，即"一边……一边……"。（trompling：此处应为 trampling，意为"践踏，踩踏"，trample 的 ing 形式；ooze：渗出）

② nightmare：噩梦

③ curb：马路牙子

④ rent：租用

⑤ dart：快速投掷

the living-room was full of boarders. Her Dad was there, too. Her Mama would be in the kitchen. They were all hanging around waiting for dinner-time.

She went into the first of the three rooms that the family kept for themselves. She put Ralph down on the bed where her Dad and Mama slept and gave him a string of beads to play with. From behind the closed door of the next room she could hear the sound of voices, and she decided to go inside.

Hazel and Etta stopped talking when they saw her. Etta was sitting in the chair by the window, painting her toenails with the red polish. Her hair was done up in steel rollers and there was a white dab of face cream on a little place under her chin where a pimple had come out.① Hazel was flopped② out lazy on the bed as usual.

'What were you all jawing about?'

'It's none of your nosy business,' Etta said. 'Just you hush up③ and leave us alone.'

'It's my room just as much as it is either one of yours. I have as good a right in here as you do.' Mick strutted from one corner to the other until she had covered all the floor space. 'But then I don't care anything about picking any fight. All I want are my own rights.'

Mick brushed back her shaggy④ bangs with the palm of her hand. She had done this so often that there was a little row of cowlicks above her forehead. She quivered⑤ her nose and made faces at herself in the mirror. Then she began walking around the room again.

Hazel and Etta were O.K. as far as sisters went. But Etta was like she was full of worms. All she thought about was movie stars and getting in the movies. Once she had written to Jeanette MacDonald

---

① 参考译文：她的头发用铁发卷卷了起来，下巴上有一小块地方涂着一点白色的面霜。
② flop：猛然躺下
③ hush up：保持沉默
④ shaggy：蓬乱的
⑤ quiver：微颤，抖动

and had got a typewritten[①] letter back saying that if ever she came out to Hollywood she could come by and swim in her swimming pool. And ever since that swimming pool had been preying on Etta's mind. All she thought about was going to Hollywood when she could scrape up the bus fare and getting a job as a secretary and being buddies with Jeanette MacDonald and getting in the movies herself.[②]

She primped all the day long. And that was the bad part. Etta wasn't naturally pretty like Hazel. The main thing was she didn't have any chin. She would pull at her jaw and go through a lot of chin exercises she had read in a movie book. She was always looking at her side profile[③] in the mirror and trying to keep her mouth set in a certain way. But it didn't do any good. Sometimes Etta would hold her face with her hands and cry in the night about it.

Hazel was plain lazy. She was good-looking but thick[④] in the head. She was eighteen years old, and next to Bill she was the oldest of all the kids in the family. Maybe that was the trouble. She got the first and biggest share of everything—the first whack[⑤] at the new clothes and the biggest part of any special treat. Hazel never had to grab for[⑥] anything and she was soft.

'Are you just going to tramp around the room all day? It makes me sick to see you in those silly boy's clothes. Somebody ought to clamp down on you, Mick Kelly, and make you behave,' Etta said.

'Shut up,' said Mick. 'I wear shorts because I don't want to wear your old hand-me-downs. I don't want to be like either of you and I don't want to look like either of you. And I won't. That's why I wear shorts. I'd rather be a boy any day, and I wish I could move in with

---

① typewritten：用打字机打出的

② 参考译文：她一心想着，等她攒够车票钱就去好莱坞，找份秘书的工作，跟珍尼特·麦克唐纳成为闺蜜，然后自己也去演电影。句中 all 为主语，she thought about 为省略 that 的定语从句修饰 all，三个并列的动名词 going、getting 和 being 为表语。（scrape up：积攒，积蓄；secretary：秘书）

③ profile：轮廓；外形

④ thick：迟钝的

⑤ whack：一份

⑥ grab for：试图获得

Bill.'

Mick scrambled[①] under the bed and brought out a large hatbox. As she carried it to the door both of them called after her, 'Good riddance!'

Bill had the nicest room of anybody in the family. Like a den—and he had it all to himself—except for Bubber. Bill had pictures cut out from magazines tacked on the walls, mostly faces of beautiful ladies, and in another corner were some pictures Mick had painted last year herself at the free art class.[②] There was only a bed and a desk in the room.

Bill was sitting hunched[③] over the desk, reading *Popular Mechanics*. She went up behind him and put her arms around his shoulders. 'Hey, you old son-of-a-gun.'

He did not begin tussling with her like he used to do. 'Hey,' he said, and shook his shoulders a little.

'Will it bother you if I stay in here a little while?'

'Sure—I don't mind if you want to stay.'

Mick knelt[④] on the floor and untied the string[⑤] on the big hatbox. Her hands hovered over the edge of the lid, but for some reason she could not make up her mind to open it.

'I been thinking about what I've done on this already,' she said. 'And it may work and it may not.'

Bill went on reading. She still knelt over the box, but did not open it. Her eyes wandered over to Bill as he sat with his back to her. One of his big feet kept stepping on the other as he read. His shoes were scuffed[⑥]. Once their Dad had said that all Bill's dinners went to

---

① scramble：快速爬行（scramble 的过去式）

② 参考译文：比尔在墙上钉满了从杂志上剪下来的照片，大都是美女的脸部特写。在另外一角，挂着米克去年上免费美术班时画的一些画。本句为 and 连接的并列句，前半句主结构为 Bill had pictures tacked on the walls，cut out from magazines 为过去分词作后置定语修饰 pictures。（have sth done 意为"让某物被……"；tack：用平头钉钉）

③ hunched：缩成一团的

④ kned：跪（过去式为 knelt）

⑤ string：线，细绳

⑥ scuffed：磨损的；磨破的

his feet and his breakfast to one ear and his supper to the other ear. That was a sort of mean[①] thing to say and Bill had been sour over[②] it for a month, but it was funny. His ears flared out[③] and were very red, and though he was just out of high school he wore a size thirteen shoe. He tried to hide his feet by scraping one foot behind the other when he stood up, but that only made it worse.

Mick opened the box a few inches and then shut it again. She felt too excited to look into it now. She got up and walked around the room until she could calm down a little. After a few minutes she stopped before the picture she had painted at the free government art class for school kids last winter. There was a picture of a storm on the ocean and a sea gull[④] being dashed through the air by the wind. It was called 'Sea Gull with Back Broken in Storm.' The teacher had described the ocean during the first two or three lessons, and that was what nearly everybody started with[⑤]. Most of the kids were like her, though, and they had never really seen the ocean with their own eyes.

That was the first picture she had done and Bill had tacked it on his wall. All the rest of her pictures were full of people. She had done some more ocean storms at first—one with an airplane crashing down and people jumping out to save themselves, and another with a trans-Atlantic liner going down and all the people trying to push and crowd into one little lifeboat.[⑥]

Mick went into the closet of Bill's room and brought out some other pictures she had done in the class—some pencil drawings, some water-colors, and one canvas with oils. They were all full of people. She had imagined a big fire on Broad Street and painted how she

① mean：不善良的，刻薄的

② be sour over：为……闷闷不乐

③ flare out：向外展开，指物体或形状从一端逐渐向外扩展

④ sea gull：海鸥

⑤ start with：开始于

⑥ 参考译文：起初，她还画过一些海上风暴的画——有一张画的是一架正在坠落的飞机，人们纷纷跳机逃命；另一张画的是一艘横渡大西洋的轮船正在沉没，所有人都争抢着往一条小救生船上挤。

thought it would be. The flames were bright green and orange and Mr. Brannon's restaurant and the First National Bank were about the only buildings left. People were lying dead in the streets and others were running for their lives. One man was in his nightshirt and a lady was trying to carry a bunch of bananas with her. Another picture was called 'Boiler Busts in Factory,' and men were jumping out of[①] windows and running while a knot of kids in overalls stood scrouged together, holding the buckets of dinner they had brought to their Daddies. The oil painting was a picture of the whole town fighting on Broad Street. She never knew why she had painted this one and she couldn't think of the right name for it. There wasn't any fire or storm or reason you could see in the picture why all this battle[②] was happening. But there were more people and more moving around than in any other picture. This was the best one, and it was too bad that she couldn't think up[③] the real name. In the back of her mind somewhere she knew what it was.

Mick put the picture back on the closet shelf. None of them were any good much. The people didn't have fingers and some of the arms were longer than the legs. The class had been fun, though. But she had just drawn whatever came into her head[④] without reason—and in her heart it didn't give her near the same feeling that music did. Nothing was really as good as music.

Mick knelt down on the floor and quickly lifted the top of the big hatbox[⑤]. Inside was a cracked ukulele strung with two violin strings, a guitar string and a banjo[⑥] string. The crack on the back of the ukulele had been neatly mended with sticking plaster and the round hole in

---

① jump out of：从……里跳出来
② battle：战斗
③ think up：想出（主意或计划）
④ come into one's head：想到
⑤ hatbox：帽盒
⑥ banjo：班卓琴；五弦琴

the middle was covered by a piece of wood.[①] The bridge of a violin held up[②] the strings at the end and some sound-holes had been carved on either side. Mick was making herself a violin. She held the violin in her lap. She had the feeling she had never really looked at it before. Some time ago she made Bubber a little play mandolin out of a cigar box with rubber bands, and that put the idea into her head. Since that she had hunted all over everywhere for the different parts and added a little to the job every day. It seemed to her she had done everything except use her head.

'Bill, this don't look like any real violin I ever saw.'

He was still reading—'Yeah—?'

'It just don't look right. It just don't—'

She had planned to tune the fiddle[③] that day by screwing the pegs[④]. But since she had suddenly realized how all the work had turned out she didn't want to look at it. Slowly she plucked[⑤] one string after another. They all made the same little hollow-sounding ping.

'How anyway will I ever get a bow? Are you sure they have to be made out of just horses' hair?'

'Yeah,' said Bill impatiently.

'Nothing like thin wire or human hair strung on a limber stick would do?'

Bill rubbed his feet against each other and didn't answer.

Anger made beads of sweat come out on her forehead[⑥]. Her voice was hoarse. 'It's not even a bad violin. It's only a cross between a mandolin[⑦] and a ukulele. And I hate them. I hate them—'

---

① 参考译文：琴背面的裂缝已经用胶布小心粘好，琴中间的圆孔盖上了一片木头。（crack：裂缝；ukulele：尤克里里琴）

② hold up：举起

③ tune the fiddle：给小提琴调音（fiddle：提琴）

④ screw the pegs：拧紧琴栓（peg：弦钮，琴栓）

⑤ pluck：拉，拽

⑥ forehead：前额

⑦ mandolin：曼陀林（一种琵琶乐器）

Bill turned around.

'It's all turned out wrong. It won't do. It's no good.'

'Pipe down[①],' said Bill. 'Are you just carrying on about that old broken ukulele you've been fooling with? I could have told you at first it was crazy to think you could make any violin. That's one thing you don't sit down and make— you got to buy them. I thought anybody would know a thing like that. But I figured it wouldn't hurt yon if you found out for yourself.'

Sometimes she hated Bill more than anyone else in the world. He was different entirely[②] from what he used to be. She started to slam the violin down on the floor and stomp on it, but instead she put it back roughly into the hatbox.[③] The tears were hot in her eyes as fire. She gave the box a kick and ran from the room without looking at Bill.

As she was dodging[④] through the hall to get to the back yard she ran into her Mama.

'What's the matter with you? What have you been into now?'

Mick tried to jerk[⑤] loose, but her Mama held on to her arm. Sullenly she wiped the tears from her face with the back of her hand. Her Mama had been in the kitchen and she wore her apron[⑥] and house-shoes. As usual she looked as though she had a lot on her mind and didn't have time to ask her any more questions.[⑦]

'Mr. Jackson has brought his two sisters to dinner and there won't be but just enough chairs, so today you're to eat in the kitchen with Bubber.'

---

① pipe down：安静下来，例：Would you pipe down? I want to hear what he wants to say. 你们能不能安静下来？我要听听他想说什么。

② entirely：完全地，彻底地

③ 参考译文：她猛地把小提琴摔到地上，一通猛踩，但接着，又把琴草草收进帽盒里。（stomp on：践踏，踩踏）

④ dodge：躲闪

⑤ jerk：猝然一动，猛地一拉

⑥ apron：围裙

⑦ 参考译文：她跟平时一样，似乎心事重重，没有时间再问米克问题。（have a lot on one's mind：心事重重）

'That's hunky-dory with me,' Mick said.

Her Mama let her go and went to take off her apron. From the dining-room there came the sound of the dinner bell and a sudden glad outbreak of talking. She could hear her Dad saying how much he had lost by not keeping up his accident insurance① until the time he broke his hip. That was one thing her Dad could never get off his mind—ways he could have made money and didn't. There was a clatter② of dishes, and after a while the talking stopped.

Mick leaned on the banisters③ of the stairs. The sudden crying had started her with the hiccups④. It seemed to her as she thought back over the last month that she had never really believed in her mind that the violin would work.⑤ But in her heart she had kept making herself believe. And even now it was hard not to believe a little. She was tired out. Bill wasn't ever a help with anything now. She used to think Bill was the grandest person in the world. She used to follow after him every place he went—out fishing in the woods, to the clubhouses he built with other boys, to the slot machine in the back of Mr. Brannon's restaurant—everywhere. Maybe he hadn't meant to let her down like this. But anyway they could never be good buddies again.

In the hall there was the smell of cigarettes and Sunday dinner. Mick took a deep breath and walked back toward the kitchen. The dinner began to smell good and she was hungry. She could hear Portia's voice as she talked to Bubber, and it was like she was half-singing something or telling him a story.

'And that is the various reason why I'm a whole lot more fortunate⑥ than most colored girls,' Portia said as she opened the door.

'Why?' asked Mick.

---

① insurance：保险
② clatter：哗啦声
③ banister：（楼梯的）栏杆，扶手
④ hiccup：打嗝
⑤ 参考译文：她回顾过去的一个月，觉得在心里似乎从未真正相信过那把小提琴能用。It seemed...that... 为主结构，中间插入 as 引导的时间状语从句。
⑥ fortunate：幸运的

Portia and Bubber were sitting at the kitchen table eating their dinner. Portia's green print dress was cool-looking against her dark brown skin. She had on green earrings and her hair was combed very tight and neat.

'You all time pounce in on the very tail of what somebody say and then want to know all about it,' Portia said. She got up and stood over the hot stove, putting dinner on Mick's plate. 'Bubber and me was just talking about my Grandpapa's home out on the Old Sardis Road. I was telling Bubber how he and my uncles owns the whole place themself. Fifteen and a half acre.[①] They always plants four of them in cotton, some years swapping[②] back to peas to keep the dirt rich, and one acre on a hill is just for peaches. They have a mule[③] and a breed sow[④] and all the time from twenty to twenty-five laying hens and fryers[⑤]. They haves a vegetable patch and two pecan trees and plenty figs and plums and berries. This here is the truth. Not many white farms has done with their land good as my Grandpapa.'

Mick put her elbows[⑥] on the table and leaned over her plate. Portia had always rather talk about the farm than anything else, except about her husband and brother. To hear her tell it you would think that colored farm was the very White House itself.

'The home started with just one little room. And through the years they done built on until there's space for my Grandpapa, his four sons and their wives and childrens, and my brother Hamilton.[⑦] In the parlor they haves a real organ and a gramophone[⑧]. And on the

---

① 参考译文：我告诉巴伯我外公和舅舅们拥有整片那个地方，足足有十五英亩半。本句由how引导宾语从句，但从句中的谓语表达有误，主语为复数，应使用own。

② swap：调整

③ mule：骡子

④ breed sow：种猪（更多使用breeding sow）

⑤ fryer：（适于炸食的）仔鸡，雏鸡

⑥ elbow：手肘

⑦ 参考译文：那么多年来，他们一直在建房子，最后，房子大得足够我外公、他的四个儿子和他们的老婆孩子住，还能装下我的弟弟汉密尔顿。本句英文主结构正确的表达应为they had built on...，过去完成时表达在过去多年里的持续动作。此处原文作者是为了表达波西娅并不纯正的英文。（build on：持续在建）

⑧ gramophone：留声机，唱机

wall they haves a large picture of my Grandpapa taken in his lodge uniform[①]. They cans all the fruit and vegetables and no matter how cold and rainy the winter turns they pretty near always haves plenty to eat.'

'How come you don't go live with them, then?' Mick asked.

Portia stopped peeling[②] her potatoes and her long, brown fingers tapped on the table in time to her words. 'This here the way it is. See—each person done built on his room for his family. They all done worked hard during all these years. And of course times is hard for everybody now. But see—I lived with my Grandpapa when I were a little girl. But I haven't never done any work out there since. Any time, though, if me and Willie and Highboy gets in bad trouble us can always go back.[③]'

'Didn't your Father build on a room? '

Portia stopped chewing. 'Whose Father? You mean my Father?'

'Sure,' said Mick.

'You know good and well my Father is a colored[④] doctor right here in town.'

Mick had heard Portia say that before, but she had thought it was a tale. How could a colored man be a doctor?

'This here the way it is. Before the tune my Mama married my Father she had never known anything but real kindness. My Grandpa is Mister Kind hisself. But my Father is different from him as day is from night.'

'Mean[⑤]? 'asked Mick.

'No, he not a mean man,' Portia said slowly. 'It just that

---

① lodge uniform：会社制服（lodge：共济会等会社的地方分会，集会处）

② peel：削皮

③ 参考译文：但从那以后我在那儿就没干过活儿。不过无论什么时候，如果我和威利、海博埃碰到了麻烦，我们随时都可以回去。本句表达同样为不纯正的黑人英语，正确的为：But I haven ever done any work out there since. Any time, though, if Willie, Highboy and I get in bad trouble we can always go back.（get in trouble：陷入麻烦）

④ colored：有色人种的（主要指黑人）

⑤ mean：刻薄的，残酷的

something is the matter. My Father not like other colored mens. This here is hard to explain. My Father all the time studying by hisself. And a long time ago he taken up[①] all these notions[②] about how a family ought to be. He bossed over ever little thing in the house and at night he tried to teach us children lessons.'

'That don't sound so bad to me,' said Mick.

'Listen here. You see most of the time he were very quiet. But then some nights he would break out in a kind of fit. He could get madder than any man I ever seen.[③] Everybody who know my Father say that he was a sure enough crazy man. He done wild, crazy things and our Mama quit[④] him. I were ten years old at the time. Our Mama taken us children with her to Grandpapa's farm and us were raised out there. Our Father all the time wanted us to come back. But even when our Mama died us children never did go home to live. And now my Father stay all by hisself.'

Mick went to the stove and filled her plate a second time. Portia's voice was going up and down like a song, and nothing could stop her now.

'I doesn't see my Father much—maybe once a week—but I done a lot of thinking about him. I feels sorrier for him than anybody I knows. I expect he done read more books than any white man in this town. He done read more books and he done worried about more things. He full of books and worrying. He done lost God and turned his back to religion. All his troubles come down just to that.'

Portia was excited. Whenever she got to talking about God—or Willie, her brother, or Highboy, her husband—she got excited.

'Now, I not a big shouter[⑤]. I belongs to the Presbyterian Church

---

① take up：采取行动

② notion：概念，想法；一时的念头，突发的奇想

③ 参考译文：但有些晚上他会大发脾气，他生气的样子比我见过的任何人都凶。（in a fit：大发脾气，fit 有“愤怒”的意思；madder：更加疯狂的，mad 的比较级）

④ quit：放弃

⑤ shouter：高呼者，呼喊派

and us don't hold with all this rolling on the floor and talking in tongues. Us don't get sanctified[1] every week and wallow around[2] together. In our church we sings and lets the preacher[3] do the preaching. And tell you the truth I don't think a little singing and a little preaching would hurt you, Mick. You ought to take your little brother to the Sunday School and also you plenty big enough to sit in church[4]. From the biggity way you been acting lately it seem to me like you already got one toe in the pit[5].'

'Nuts,' Mick said.

'Now Highboy he were Holiness boy before us were married. He loved to get the spirit ever Sunday and shout and sanctify hisself. But after us were married I got him to join with me, and although it kind of hard to keep him quiet sometime I think he doing right well.'

'I don't believe in God any more than I do Santa Oaus,' Mick said.

'You wait a minute! That's why it sometime seem to me you favor my Father more than any person I ever knowed.'

'Me? You say I favor[6] him?'

'I don't mean in the face or in any kind of looks. I was speaking about the shape and color of your souls.'

Bubber sat looking from one to the other. His napkin[7] was tied around his neck and in his hand he still held his empty spoon. 'What all does God eat?' he asked.

Mick got up from the table and stood in the doorway[8], ready to leave. Sometimes it was fun to devil[9] Portia. She started on the same tune and said the same thing over and over—like that was all she

---

① sanctify：使净化
② wallow around：四处游荡
③ preacher：传道者；牧师
④ church：教堂
⑤ pit：深坑（get one toe in the pit：一只脚迈进火坑）
⑥ favor：（非正式）长得像（大多数时候意为“喜欢”）
⑦ napkin：餐巾
⑧ doorway：门口，门道
⑨ devil：困扰，使担忧，折腾

knew.

'Folks like you and my Father who don't attend the church can't never have nair peace at all. Now take me here—I believe and I haves peace. And Bubber, he haves his peace too. And my Highboy and my Willie likewise[①]. And it seem to me just from looking at him this here Mr. Singer haves peace too. I done felt that the first time I seen him.'

'Have it your own way,' Mick said. 'You're crazier than any father of yours could ever be.'

'But you haven't never loved God nor even nair person. You hard and tough as cowhide[②]. But just the same I knows you. This afternoon you going to roam all over the place without never being satisfied. You going to traipse[③] all around like you haves to find something lost. You going to work yourself up with excitement. Your heart going to beat hard enough to kill you because you don't love and don't have peace. And then some day you going to bust loose and be ruined[④]. Won't nothing help you then.'

'What, Portia?' Bubber asked. 'What kind of things does He eat?'

Mick laughed and stamped[⑤] out of the room.

She did roam around the house during the afternoon because she could not get settled. Some days were just like that. For one thing the thought of the violin kept worrying her. She could never have made it like a real one—and after all those weeks of planning the very thought of it made her sick. But how could she have been so sure the idea would work? So dumb? Maybe when people longed for a thing that bad the longing made them trust in anything that might give it to them.

Mick did not want to go back into the rooms where the family

---

① likewise：同样地；也
② cowhide：牛皮
③ traipse：闲逛；游荡
④ ruin：破坏
⑤ stamp：跺脚

stayed. And she did not want to have to talk to any of the boarders[1]. No place was left but the street—and there the sun was too burning hot. She wandered aimlessly up and down the hall and kept pushing back her rumpled hair with the palm of her hand. 'Hell,' she said aloud to herself. 'Next to a real piano I sure would rather have some place to myself than anything I know.'

That Portia had a certain kind of niggery[2] craziness, but she was O.K. She never would do anything mean to Bubber or Ralph on the sly[3] like some colored girls. But Portia had said that she never loved anybody. Mick stopped walking and stood very still, rubbing[4] her fist on the top of her head. What would Portia think if she really knew? Just what would she think?

She had always kept things to herself. That was one sure truth.

Mick went slowly up the stairs. She passed the first landing and went on to the second. Some of the doors were open to make a draught and there were many sounds in the house. Mick stopped on the last flight of stairs and sat down. If Miss Brown turned on her radio she could hear the music. Maybe some good program would come on.

She put her head on her knees and tied knots in the strings of her tennis shoes. What would Portia say if she knew that always there had been one person after another? And every time it was like some part of her would bust[5] in a hundred pieces.

But she had always kept it to herself and no person had ever known.

Mick sat on the steps a long time. Miss Brown did not turn on

---

① boarder：寄宿者，房客

② niggery：黑人般的（nigger 的派生词）

③ on the sly：偷偷地；冷不防地，例：She often writes to her boy friend at school. 她在学校经常偷偷给男朋友写信。

④ rub：摩擦

⑤ bust：打破，炸破

her radio and there was nothing but the noises that people made.[①] She thought a long time and kept hitting her thighs with her fists. Her face felt like it was scattered[②] in pieces and she could not keep it straight. The feeling was a whole lot worse than being hungry for any dinner, yet it was like that. I want—I want—I want—was all that she could think about—but just what this real want was she did not know.

After about an hour there was the sound of a doorknob[③] being turned on the landing above. Mick looked up quickly and it was Mister Singer. He stood in the hall for a few minutes and his face was sad and calm. Then he went across to the bathroom. His company did not come out with him. From where she was sitting she could see part of the room, and the company was asleep on the bed with a sheet pulled over him. She waited for Mister Singer to come out of the bathroom. Her cheeks were very hot and she felt them with her hands. Maybe it was true that she came up on these top steps sometimes so she could see Mister Singer while she was listening to Miss Brown's radio on the floor below.[④] She wondered what kind of music he heard in his mind that his ears couldn't hear. Nobody knew. And what kind of things he would say if he could talk. Nobody knew that either[⑤].

Mick waited, and after a while he came out into the hall again. She hoped he would look down and smile at her. And then when he got to his door he did glance down and nod his head. Mick's grin was wide and trembling[⑥]. He went into his room and shut the door. It might have been he meant to invite her in to see him. Mick wanted suddenly to go into his room. Sometime soon when he didn't have company she would really go in and see Mister Singer. She really

---

① 参考译文：布朗小姐并没有打开收音机，除了人们的嘈杂声，再没有别的声音了。（turn on：打开；nothing but：只有）

② scattered：零散的

③ doorknob：球形门把手

④ 参考译文：也许，她有时候到最上面的楼梯来，的确是为了一边听楼下布朗小姐的收音机，一边还可以看见辛格先生。（It was/is true tha...：确实……；while：与……同时）

⑤ either：用于否定句，表示“也不”，与刚提过的人或事物类似或有关联。

⑥ tremble：发抖（trembling 为 tremble 的现在分词）

would do that.

The hot afternoon passed slowly and Mick still sat on the steps by herself. The fellow Motsart's music was in her mind again. It was funny, but Mister Singer reminded her of[①] this music. She wished there was some place where she could go to hum it out loud. Some kind of music was too private to sing in a house cram full of people. It was funny, too, how lonesome[②] a person could be in a crowded house. Mick tried to think of some good private place where she could go and be by herself and study about this music. But though she thought about this a long time she knew in the beginning that there was no good place.

---

① remind sb. of sth. 使某人想起某事，例：I bought this card to remind you of your birthday. 我买这张卡片是要提醒你的生日到了。

② lonesome：孤单的

4

LATE IN the afternoon Jake Blount awoke with the feeling that he had slept enough. The room in which he lay was small and neat, furnished with a bureau, a table, a bed, and a few chairs.① On the bureau an electric fan turned its face slowly from one wall to another, and as the breeze from it passed Jake's face he thought of cool water. By the window a man sat before the table and stared down at a chess game laid out② before him. In the daylight the room was not familiar to Jake, but he recognized the man's face instantly③ and it was as though he had known him a very long time.

Many memories were confused in Jake's mind. He lay motionless with his eyes open and his hands turned palm④ upward. His hands were huge and very brown against the white sheet. When he held them up to his face he saw that they were scratched and bruised—and the veins were swollen as though he had been grasping hard at something for a long time.⑤ His face looked tired and unkempt. His brown hair fell down over his forehead and his mustache⑥ was awry. Even his wing-shaped eyebrows were rough and tousled. As he lay

---

① 参考译文：他躺着的这个房间小而整洁，有一张书桌、一张饭桌、一张床和几把椅子。（furnish：配备了……家具，即词组 furnished with；bureau：办公桌；table：餐桌）

② lay out：摆放，布置（laid 为过去分词，被动式作后置定语）

③ instantly：立即，马上

④ palm：手掌，手心

⑤ 参考译文：他把手举到面前，上面布满抓痕和淤青——血管都突出着，好像他一直抓着什么东西抓了很久。（scratch：抓，搔；grasp：抓住）

⑥ mustache：胡子

there his lips moved once or twice and his mustache jerked with a nervous quiver[1].

After a while he sat up and gave himself a thump on the side of his head with one of his big fists to straighten himself out. When he moved, the man playing chess looked up quickly and smiled at[2] him.

'God, I'm thirsty,' Jake said. 'I feel like the whole Russian army marched through my mouth in its stocking feet.'

The man looked at him, still smiling, and then suddenly he reached down on the other side of the table and brought up a frosted[3] pitcher of ice water and a glass. Jake drank in great panting gulps—standing half-naked in the middle of the room, his head thrown back and one of his hands closed in a tense fist. He finished four glasses before he took a deep breath and relaxed a little.

Instantly certain recollections came to him. He couldn't remember coming home with this man, but things that had happened later were clearer now.[4] He had waked up soaking in a tub of cold water, and afterward they drank coffee and talked. He had got a lot of things off his chest and the man had listened. He had talked himself hoarse, but he could remember the expressions on the man's face better than anything that was said. They had gone to bed in the morning with the shade pulled down so no light could come in. At first he would keep waking up with nightmares and have to turn the light on to get himself clear again. The light would wake this fellow also, but he hadn't complained at all.

'How come you didn't kick me out[5] last night?'

The man only smiled again. Jake wondered why he was so quiet. He looked around for his clothes and saw that his suitcase[6] was on the

---

① quiver：抖动

② smile at：冲……微笑

③ frosted：磨砂（玻璃）的

④ 参考译文：他不记得跟这个男人回家了，但之后发生的事情现在越来越清晰。（remember doing：记得做过某事，例：I remember finishing my homework. 我记得我写完作业了。）

⑤ kick sb. out：赶某人出去

⑥ suitcase：手提箱

floor by the bed. He couldn't remember how he had got it back from the restaurant where he owed for the drinks. His books, a white suit, and some shirts were all there as he had packed[①] them. Quickly he began to dress himself.

An electric coffee-pot was perking on the table by the time he had his clothes on. The man reached into the pocket[②] of the vest that hung over the back of a chair. He brought out a card and Jake took it questioningly[③]. The man's name—John Singer—was engraved[④] in the center, and beneath this, written in ink with the same elaborate[⑤] precision[⑥] as the engraving, there was a brief[⑦] message.

I am a deaf-mute, but I read the lips and understand what is said to me. Please do not shout.

The shock made Jake feel light and vacant. He and John Singer just looked at each other.

'I wonder how long it would have taken me to find that out,' he said.

Singer looked very carefully at his lips when he spoke—he had noticed that before. But a dummy[⑧]!

They sat at the table and drank hot coffee out of blue cups. The room was cool and the half-drawn shades softened the hard glare from the windows. Singer brought from his closet a tin box that contained a loaf of bread, some oranges, and cheese. He did not eat much, but sat leaning back in his chair with one hand in his pocket. Jake ate hungrily. He would have to leave the place immediately[⑨] and think

---

① pack：打包、收拾行李（packed 为过去分词）
② pocket：口袋
③ questioningly：怀疑地；不确定地
④ engrave：雕刻；刻上；铭记
⑤ elaborate：精细的
⑥ precision：精度，（数）精密度
⑦ brief：简短的；扼要的
⑧ dummy：笨蛋；哑巴
⑨ immediately：立即，马上

things over. As long as he was stranded he ought to scout around for some sort of job in a hurry. The quiet room was too peaceful and comfortable to worry in—he would get out and walk by himself for a while.

'Are there any other deaf-mute people here?' he asked. 'You have many friends?'

Singer was still smiling. He did not catch on to the words at first, and Jake had to repeat them. Singer raised his sharp, dark eyebrows and shook his head.

'Find it lonesome?'

The man shook his head in a way that might have meant either yes or no. They sat silently for a little while and then Jake got up to leave. He thanked Singer several times for the night's lodging, moving his lips carefully so that he was sure to be understood. The mute only smiled again and shrugged① his shoulders. When Jake asked if he could leave his suitcase under the bed for a few days the mute nodded that he could.

Then Singer took his hands from his pocket and wrote carefully on a pad of paper with a silver② pencil. He shoved the pad③ over toward Jake.

I can put a mattress④ on the floor and you can stay here until you find a place. I am out most of the day. It will not be any trouble.

Jake felt his lips tremble with a sudden feeling of gratefulness⑤. But he couldn't accept. 'Thanks,' he said, 'I already got a place.'

As he was leaving the mute handed him a pair of blue overalls⑥,

---

① shrug：耸肩（表示冷淡、厌恶、不知情等）
② silver：银的；银色的
③ pad：便笺笺簿
④ mattress：床垫，褥垫
⑤ gratefulness：感激，感恩
⑥ overall：罩衫；工作服

rolled into a tight bundle[1], and seventy-five cents. The overalls were filthy and as Jake recognized them they aroused[2] in him a whirl of[3] sudden memories from the past week. The money, Singer made him understand, had been in his pockets.

'Adios,' Jake said. 'I'll be back sometime soon.'

He left the mute standing in the doorway with his hands still in his pockets and the half-smile on his face.[4] When he had gone down several steps of the stairs he turned and waved. The mute waved back to him and closed his door.

Outside the glare was sudden and sharp against his eyes. He stood on the sidewalk before the house, too dazzled at first by the sunlight to see very clearly. A youngun was sitting on the banisters of the house. He had seen her somewhere before. He remembered the boy's shorts she was wearing and the way she squinted her eyes.

He held up thc dirty roll of overalls. 'I want to throw these away. Know where I can find a garbage can?'

The kid jumped down from the banisters. 'It's in the back yard. I'll show you.'

He followed her through the narrow, dampish alley at the side of the house. When they came to the back yard Jake saw that two Negro men were sitting on the back steps. They were both dressed in white suits and white shoes. One of the Negroes was very tall and his tie and socks were brilliant green. The other was a light mulatto[5] of average height. He rubbed a tin harmonica across his knee. In contrast with his tall companion his socks and tie were a hot red.

The kid pointed to the garbage can[6] by the back fence and then turned to the kitchen window. 'Portia!' she called. 'Highboy and

---

① bundle：捆；束

② arouse：引起

③ a whirl of：一连串混乱的

④ 参考译文：他走了，哑巴站在门口，双手依然插在口袋里，脸上留着还未褪去的笑容。（leave sb. doing：留下某人独自做某事）

⑤ mulatto：白黑混血儿

⑥ garbage can：垃圾桶，垃圾箱

Willie here waiting for you.'

A soft voice answered from the kitchen. 'You neen[①] holler so loud. I know they is. I putting on my hat right now.'

Jake unrolled the overalls before throwing them away. They were stiff with mud. One leg was torn and a few drops of blood stained the front. He dropped them in the can. A Negro girl came out of the house and joined the white-suited boys on the steps. Jake saw that the youngun in shorts was looking at him very closely. She changed her weight from one foot to the other and seemed excited.

'Are you kin[②] to Mister Singer?' she asked.

'Not a bit.'

'Good friend?'

'Good enough to spend the night with him.'

'I just wondered—'

'Which direction is Main Street? '

She pointed to the right. 'Two blocks down this way.'

Jake combed his mustache with his fingers and started off. He jingled[③] the seventy-five cents in his hand and bit his lower lip until it was mottled[④] and scarlet[⑤]. The three Negroes[⑥] were walking slowly ahead of him, talking among themselves. Because he felt lonely in the unfamiliar[⑦] town he kept close behind them and listened. The girl held both of them by the arm. She wore a green dress with a red hat and shoes. The boys walked very close to her.

'What we got planned for this evening?' she asked.

'It depend entirely upon you, Honey,' the tall boy said. 'Willie and me don't have no special plans.'

---

① 此处 neen 为口语，是 needn't 吞音后的发音。

② kin：（人）有亲戚关系的（be kin to sb.：与……有亲属关系：表示与某人或某物有密切的关系，通常指家庭成员或亲戚。）

③ jingle：使发出丁零声

④ mottled：斑驳的，杂色的

⑤ scarlet：深红的，鲜红色的

⑥ negro：黑种人，黑人

⑦ unfamiliar：不熟悉的

She looked from one to the other. 'You all got to decide.'

'Well—' said the shorter boy in the red socks. 'Highboy and me thought m-maybe us three go to church.'

The girl sang her answer in three different tones. 'O—K—And after church I got a notion[①] I ought to go and set with Father for a while—just a short while.' They turned at the first corner, and Jake stood watching them a moment before walking on.

The main street was quiet and hot, almost deserted. He had not realized until now that it was Sunday—and the thought of this depressed him.[②] The awnings[③] over the closed stores were raised and the buildings had a bare look in the bright sun. He passed the New York Cafe. The door was open, but the place looked empty and dark. He had not found any socks to wear that morning, and the hot pavement burned through the thin soles of his shoes.[④] The sun felt like a hot piece of iron pressing down on his head. The town seemed more lonesome than any place he had ever known. The stillness of the street gave him a strange feeling. When he had been drunk the place had seemed violent and riotous[⑤]. And now it was as though everything had come to a sudden, static halt.

He went into a fruit and candy store to buy a paper. The Help-Wanted[⑥] column[⑦] was very short. There were several calls for young men between twenty-five and forty with automobiles to sell various products on commission.[⑧] These he skipped over quickly. An advertisement for a truck-driver held his attention for a few minutes.

① notion：打算

② 参考译文：直到现在，他才意识到今天是周日——想到这里，他觉得很沮丧。not...until...：直到……才……，此处连接 realize 的宾语从句。（depress：使沮丧）

③ awning：（建）遮阳篷；遮雨篷

④ 参考译文：那天早晨他没找到袜子穿，炽热的人行道透过薄薄的鞋底烤着他的双脚。（pavement：人行道；sole：鞋底）

⑤ riotous：暴乱的

⑥ Help-Wanted：（通常刊登在报纸上的）急聘启事

⑦ column：专栏

⑧ 参考译文：有几家招聘二十五至四十岁的年轻人，要有车，通过销售各种产品抽取佣金。（automobile：汽车，发动器；on commission：抽取佣金）

But the notice at the bottom[①] interested him most It read:

Wanted—Experienced Mechanic. Sunny Dixie Show. Apply Corner Weavers Lane & 15th Street.

Without knowing it he had walked back to the door of the restaurant where he had spent his time during the past two weeks. This was the only place on the block besides the fruit store which was not closed. Jake decided suddenly to drop in and see Biff Brannon.

The café was very dark after the brightness[②] outside. Everything looked dingier[③] and quieter than he had remembered it. Brannon stood behind the cash register[④] as usual, his arms folded over his chest. His good-looking plump wife sat filing her fingernails[⑤] at the other end of the counter. Jake noticed that they glanced at each other as he came in.

'Afternoon,' said Brannon.

Jake felt something in the air. Maybe the fellow was laughing because he remembered things that had happened when he was drunk. Jake stood wooden and resentful[⑥]. 'Package of Target, please.' As Brannon reached beneath the counter for the tobacco Jake decided that he was not laughing. In the daytime the fellow's face was not as hard-looking as it was at night He was pale as though he had not slept, and his eyes had the look of a weary[⑦] buzzard's.

'Speak up,' Jake said. 'How much do I owe you?'

Brannon opened a drawer and put on the counter a public-school tablet. Slowly he turned over the pages and Jake watched him. The tablet looked more like a private notebook than the place where he

---

① at the bottom：在底部，在底端

② brightness：光亮；明亮

③ dingy：昏暗的

④ cash register：收银机

⑤ fingernail：指甲；手指甲

⑥ resentful：充满忿恨的

⑦ weary：疲倦的；厌烦的；令人厌烦的

kept his regular accounts[①]. There were long lines of figures, added, divided, and subtracted[②], and little drawings. He stopped at a certain page and Jake saw his last name written at the corner. On the page there were no figures—only small checks and crosses. At random[③] across the page were drawn little round, seated cats with long curved lines for tails. Jake stared. The faces of the little cats were human and female. The faces of the little cats were Mrs. Brannon.

'I have checks here for the beers,' Brannon said. 'And crosses for dinners and straight lines for the whiskey. Let me see—' Brannon rubbed his nose and his eyelids drooped down. Then he shut the tablet. 'Approximately[④] twenty dollars.'

'It'll take me a long time,' Jake said. 'But maybe you'll get it.'

'There's no big hurry.'

Jake leaned against the counter. 'Say, what kind of a place is this town?'

'Ordinary,' Brannon said. 'About like any other place the same size.'

'What population?'

'Around thirty thousand.'

Jake opened the package of tobacco and rolled[⑤] himself a cigarette. His hands were shaking. 'Mostly mills[⑥]?'

'That's right. Four big cotton mills—those are the main ones. A hosiery factory. Some gins[⑦] and sawmills.'

'What kind of wages?'

'I'd say around ten or eleven a week on the average—but then of course they get laid off now and then. What makes you ask all this? You mean to try to get a job in a mill?'

---

① account：账目
② subtracted：减掉的，除去的
③ at random：任意地，随意地
④ approximately：大约，大概
⑤ roll：卷，绕
⑥ mill：作坊；工厂
⑦ gins：弹棉机；轧花机

Jake dug his fist into his eye and rubbed it sleepily. 'Don't know. I might and I might not.' He laid the newspaper on the counter and pointed out the advertisement[①] he had just read. 'I think I'll go around and look into this.'

Brannon read and considered. 'Yeah,' he said finally. 'I've seen that show. It's not much— just a couple of contraptions[②] such as a flying-jinny and swings. It corrals the colored people and mill hands and kids. They move around to different vacant lots in town.'

'Show me how to get there.'

Brannon went with him to the door and pointed out[③] the direction. 'Did you go on home with Singer this morning?'

Jake nodded.

'What do you think of him?'

Jake bit his lips. The mute's face was in his mind very clearly. It was like the face of a friend he had known for a long time. He had been thinking of the man ever since he had left his room. 'I didn't even know he was a dummy,' he said finally.

He began walking again down the hot, deserted street. He did not walk as a stranger in a strange town. He seemed to be looking for someone. Soon he entered one of the mill districts[④] bordering the river. The streets became narrow and unpaved[⑤] and they were not empty any longer. Groups of dingy, hungry-looking children called to each other and played games. The two-room shacks, each one like the other, were rotten and unpainted. The stink of food and sewage[⑥] mingled with the dust in the air. The falls up the river made a faint rushing sound. People stood silently in doorways or lounged[⑦] on steps. They looked at Jake with yellow, expressionless faces. He stared

---

① advertisement：广告
② contraption：奇妙的装置
③ point out：指出
④ district：地区；行政区
⑤ unpaved：没有铺石砖的，没有铺柏油的
⑥ sewage：污水
⑦ lounge：懒洋洋地坐着

back at them with wide, brown eyes. He walked jerkily, and now and then he wiped his mouth with the hairy back of his hand.

At the end of Weavers Lane there was a vacant block. It had once been used as a junk yard for old automobiles. Rusted pieces of machinery and torn inner tubes still littered the ground. A trailer was parked in one corner of the lot, and nearby was a flying-jinny partly covered with canvas[①].

Jake approached[②] slowly. Two little younguns in overalls stood before the flying-jinny. Near them, seated on a box, a Negro man drowsed in the late sunshine, his knees collapsed against each other. In one hand he held a sack of melted chocolate.[③] Jake watched him stick his fingers in the miry[④] candy and then lick them slowly.

'Who's the manager of this outfit[⑤]?'

The Negro thrust his two sweet fingers between his lips and rolled over them with his tongue. 'He a red-headed man,' he said when he had finished. 'That all I know, Cap'n.'

'Where's he now? '

'He over there behind that largest wagon.'

Jake slipped off his tie as he walked across the grass and staffed it into his pocket. The sun was beginning to set in the west. Above the black line of housetops the sky was warm crimson. The owner of the show stood smoking a cigarette by himself. His red hair sprang up like a sponge on the top of his head and he stared at Jake with gray, flabby eyes.

'You the manager?'

'Uh-huh. Patterson's my name.'

'I come about the job in this morning's paper.'

'Yeah. I don't want no greenhorn[⑥]. I need an experienced

① canvas：帆布

② approach：走近，靠近

③ 参考译文：旁边有个黑人坐在箱子上，在夕阳下昏昏欲睡，两个膝盖瘫软地靠在一起，一只手还拿着一袋融化了的巧克力。（drowse：打瞌睡；collapse：瘫坐）

④ miry：泥泞的，脏的

⑤ outfit：机构

⑥ greenhorn：生手；初学者

mechanic.'

'I got plenty of experience,' Jake said.

'What you ever done?'

'I've worked as a weaver and loom-fixer. I've worked in garages and an automobile assembly shop. All sorts of different things.'

Patterson guided him toward the partly covered flying-jinny. The motionless wooden horses were fantastic in the late afternoon sun. They pranced up① statically②, pierced by their dull gilt bars. The horse nearest Jake had a splintery wooden crack in its dingy rump and the eyes walled blind and frantic, shreds of paint peeled from the sockets.③ The motionless④ merry-go-round seemed to Jake like something in a liquor dream.

'I want a experienced mechanic to run this and keep the works in good shape,' Patterson said.

'I can do that all right.'

'It's a two-handed job,' Patterson explained. 'You're in charge of the whole attraction. Besides looking after the machinery you got to keep the crowd in order. You got to be sure that everybody gets on has a ticket. You got to be sure that the tickets are O.K. and not some old dance-hall ticket. Everybody wants to ride them horses, and you'd be surprised what niggers will try to put over on you when they don't have no money. You got to keep three eyes open all the time.'

Patterson led him to the machinery⑤ inside the circle of horses and pointed out the various parts. He adjusted a lever and the thin jangle⑥ of mechanical music began. The wooden cavalcade⑦ around them seemed to cut them off from the rest of the world. When

---

① prance up：（马）腾跃

② statically：静止地

③ 参考译文：最靠近杰克的那匹马，脏乎乎的木头屁股上有细碎的裂纹，两只眼睛好像是瞎了一样，它神情狂躁，眼窝处的油漆也一片片剥落。从表达看，本句原文 walled 应为 were。（dingy：肮脏的；rump：臀部，尾部）

④ motionless：静止的；不运动的

⑤ machinery：机器

⑥ jangle：刺耳声，金属撞击声

⑦ cavalcade：（车或马的）队列

the horses stopped, Jake asked a few questions and operated the mechanism himself.

'The fellow I had quit on me,' Patterson said when they had come out again into the lot. 'I always hate to break in a new man.'

'When do I start?'

'Tomorrow afternoon. We run six days and nights a week—beginning at four and shutting up at twelve. You're to come about three and help get things going. And it takes about a hour after the show to fold up for the night.'

'What about pay?'

'Twelve dollars.'

Jake nodded, and Patterson held out a dead-white, boneless[①] hand with dirty fingernails.

It was late when he left the vacant lot. The hard, blue sky had blanched and in the east there was a white moon. Dusk softened the outline of the houses along the street. Jake did not return immediately through Weavers Lane, but wandered in the neighborhoods nearby. Certain smells, certain voices heard from a distance, made him stop short now and then by the side of the dusty street. He walked erratically, jerking[②] from one direction to another for no purpose. His head felt very light, as though it were made of thin glass. A chemical change was taking place in him. The beers and whiskey[③] he had stored so continuously in his system set in a reaction. He was sideswiped by drunkenness. The streets which had seemed so dead before were quick with life. There was a ragged[④] strip of grass bordering[⑤] the street, and as Jake walked along the ground seemed to rise nearer to his face. He sat down on the border of grass and leaned against a telephone pole.

---

① boneless：无骨的；去骨的（此处根据上下文应为 bony，意为"瘦骨嶙峋的"。）

② jerk：使……猝然一动；猝然一动，例：Mr. Griffin jerked forward in his chair. 格里芬先生在椅子上猛地向前一动。

③ whiskey：威士忌酒

④ ragged：高低不平的，参差不齐的

⑤ border：接壤

He settled himself comfortably, crossing his legs Turkish fashion and smoothing down the ends of his mustache. Words came to him and dreamily[①] he spoke them aloud to himself.

'Resentment is the most precious flower of poverty.[②] Yeah.'

It was good to talk. The sound of his voice gave him pleasure. The tones seemed to echo and hang on the air so that each word sounded twice.[③] He swallowed and moistened his mouth to speak again. He wanted suddenly to return to the mute's quiet room and tell him of the thoughts that were in his mind. It was a queer[④] thing to want to talk with a deaf-mute. But he was lonesome.

The street before him dimmed with the coming evening. Occasionally[⑤] men passed along the narrow street very close to him, talking in monotones to each other, a cloud of dust rising around their feet with each step. Or girls passed by together, or a mother with a child across her shoulder. Jake sat numbly[⑥] for some time, and at last he got to his feet and walked on.

Weavers Lane was dark. Oil lamps[⑦] made yellow, trembling patches of light in the doorways and windows. Some of the houses were entirely dark and the families sat on their front steps with only the reflections from a neighboring house to see by. A woman leaned out of a window and splashed[⑧] a pail of dirty water into the street. A few drops of it splashed on Jake's face. High, angry voices could be heard from the backs of some of the houses. From others there was the peaceful sound of a chair slowly rocking.

Jake stopped before a house where three men sat together on the front steps. A pale yellow light from inside the house shone on them.

---

① dreamily：梦似地，朦胧地

② 参考译文：愤慨是贫穷最宝贵的花朵。（resentment：怨恨，愤恨）

③ 参考译文：声音似乎回荡着，萦绕在空中，每个词都响了两次。（echo：回响，回音；so that：所以）

④ queer：奇怪的

⑤ occasionally：偶尔；间或

⑥ numbly：麻木地；木然地

⑦ oil lamp：油灯

⑧ splash：泼洒；把（水、泥等）泼在……上

Two of the men wore overalls but no shirts and were barefooted. One of these was tall and loose-jointed[①]. The other was small and he had a running sore on the corner of his mouth. The third man was dressed in shirt and trousers. He held a straw hat on his knee.

'Hey,' Jake said.

The three men stared at him with mill-sallow, dead-pan faces. They murmured[②] but did not change their positions[③]. Jake pulled the package of Target from his pocket and passed it around. He sat down on the bottom step and took off his shoes. The cool, damp[④] ground felt good to his feet.

'Working now?'

'Yeah,' said the man with the straw hat. 'Most of the time.'

Jake picked between his toes. 'I got the Gospel[⑤] in me,' he said. "I want to tell it to somebody.'

The men smiled. From across the narrow street there was the sound of a woman singing. The smoke from their cigarettes hung close around them in the still air. A little youngun passing along the street stopped and opened his fly to make water.

'There's a tent around the corner and it's Sunday,' the small man said finally. 'You can go there and tell all the Gospel you want.'

'It's not that kind. It's better. It's the truth.'

'What kind?'

Jake sucked his mustache and did not answer. After a while he said, 'You ever have any strikes[⑥] here?'

'Once,' said the tall man. They had one of these here strikes around six years ago.'

'What happened?'

---

① loose-jointed：关节松弛的

② murmur：低声说

③ position：位置；站位

④ damp：潮湿的

⑤ Gospel：福音，也有“真理”的意思。

⑥ strike：罢工

The man with the sore on his mouth shuffled[1] his feet and dropped the stub of his cigarette to the ground. 'Well—they just quit work because they wanted twenty cents a hour. There was about three hundred did it. They just hung around the streets all day. So the mill sent out trucks, and in a week the whole town was swarming with folks come here to get a job.'

Jake turned so that he was facing them. The men sat two steps above him so that he had to raise his head to look into their eyes. 'Don't it make you mad?' he asked.

'How do you mean—mad?'

The vein in Jake's forehead was swollen[2] and scarlet. 'Christamighty, man! I mean mad-m-a-d-mad.' He scowled[3] up into their puzzled, sallow faces. Behind them, through the open front door he could see the inside of the house. In the front room there were three beds and a wash-stand[4]. In the back room a barefooted woman sat sleeping in a chair. From one of the dark porches nearby there was the sound of a guitar.

'I was one of them come in on the trucks,' the tall man said.

'That makes no difference[5]. What I'm trying to tell you is plain and simple. The bastards[6] who own these mills are millionaires. While the doffers and carders and all the people behind the machines who spin and weave the cloth can't hardly make enough to keep their guts quiet. See? So when you walk around the streets and think about it and see hungry, worn-out people and ricket-legged younguns, don't it make you mad? Don't it?'

Jake's face was flushed[7] and dark and his lips trembled. The three

---

① shuffle：拖着脚走

② swollen：肿大的；水涨的

③ scowl：皱眉；怒视

④ wash-stand：洗脸台

⑤ make no difference：无区别，不起作用，例：The size makes no difference in the price. 尺寸大小不影响价格。

⑥ bastard：私生子

⑦ flushed：激动的；心情愉快的

men looked at him warily. Then the man in the straw hat began to laugh.

'Go on and snicker. Sit there and bust your sides open.'

The men laughed in the slow and easy way that three men laugh at one. Jake brushed the dirt from the soles of his feet and put on his shoes. His fists were closed tight and his mouth was contorted with an angry sneer. 'Laugh—that's all you're good for. I hope you sit there and snicker 'til you rot!' As he walked stiffly[①] down the street, the sound of their laughter and catcalls still followed him.

The main street was brightly lighted. Jake loitered[②] on a corner, fondling[③] the change in his pocket. His head throbbed, and although the night was hot a chill passed through his body. He thought of the mute and he wanted urgently to go back and sit with him awhile[④]. In the fruit and candy store where he had bought the newspaper that afternoon he selected a basket of fruit wrapped in cellophane. The Greek behind the counter said the price was sixty cents, so that when he had paid he was left with only a nickel. As soon as he had come out of the store the present seemed a funny one to take a healthy man. A few grapes hung down below, the cellophane, and he picked them off hungrily.

Singer was at home when he arrived. He sat by the window with the chess game laid out before him on the table. The room was just as Jake had left it, with the fan turned on and the pitcher of ice water beside the table.[⑤] There was a panama hat on the bed and a paper parcel, so it seemed that the mute had just come in. He jerked his head toward the chair across from him at the table and pushed the chessboard[⑥] to one side. He leaned back with his hands in his pockets,

---

① stiffly：顽固地；僵硬地

② loiter：闲荡；徘徊

③ fondle：轻抚，抚弄（某物）

④ awhile：片刻；一会儿

⑤ 参考译文：房间还是杰克离开时的样子，电扇开着，那罐冰水放在桌子旁边。（just as：正如，正当；pitcher：水罐，a pitcher of water 一罐水）

⑥ chessboard：棋盘

and his face seemed to question Jake about what had happened since he had left.

Jake put the fruit on the table. 'For this afternoon,' he said. 'The motto has been: Go out and find an octopus and put socks on it.'

The mute smiled, but Jake could not tell if he had caught what he had said. The mute looked at the fruit with surprise and then undid the cellophane wrappings①. As he handled the fruits there was something very peculiar② in the fellow's face. Jake tried to understand this look and was stumped③. Then Singer smiled brightly.

'I got a job this afternoon with a sort of show. I'm to run the flying-jinny.'

The mute seemed not at all surprised. He went into the closet and brought out a bottle of wine and two glasses. They drank in silence. Jake felt that he had never been in such a quiet room. The light above his head made a queer reflection of himself in the glowing wineglass he held before him—the same caricature of himself he had noticed many times before on the curved surfaces of pitchers or tin mugs—with his face egg-shaped and dumpy and his mustache straggling almost up to his ears.④ Across from him the mute held his glass in both hands. The wine began to hum through Jake's veins and he felt himself entering again the kaleidoscope⑤ of drunkenness. Excitement made his mustache tremble jerkily. He leaned forward with his elbows on his knees and fastened a wide, searching gaze on Singer.

'I bet I'm the only man in this town that's been mad—I'm talking about really mean mad— for ten solid long years. I damn near got in a fight just a little while ago. Sometimes it seems to me like I

---

① wrapping：包装材料

② peculiar：奇怪的；独特的

③ stump：把（某人）难住（stumped 为过去分词）

④ 参考译文：头顶上的灯光将自己的影子投在面前闪亮的玻璃杯上，很奇怪的影子——以前，他很多次都注意到自己在罐子或锡杯的弯曲表面上投下的影子，跟现在一模一样——脸是鸡蛋形状，矮墩墩的，胡子乱七八糟，都快长到耳朵上了。本句原文较长，巧妙地用两个破折号进行解释说明。（reflection：反射；wineglass：酒杯；mug：杯子）

⑤ kaleidoscope：万花筒

might even be crazy. I just don't know.'

Singer pushed the wine toward his guest. Jake drank from the bottle and rubbed the top of his head.

'You see, it's like I'm two people. One of me is an educated man. I been in some of the biggest libraries in the country. I read. I read all the time. I read books that tell the pure[①] honest truth. Over there in my suitcase I have books by Karl Marx and Thorstein Veblen and such writers as them. I read them over and over, and the more I study the madder I get. I know every word printed on every page. To begin with I like words. Dialectic materialism—Jesuitical prevarication'—Jake rolled the syllables in his mouth with loving solemnity—'teleological propensity.'

The mute wiped his forehead with a neatly folded handkerchief.

'But what I'm getting at is this. When a person knows and can't make the others understand, what does he do?'

Singer reached for a wineglass, filled it to the brim[②], and put it firmly into Jake's bruised hand. 'Get drunk, huh?' Jake said with a jerk of his arm that spilled drops of wine on his white trousers. 'But listen! Wherever you look there's meanness and corruption. This room, this bottle of grape wine, these fruits in the basket, are all products of profit and loss. A fellow can't live without giving his passive acceptance[③] to meanness. Somebody wears his tail to a frazzle for every mouthful we eat and every stitch we wear—and nobody seems to know. Everybody is blind, dumb, and blunt-headed—stupid and mean.'

Jake pressed his fists to his temples[④]. His thoughts had careened[⑤] in several directions and he could not get control of them. He wanted to go berserk. He wanted to get out and fight violently with someone in a crowded street.

---

① pure：纯粹的

② brim：（容器的）口，边沿，（to the brim：斟满酒，满到杯）

③ passive acceptance：被动的接受

④ temple：太阳穴

⑤ careen：猛冲

Still looking at him with patient interest, the mute took out his silver pencil. He wrote very carefully on a slip of paper, Are you Democrat or Republican? and passed the paper across the table. Jake crumpled① it in his hand. The room had begun to turn around him again and he could not even read.

He kept his eyes on the mute's face to steady② himself. Singer's eyes were the only things in the room that did not seem to move. They were varied③ in color, flecked④ with amber⑤, gray, and a soft brown. He stared at them so long that he almost hypnotized⑥ himself. He lost the urge to be riotous⑦ and felt calm again. The eyes seemed to understand all that he had meant to say and to hold some message for him. After a while the room was steady again.

'You get it,' he said in a blurred⑧ voice. 'You know what I mean.'

From afar off there was the soft, silver ring of church bells. The moonlight was white on the roof next door and the sky was a gentle summer blue. It was agreed without words that Jake would stay with Singer a few days until he found a room. When the wine was finished the mute put a mattress on the floor beside the bed. Without removing any of his clothes Jake lay down and was instantly asleep.

---

① crumpled：压皱，弄皱（crumple 的过去式）
② steady：使坚定
③ varied：各种各样的；各不相同的
④ fleck：使起斑点；使有斑驳（flecked with：夹杂着……颜色）
⑤ amber：琥珀色
⑥ hypnotize：催眠；使着迷，恍惚
⑦ riotous：（人群）骚乱的，狂躁的
⑧ blurred：模糊的，不清晰的

5

FAR FROM the main street, in one of the Negro sections of the town, Doctor Benedict Mady Copeland sat in his dark kitchen alone. It was past nine o'clock and the Sunday bells were silent now. Although the night was very hot, there was a small fire in the round-bellied wood stove. Doctor Copeland sat close to it, leaning forward in a straight-backed kitchen chair with his head cupped in his long, slender① hands. The red glow from the chinks of the stove shone on his face—in this light his heavy lips looked almost purple against his black skin, and his gray hair, tight against his skull like a cap of lamb's wool, took on a bluish color also. He sat motionless in this position for a long time. Even his eyes, which stared from behind the silver rims of his spectacles, did not change their fixed, somber② gaze③. Then he cleared his throat harshly, and picked up a book from the floor beside his chair. All around him the room was very dark, and he had to hold the book close to the stove to make out④ the print⑤. Tonight he read Spinoza. He did not wholly⑥ understand the intricate⑦ play of ideas and the complex phrases, but as he read he sensed a strong, true purpose behind the words and he felt that he almost understood.

---

① slender：苗条的
② somber：忧郁的
③ gaze：凝视；注视
④ make out：辨认出
⑤ print：文字，印刷字体
⑥ wholly：完全地
⑦ intricate：复杂的；错综的，缠结的

Often at night the sharp jangle[①] of the doorbell would rouse him from his silence, and in the front room he would find a patient with a broken bone or with a razor[②] wound. But this evening he was not disturbed. And after the solitary hours spent sitting in the dark kitchen it happened that he began swaying slowly from side to side and from his throat there came a sound like a kind of singing moan.[③] He was making this sound when Portia came.

Doctor Copeland knew of her arrival in advance[④]. From the street outside he caught the sound of a harmonica playing a blues song and he knew that the music was played by William, his son. Without turning on the light he went through the hall and opened the front door. He did not step out on the porch, but stood in the dark behind the screen. The moonlight was bright and the shadows of Portia and William and Highboy lay black and solid on the dusty street. The houses in the neighborhood had a miserable[⑤] look. Doctor Copeland's house was different from any other building nearby. It was built solidly of brick and stucco[⑥]. Around the small front yard there was a picket fence. Portia said goodbye to her husband and brother at the gate and knocked on the screen door.

'How come you sit here in the dark like this?'

They went together through the dark hall back to the kitchen.

'You haves grand electric lights. It don't seem natural why you all the time sitting in the dark like this.'

Doctor Copeland twisted the bulb suspended over the table and the room was suddenly very bright. 'The dark suits me,' he said.

The room was clean and bare. On one side of the kitchen table

---

① jangle：刺耳声，金属撞击声

② razor：剃刀

③ 参考译文：他在昏暗的厨房里独自坐了好几个小时，开始慢慢地左右摇晃起来，从喉咙里发出一种像唱歌一样的呻吟。本句中 spent 为过去分词，指独自坐的几个小时，spend+ 一段时间 +doing，表示“花费一段时间做某事”。

④ in advance：提前，例：The subject of the talk is announced a week in advance. 会谈的主题提前一周宣布。

⑤ miserable：悲惨的；痛苦的

⑥ stucco：（涂墙壁或天花板的）灰泥

there were books and an inkstand[1]—on the other side a fork, spoon, and plate. Doctor Copeland held himself bolt upright with his long legs crossed and at first Portia sat stiffly, too. The father and daughter had a strong resemblance[2] to each other—both of them had the same broad, flat noses, the same mouths and foreheads. But Portia's skin was very light when compared to her Father's.

'It sure is roasting in here,' she said. 'Seems to me you would let this here fire die down except when you cooking.'

'If you prefer we can go up to my office,' Doctor Copeland said.

'I be all right, I guess. I don't prefer.'

Doctor Copeland adjusted his silver-rimmed[3] glasses and then folded his hands in his lap. 'How have you been since we were last together? You and your husband—and your brother?'

Portia relaxed and slipped her feet out of her pumps. 'Highboy and Willie and me gets along just fine.'

'William still boards with you?'

'Sure he do,' Portia said. 'You see—us haves our own way of living and our own plan. Highboy—he pay the rent[4]. I buys all the food out of my money. And Willie—he tends to all of our church dues,[5] insurance[6], lodge dues, and Saturday Night. Us three haves our own plan and each one of us does our parts.'

Doctor Copeland sat with his head bowed, pulling at his long fingers until he had cracked all of his joints. The clean cuffs of his sleeves hung down[7] past his wrists—below them his thin hands seemed lighter in color than the rest of his body and the palms were soft yellow. His hands had always an immaculate[8], shrunken[9] look, as

---

① inkstand：墨水瓶；墨水台（等于 inkwell）
② resemblance：相像；相似
③ silver-rimmed：银边的
④ rent：租金
⑤ due：税捐（church due：教堂税；lodge due：房屋税）
⑥ insurance：保险费
⑦ hang down：挂下来，下垂（hung 为 hang 的过去式及过去分词，文中为过去分词）
⑧ immaculate：洁净的；无瑕疵的
⑨ shrunken：皱缩的

though they had been scrubbed[1] with a brush and soaked[2] for a long time in a pan of water.

'Here, I almost forgot what I brought,' Portia said. 'Haves you had your supper yet?'

Doctor Copeland always spoke so carefully that each syllable seemed to be filtered through[3] his sullen[4], heavy lips. 'No, I have not eaten.'

Portia opened a paper sack she had placed on the kitchen table. 'I done brought a nice mess of collard greens and I thought maybe we have supper together. I done brought a piece of side meat, too. These here greens need to be seasoned with[5] that. You don't care if the collards is just cooked in meat, do you?'

'It does not matter.'

'You still don't eat nair[6] meat?'

'No. For purely private reasons I am a vegetarian, but it does not matter if you wish to cook the collards with a piece of meat.'

Without putting on her shoes Portia stood at the table and carefully began to pick over the greens. 'This here floor sure do feel good to my feets. You mind if I just walk around like this without putting back on them tight, hurting pumps?'

'No,' said Doctor Copeland. 'That will be all right.'

'Then—us'll have these nice collards and some hoecake[7] and coffee. And I, going to cut me off a few slices of this here white meat and fry it for myself.'

Doctor Copeland followed Portia with his eyes. She moved slowly around the room in her stockinged feet, taking down the

---

① scrub：用力擦洗，刷洗
② soak：浸泡
③ filter through：缓慢地，逐渐传播
④ sullen：愠怒的，不高兴的
⑤ be seasoned with：加……调味
⑥ nair：（有误表达）此处意指 no，即不吃肉。
⑦ hoecake：玉米饼

scrubbed[1] pans from the wall, building up the fire, washing the grit[2] from the collards. He opened his mouth to speak once and then composed his lips again.

'So you and your husband and your brother have your own cooperative[3] plan,' he said finally.

'That's right.'

Doctor Copeland jerked at his fingers and tried to pop the joints again. 'Do you intend to plan for children?'

Portia did not look at her father. Angrily she sloshed[4] the water from the pan of collards. 'There be some things,' she said, 'that seem to me to depend entirely upon God.'

They did not say anything else. Portia left the supper to cook on the stove and sat silently with her long hands dropping down limp between her knees. Doctor Copeland's head rested on his chest as though he slept. But he was not sleeping; now and then a nervous tremor[5] would pass over his face. Then he would breathe deeply and compose his face again. Smells of the supper began to fill the stifling[6] room. In the quietness the clock on top of the cupboard sounded very loud, and because of what they had just said to each other the monotonous ticking was like the word 'children, children,' said over and over.[7]

He was always meeting one of them—crawling naked on a floor or engaged in a game of marbles or even on a dark street with his arms around a girl. Benedict Copeland, the boys were all called. But for the girls there were such names as Benny Mae or Madyben or Benedine

---

① scrubbed：擦洗过的（scrub 的过去分词）

② grit：沙砾，沙粒

③ cooperative：合作的；合作社的

④ slosh：泼溅；搅动

⑤ tremor：震颤

⑥ stifling：令人窒息的；沉闷的

⑦ 参考译文：在一片沉寂中，橱柜上面的钟表走动的声音很大，因为他们刚刚谈过的话题，所以，钟表单调的嘀嗒声像是一遍遍地在重复一个词："孩子，孩子。"（monotonous：单调的）

Madine. He had counted[①] one day, and there were more than a dozen named for him.

But all his life he had told and explained and exhorted[②]. You cannot do this, he would say. There are all reasons why this sixth or fifth or ninth child cannot be, he would tell them. It is not more children we need but more chances for the ones already on the earth. Eugenic Parenthood for the Negro Race was what he would exhort them to. He would tell them in simple words, always the same way, and with the years it came to be a sort of[③] angry poem which he had always known by heart.

He studied and knew the development of any new theory. And from his own pocket he would distribute the devices to his patients himself. He was by far the first doctor in the town to even think of such. And he would give and explain and give and tell them. And then deliver maybe two score times a week. Madyben and Benny Mae.

That was only one point. Only one.

All of his life he knew that there was a reason for his working. He always knew that he was meant to[④] teach his people. All day he would go with his bag from house to house and on all things he would talk to them.

After the long day a heavy tiredness would come in him. But in the evening when he opened the front gate the tiredness would go away. There were Hamilton and Karl Marx and Portia and little William. There was Daisy, too.

Portia took the lid from the pan on the stove and stirred the collards with a fork. 'Father—' she said after a while.

Doctor Copeland cleared his throat[⑤] and spat into a handkerchief[⑥].

---

① count：计算
② exhorted：忠告，劝诫
③ a sort of：一种
④ be meant to do：注定要做
⑤ clear one's throat：清嗓子
⑥ handkerchief：手帕

His voice was bitter and rough. 'Yes?'

'Less us quit this here quarreling with each other.'

'We were not quarreling,' said Doctor Copeland.

'It don't take words to make a quarrel,' Portia said. 'It look to me like us is always arguing even when we sitting perfectly quiet like this. It just this here feeling I haves. I tell you the truth—ever time I come to see you it mighty near wears me out[①]. So less us try not to quarrel in any way no more.'

'It is certainly not my wish to quarrel. I am sorry if you have that feeling, Daughter.'

She poured out coffee and handed one cup unsweetened[②] to her father. In her own portion she put several spoons of sugar. 'I getting hungry and this will taste good to us. Drink your coffee while I tell you something which happened to us a piece back. Now that it all over it seem a little bit funny, but we got plenty reason not to laugh too hard.'

'Go ahead,' said Doctor Copeland.

'Well—sometime back a real fine-looking, dressed-up colored man come in town here. He called hisself Mr. B. F. Mason and said he come from Washington, D. C. Ever day he would walk up and down the street with a walking-cane and a pretty colored shirt on. Then at night he would go to the Society Cafe. He eaten finer than any man in this town. Ever night he would order hisself a bottle of gin[③] and two pork chops for his supper. He always had a smile for everybody and was always bowing around to the girls and holding a door open for you to come in or go out. For about a week he made hisself mighty pleasant wherever he were.[④] Peoples begun to ask questions

① wear sb. out：使某人筋疲力尽

② unsweetened：未加糖的

③ gin：杜松子酒

④ 参考译文：他对每个人都笑容可掬，对身边所有女孩都鞠躬致敬，进来出去时会为你拉门。也就一个星期的时间，他无论去哪里，都成为受欢迎的人。本句原文用进行时态表示习惯性发生的动作和事情。

and wonder about this rich Mr. B. F. Mason. Then pretty soon, after he acquaints[①] hisself, he begun to settle down to business.'

Portia spread out her lips and blew into her saucer[②] of coffee. 'I suppose you done read in the paper about this Government Pincher business for old folks?'

Doctor Copeland nodded. 'Pension,' he said.

'Well—he were connected with that. He were from the government. He had to come down from the President in Washington, D. C, to join everbody up for the Government Pinchers. He went around from one door to the next explaining how you pay one dollar down to join and after that twenty-five cents a week—and how when you were forty-five year old the government would pay you fifty dollars ever month of your life.[③] All the peoples I know were very excited about this. He give everbody that joined a free picture of the President with his name signed under it. He told how at the end of six months there were going to be free uniforms for ever member. The club was called the Grand League of Pincheners for Colored Peoples—and at the end of two months everbody was going to get a orange ribbon[④] with a G. L. P. C. P.[⑤] on it to stand for the name. You know, like all these other letter things in the government. He come around from house to house with this little book and everbody commenced[⑥] to join. He wrote their names down and took the money. Ever Saturday he would collect. In three weeks this Mr. B. F. Mason had joined up so many peoples he couldn't get all the way around on Saturday. He have to pay somebody to take up the collections in each three four blocks. I collected early ever Saturday

---

① acquaint：使熟悉；使认识

② saucer：茶托；碟子

③ 参考译文：他挨家挨户地跟人们解释，你交一块钱定金加入这个计划，然后每周交两毛五分钱——等你到四十五岁时，政府会每个月发给你五十块钱，一直付到你死的时候。（pay money down：部分支付，即支付定金。）

④ ribbon：带；缎带；（勋章等的）绶带；带状物；勋表

⑤ G. L. P. C. P.：指前文中提到的俱乐部的全称 the Grand League of Pincheners for Colored Peoples。

⑥ commence：开始，着手

for near where we live and got that quarter. Course Willie had joined at the beginning for him and Highboy and me.'

'I have come across many pictures of the President in various houses near where you live and I remember hearing[①] the name Mason mentioned,' said Doctor Copeland. 'He was a thief?'

'He were,' said Portia. 'Somebody begun to find out about this Mr. B. F. Mason and he were arrested. They find out he were from just plain Atlanta and hadn't never smelled no Washington, D. C, or no President. All the money were hid or spent. Willie had just throwed away seven dollars and fifty cents.'

Doctor Copeland was excited. 'That is what I mean by—'

'In the hereafter[②],' Portia said, 'that man sure going to wake up with a hot pitchfork[③] in his gut. But now that it all over it do seem a little bit funny, but of course we got plenty reason not to laugh too hard.'

'The Negro race of its own accord climbs up on the cross on every Friday,' said Doctor Copeland.

Portia's hands shook and coffee trickled[④] down from the saucer she was holding. She licked it from her arm. 'What, you mean?'

'I mean that I am always looking. I mean that if I could just find ten Negroes—ten of my own people—with spine[⑤] and brains and courage who are willing to give all that they have—'

Portia put down the coffee. 'Us was not talking about anything like that.'

'Only four Negroes,' said Doctor Copeland. 'Only the sum of Hamilton and Karl Marx and William and you. Only four Negroes with these real true qualities[⑥] and backbone[⑦]—'

---

① remember doing sth.：记得做过某事；表示回忆起过去曾经做过的事情。
② hereafter：今后，从此以后
③ pitchfork：干草叉；长柄草耙
④ trickled：使……滴；使……淌；使……细细地流
⑤ spine：脊柱，脊椎；刺
⑥ quality：质量
⑦ backbone：脊梁骨，脊椎

'Willie and Highboy and me have backbone,' said Portia angrily. 'This here is a hard world and it seem to me us three struggles along pretty well.'

For a minute they were silent. Doctor Copeland laid his spectacles[①] on the table and pressed his shrunken fingers to his eyeballs.

'You all the time using that word—Negro,' said Portia. 'And that word haves a way of hurting people's feelings. Even old plain nigger[②] is better than that word. But polite peoples—no matter what shade they is—always says colored.'

Doctor Copeland did not answer.

'Take Willie and me. Us aren't all the way colored. Our Mama was real light and both of us haves a good deal of white folks' blood in us. And Highboy— he Indian. He got a good part Indian in him. None of us is pure colored and the word you all the time using haves a way of hurting people's feelings.'

'I am not interested in subterfuges[③],' said Doctor Copeland. 'I am interested only in real truths.'

'Well, this here is a truth. Everybody is scared of you. It sure would take a whole lot of gin to get Hamilton or Buddy or Willie or my Highboy to come in this house and sit with you like I does.[④] Willie say he remember you when he were only a little boy and he were afraid of his own father then.'

Doctor Copeland coughed harshly and cleared his throat.

'Everbody haves feelings—no matter who they is—and nobody is going to walk in no house where they certain their feelings will be hurt. You the same way. I seen your feelings injured too many times by white peoples not to know that.'

---

① spectacle：眼镜

② nigger：黑鬼（蔑称）；社会地位低下的人

③ subterfuge：托词

④ 参考译文：汉密尔顿、巴迪、威利，还有我的海博埃，他们得喝很多杜松子酒才敢到这儿来，像我一样跟你坐坐。It takes...to do sth. 意为“花费……（时间、金钱）做某事”，例：It took me three hours to finish the article. 我花了三个小时读完那篇文章。

'No,' said Doctor Copeland. 'You have not seen my feelings injured.'

'Course I realize that Willie or my Highboy or me—that none of us is scholars. But Highboy and Willie is both good as gold. There just is a difference between them and you.'

'Yes,' said Doctor Copeland.

'Hamilton or Buddy or Willie or me—none of us ever cares to talk like you. Us talk like our own Mama and her peoples and their peoples before them. You think out everthing in your brain. While us rather talk from something in our hearts that has been there for a long time. That's one of them differences.'

'Yes,' said Doctor Copeland.

'A person can't pick up they children and just squeeze[①] them to which-a-way they wants them to be[②]. Whether it hurt them or not. Whether it right or wrong. You done tried that hard as any man could try. And now I the only one of us that would come in this here house and sit with you like this.'

The light was very bright in Doctor Copeland's eyes and her voice was loud and hard. He coughed and his whole face trembled. He tried to pick up the cup of cold coffee, but his hand would not hold it steadily. The tears came up to his eyes and he reached for his glasses to try to hide them.

Portia saw and went up to him quickly. She put her arms around his head and pressed[③] her cheek to his forehead. 'I done hurt my Father's feelings,' she said softly.

His voice was hard. 'No. It is foolish and primitive[④] to keep repeating this about hurt feelings.'

The tears went slowly down his cheek and the fire made them take on the colors of blue and green and red. 'I be really and truly

① squeeze：挤，榨
② 参考译文：人们不能抓起自己的孩子，把他们按照自己的想法变成自己想要的样子。
③ press：压，按
④ primitive：原始的（此处意为"幼稚的"。）

sorry,' said Portia.

Doctor Copeland wiped his face with his cotton handkerchief. 'It is all right.'

'Less us not ever quarrel[①] no more. I can't stand this here fighting between us. It seem to me that something real bad come up in us ever time we be together. Less us never quarrel like this no more.'

'No,' said Doctor Copeland. 'Let us not quarrel.'

Portia sniffled[②] and wiped her nose with the back of her hand. For a few minutes she stood with her arms around her father's head. Then after a while she wiped her face for a final time and went over to the pot of greens on the stove.

'It mighty nigh time for these to be tender[③],' she said cheerfully. 'Now I think I'll start making some of them good little hoecakes to go along with them.'

Portia moved slowly around the kitchen in her stockinged feet and her father followed her with his eyes. For a while again they were silent.

With his eyes wet, so that the edges of things were blurred, Portia was truly like her mother.[④] Years ago Daisy had walked like that around the kitchen, silent and occupied[⑤]. Daisy was not black as he was—her skin had been like the beautiful color of dark honey. She was always very quiet and gentle. But beneath that soft gentleness there was something stubborn in her, and no matter how conscientiously he studied it all out, he could not understand the gentle stubbornness in his wife.[⑥]

---

① quarrel：争辩，争吵

② sniffle：抽鼻子；抽噎

③ tender：柔软的

④ 参考译文：他的眼里还有泪花，看东西轮廓都是模糊的。波西娅真的很像她妈妈。本句 with 后为宾语加宾语补足语成分，wet 形容词起补充说明作用，so that... 引导的结果为“眼睛湿润”的结果，同时也是科普兰医生看着波西娅像她妈妈的缘由。

⑤ occupied：忙碌的

⑥ 参考译文：但在那种柔软的温和背后，她身上还有一种倔强。无论他多么认真地去研究，始终也无法理解妻子身上这种温柔的倔强。本句将并列分句直接拆译成两个完整的句子；并列句的后半句又包含了 no matter how 引导的让步状语从句。（conscientiously：认真地）

He would exhort her and he would tell her all that was in his heart and still she was gentle. And still she would not listen to him but would go on her own way.

Then later there were Hamilton and Karl Marx and William and Portia. And this feeling of real true purpose for them was so strong that he knew exactly how each thing should be with them. Hamilton would be a great scientist and Karl Marx a teacher of the Negro race and William a lawyer to fight against injustice[①] and Portia a doctor for women and children.

And when they were even babies he would tell them of the yoke they must thrust from their shoulders—the yoke of submission[②] and slothfulness[③]. And when they were a little older he would impress upon them that there was no God, but that their lives were holy and for each one of them there was this real true purpose. He would tell it to them over and over, and they would sit together far away from him and look with their big Negro-children eyes at their mother. And Daisy would sit without listening, gentle and stubborn.

Because of the true purpose for Hamilton, Karl Marx, William, and Portia, he knew how every detail should be. In the autumn of each year he took them all into town and bought for them good black shoes and black stockings. For Portia he bought black woolen material for dresses and white linen for collars and cuffs[④]. For the boys there was black wool for trousers and fine white linen for shirts. He did not want them to wear bright-colored, flimsy clothes. But when they went to school those were the ones they wished to wear, and Daisy said that they were embarrassed and that he was a hard father. He knew how the house should be. There could be no fanciness—no gaudy calendars or lace pillows[⑤] or knickknacks—but everything in the house must be

---

① injustice：不公平，不公正
② submission：屈服，服从
③ slothfulness：怠惰，懒惰
④ cuff：袖口
⑤ pillow：枕头

plain and dark and indicative of work and the real true purpose.

Then one night he found that Daisy had pierced holes in little Portia's ears for earrings. And another time a kewspie doll with feather skirts was on the mantelpiece① when he came home, and Daisy was gentle and hard and would not put it away. He knew, too, that Daisy was teaching the children the cult② of meekness③. She told them about hell and heaven. Also she convinced them of ghosts and of haunted places. Daisy went to church every Sunday and she talked sorrowfully to the preacher of her own husband. And with her stubbornness she always took the children to the church, too, and they listened.

The whole Negro race was sick, and he was busy all the day and sometimes half the night. After the long day a great weariness④ would come in him, but when he opened the front gate of his home the weariness would go away. Yet when he went into the house William would be playing music on a comb wrapped in toilet paper, Hamilton and Karl Marx would be shooting craps for their lunch money, Portia would be laughing with her mother.⑤

He would start all over with them, but in a different way. He would bring out their lessons and talk with them. They would sit close together and look at their mother. He would talk and talk, but none of them wanted to understand.

The feeling that would come on him was a black, terrible, Negro feeling. He would try to sit in his office and read and meditate until he could be calm and start again. He would pull down the shades of the room so that there would be only the bright light and the books and

---

① mantelpiece：壁炉台，壁炉架

② cult：（对生活方式、看法、观念等的）狂热

③ meekness：温顺

④ weariness：疲倦，疲劳

⑤ 参考译文：然而，等他真的走进屋门，往往会发现，威廉在梳子上包了卫生纸，正在用梳子弹奏音乐，汉密尔顿和卡尔·马克思正在掷骰子赌午饭钱，而波西娅正在跟妈妈一起笑。本句为 when 引导的时间状语从句，后面跟着三句并列主句，在翻译中，为了衔接，增译了“往往会发现”；同时，将作定语的 wrapped in toilet paper 也拆译为小分句，增加了行文流畅度。（crap：双骰儿赌博；掷骰子赌博）

the feeling of meditation[1]. But sometimes this calmness would not come. He was young, and the terrible feeling would not go away with study.

Hamilton, Karl Marx, William, and Portia would be afraid of him and look at their mother—and sometimes when he realized this the black feeling would conquer[2] him and he knew not what he did.

He could not stop those terrible things, and afterward he could never understand.

'This here supper sure smells good to me,' said Portia. 'I expect us better eat now because Highboy and Willie liable[3] to come trooping in any minute.'

Doctor Copeland settled his spectacles and pulled his chair up to the table. 'Where have your husband and William been spending the evening?'

They been throwing horseshoes. This here Raymond Jones haves a horseshoe place in his back yard. This Raymond and his sister, Love Jones, plays ever night. Love is such a ugly girl[4] I don't mind about Highboy or Willie going around to their house any time they wishes. But they said they would come back for me at quarter to ten and I expecting them now any minute.'

'Before I forget,' said Doctor Copeland. 'I suppose you hear frequently[5] from Hamilton and Karl Marx.'

'I does from Hamilton. He practically taken over all the work on our Grandpapa's place. But Buddy, he in Mobile—and you know he were never a big hand at writing letters. However, Buddy always haves such a sweet way with peoples that I don't ever worry concerning him. He the kind to always get along right well.'

They sat silently at the table before the supper. Portia kept

---

① meditation：沉思，冥想
② conquer：击败，战胜
③ liable：有可能的
④ 此处应为 an ugly girl，ugly 为元音音素开头。
⑤ frequently：频繁地

looking up at the clock on the cupboard because it was time for Highboy and Willie to come. Doctor Copeland bent his head over the plate. He held the fork in his hand as though it were heavy, and his fingers trembled. He only tasted the food and with each mouthful[①] he swallowed hard. There was a feeling of strain[②], and it seemed as though both of them wanted to keep up[③] some conversation.

Doctor Copeland did not know how to begin. Sometimes he thought that he had talked so much in the years before to his children and they had understood so little that now there was nothing at all to say.[④] After a while he wiped his mouth with his handkerchief and spoke in an uncertain voice.

'You have hardly mentioned yourself. Tell me about your job and what you have been doing lately.'

'Course I still with the Kellys,' said Portia. 'But I tells you, Father, I don't know how long I going to be able to keep on with them. The work is hard and it always take me a long time to get through. However, that don't bother me none. It about the pay I worries about. I suppose to get three dollars a week —but sometimes Mrs. Kelly likes a dollar or fifty cents of paying me the full amount. Course she always catches up on it soon as she able. But it haves a way of leaving me in a pinch[⑤].'

'That is not right,' said Doctor Copeland. 'Why do you stand for it?'

'It ain't her fault. She can't help it,' said Portia. 'Half the folks in that house don't pay the rent[⑥], and it a big expense to keep everthing up. I tell you the truth—the Kellys is just barely keeping one jump

---

① mouthful：一口；满口

② strain：紧张

③ keep up：使……继续，此处指维持对话。

④ 参考译文：有时候，他觉得以前跟孩子们说得太多了，他们几乎都听不懂，所以现在也就无话可说了。本文主句为一般过去时态，thought 后的宾语从句时间线在此之前，故采用过去完成时态表达；so...that... 表示“如此……以至于……”，表示因果关系。

⑤ in a pinch：在必要的时候，例：In a pinch, you could go home on foot. 必要时，你可以走路回家。

⑥ pay the rent：支付房租

ahead of the sheriff[①]. They having a mighty hard time.'

'There ought to be some other job you can get.'

'I know. But the Kellys is really grand white peoples to work for. I really fond of them as I can be. Them three little children is just like some of my own kinfolks[②]. I feel like I done really raised Bubber and the baby. And although Mick and me is always getting into some kind of quarrel together, I haves a real close fondness[③] for her, too.'

'But you must think of yourself,' said Doctor Copeland.

'Mick, now—' said Portia. 'She a real case. Not a soul know how to manage that child. She just as biggity and headstrong as she can be. Something going on in her all the time. I haves a funny feeling about that child. It seem to me that one of these days she going to really surprise somebody. But whether that going to be a good surprise or a bad surprise I just don't know. Mick puzzle me sometimes. But still I really fond of her.'

'You must look out for[④] your own livelihood first.'

'As I say, it ain't Mrs. Kelly's fault. It cost so much to run that big old house and the rent just don't be paid. Ain't but one person in the house who pay a decent amount for his room and pay it on the dot without fail. And that man only been living there a short while. He one of these here deaf-and-dumb[⑤] folks. He the first one of them I ever seen close up—but he a mighty fine white man. '

'Tall, thin, with gray and green eyes?' asked Doctor Copeland suddenly. 'And always polite to everyone and very well dressed? Not like someone from this town—more like a Northerner or maybe a Jew?'

'That him,' said Portia.

Eagerness came into Doctor Copeland's face. He crumbled his

---

① sheriff:（高等法院的）司法干事
② kinfolk：亲属
③ fondness：爱好；喜爱
④ look out for：关注某人或某事
⑤ deaf-and-dumb：聋哑的

hoecake into the collard juice in his plate and began to eat with a new appetite. 'I have a deaf-mute patient,' he said.

'How come you acquainted[①] with Mr. Singer?' asked Portia.

Doctor Copeland coughed and covered his mouth with his handkerchief. 'I have just seen him several times.'

'I better clean up now,' said Portia. 'It sure enough time for Willie and my Highboy. But with this here real sink and grand running water these little dishes won't take me two winks.'

The quiet insolence of the white race was one thing he had tried to keep out of his mind for years. When the resentment would come to him he would cogitate[②] and study. In the streets and around white people he would keep the dignity[③] on his face and always be silent. When he was younger it was 'Boy'—but now it was 'Uncle.' 'Uncle, run down to that filling station on the corner and send me a mechanic.' A white man in a car had called out those words to him not long ago. 'Boy, give me a hand with this.' 'Uncle, do that.' And he would not listen, but would walk on with the dignity in him and be silent.

A few nights ago a drunken white man had come up to him and begun pulling him along the street. He had his bag with him and he was sure someone was hurt. But the drunkard had pulled him into a white man's restaurant and the white men at the counter had begun hollering[④] out with their insolence[⑤]. He knew that the drunkard was making fun of[⑥] him. Even then he had kept the dignity[⑦] in him.

But with this tall, thin white man with the gray-green eyes something had happened that had never happened to him with any white man before.

---

① acquaint：认识，熟悉
② cogitate：认真思考，深思熟虑
③ dignity：尊严；高贵；端庄
④ holler：大声叫喊
⑤ insolence：傲慢；傲慢无礼的行为
⑥ make fun of：取笑，嘲笑
⑦ dignity：尊严，自尊

It came about on a dark, rainy night several weeks ago. He had just come from a maternity case and was standing in the rain on a corner. He had tried to light a cigarette and one by one the matches in his box fizzled out[①]. He had been standing with the unlighted cigarette in his mouth when the white man stepped up[②] and held for him a lighted match. In the dark with the flame between them they could see each other's faces. The white man smiled at him and lighted for him his cigarette. He did not know what to say, for nothing like that had ever happened to him before.

They had stood for a few minutes on the street corner together, and then the white man had handed him his card. He wanted to talk to the white man and ask him some questions, but he did not know for sure if he could really understand. Because of the insolence of all the white race he was afraid to lose his dignity in friendliness.

But the white man had lighted his cigarette and smiled and seemed to want to be with him. Since then he had thought this over many times.

'I have a deaf-mute patient,' said Doctor Copeland to Portia. The patient is a boy five years of age. And somehow I cannot get over the feeling that I am to blame for his handicap.[③] I delivered him, and after two post-delivery[④] visits of course I forgot about him. He developed ear trouble, but the mother paid no attention to the discharges from his ears and did not bring him to me. When it was finally brought to my attention it was too late. Of course he hears nothing and of course he therefore cannot speak. But I have watched him carefully, and it seems to me that if he were normal he would be a very intelligent[⑤] child.'

---

① fizzle out：逐渐消失（此处意为火柴一根根熄灭。）

② step up：走上前去

③ 参考译文：不知为什么，我总觉得自己要为他的残疾负责任。本句 feeling 后跟的 that 从句为同位语从句。（get over：克服；blame for：为……负责；handicap：障碍；缺陷）

④ post-delivery：产后

⑤ intelligent：聪明的

'You always had a great interest in little children,' said Portia. 'You care a heap more about them than about grown peoples, don't you?'

'There is more hope in the young child,' said Doctor Copeland. 'But this deaf boy—I have been meaning to make inquiries[1] and find if there is some institution that would take him.'

'Mr. Singer would tell you. He a truly kind white man and he not a bit biggity.'

'I do not know—' said Doctor Copeland. 'I have thought once or twice about writing him a note and seeing if he could give me information.'

'Sure I would if I was you. You a grand letter-writer and I would give it to Mr. Singer for you,' said Portia. 'He come down in the kitchen two-three weeks ago with a few shirts he wanted me to rinse out for him. Them shirts were no more dirty than if Saint John the Baptist hisself had been wearing them. All I had to do were dip[2] them in warm water and give the collars a small rub and press them. But that night when I taken them five clean shirts up to his room you know how much he give me?'

'No.'

'He smile like he always do and hand over to me a dollar. A whole dollar just for them little shirts. He one really kind and pleasant white man and I wouldn't be afraid to ask him any question. I wouldn't even mind writing that nice white man a letter myself. You go right ahead and do it, Father, if you wants to.'

'Perhaps I will,' said Doctor Copeland.

Portia sat up suddenly and began arranging her tight, oily hair. There was the faint[3] sound of a harmonica and then gradually the music grew louder. 'Here come Willie and Highboy,' Portia said. 'I

---

① make inquiries：调查；询问

② dip：浸泡

③ faint：模糊的，微弱的

got to go out now and meet them. You take care of yourself now, and send me a word if you needs me for anything. I did[1] enjoy the supper with you and the talking very much.'

The music from the harmonica[2] was very clear now, and they could tell that Willie was playing while he waited at the front gate.

'Wait a minute,' said Doctor Copeland. 'I have only seen your husband with you about two times and I believe we have never really met each other. And it has been three years since William has visited his father. Why not tell them to drop in for a little while?'

Portia stood in the doorway, fingering her hair and her earrings.

'Last time Willie come in here you hurted his feelings. You see you don't understand just how—'

'Very well,' said Doctor Copeland. 'it was only a suggestion.'

'Wait,' said Portia. 'I going to call them. I going to invite them in right now.'

Doctor Copeland lighted a cigarette and walked up and down[3] the room. He could not straighten his glasses to just the right position and his fingers kept trembling. From the front yard there was the sound of low voices. Then heavy footsteps were in the hall and Portia, William, and Highboy entered the kitchen.

'Here we is,' said Portia. 'Highboy, I don't believe you and my Father has ever truly been introduced to each other. But you knows who each other is.'

Doctor Copeland shook hands with both of them. Willie hung back shyly against the wall, but Highboy stepped forward and bowed formally. 'I has always heard so much about you,' he said. 'I be very pleased to make your acquaintance[4].'

Portia and Doctor Copeland brought in chairs from the hall and

---

① did：（do 的过去式）用于强调主要动词，意为"确实，的确"。

② harmonica：口琴；玻璃琴

③ walk up and down：走来走去

④ make one's acquaintance：与某人初次相识

the four of them sat around the stove[1]. They were silent and uneasy. Willie gazed nervously around the room—at the books on the kitchen table, the sink[2], the cot against the wall, and at his father. Highboy grinned[3] and picked at his tie. Doctor Copeland seemed about to speak, and then he wet his lips and was still silent.

'Willie, you were going pretty good with your harp,' said Portia finally. 'Look to me like you and Highboy must of got into somebody's gin bottle.'

'No, ma'am,' said Highboy very politely. 'Us haven't had anything since Saturday. Us have just been enjoying our horseshoe[4] game.'

Doctor Copeland still did not speak, and they all kept glancing at him and waiting. The room was close and the quietness made everyone nervous.

'I do haves the hardest time with them boys' clothes,' Portia said. 'I washes both of them white suits ever Saturday and I presses them twice a week. And look at them now. Course they don't wear them except when they gets home from work. But after two days they seems to be potty black. I ironed[5] them pants just last night and now there not a crease left.'

Still Doctor Copeland was silent. He kept his eyes on his son's face, but when Willie noticed this he bit his rough, blunt fingers and stared at his feet. Doctor Copeland felt his pulse hammering at his wrists and temples. He coughed and held his fist to his chest. He wanted to speak to his son, but he could think of nothing to say. The old bitterness[6] came up in him and he did not have time to cogitate and push it down. His pulse hammered in him and he was confused.

---

① stove：（取暖或烹饪用的）炉子，火炉
② sink：洗涤槽，水槽
③ grin：露齿笑
④ horseshoe：马蹄铁；U 形物
⑤ iron：用熨斗熨衣服
⑥ bitterness：痛苦；悲痛

But they all looked at him, and the silence was so strong that he had to speak.

His voice was high and it did not sound as though it came from himself. 'William, I wonder how much of all the things I have said to you when you were a child have stayed in your mind.[①]'

'I don't know what you m-m-means,' Willie said.

The words came before Doctor Copeland knew what he would say. 'I mean that to you and Hamilton and Karl Marx I gave all that was in me. And I put all of my trust and hope in you. And all I get is blank misunderstanding and idleness[②] and indifference[③]. Of all I have put in nothing has remained. All has been taken away from me. All that I have tried to do—'

'Hush,' said Portia. 'Father, you promised me that us would not quarrel. This here is crazy. Us can't afford to quarrel.'

Portia got up and started toward the front door. Willie and Highboy followed quickly. Doctor Copeland was the last to come.

They stood in the dark before the front door. Doctor Copeland tried to speak, but his voice seemed lost somewhere deep inside him. Willie and Portia and Highboy stood in a group together.

With one arm Portia held to her husband and brother and with the other she reached out to Doctor Copeland. 'Less us all make up now before us goes. I can't stand this here fighting between us. Less us not ever quarrel no more.'

In silence Doctor Copeland shook hands again with each of them. 'I am sorry,' he said.

'It quite all right with me,' said Highboy politely.

'It quite all right with me too,' Willie mumbled.

Portia held all of their hands together. 'Us just can't afford to

---

① 参考译文：威廉，不知道（你）小时候我跟你说过的那些话，你还记得多少。本句套了较多从句成分，wonder 后跟了宾语从句，主结构为 how much have stayed in your mind；主结构中包含了定语从句 I have said to you 来修饰 things，定语从句中又套了时间状语从句。

② idleness：懒惰

③ indifference：漠不关心，冷淡

quarrel[1].'

They said goodbye, and Doctor Copeland watched them from the dark front porch as they went together up the street. Their footsteps as they walked away had a lonesome sound and he felt weak and tired. When they were a block away William began playing his harmonica again. The music was sad and empty. He stayed on the front porch until he could neither see nor hear them any longer.

Doctor Copeland turned off the lights in his house and sat in the dark before the stove. But peace would not come to him. He wanted to remove Hamilton and Karl Marx and William from his mind. Each word that Portia had said to him came back in a loud, hard way to his memory. He got up suddenly and turned on the light. He settled himself at the table with his books by Spinoza and William Shakespeare and Karl Marx. When he read the Spinoza aloud to himself the words had a rich, dark sound.

He thought of the white man of whom they had spoken. It would be good if the white man could help him with Augustus Benedict Mady Lewis, the deaf patient. It would be good to write to the white man even if he did not have this reason and these questions to ask. Doctor Copeland held his head in his hands and from his throat there came the strange sound like a kind of singing moan[2]. He remembered the white man's face when he smiled behind the yellow match flame on that rainy night—and peace was in him.

---

① can't afford to do sth.：无法承担做某事，例：I can't afford to buy anything they want. 我负担不起他们想买的任何东西。

② moan：呻吟声；抱怨声

6

BY MIDSUMMER Singer had visitors more often than any other person in the house. From his room in the evening there was nearly always the sound of a voice. After dinner at the New York Café he bathed and dressed himself in one of his cool wash suits and as a rule did not go out again. The room was cool and pleasant. He had an icebox in the closet① where he kept bottles of cold beer and fruit drinks. He was never busy or in a hurry②. And always he met his guests at the door with a welcome smile.

Mick loved to go up to Mister Singer's room. Even if he was a deaf-and-dumb mute he understood every word she said to him. Talking with him was like a game. Only there was a whole lot more to it than any game. It was like finding out new things about music. She would tell him some of her plans that she would not tell anybody else. He let her meddle③ with his cute little chess men. Once when she was excited and caught her shirttail in the electric fan he acted in such a kindly way that she was not embarrassed at all.④ Except for her Dad, Mister Singer was the nicest man she knew.

When Doctor Copeland wrote the note to John Singer about

---

① closet：壁橱

② in a hurry：匆忙地；急于，例：I was in a hurry to catch the train, so I didn't have time to eat breakfast. 我急着赶火车，所以没时间吃早饭。

③ meddle：乱弄（meddle with：弄乱，摆弄）

④ 参考译文：有一次，她很兴奋，衬衫下摆卷进了电风扇，他表现得那么和善，没让她感觉到一丁点尴尬。such...that... 与 so...that... 类似，也表示“如此……，以至于……”，such 后常跟名词。

Augustus Benedict Mady Lewis there was a polite reply and an invitation for him to make a call[①] when he found the opportunity. Doctor Copeland went to the back of the house and sat with Portia awhile in the kitchen. Then he climbed the stairs to the white man's room. There was truly none of the quiet insolence about this man. They had a lemonade[②] together and the mute wrote down the answer to the questions he wished to know. This man was different from any person of the white race whom Doctor Copeland had ever encountered. Afterward he pondered[③] about this white man a long time. Then later, inasmuch as[④] he had been invited in a cordial manner to return, he made another visit.

Jake Blount came every week. When he walked up to Singer's room the whole stairway shook. Usually he carried a paper sack[⑤] of beers. Often his voice would come out loud and angry from the room. But before he left his voice gradually quieted. When he descended[⑥] the stairs he did not carry the sack of beers any longer, and he walked away thoughtfully without seeming to notice where he was going.

Even Biff Brannon came to the mute's room one night. But as he could never stay away from the restaurant for long, he left in a half-hour.

Singer was always the same to everyone. He sat in a straight chair by the window with his hands stuffed[⑦] tight into his pockets, and nodded or smiled to show his guests that he understood.

If he did not have a visitor in the evening, Singer went to a late movie. He liked to sit back and watch the actors talking and walking about on the screen. He never looked at the title of a picture before going into a movie, and no matter what was showing he watched each scene with equal interest.

---

① make a call：打电话
② lemonade：柠檬水
③ ponder：思考
④ inasmuch as：由于；因为
⑤ sack：麻布（或厚纸、塑料等）大袋；一袋
⑥ descend：从……下来
⑦ stuffed：塞满了的

Then, one day in July, Singer suddenly went away without warning. He left the door of his room open, and on the table in an envelope[①] addressed to Mrs. Kelly there were four dollars for the past week's rent. His few simple possessions[②] were gone and the room was very clean and bare. When his visitors came and saw this empty room they went away with hurt surprise. No one could imagine why he had left like this.

Singer spent all of his summer vacation in the town where Antonapoulos was being kept in the asylum[③]. For months he had planned this trip and imagined about each moment they would have together. Two weeks beforehand his hotel reservation had been made and for a long time he had carried his railroad[④] ticket in an envelope in his pocket.

Antonapoulos was not changed at all. When Singer came into his room he ambled placidly to meet his friend. He was even fatter than before, but the dreamy smile on his face was just the same. Singer had some packages in his arms and the big Greek gave them his first attention. His presents were a scarlet dressing-gown, soft bedroom slippers, and two monogrammed nightshirts. Antonapoulos looked beneath all the tissue papers in the boxes very carefully. When he saw that nothing good to eat had been concealed there, he dumped the gifts disdainfully[⑤] on his bed and did not bother with them any more.

The room was large and sunny. Several beds were spaced in a row together. Three old men played a game of slapjack in a corner. They did not notice Singer or Antonapoulos, and the two friends sat alone on the other side of the room.

It seemed to Singer that years had passed since they had been together. There was so much to say that his hands could not shape the signs with speed enough. His green eyes burned and sweat glittered[⑥]

---

① envelope：信封
② possession：财产；所有物
③ asylum：收容所；避难所
④ railroad：铁路
⑤ disdainfully：轻视地；蔑视地
⑥ glitter：灿烂；闪烁；辉耀

on his forehead. The old feeling of gaiety and bliss was so quick in him again that he could not control himself.

Antonapoulos kept his dark, oily eyes on his friend and did not move. His hands fumbled① languidly with the crotch of his trousers. Singer told him, among other things, about the visitors who had been coming to see him. He told his friend that they helped take his mind away from his lonesomeness. He told Antonapoulos that they were strange people and always talking—but that he liked to have them come. He drew quick sketches of Jake Blount and Mick and Doctor Copeland. Then as soon as he saw that Antonapoulos was not interested Singer crumpled the sketches and forgot about them. When the attendant② came in to say that their time was up, Singer had not finished half of the things he wanted to say.③ But he left the room very tired and happy.

The patients could receive their friends only on Thursday and Sunday. On the days when he could not be with Antonapoulos, Singer walked up and down in his room at the hotel.

His second visit to his friend was like the first, except that the old men in the room watched them listlessly④ and did not play slapjack.

After much trouble Singer obtained⑤ permission to take Antonapoulos out with him for a few hours. He planned each detail of the little excursion⑥ in advance. They drove out into the country in a taxi, and then at four-thirty they went to the dining-room at the hotel. Antonapoulos greatly enjoyed his extra meal. He ordered half the dishes on the menu and ate very greedily⑦. But when he had finished he would not leave. He held to the table. Singer coaxed him and the

---

① fumble：摸索；笨拙地行动

② attendant：服务员，侍者

③ 参考译文：看护走进来对他们说时间到了，这时辛格的话连一半还没说完。本句为时间状语从句，主结构内含定语从句。time is up 表示"时间到了"。

④ listlessly：百无聊赖地；倦怠地

⑤ obtain：获取

⑥ excursion：（尤指集体）远足；短途旅行

⑦ greedily：贪食地；贪婪地

cab driver wanted to use force. Antonapoulos sat stolidly and made obscene[①] gestures[②] when they came too close to him. At last Singer bought a bottle of whiskey from the hotel manager and lured[③] him into the taxi again. When Singer threw the unopened bottle out of the window Antonapoulos wept with disappointment and offense. The end of their little excursion made Singer very sad.

His next visit was the last one, for his two weeks' vacation was almost over. Antonapoulos had forgotten what had happened before. They sat in their same corner of the room. The minutes slipped by quickly. Singer's hands talked desperately[④] and his narrow face was very pale. At last it was time for him to go. He held his friend by the arm and looked into his face in the way that he used to do when they parted each day before work. Antonapoulos stared at him drowsily[⑤] and did not move. Singer left the room with his hands stuffed hard into his pockets.

Soon after Singer returned to his room at the boarding-house, Mick and Jake Blount and Doctor Copeland began to come again. Each one of them wanted to know where he had been and why he had not let them know about his plans. But Singer pretended that he did not understand their questions, and his smile was inscrutable.

One by one they would come to Singer's room to spend the evening with him. The mute was always thoughtful and composed. His many-tinted gentle eyes were grave as a sorcerer's. Mick Kelly and Jake Blount and Doctor Copeland would come and talk in the silent room—for they felt that the mute would always understand whatever they wanted to say to him.[⑥] And maybe even more than that.

---

① obscene：淫秽的；猥亵的

② gesture：手势

③ lure：诱惑；引诱

④ desperately：拼命地；绝望地

⑤ drowsily：昏昏欲睡地；恹恹地

⑥ 参考译文：米克·凯利、杰克·布朗特和科普兰医生经常来到这个寂静的屋子里说话——他们觉得，无论对哑巴说什么，他都会明白。for 引导原因状语从句，表示补充说明；whatever 引导宾语从句，表示“无论什么”，相当于 anything what。

Part Two

1

THIS SUMMER was different from any other time Mick could remember. Nothing much happened that she could describe to herself in thoughts or words—but there was a feeling of change. All the time she was excited. In the morning she couldn't wait to get out of bed and start going for the day. And at night she hated like hell to have to sleep again.

Right after breakfast she took the kids out, and except for meals they were gone most of the day.① A good deal of the time they just roamed② around the streets—with her pulling Ralph's wagon and Bubber following along behind. Always she was busy with thoughts and plans. Sometimes she would look up suddenly and they would be way off in some part of town she didn't even recognize③. And once or twice they ran into Bill on the streets and she was so busy thinking he had to grab④ her by the arm to make her see him.

Early in the mornings it was a little cool and their shadows stretched out⑤ tall on the sidewalk in front of them. But in the middle of the day the sky was always blazing hot. The glare was so bright it hurt to keep your eyes open. A lot of times the plans about the

---

① 参考译文：一吃完早饭，她就把孩子们带出去，除了吃饭时间，他们白天基本不在家。right 后加时间状语，指"一做完某事就……"。(except for：除了……以外)

② roam：漫游

③ recognize：认出

④ grab：抓住；攫取

⑤ stretch out：伸展开来

things that were going to happen to her were mixed up[①] with ice and snow. Sometimes it was like she was out in Switzerland and all the mountains were covered with snow and she was skating on cold, greenish-colored ice. Mister Singer would be skating with her. And maybe Carole Lombard[②] or Arturo Toscanini[③] who played on the radio. They would be skating together and then Mister Singer would fall through the ice and she would dive in without regard for peril and swim under the ice and save his life.[④] That was one of the plans always going on in her mind.

Usually after they had walked awhile she would park Bubber and Ralph in some shady place. Bubber was a swell kid and she had trained him pretty good. If she told him not to go out of hollering distance from Ralph she wouldn't ever find him shooting marbles with kids two or three blocks away. He played by himself near the wagon, and when she left them she didn't have to worry much. She either went to the library and looked at the National Geographic or else just roamed around and thought some more. If she had any money she bought a dope or a Milky Way at Mister Brannon's. He gave kids a reduction[⑤]. He sold them nickel[⑥] things for three cents.

But all the time—no matter what she was doing—there was music. Sometimes she hummed to herself as she walked, and other times she listened quietly to the songs inside her. There were all kinds of music in her thoughts. Some she heard over radios, and some was in her mind already without her ever having heard it anywhere.

---

① be mixed up：与……混在一起

② Carole Lombard：卡罗尔·隆巴德，20世纪30年代美国著名女演员，主演的电影包括《我的高德弗里》《毫不神圣》等。

③ Arturo Toscanini：阿图罗·托斯卡尼尼，意大利著名指挥家。在美国，众多音乐爱好者通过广播、电视节目及众多歌剧与交响乐录音知悉了这位音乐大师，使托斯卡尼尼成为一个家喻户晓的名字。

④ 参考译文：他们一起溜冰，然后辛格先生掉进了冰窟窿，她则会不顾一切地跳进去，在冰下游着把他救上来。从本句谓语使用 would do 可以看出本句为虚拟语气，通过后文"这个计划一直萦绕在她的脑海中"得到进一步验证。

⑤ reduction：减价，折扣

⑥ nickel：（美国和加拿大的）五分镍币

In the night-time, as soon as the kids were in bed, she was free. That was the most important time of all. A lot of things happened when she was by herself and it was dark. Right after supper she ran out of the house again. She couldn't tell anybody about the things she did at night, and when her Mama asked her questions she would answer with any little tale that sounded reasonable. But most of the time if anybody called her she just ran away like she hadn't heard. That went for everybody except her Dad. There was something about her Dad's voice she couldn't run away from. He was one of the biggest, tallest men in the whole town. But his voice was so quiet and kindly that people were surprised when he spoke. No matter how much of a hurry she was in, she always had to stop when her Dad called.①

This summer she realized something about her Dad she had never known before. Up until then she had never thought about him as being a real separate② person. A lot of times he would call her. She would go in the front room where he worked and stand by him a couple of minutes—but when she listened to him her mind was never on the things he said to her. Then one night she suddenly realized about her Dad. Nothing unusual happened that night and she didn't know what it was that made her understand. Afterward she felt older and as though she knew him as good as she could know any person.

It was a night in late August and she was in a big rush. She had to be at this house by nine o'clock, and no maybe either.③ Her Dad called and she went into the front room. He was sitting slumped over④ his workbench⑤. For some reason it never did seem natural to see him there. Until the time of his accident last year he had been a painter and

---

① 参考译文：不管她多着急，只要爸爸一喊她，她总是不得不停住脚步。（no matter how：无论如何）

② separate：单独的

③ 参考译文：她必须九点以前赶到那所房子，不容商量。（no maybe either：此处表示没有商量的可能性。）

④ slump over：弯着身子坐，伏

⑤ workbench：工作台，手工台

carpenter[1]. Before daylight every morning he would leave the house in his overalls, to be gone all day. Then at night sometimes he fiddled[2] around with clocks as an extra work. A lot of times he had tried to get a job in a jewelry[3] store where he could sit by himself at a desk all day with a clean white shirt on and a tie. Now when he couldn't carpenter any more he had put a sign at the front of the house reading 'Clocks and Watches Repaired Cheap.' But he didn't look like most jewelers—the ones downtown were quick, dark little Jew men. Her Dad was too tall for his workbench, and his big bones seemed joined together in a loose way.

Her Dad just stared at her. She could tell he didn't have any reason for calling. He only wanted real bad to talk to her. He tried to think of some way to begin. His brown eyes were too big for his long, thin face, and since he had lost every single hair the pale, bald[4] top of his head gave him a naked[5] look. He looked at her without speaking and she was in a hurry. She had to be at that house by nine sharp and there was no time to waste. Her Dad saw she was in a hurry and he cleared his throat.

'I got something for you,' he said. 'Nothing much, but maybe you can treat yourself with it.'

He didn't have to give her any nickel or dime just because he was lonesome and wanted to talk. Out of what he made he only kept enough to have beer about twice a week.[6] Two bottles were on the floor by his chair now, one empty and one just opened. And whenever he drank beer he liked to talk to somebody. Her Dad fumbled with his belt and she looked away. This summer he had gotten like a kid about hiding those nickels and dimes[7] he kept for himself. Sometimes he hid

---

① carpenter：木匠

② fiddle with：调整，处理（fiddle with clocks 意为“修表”。）

③ jewelry：珠宝，首饰

④ bald：秃头的

⑤ naked：裸露的

⑥ 参考译文：他赚的钱，只够他大约每星期喝两次啤酒。

⑦ dime：（美国和加拿大的）10 分铸币

them in his shoes, and other times in a little slit he had cut in his belt. She only halfway[1] wanted to take the dime, but when he held it out her hand was just naturally open and ready.

'I got so much work to do I don't know where to begin,' he said.

That was just the opposite to the truth, and he knew it good as she did. He never had many watches to fix, and when he finished he would fool around the house doing any little job that was needed.[2] Then at night he sat at his bench, cleaning old springs and wheels and trying to make the work last out until bedtime. Ever since he broke his hip and couldn't work steady he had to be doing something every minute.

'I been thinking a lot tonight,' her Dad said. He poured out[3] his beer and sprinkled[4] a few grains of salt on the back of his hand. Then he licked up the salt and took a swallow out of the glass.

She was in such a hurry that it was hard to stand still. Her Dad noticed this. He tried to say something—but he had not called to tell her anything special. He only wanted to talk with her for a little while. He started to speak and swallowed. They just looked at each other. The quietness grew out longer and neither of them could say a word.

That was when she realized about her Dad. It wasn't like she was learning a new fact—she had understood it all along in every way except with her brain. Now she just suddenly knew that she knew about her Dad. He was lonesome and he was an old man. Because none of the kids went to him for anything and because he didn't earn much money he felt like he was cut off from the family.[5] And in his

---

① halfway：一定程度上，部分地

② 参考译文：他根本没有多少表要修，干完那点活儿，他便总是在家里到处转悠，找些杂七杂八的事干。（fool around：闲逛）

③ pour out：倒出

④ sprinkle：撒

⑤ 参考译文：从来没有哪个孩子会因为什么事情来找他，而且他赚的钱也不多。因此，他觉得自己被家人孤立了。本句包含两个原因状语从句，之后才引出主结构；而译文则进行拆译，用"因此"进行连接。

lonesomeness he wanted to be close to one of his kids—and they were all so busy that they didn't know it. He felt like he wasn't much real use to anybody.

She understood this while they were looking at each other. It gave her a queer feeling. Her Dad picked up a watch spring and cleaned it with a brush dipped in gasoline[①].

'I know you're in a hurry. I just hollered to say hello.'

'No, I'm not in any rush,' she said. 'Honest.'

That night she sat down in a chair by his bench and they talked awhile. He talked about accounts and expenses and how things would have been if he had just managed in a different way. He drank beer, and once the tears came to his eyes and he snuffled his nose against his shirt-sleeve. She stayed with him a good while that night. Even if she was in an awful hurry. Yet for some reason she couldn't tell him about the things in her mind—about the hot, dark nights.

These nights were secret, and of the whole summer they were the most important time. In the dark she walked by herself and it was like she was the only person in the town. Almost every street came to be as plain to her in the nighttime as her own home block. Some kids were afraid to walk through strange places in the dark, but she wasn't. Girls were scared a man would come out from somewhere and put his teapot in them like they was married. Most girls were nuts[②]. If a person the size of Joe Louis[③] or Mountain Man Dean[④] would jump out at her and want to fight she would run. But if it was somebody within twenty pounds her weight she would give him a good sock[⑤] and go right on[⑥].

The nights were wonderful, and she didn't have time to think

① gasoline：汽油

② nut：怪人，疯子

③ Joe Louis：乔·路易斯，美国著名黑人拳击手。

④ Mountain Man Dean："山人"迪恩，原名 Frank Simmons Leavitt（1891—1953），著名职业摔跤手。"山人"为其台上绰号。

⑤ sock：重击

⑥ go right on：一直干下去

about such things as being scared. Whenever she was in the dark she thought about music. While she walked along the streets she would sing to herself. And she felt like the whole town listened without knowing it was Mick Kelly.

She learned a lot about music during these free nights in the summer-time. When she walked out in the rich parts of town every house had a radio. All the windows were open and she could hear the music very marvelous①. After a while she knew which houses tuned in for the programs she wanted to hear. There was one special house that got all the good orchestras②. And at night she would go to this house and sneak into③ the dark yard to listen. There was beautiful shrubbery④ around this house, and she would sit under a bush near the window. And after it was all over she would stand in the dark yard with her hands in her pockets and think for a long time. That was the realest part of all the summer—her listening to this music on the radio and studying about it.

'Cerra fa puerta, señor⑤,' Mick said.

Bubber was sharp as a briar. 'Haga me usted el favor, señorita⑥,' he answered as a comeback.

It was grand to take Spanish at Vocational. There was something about speaking in a foreign language that made her feel like she'd been around a lot. Every afternoon since school had started she had fun speaking the new Spanish words and sentences. At first Bubber was stumped, and it was funny to watch his face while she talked the foreign language. Then he caught on in a hurry, and before long he could copy everything she said. He remembered the words he learned, too. Of course he didn't know what all the sentences meant, but she

① marvelous：了不起的；非凡的
② orchestra：管弦乐队
③ sneak into：偷偷摸摸地进入
④ shrubbery：灌木林
⑤ 参考译文：请关门，先生。原文为西班牙语。
⑥ 参考译文：请您帮个忙，小姐。原文为西班牙语。

didn't say them for the sense they made, anyway.[①] After a while the kid learned so fast she gave out of Spanish and just gabbled[②] along with made-up sounds. But it wasn't long before he caught her out at that—nobody could put a thing over on old Bubber Kelly.

'I'm going to pretend[③] like I'm walking into this house for the first time,' Mick said. 'Then I can tell better if all the decorations[④] look good or not.'

She walked out on the front porch and then came back and stood in the hall. All day she and Bubber and Portia and her Dad had been fixing the hall and the dining-room for the party. The decoration was autumn leaves and vines and red crêpe[⑤] paper. On the mantelpiece in the dining-room and sticking up behind the hat rack there were bright yellow leaves. They had trailed[⑥] vines along the walls and on the table where the punch bowl would be. The red crêpe paper hung down in long fringes from the mantel and also was looped around the backs of the chairs.[⑦] There was plenty decoration. It was O.K.

She rubbed her hand on her forehead and squinted her eyes. Bubber stood beside her and copied every move she made. 'I sure do want this party to turnout all right. I sure do.'

This would be the first party she had ever given. She had never even been to more than four or five. Last summer she had gone to a prom party. But none of the boys asked her to prom or dance, she just stood by the punch bowl until all the refreshments were gone and

---

① 参考译文：当然，他并不能完全理解那些句子的意思，但她说西班牙语反正也不是因为这些话的意思。此处指米克说西班牙语句子只是为了将所学的句子说出来，而不是真的在表达什么意思。

② gabble：急促而含糊地说话

③ pretend：假装，伪装

④ decoration：装饰品

⑤ crêpe：绉纱，绉绸

⑥ trail：（使植物）蔓生；蔓延

⑦ 参考译文：铺在壁炉上的红色绉纱纸垂着长长的流苏，椅背上也绕了一圈垂着流苏的红色绉纱纸。（fringe：流苏；mantel：壁炉架）

then went home.[1] This party was not going to be a bit like that one. In a few hours now the people she had invited would start coming and the to-do would begin.

It was hard to remember just how she got the idea of this party. The notion came to her soon after she started at Vocational. High School was swell. Everything about it was different from grammar School. She wouldn't have liked it so much if she had had to take a stenographic[2] course like Hazel and Etta had done—but she got special permission and took mechanical shop like a boy. Shop and Algebra and Spanish were grand. English was mighty hard. Her English teacher was Miss Minner. Everybody said Miss Minner had sold her brains to a famous doctor for ten thousand dollars, so that after she was dead he could cut them up and see why she was so smart. On written lessons she cracked such questions as 'Name eight famous contemporaries[3] of Doctor Johnson,' and 'Quote ten lines from 'The Vicar of Wakefield.' She called on people by the alphabet[4] and kept her grade book open during the lessons. And even if she was brainy she was an old sourpuss[5]. The Spanish teacher had traveled once in Europe. She said that in France the people carried home loaves of bread without having them wrapped up[6]. They would stand talking on the streets and hit the bread on a lamp post[7]. And there wasn't any water in France—only wine.

In nearly all ways Vocational was wonderful. They walked back and forth in the hall between classes, and at lunch period students hung around[8] the gym. Here was the thing that soon began to bother

---

① 参考译文：却没有一个男孩邀请她散步或者跳舞，她只能站在潘趣酒大碗旁边。最后，所有茶点都吃光了，她便回家了。（punch：潘趣酒，一种果汁鸡尾酒，有的会加碳酸水或苏打水，通常调味后在底部混有葡萄酒或蒸馏酒。）

② stenographic：速记的

③ contemporary：同龄，同辈人

④ by the alphabet：按照字母表顺序

⑤ sourpuss：讨人嫌的人

⑥ wrap up：包起来

⑦ lamp post：灯柱，灯杆

⑧ hang around：闲荡；徘徊

her. In the halls the people would walk up and down together and everybody seemed to belong to some special bunch. Within a week or two she knew people in the halls and in classes to speak to them—but that was all. She wasn't a member of any bunch. In Grammar School she would have just gone up to any crowd she wanted to belong with and that would have been the end of the matter. Here it was different.

During the first week she walked up and down the halls by herself and thought about this. She planned about being with some bunch almost as much as she thought of music. Those two ideas were in her head all the time. And finally she got the idea of the party.

She was strict with[①] the invitations. No Grammar School kids and nobody under twelve years old. She just asked people between thirteen and fifteen. She knew everybody she invited good enough to speak to them in the halls—and when she didn't know their names she asked to find out. She called up those who had a telephone, and the rest she invited at school.

On the telephone she always said the same thing. She let Bubber stick in his ear[②] to listen.'This is Mick Kelly,' she said. If they didn't understand the name she kept on until they got it. I'm having a prom[③] party at eight o'clock Saturday night and I'm inviting you now. I live at 103 Fourth Street, Apartment A.' That Apartment A sounded swell on the telephone. Nearly everybody said they would be delighted. A couple of tough boys tried to be smarty and kept on asking her name over and over. One of them tried to act cute and said, 'I don't know you.' She squelched[④] him in a hurry: 'You go eat grass!' Outside of that wise guy there were ten boys and ten girls and she knew that they were all coming. This was a real party, and it would be better and different from any party she had ever gone to or heard about before.

Mick looked over the hall and dining-room one last time. By

---

① be strict with：对……要求严格

② stick in one's ear：附耳，把耳朵贴过来

③ prom：舞会（为中学生举办的正式舞会或聚会，通常在高中学年即将结束时举行）

④ squelch：制止

the hatrack she stopped before the picture of Old Dirty-Face. This was a photo of her Mama's grandfather. He was a major way back in the Civil War and had been killed in a battle. Some kid once drew eyeglasses and a beard on his picture, and when the pencil marks were erased it left his face all dirty. That was why she called him Old Dirty-Face. The picture was in the middle of a three-part frame[①]. On both sides were pictures of his sons. They looked about Bubber's age. They had on uniforms and their faces were surprised. They had been killed in battle also. A long time ago.

'I'm going to take this down for the party. I think it looks common. Don't you?'

'I don't know,' Bubber said. 'Are we common, Mick?'

'I'm not.'

She put the picture underneath the hat rack. The decoration was O.K. Mister Singer would be pleased when he came home. The rooms seemed very empty and quiet. The table was set for supper. And then after supper it would be time for the party. She went into the kitchen to see about the refreshments[②].

'You think everything will be all right?' she asked Portia.

Portia was making biscuits[③]. The refreshments were on top of the stove. There were peanut[④] butter and jelly sandwiches and chocolate snaps and punch. The sandwiches were covered with a damp dishcloth[⑤]. She peeped[⑥] at them but didn't take one.

'I done told you forty times that everything going to be all right,' Portia said. 'Just soon as I come back from fixing supper at home I going to put on that white apron and serve the food real nice. Then I going to push off[⑦] from here by nine-thirty. This here is Saturday

---

① frame：框架；结构
② refreshment：茶点
③ biscuit：饼干
④ peanut：花生
⑤ dishcloth：抹布
⑥ peep：窥视，偷看
⑦ push off：离开

night and Highboy and Willie and me haves our plans, too.'

'Sure,' Mick said. 'I just want you to help out till things sort of get started—you know.'

She gave in and took one of the sandwiches. Then she made Bubber stay with Portia and went into the middle room. The dress she would wear was laying out on the bed. Hazel and Etta had both been good about lending her their best clothes—considering that they weren't supposed to come to the party. There was Etta's long blue crêpe de chine evening dress and some white pumps and a rhinestone[①] tiara[②] for her hair. These clothes were really gorgeous[③]. It was hard to imagine how she would look in them.

The late afternoon had come and the sun made long, yellow slants through the window. If she took two hours over dressing for the party it was time to begin now. When she thought about putting on the fine clothes she couldn't just sit around and wait. Very slowly she went into the bathroom and shucked off her old shorts and shirt and turned on the water. She scrubbed the rough parts of her heels and her knees and especially her elbows. She made the bath take a long time.

She ran naked into the middle room and began to dress. Silk teddies she put on, and silk stockings. She even wore one of Etta's brassieres[④] just for the heck of it. Then very carefully she put on the dress and stepped into the pumps. This was the first time she had ever worn an evening dress. She stood for a long time before the mirror. She was so tall that the dress came up two or three inches above her ankles—and the shoes were so short they hurt her. She stood in front of the mirror a long tune, and finally decided she either looked like a sap or else she looked very beautiful. One or the other.

Six different ways she tried out her hair. The cowlicks[⑤] were a

---

① rhinestone：人造钻石；莱茵石
② tiara：女式冕状头饰；（罗马教皇的）三重冕
③ gorgeous：美丽动人的；令人愉快的；绚丽的，华丽的
④ brassiere：胸罩
⑤ cowlick：额头翘起的一绺头发

little trouble, so she wet her bangs and made three spit curls. Last of all she stuck the rhinestones in her hair and put on plenty of lipstick and paint.[1] When she finished she lifted up her chin and half-closed eyes like a movie star. Slowly she turned her face from one side to the other. It was beautiful she looked—just beautiful.

She didn't feel like herself at all. She was somebody different from Mick Kelly entirely. Two hours had to pass before the party would begin, and she was ashamed for any of the family to see her dressed so far ahead of time. She went into the bathroom again and locked[2] the door. She couldn't mess up[3] her dress by sitting down, so she stood in the middle of the floor. The close walls around her seemed to press in all the excitement. She felt so different from the old Mick Kelly that she knew this would be better than anything else in all her whole life—this party.

'Yippee! The punch!'

'The cutest dress—'

'Say! You solve that one about the triangle forty-six by twen—'

'Lemme by! Move out my way!'

The front door slammed[4] every second as the people swarmed into[5] the house. Sharp voices and soft voices sounded together until there was just one roaring noise. Girls stood in bunches in their long, fine evening dresses, and the boys roamed around in clean duck pants or R.O.T.C. uniforms or new dark fall suits.[6] There was so much commotion that Mick couldn't notice any separate face or person. She

---

① 参考译文：最后，她把水晶头冠卡在头发上，涂了很多口红，还有腮红。（rhinestone：人造钻石，莱茵石，此处指水晶头冠；lipstick：口红；paint：颜料，此处指腮红。）

② lock：锁上

③ mess up：搞糟，弄脏

④ slam：砰地关上

⑤ swarm into：蜂拥而入

⑥ 参考译文：女孩们扎堆站在一起，穿着漂亮的长晚礼服；男孩们则到处闲逛，他们穿着洁净的帆布裤子，或者后备军官训练队制服，或者崭新的深色秋季新装。本句非常形象地描绘了男孩和女孩参加晚会的不同状态，女孩们就像参加选秀，男孩们则较随意。（R.O.T.C.：Reserve Officers' Training Corps，指的是预备役军官训练营。）

stood by the hat rack and stared around at the party as a whole.

'Everybody get a prom card and start signing up[1].'

At first the room was too loud for anyone to hear and pay attention. The boys were so thick around the punch bowl that the table and the vines didn't show at all. Only her Dad's face rose up above the boys' heads as he smiled and dished up the punch into the little paper cups. On the seat of the hatrack beside her were a jar of candy and two handkerchiefs. A couple of girls thought it was her birthday, and she had thanked them and unwrapped the presents without telling them she wouldn't be fourteen for eight more months. Every person was as clean and fresh and dressed up as she was. They smelled good. The boys had their hair plastered[2] down wet and slick. The girls with their different-colored long dresses stood together, and they were like a bright hunk of flowers. The start was marvelous[3]. The beginning of this party was O.K.

'I'm part Scotch Irish and French and—'

'I got German blood—'

She hollered[4] about the prom cards one more time before she went into the dining-room. Soon they began to pile in[5] from the hall. Every person took a prom card and they lined up in bunches against the walls of the room. This was the real start now.

It came all of a sudden in a very queer way—this quietness. The boys stood together on one side of the room and the girls were across from them. For some reason every person quit making noise at once. The boys held their cards and looked at the girls and the room was very still. None of the boys started asking for proms like they were supposed to do. The awful quietness got worse and she had not been to enough parties to know what she should do. Then the boys started

---

① sign up：签约参加
② plaster：把（头发）梳平
③ marvelous：了不起的；不平常的
④ holler about：抱怨，发牢骚
⑤ pile in：迅速进入

punching each other and talking. The girls giggled[1]—but even if they didn't look at the boys you could tell they only had their minds on whether they were going to be popular or not. The awful quietness was gone now, but there was something jittery[2] about the room.

After a while a boy went up to a girl named Delores Brown. As soon as he had signed her up the other boys all began to rush Delores at once. When her whole card was full they started on another girl, named Mary. After that everything suddenly stopped again. One or two extra girls got a couple of proms—and because she was giving the party three boys came up to her. That was all.

The people just hung around in the dining-room and the hall. The boys mostly flocked around the punch bowl and tried to show off[3] with each other. The girls bunched together and did a lot of laughing to pretend like they were having a good time. The boys thought about the girls and the girls thought about the boys. But all that came of it was a queer feeling in the room.

It was then she began to notice Harry Minowitz. He lived in the house next door and she had known him all her life. Although he was two years older she had grown faster than him, and in the summer-time they used to wrestle[4] and fight out on the plot of grass by the street. Harry was a Jew boy, but he did not look so much like one. His hair was light brown and straight. Tonight he was dressed very neat, and when he came in the door he had hung a grown man's panama hat with a feather in it on the hat rack.

It wasn't his clothes that made her notice him. There was something changed about his face because he was without the horn-

---

① giggle：咯咯地笑，咯咯地笑着说
② jittery：紧张不安的
③ show off：炫耀，卖弄
④ wrestle：摔跤，搏斗

rimmed[①] specs[②] he usually wore. A red, droopy[③] sty[④] had come out on one of his eyes and he had to cock his head sideways like a bird in order to see. His long, thin hands kept touching around his sty as though it hurt him. When he asked for punch he stuck the paper cup right into her Dad's face. She could tell he needed his glasses very bad. He was nervous and kept bumping into people. He didn't ask any girl to prom except her—and that was because it was her party.

All the punch had been drunk. Her Dad was afraid she would be embarrassed, so he and her Mama had gone back to the kitchen to make lemonade. Some of the people were on the front porch and the sidewalk. She was glad to get out in the cool night air. After the hot, bright house she could smell the new autumn in the darkness.

Then she saw something she hadn't expected. Along the edge of the sidewalk and in the dark street there was a bunch of neighborhood kids. Pete and Sucker Wells and Baby and Spareribs—the whole gang that started at below Bubber's age and went on up to over twelve. There were even kids she didn't know at all who had somehow smelled a party and come to hang around.[⑤] And there were kids her age and older that she hadn't invited either because they had done something mean to her or she had done something mean to them. They were all dirty and in plain shorts or draggle-tailed knickers[⑥] or old everyday dresses. They were just hanging around in the dark to watch the party. She thought of two feelings when she saw those kids—one was sad and the other was a kind of warning.

'I got this prom with you.' Harry Minowitz made out like he was reading on his card, but she could see nothing was written on it.

---

① horn-rimmed：（指眼镜）角质架的

② specs：眼镜，即 spectacles。

③ droopy：下垂的；没有精神的

④ sty：睑腺炎，麦粒肿

⑤ 参考译文：还有些孩子她根本不认识，他们不知怎的都嗅到了派对的味道，到附近来转悠。本句 she didn't know at all 和 who had somehow smelled a party and come to hang around 均为定语从句修饰 kids。

⑥ knickers：灯笼裤

Her Dad had come onto the porch and blown the whistle[①] that meant the beginning of the first prom.

'Yeah,' she said. 'Let's get going.'

They started out[②] to walk around the block. In the long dress she still felt very ritzy. 'Look yonder at Mick Kelly!' one of the kids in the dark hollered. 'Look at her!' She just walked on like she hadn't heard, but it was that Spare-ribs, and some day soon she would catch him. She and Harry walked fast along the dark sidewalk, and when they came to the end of the street they turned down[③] another block.

'How old are you now, Mick—thirteen?'

'Going on fourteen.'

She knew what he was thinking. It used to worry her all the time. Five feet six inches[④] tall and a hundred and three pounds, and she was only thirteen. Every kid at the party was a runt[⑤] beside her, except Harry, who was only a couple of inches shorter. No boy wanted to prom with a girl so much taller than him. But maybe cigarettes would help stunt[⑥] the rest of her growth.

'I grew three and a fourth inches just in last year,' she said.

'Once I saw a lady at the fair who was eight and a half feet tall. But you probably won't grow that big.'

Harry stopped beside a dark crêpe myrtle[⑦] bush. Nobody was in sight. He took something out of his pocket and started fooling with whatever it was. She leaned over to see—it was his pair of specs and he was wiping them with his handkerchief.

'Pardon me,' he said. Then he put on his glasses and she could hear him breathe deep.

'You ought to wear your specs all the time.'

---

① whistle：口哨
② start out：开始出发
③ turn down：转弯
④ inch：英寸（inches 为复数形式）
⑤ runt：小个子
⑥ stunt：阻碍……的正常生长或发展
⑦ myrtle：桃金娘；桃金娘科植物

'Yeah.'

'How come you go around without them?'

The night was very quiet and dark. Harry held her elbow when they crossed the street.

'There's a certain young lady back at the party that thinks it's sissy for a fellow to wear glasses. This certain person—oh well, maybe I am a—'

He didn't finish. Suddenly he tightened up[①] and ran a few steps and sprang for a leaf about four feet above his head. She just could see that high leaf in the dark. He had a good spring to his jumping and he got it the first time. Then he put the leaf in his mouth and shadow-boxed for a few punches in the dark. She caught up with him.

As usual a song was in her mind. She was humming to herself.

'What's that you're singing? '

'It's a piece by a fellow named Mozart'

Harry felt pretty good. He was sidestepping with his feet like a fast boxer. 'That sounds like a sort of German name.'

'I reckon so.[②]'

'Fascist[③]?' he asked.

'What?'

'I say is that Mozart a Fascist or a Nazi? '

Mick thought a minute. 'No. They're new, and this fellow's been dead some time.'

'It's a good thing.' He began punching in the dark again. He wanted her to ask why.

'I say it's a good thing,' he said again.

'Why? '

'Because I hate Fascists. If I met one walking on the street I'd kill him.'

---

① tighten up：拉紧，绷紧

② 参考译文：我猜是的。（reckon：料想，认为）

③ fascist：法西斯主义者

She looked at Harry. The leaves against the street light made quick, freckly[①] shadows on his face. He was excited.

'How come?' she asked.

'Gosh! Don't you ever read the paper? You see, it's this way—'

They had come back around the block. A commotion was going on at her house. People were yelling[②] and running on the sidewalk. A heavy sickness came in her belly.

'There's not time to explain unless we prom around the block again. I don't mind telling you why I hate Fascists. I'd like to tell about it.'

This was probably the first chance he had got to spiel[③] these ideas out to somebody. But she didn't have time to listen. She was busy looking at what she saw in the front of her house. 'O.K. I'll see you later.' The prom was over now, so she could look and put her mind on the mess she saw.

What had happened while she was gone? When she left the people were standing around in the fine clothes and it was a real party. Now—after just five minutes—the place looked more like a crazy house. While she was gone those kids had come out of the dark and right into the party itself. The nerve they had! There was old Pete Wells banging out of the front door with a cup of punch in his hand. They bellowed[④] and ran and mixed with the invited people—in their old loose-legged knickers and everyday clothes.

Baby Wilson messed around[⑤] on the front porch—and Baby wasn't more than four years old. Anybody could see she ought to be[⑥] home in bed by now, same as Bubber. She walked down the steps one at a time, holding the punch high up[⑦] over her head. There was no

---

① freckly：多雀斑的
② yell：叫喊
③ spiel：喋喋不休地高谈阔论
④ bellow：大声吼叫
⑤ mess around：瞎混，打发时间
⑥ ought to do sth.：应该，应当
⑦ high up：在高处

reason for her to be here at all. Mister Brannon was her uncle and she could get free candy and drinks at his place any time she wanted to. As soon as she was on the sidewalk Mick caught her by the arm. 'You go right home, Baby Wilson. Go on, now.' Mick looked around to see what else she could do to straighten things out again like they ought to be. She went up to Sucker Wells. He stood farther down the sidewalk, where it was dark, holding his paper cup and looking at everybody in a dreamy way. Sucker was seven years old and he had on shorts. His chest and feet were naked. He wasn't causing any of the commotion[①], but she was mad as hell at what had happened.

She grabbed Sucker by the shoulders and began to shake him. At first he held his jaws tight, but after a minute his teeth began to rattle[②]. 'You go home, Sucker Wells. You quit hanging around where you're not invited.' When she let him go, Sucker tucked his tail[③] and walked slowly down the street. But he didn't go all the way home. After he got to the corner she saw him sit down on the curb and watch the party where he thought she couldn't see him.[④]

For a minute she felt good about shaking the spit out of[⑤] Sucker. And then right afterward she had a bad worry feeling in her and she started to let him come back. The big kids were the ones who messed up everything. Real brats[⑥] they were, and with the worst nerve she had ever seen. Drinking up the refreshments and ruining the real party into all this commotion. They slammed through the front door and hollered and bumped into each other. She went up to Pete Wells because he was the worst of all. He wore his football helmet[⑦] and butted into people. Pete was every bit of fourteen, yet he was still

---

① commotion：骚动；骚乱

② rattle：发出咔嗒咔嗒声

③ tuck one's tail：夹起尾巴（形容羞愧慌乱）

④ 参考译文：他走到街角，她看见他在路边坐了下来，望着派对上的人，他以为这样便会逃过她的目光了。本句中 where he thought she couldn't see him 为定语从句修饰 party，表示萨克觉得米克在派对上不会注意到自己。（curb：路边）

⑤ shake the spit out of sb.：摆脱某人

⑥ brat：乳臭未干的小孩；顽童

⑦ helmet：钢盔，头盔

stuck in the seventh grade. She went up to him, but he was too big to shake like Sucker. When she told him to go home he shimmied[①] and made a nosedive[②] at her.

'I been in six different states. Florida, Alabama—'

'Made out of silver cloth with a sash—'

The party was all messed up. Everybody was talking at once. The invited people from Vocational were mixed with the neighborhood gang. The boys and the girls still stood in separate bunches, though—and nobody prommed. In the house the lemonade was just about gone. There was only a little puddle of[③] water with floating lemon peels at the bottom of the bowl. Her Dad always acted too nice with kids. He had served out the punch to anybody who stuck a cup at him. Portia was serving the sandwiches when she went into the dining-room. In five minutes they were all gone. She only got one—a jelly kind with pink sops come through the bread.

Portia stayed in the dining-room to watch the party. 'I having too good a time to leave,' she said. 'I done sent word to Highboy and Willie to go on with the Saturday Night without me. Everbody so excited here I going to wait and see the end of this party.'

Excitement—that was the word. She could feel it all through the room and on the porch and the sidewalk. She felt excited, too. It wasn't just her dress and the beautiful way her face looked when she passed by the hat rack mirror and saw the red paint on her cheeks and the rhinestone tiara in her hair. Maybe it was the decoration and all these Vocational people and kids being jammed[④] together.

'Watch her run!'

'Ouch! Cut it out—'

'Act your age!'

A bunch of girls were running down the street, holding up their

① shimmy：（抖动着肩膀和臀部）跳希米舞（shimmied 为过去式）
② make a nosedive at sb.：直冲向某人
③ a little puddle of：一小滩……
④ jammed：堵塞的；拥挤的

dresses and with the hair flying out behind them. Some boys had cut off the long, sharp spears of a Spanish bayonet bush and they were chasing[①] the girls with them. Freshmen in Vocational all dressed up for a real prom party and acting just like kids. It was half play like and half not play like at all. A boy came up to her with a sticker and she started running too.

The idea of the party was over entirely now. This was just a regular playing-out. But it was the wildest[②] night she had ever seen. The kids had caused it. They were like a catching sickness, and their coming to the party made all the other people forget about high school and being almost grown.[③] It was like just before you take a bath in the afternoon when you might wallow[④] around in the back yard and get plenty dirty just for the good feel of it before getting into the tub[⑤]. Everybody was a wild kid playing out on Saturday night—and she felt like the very wildest of all.

She hollered and pushed and was the first to try any new stunt[⑥]. She made so much noise and moved around so fast she couldn't notice what anybody else was doing. Her breath wouldn't come fast enough to let her do all the wild things she wanted to do.

'The ditch[⑦] down the street! The ditch! The ditch!'

She started for it first. Down a block they had put in new pipes[⑧] under the street and dug a swell deep ditch. The flambeaux around the edge were bright and red in the dark. She wouldn't wait to climb down. She ran until she reached the little wavy[⑨] flames and then she

---

① chase：追赶

② wildest：狂热的

③ 参考译文：他们就像一场传染病，他们来到派对上，便让所有人都忘记了高中，忘记了长大。（catching sickness：传染病；forget about sth.：忘记某事；forget doing sth.：忘记做过了某事）

④ wallow：打滚

⑤ tub：浴盆；桶

⑥ stunt：绝技

⑦ ditch：沟渠，壕沟

⑧ pipe：管线，管道

⑨ wavy：波动起伏的

jumped.

With her tennis shoes she would have landed like a cat—but the high pumps made her slip and her stomach hit this pipe. Her breath was stopped. She lay quiet with her eyes closed.

The party—For a long time she remembered how she thought it would be, how she imagined the new people at Vocational. And about the bunch she wanted to be with every day. She would feel different in the halls now, knowing that they were not something special but like any other kids. It was O.K. about the ruined party. But it was all over. It was the end.

Mick climbed out of the ditch. Some kids were playing around the little pots of flames. The fire made a red glow and there were long, quick shadows. One boy had gone home and put on a dough-face bought in advance for Halloween. Nothing was changed about the party except her.

She walked home slowly. When she passed kids she didn't speak or look at them. The decoration in the hall was torn down[①] and the house seemed very empty because everyone had gone outside. In the bathroom she took off the blue evening dress. The hem[②] was torn and she folded it so the raggedy[③] place wouldn't show. The rhinestone tiara was lost somewhere. Her old shorts and shirt were lying on the floor just where she had left them. She put them on. She was too big to wear shorts any more after this. No more after this night. Not any more.

Mick stood out on the front porch. Her face was very white without the paint. She cupped her hands before her mouth and took a deep breath. 'Everybody go home! The door is shut! The party is over!'

In the quiet, secret night she was by herself again. It was not

① torn down：扯下

② hem：褶边；下摆

③ raggedy：破烂的，褴褛的

late—yellow squares of light showed in the windows of the houses along the streets. She walked slow, with her hands in her pockets and her head to one side. For a long time she walked without noticing the direction.

Then the houses were far apart from each other and there were yards with big trees in them and black shrubbery. She looked around and saw she was near this house where she had gone so many times in the summer. Her feet had just taken her here without her knowing. When she came to the house she waited to be sure no person could see. Then she went through the side yard.

The radio was on as usual. For a second she stood by the window and watched the people inside. The bald-headed① man and the gray-haired lady were playing cards at a table. Mick sat on the ground. This was a very fine and secret place. Close around were thick cedars② so that she was completely hidden by herself. The radio was no good tonight—somebody sang popular songs that all ended in the same way. It was like she was empty. She reached in her pockets and felt around with her fingers. There were raisins and a buckeye③ and a string of beads—one cigarette with matches. She lighted the cigarette and put her arms around her knees. It was like she was so empty there wasn't even a feeling or thought in her.

One program came on after another, and all of them were punk. She didn't especially④ care. She smoked and picked a little bunch of grass blades. After a while a new announcer⑤ started talking. He mentioned Beethoven. She had read in the library about that musician—his name was pronounced⑥ with an a and spelled with double e. He was a German fellow like Mozart. When he was living

---

① bald-headed：秃头的
② cedar：雪松，香柏
③ buckeye：七叶树
④ especially：特别；尤其
⑤ announcer：广播员；宣告者
⑥ pronounced：发音（pronounce 的过去分词，表被动）

he spoke in a foreign language and lived in a foreign place—like she wanted to do. The announcer said they were going to play his third symphony[①]. She only halfway listened because she wanted to walk some more and she didn't care much what they played. Then the music started. Mick raised her head and her fist went up to her throat.

How did it come? For a minute the opening balanced from one side to the other. Like a walk or march. Like God strutting in the night. The outside of her was suddenly froze and only that first part of the music was hot inside her heart. She could not even hear what sounded after, but she sat there waiting and froze, with her fists[②] tight. After a while the music came again, harder and loud. It didn't have anything to do with God. This was her, Mick Kelly, walking in the daytime and by herself at night. In the hot sun and in the dark with all the plans and feelings. This music was her—the real plain her.

She could not listen good enough to hear it all. The music boiled inside her. Which? To hang on to certain wonderful parts and think them over so that later she would not forget—or should she let go and listen to each part that came without thinking or trying to remember?[③] Golly! The whole world was this music and she could not listen hard enough. Then at last the opening music came again, with all the different instruments bunched together for each note like a hard, tight fist that socked at her heart. And the first part was over.

This music did not take a long time or a short time. It did not have anything to do with time going by at all. She sat with her arms held tight around her legs, biting her salty knee very hard. It might have been five minutes she listened or half the night. The second part was black-colored—a slow march. Not sad, but like the whole world was dead and black and there was no use thinking back how it was

---

① symphony：交响乐

② fist：拳头

③ 参考译文：牢牢抓住某些精彩的部分，反复思考，这样以后她就不会忘记了——或许她应该放手，先听完所有部分，并不仔细思考或试图记住？本句细致描写了音乐可以带给人的迷思，一首引起共鸣的音乐带给人诸多思考，正如米克此时的感受。（hang on to：紧紧抓住）

before. One of those horn[①] kind of instruments played a sad and silver tune. Then the music rose up[②] angry and with excitement underneath. And finally the black march[③] again.

But maybe the last part of the symphony[④] was the music she loved the best—glad and like the greatest people in the world running and springing up[⑤] in a hard, free way. Wonderful music like this was the worst hurt there could be. The whole world was this symphony, and there was not enough of her to listen.

It was over, and she sat very stiff with her arms around her knees. Another program came on the radio and she put her fingers in her ears. The music left only this bad hurt in her, and a blankness. She could not remember any of the symphony, not even the last few notes. She tried to remember, but no sound at all came to her. Now that it was over there was only her heart like a rabbit and this terrible hurt.

The radio and the lights in the house were turned off. The night was very dark. Suddenly Mick began hitting her thigh with her fists. She pounded the same muscle[⑥] with all her strength until the tears came down her face. But she could not feel this hard enough. The rocks under the bush were sharp. She grabbed a handful of them and began scraping them up and down on the same spot until her hand was bloody. Then she fell back to the ground and lay looking up at the night. With the fiery[⑦] hurt in her leg she felt better. She was limp[⑧] on the wet grass, and after a while her breath came slow and easy again.

Why hadn't the explorers known by looking at the sky that the world was round? The sky was curved[⑨], like the inside of a huge glass ball, very dark blue with the sprinkles of bright stars. The

---

① horn：喇叭，号角
② rise up：（音调）上升
③ march：进行曲
④ symphony：交响乐
⑤ spring up：出现
⑥ muscle：肌肉
⑦ fiery：燃烧的（fiery hurt：意为“火辣辣的疼”。）
⑧ limp：不直挺的；无力的，跛着脚的
⑨ curved：弧形的

night was quiet. There was the smell of warm cedars[①]. She was not trying to think of the music at all when it came back to her. The first part happened ih her mind just as it had been played. She listened in a quiet, slow way and thought the notes out like a problem in geometry[②] so she would remember. She could see the shape of the sounds very clear and she would not forget them.

Now she felt good. She whispered some words out loud: 'Lord forgiveth me, for I knoweth not what I do.' Why did she think of that? Everybody in the past few years knew there wasn't any real God. When she thought of what she used to imagine was God she could only see Mister Singer with a long, white sheet around him. God was silent—maybe that was why she was reminded. She said the words again, just as she would speak them to Mister Singer: 'Lord forgiveth me, for I knoweth not what I do.'

This part of the music was beautiful and clear. She could sing it now whenever she wanted to. Maybe later on, when she had just waked up some morning, more of the music would come back to her. If ever she heard the symphony again there would be other parts to add to what was already in her mind.[③] And maybe if she could hear it four more times, just four more times, she would know it all. Maybe.

Once again she listened to this opening part of the music. Then the notes grew slower and soft and it was like she was sinking down[④] slowly into the dark ground.

Mick awoke with a jerk[⑤]. The air had turned chilly, and as she was coming up out of the sleep she dreamed old Etta Kelly was taking all the cover. 'Gimme some blanket—' she tried to say. Then she opened her eyes. The sky was very black and all the stars were gone.

---

① cedar：雪松；香柏

② geometry：几何学

③ 参考译文：也许，如果她能再听一次这首交响乐，她能记住更多部分。（symphony：交响乐；add to：增加）

④ sink down：下沉

⑤ jerk：肌肉抽搐

The grass was wet. She got up in a hurry because her Dad would be worried. Then she remembered the music. She couldn't tell whether the time was midnight or three in the morning, so she started beating it for home in a rush. The air had a smell in it like autumn. The music was loud and quick in her mind, and she ran faster and faster on the sidewalks leading to the home block[①].

① block：街段，街区；大楼，大厦（home block：意为"家的方向"。）

2

BY OCTOBER the days were blue and cool. Biff Brannon changed his light seersucker[①] trousers[②] for dark-blue serge[③] ones. Behind the counter of the café he installed a machine that made hot chocolate. Mick was very partial[④] to hot chocolate, and she came in three or four times a week to drink a cup. He served it to her for a nickel instead of a dime and he wanted to give it to her free. He watched her as she stood behind the counter and he was troubled and sad. He wanted to reach out his hand and touch her sunburned, tousled[⑤] hair—not as he had ever touched a woman. In him there was an uneasiness[⑥], and when he spoke to her his voice had a rough, strange sound.

There were many worries on his mind. For one thing, Alice was not well. She worked downstairs as usual from seven in the morning until ten at night, but she walked very slowly and brown circles were beneath her eyes.[⑦] It was in the business that she showed this illness most plainly. One Sunday, when she wrote out the day's menu on the typewriter, she marked the special dinner with chicken a la king

① seersucker：泡泡纱；绉条纹薄织物
② trousers：裤子，长裤（使用复数形式）
③ serge：哔叽，一种结实的羊毛布
④ partial：偏爱的
⑤ tousled：（头发等）蓬乱的，混乱的
⑥ uneasiness：不安；担忧
⑦ 参考译文：从早上七点到晚上十点，她还是照常在楼下工作，但走路非常缓慢，眼睛下面有黑眼圈。（brown circle：棕色晕轮，此处指黑眼圈。）

at twenty cents instead of fifty, and did not discover the mistake until several customers had already ordered and were ready to pay.[①] Another time she gave back two fives and three ones as change for ten dollars. Biff would stand looking at her for a long time, rubbing[②] his nose thoughtfully and with his eyes half-closed.

They did not speak of this together. At night he worked downstairs while she slept, and during the morning she managed the restaurant alone. When they worked together he stayed behind the cash register and looked after the kitchen and the tables, as was their custom. They did not talk except on matters of business, but Biff would stand watching her with his face puzzled.

Then in the afternoon of the eighth of October there was a sudden cry of pain from the room where they slept. Biff hurried upstairs. Within an hour they had taken Alice to the hospital and the doctor had removed from her a tumor[③] almost the size of a newborn child. And then within another hour Alice was dead.

Biff sat by her bed at the hospital in stunned reflection. He had been present when she died. Her eyes had been drugged and misty[④] from the ether and then they hardened like glass. The nurse and the doctor withdrew from the room. He continued to look into her face. Except for the bluish pallor there was little difference. He noted each detail about her as though he had not watched her every day for twenty-one years. Then gradually as he sat there his thoughts turned to a picture that had long been stored inside him.

The cold green ocean and a hot gold strip of sand. The little children playing on the edge of the silky line of foam. The sturdy brown baby girl, the thin little naked boys, the half-grown children

---

① 参考译文：有个星期天，她在打字机上打当日菜单，“皇家奶油鸡”的特色菜应该是五毛钱，她却标成了两毛钱，一直等到好几位顾客点完菜要付账时，她才注意到这个错误。（not...until...：直到……才……）

② rub：揉；按摩（rubbing 为 ing 形式）

③ tumor：肿瘤；肿块

④ misty：模糊的；有雾的

running and calling out to each other with sweet, shrill[①] voices. Children were here whom he knew, Mick and his niece, Baby, and there were also strange young faces no one had ever seen before.[②] Biff bowed his head.

After a long while he got up from his chair and stood in the middle of the room. He could hear his sister-in-law, Lucile, walking up and down the hall outside. A fat bee crawled across the top of the dresser, and adroitly Biff caught it in his hand and put it out the open window. He glanced at the dead face one more time, and then with widowed sedateness he opened the door that led out into the hospital corridor.

Late the next morning he sat sewing in the room upstairs. Why? Why was it that in cases of real love the one who is left does not more often follow the beloved by suicide?[③] Only because the living must bury the dead? Because of the measured[④] rites[⑤] that must be fulfilled after a death? Because it is as though the one who is left steps for a time upon a stage and each second swells to an unlimited amount of time and he is watched by many eyes? Because there is a function he must carry out? Or perhaps, when there is love, the widowed must stay for the resurrection of the beloved—so that the one who has gone is not really dead, but grows and is created for a second time in the soul of the living? Why?

Biff bent close over his sewing and meditated on many things. He sewed skillfully, and the calluses on the tips of his fingers were so hard that he pushed the needle through the cloth without a thimble[⑥].

---

① shrill：尖锐的；刺耳的

② 参考译文：里面的一些孩子他认识，米克、他的外甥女巴比，还有一些陌生的年轻面孔，以前没人见过他们。本句由两个并列句组成，同时两个并列句中分别包含一句定语从句。

③ 参考译文：在很多关于真爱的故事里，为什么一个人失去爱人之后，并不会自杀，紧随爱人而去？

④ measured：有规则的

⑤ rite：仪式

⑥ thimble：顶针

Already the mourning[①] bands had been sewn[②] around the arms of two gray suits, and now he was on the last.

The day was bright and hot, and the first dead leaves of the new autumn scraped on the sidewalks. He had gone out early. Each minute was very long. Before him there was infinite leisure. He had locked the door of the restaurant and hung on the outside a white wreath of lilies. To the funeral home he went first and looked carefully at the selection of caskets. He touched the materials of the linings[③] and tested the strength of the frames.

'What is the name of the crêpe of this one—Georgette?'

The undertaker answered his questions in an oily, unctuous voice.

'And what is the percentage of cremations in your business?'

Out on the street again Biff walked with measured formality. From the west there was a warm wind and the sun was very bright. His watch had stopped, so he turned down toward the street where Wilbur Kelly had recently put out his sign as watchmaker. Kelly was sitting at his bench in a patched bathrobe[④]. His shop was also a bedroom, and the baby Mick pulled around with her in a wagon sat quietly on a pallet on the floor. Each minute was so long that in it there was ample time for contemplation[⑤] and enquiry. He asked Kelly to explain the exact use of jewels in a watch. He noted the distorted look of Kelly's right eye as it appeared through his watchmaker's loupe. They talked for a while about Chamberlain and Munich. Then as the time was still early he decided to go up to the mute's room.

Singer was dressing for work. Last night there had come from him a letter of condolence[⑥]. He was to be a pallbearer[⑦] at the

① mourning：服丧
② sew：缝纫，缝上（sewn 为过去分词）
③ lining：（服装）衬里；内里
④ bathrobe：浴衣；睡衣
⑤ contemplation：沉思
⑥ condolence：哀悼；慰问
⑦ pallbearer：护柩者；棺侧送葬者

funeral[①]. Biff sat on the bed and they smoked a cigarette together. Singer looked at him now and then with his green observant[②] eyes. He offered him a drink of coffee. Biff did not talk, and once the mute stopped to pat him on the shoulder and look for a second into his face.[③] When Singer was dressed they went out together.

Biff bought the black ribbon at the store and saw the preacher of Alice's church. When all was arranged he came back home. To put things in order—that was the thought in his mind. He bundled up[④] Alice's clothes and personal possessions to give to Lucile. He thoroughly cleaned and straightened the bureau drawers. He even rearranged[⑤] the shelves of the kitchen downstairs and removed the gaily colored crêpe streamers from the electric fans. Then when this was done he sat in the tub and bathed himself all over. And the morning was done.

Biff bit the thread[⑥] and smoothed the black band on the sleeve of his coat. By now Lucile would be waiting for him. He and she and Baby would ride in the funeral car together. He put away the work basket and fitted the coat with the mourning band very carefully on his shoulders. He glanced swiftly around the room to see that all was well before going out again.

An hour later he was in Lucile's kitchenette. He sat with his legs crossed, a napkin over his thigh, drinking a cup of tea. Lucile and Alice had been so different in all ways that it was not easy to realize they were sisters. Lucile was thin and dark, and today she had dressed completely in black. She was fixing Baby's hair. The kid waited patiently on the kitchen table with her hands folded in her lap while her mother worked on her. The sunlight was quiet and mellow in the

---

① funeral：葬礼

② observant：善于观察的；机警的

③ 参考译文：比夫没说话，哑巴一度过来拍拍他的肩膀，盯着他的脸看了一会儿。（pat sb. on the shoulder：拍拍某人的肩膀）

④ bundle up：把……捆扎

⑤ rearrange：重新排列，重新整理

⑥ bite the thread：咬断线头

room.

'Bartholomew—' said Lucile.

'What?'

'Don't you ever start thinking backward?'

'I don't,' said Biff.

'You know it's like I got to wear blinders all the time so I won't think sideways or in the past. All I can let myself think about is going to work every day and fixing meals and Baby's future.'

That's the right attitude.'

'I been giving Baby finger waves down at the shop. But they come out so quick I been thinking about letting her have a permanent. I don't want to give it to her myself—I think maybe I'll take her up to Atlanta when I go to the cosmetologist① convention and let her get it there.'

'Motherogod! She's not but four. It's liable to scare her. And besides, permanents② tend to coarsen③ the hair.'

Lucile dipped the comb in a glass of water and mashed the curls over Baby's ears. 'No, they don't. And she wants one. Young as Baby is, she already has as much ambition as I got. And that's saying plenty.' Biff polished his nails on the palm of his hand and shook his head.'Every time Baby and I go to the movies and see those kids in all the good rôles she feels the same way I do. I swear she does, Bartholomew. I can't even get her to eat her supper afterward.'

'For goodness' sake,' Biff said.

'She's getting along so fine with her dancing and expression lessons. Next year I want her to start with the piano because I think it'll be a help for her to play some. Her dancing teacher is going to give her a solo④ in the soirée⑤. I feel like I got to push Baby all I can.

---

① cosmetologist:（医）美容师；美容品业者
② permanent：烫发
③ coarsen：使变粗；使变糙
④ solo：独舞
⑤ soirée：（法）晚会；社交聚会

Because the sooner she gets started on her career the better it'll be for both of us.'

'Motherogod!'

'You don't understand. A child with talent can't be treated like ordinary kids. That's one reason I want to get Baby out of this common neighborhood. I can't let her start to talk vulgar[①] like these brats[②] around her or run wild like they do.'

'I know the kids on this block,' Biff said. 'They're all right. Those Kelly kids across the street—the Crane boy—'

'You know good and well that none of them are up to Baby's level.'

Lucile set the last wave in Baby's hair. She pinched the kid's little cheeks to put more color in them. Then she lifted her down from the table. For the funeral Baby had on a little white dress with white shoes and white socks and even small white gloves. There was a certain way Baby always held her head when people looked at her, and it was turned that way now.[③]

They sat for a while in the small, hot kitchenette without saying anything. Then Lucile began to cry. 'It's not like we was ever very close as sisters. We had our differences and we didn't see much of each other. Maybe it was because I was so much younger. But there's something about your own blood kin, and when anything like this happens—'

Biff clucked[④] soothingly[⑤].

'I know how you two were,' she said. It wasn't all just roses with you and she. But maybe that sort of makes it worse for you now.'

Biff caught Baby under the arms and swung her up to his shoulder. The kid was getting heavier. He held her carefully as

---

① vulgar：粗俗的，庸俗的
② brat：顽童
③ 参考译文：有人望着巴比时，她总会把头那样昂着，现在就是这副姿势。
④ cluck：发出啧啧声
⑤ soothingly：安慰地

he stepped into the living-room. Baby felt warm and close on his shoulder, and her little silk[①] skirt was white against the dark cloth of his coat. She grasped one of his ears very tight with her little hand.

'Unca Biff! Watch me do the split[②].'

Gently he set Baby on her feet again. She curved both arms above her head and her feet slid slowly in opposite directions on the yellow waxed floor. In a moment she was seated with one leg stretched[③] straight in front of her and one behind. She posed with her arms held at a fancy angle, looking sideways at the wall with a sad expression.

She scrambled up[④] again. 'Watch me do a handspring. Watch me do a—'

'Honey, be a little quieter,' Lucile said. She sat down beside Biff on the plush sofa. 'Don't she remind you a little of him—something about her eyes and face?'

'Hell, no. I can't see the slightest resemblance[⑤] between Baby and Leroy Wilson.'

Lucile looked too thin and worn out for her age. Maybe it was the black dress and because she had been crying. 'After all, we got to admit he's Baby's father,' she said.

'Can't you ever forget about that man?'

'I don't know. I guess I always been a fool about two things. And that's Leroy and Baby.'

Bill's new growth of beard was blue against the pale skin of his face and his voice sounded tired. 'Don't you ever just think a thing through and find out what's happened and what ought to come from that?[⑥] Don't you ever use logic—if these are the given facts this ought to be the result?'

---

① silk：丝的；丝绸的

② do the split：劈叉

③ stretch：拉紧；伸展；伸长（stretched 在此处为过去分词做补语，表被动）

④ scramble up：爬了起来

⑤ resemblance：相似；相似之处

⑥ 参考译文：难道你不能把一件事情想清楚，搞明白原委，然后从中吸取教训吗？

'Not about him, I guess.'

Biff spoke in a weary manner and his eyes were almost closed. 'You married this certain party when you were seventeen, and afterward there was just one racket between you after another.① You divorced② him. Then two years later you married him a second time. And now he's gone off again and you don't know where he is. It seems like those facts would show you one thing—you two are not suited to each other. And that's aside from the more personal side—the sort of man this certain party happens to be anyway.'

'God knows I been realizing all along he's a heel. I just hope he won't ever knock on that door again.'

'Look, Baby,' Biff said quickly. He laced his fingers and held up his hands. 'This is the church and this is the steeple. Open the door and here are God's people.'

Lucile shook her head. 'You don't have to bother about Baby. I tell her everything. She knows about the whole mess from A to Z③.'

'Then if he comes back you'll let him stay here and sponge on you just as long as he pleases—like it was before?'

'Yeah. I guess I would. Every time the doorbell or the phone rings, every time anybody steps up on the porch, something in the back of my mind thinks about that man.'

Biff spread out the palms of his hands. 'There you are.'

The clock struck two. The room was very close and hot. Baby turned another handspring and made a split again on the waxed④ floor. Then Biff took her up into his lap. Her little legs dangled against his shin. She unbuttoned⑤ his vest and burrowed⑥ her face into him.

'Listen,' Lucile said. 'If I ask you a question will you promise to

---

① 参考译文：你十七岁就嫁给了这个人，后来你们俩之间就争吵不断。（party：一方；racket：吵闹，喧闹；one...after another：一个接着一个）

② divorce：与（某人）离婚

③ the whole mess from A to Z：事情的来龙去脉

④ waxed：上过蜡的；防水的

⑤ unbutton：解开钮扣

⑥ burrow：偎依；使……钻到（……下面）

answer me the truth?'

'Sure.'

'No matter what it is?'

Biff touched Baby's soft gold hair and laid his hand gently[1] on the side of her little head. 'Of course.'

'It was about seven years ago. Soon after we was married the first time. And he came in one night from your place with big knots[2] all over his head and told me you caught him by the neck and banged[3] his head against the side of the wall. He made up some tale about why you did it, but I want to know the real reason.'

Biff turned the wedding ring on his finger. 'I just never did like Leroy, and we had a fight In those days I was different from now.'

'No. There was some definite[4] thing you did that for. We been knowing each other a pretty long time, and I understand by now that you got a real reason for every single[5] thing you ever do. Your mind runs by reasons instead of just wants. Now, you promised you'd tell me what it was, and I want to know.'

'It wouldn't mean anything now.'

'I tell you I got to know.'

'All right,' Biff said. 'He came in that night and started drinking, and when he was drunk he shot off[6] his mouth about you. He said he would come home about once a month and beat hell out of you and you would take it. But then afterward you would step outside in the hall and laugh aloud a few times so that the neighbors in the other rooms would think you both had just been playing around and it had all been a joke.[7] That's what happened, so just forget about it.'

---

① gently：轻轻地；温柔地

② knot：结；结头

③ bang：重击；突然巨响

④ definite：一定的；确切的

⑤ single：单一的

⑥ shoot off one's mouth：大放厥词，夸夸其谈

⑦ 参考译文：过后你会走到外面走廊里，大笑好几次，这样其他屋里的邻居们便会以为你俩只是在玩闹，开玩笑而已。

Lucile sat up straight and there was a red spot on each of her cheeks. 'You see, Bartholomew, that's why I got to be like I have blinders[①] on all the time so as not to think backward or sideways. All I can let my mind stay on is going to work every day and fixing three meals here at home and Baby's career.'

'Yes.'

'I hope you'll do that too, and not start thinking backward.'

Biff leaned his head down on his chest and closed his eyes. During the whole long day he had not been able to think of Alice. When he tried to remember her face there was a queer[②] blankness in him. The only thing about her that was clear in his mind was her feet—stumpy[③], very soft and white with puffy[④] toes. The bottoms were pink and near the left heel there was a tiny brown mole. The night they were married he had taken off her shoes and stockings and kissed her feet. And, come to think of it, that was worth considerable, because the Japanese believe that the choicest part of a woman—

Biff stirred and glanced at his watch. In a little while they would leave for the church where the funeral would be held. In his mind he went through the motions of the ceremony. The church—riding dirge-paced behind the hearse[⑤] with Lucile and Baby—the group of people standing with bowed heads in the September sunshine. Sun on the white tombstones, on the fading flowers and the canvas tent covering the newly dug grave[⑥]. Then home again—and what?

'No matter how much you quarrel there's something about your own blood sister,' Lucile said.

Biff raised his head. 'Why don't you marry again? Some nice young man who's never had a wife before, who would take care of

---

① blinders：眼罩（使用复数形式）
② queer：奇怪的，异常的
③ stumpy：粗短的
④ puffy：圆肿的
⑤ hearse：灵车；棺材
⑥ grave：墓穴，坟墓

you and Baby? If you'd just forget about Leroy you would make a good man a fine wife.'

Lucile was slow to answer. Then finally she said: 'You know how we always been—we nearly all the time understand each other pretty well without any kind of throbs[1] either way. Well, that's the closest I ever want to be to any man again.'

'I feel the same way,' Biff said.

Half an hour later there was a knock on the door. The car for the funeral was parked before the house. Biff and Lucile got up slowly. The three of them, with Baby in her white silk dress a little ahead, walked in solemn quietness outside.

Biff kept the restaurant closed during the next day. Then in the early evening he removed the faded wreath of lilies from the front door and opened the place for business again.[2] Old customers came in with sad faces and talked with him a few minutes by the cash register before giving their orders. The usual crowd was present—Singer, Blount, various men who worked in stores along the block and in the mills down on the river. After supper Mick Kelly showed up with her little brother and put a nickel into the slot machine. When she lost the first coin she banged on the machine with her fists and kept opening the receiver to be sure that nothing had come down.[3] Then she put in another nickel and almost won the jackpot[4]. Coins came clattering out and rolled along the floor. The kid and her little brother both kept looking around pretty sharp as they picked them up, so that no customer would put his foot on one before they could get to it. The mute was at the table in the middle of the room with his dinner before him. Across from him Jake Blount sat drinking beer, dressed in his

① throb：悸动

② 参考译文：傍晚时分，他把枯萎的百合花花环从前门取了下来，打开门，重新开始营业。（faded：褪色的；lily：百合花）

③ 参考译文：第一枚硬币被吞了之后，她用两只拳头砰砰猛砸机器，不断地打开出口，确认没有任何东西出来。

④ jackpot：头奖

Sunday clothes, and talking. Everything was the same as it had always been before. After a while the air became gray with cigarette smoke and the noise increased. Biff was alert[①], and no sound or movement escaped[②] him.

'I go around,' Blount said. He leaned earnestly[③] across the table and kept his eyes on the mute's face. 'I go all around and try to tell them. And they laugh. I can't make them understand anything. No matter what I say I can't seem to make them see, the truth.'

Singer nodded and wiped his mouth with his napkin. His dinner had got cold because he couldn't look down to eat, but he was so polite that he let Blount go on talking.

The words of the two children at the slot machine[④] were high and clear against the coarser voices of the men. Mick was putting her nickels back into the slot. Often she looked around at the middle table, but the mute had his back turned to her and did not see.

'Mister Singer's got fried chicken for his supper and he hasn't eaten one piece yet,' the little boy said.

Mick pulled down[⑤] the lever of the machine very slowly. 'Mind your own business.'

'You're always going up to his room or some place where you know he'll be.'

'I told you to hush, Bubber Kelly.'

'You do.'

Mick shook him until his teeth rattled and turned him around toward the door. 'You go on home to bed. I already told you I get a bellyful[⑥] of you and Ralph in the daytime, and I don't want you hanging around me at night when I'm supposed to be free.'

---

① alert：警惕的，警觉的
② escape：逃脱；逃过
③ earnestly：认真地；诚挚地
④ slot machine：自动售货机（尤指一种俗称吃角子老虎的赌具）
⑤ pull down：拉下来
⑥ bellyful：满腹；过量

Bubber held out his grimy[1] little hand. Well, give me a nickel, then.' When he had put the money in his shirt pocket he left for home.

Biff straightened his coat and smoothed back his hair. His tie was solid black, and on the sleeve of his gray coat there was the mourning band that he had sewn there. He wanted to go up to the slot machine and talk with Mick, but something would not let him. He sucked[2] in his breath sharply and drank a glass of water. A dance orchestra[3] came in on the radio, but he did not want to listen. All the tunes in the last ten years were so alike he couldn't tell one from the other. Since1928 he had not enjoyed music. Yet when he was young he used to play the mandolin, and he knew the words and the melody[4] of every current[5] song.

He laid his finger on the side of his nose and cocked his head to one side. Mick had grown so much in the past year that soon she would be taller than he was. She was dressed in the red sweater and blue pleated skirt she had worn every day since school started. Now the pleats had come out and the hem dragged loose around her sharp, jutting[6] knees. She was at the age when she looked as much like an overgrown[7] boy as a girl. And on that subject why was it that the smartest people mostly missed that point? By nature all people are of both sexes. So that marriage and the bed is not all by any means. The proof? Real youth and old age. Because often old men's voices grow high and reedy[8] and they take on a mincing[9] walk. And old women sometimes grow fat and their voices get rough and deep and they grow dark little mustaches. And he even proved it himself—the part of

---

① grimy：肮脏的，污秽的
② suck：吸，吮
③ orchestra：（大型的）管弦乐队
④ melody：旋律
⑤ current：现在的；流行的
⑥ jutting：突出来的
⑦ overgrown：生长过快的
⑧ reedy：似笛声的，形容声音过尖
⑨ mincing：装腔作势的

him that sometimes almost wished he was a mother and that Mick and Baby were his kids. Abruptly Biff turned from the cash register.

The newspapers were in a mess. For two weeks he hadn't filed a single one. He lifted a stack of them from under the counter. With a practiced eye he glanced from the masthead to the bottom of the sheet. Tomorrow he would look over the stacks of them in the back room and see about changing the system of files. Build shelves and use those solid boxes canned goods were shipped in for drawers. Chronologically from October 27, 1918, on up to the present date. With folders and top markings outlining historical events. Three sets of outlines—one international beginning with the Armistice and leading through the Munich aftermath, the second national, the third all the local dope from the time Mayor Lester shot his wife at the country club up to the Hudson Mill fire.① Everything for the past twenty years docketed and outlined and complete. Biff beamed② quietly behind his hand as he rubbed his jaw. And yet Alice had wanted him to haul out③ the papers so she could turn the room into a ladies' toilet. That was just what she had nagged him to do, but for once he had battered her down. For that one time.

With peaceful absorption④ Biff settled down to the details of the newspaper before him. He read steadily and with concentration, but from habit some secondary part of him was alert to everything around him.⑤ Jake Blount was still talking, and often he would hit his fist on the table. The mute sipped⑥ beer. Mick walked restlessly around the radio and stared at the customers. Biff read every word in the first paper and made a few notes on the margins.

---

① 参考译文：三种不同的标记方法——第一种是标注国际事件，从停战协议一直到慕尼黑事件；第二种是标记国内事件；第三种标注地方新闻，从莱斯特市长在乡村俱乐部射杀妻子到哈德逊工厂的大火。本句虽长，但脉络清晰，由三句独立结构组成，中间省略谓语 be。

② beam：绽开笑容

③ haul out：拉出；拖出

④ absorption：全神贯注，专心致志

⑤ 参考译文：他看得很慢，很专注，但出于习惯，他还有一只眼睛警惕着周围的一切。

⑥ sip：小口喝，抿

Then suddenly he looked up with a surprised expression. His mouth had been open for a yawn[①] and he snapped[②] it shut. The radio swung into an old song that dated back to the time when he and Alice were engaged. 'Just a Baby's Prayer at Twilight.' They had taken the streetcar[③] one Sunday to Old Sardis Lake and had rented a rowboat. At sunset[④] he played on the mandolin while she sang. She had on a sailor hat, and when he put his arm around her waist she—Alice—

A dragnet[⑤] for lost feelings. Biff folded the newspapers and put them back under the counter. He stood on one foot and then the other. Finally he called across the room to Mick.'You're not listening, are you?'

Mick turned off the radio. 'No. Nothing on tonight.'

All of that he would keep out of his mind, and concentrate on something else. He leaned over the counter and watched one customer after another. Then at last his attention rested on the mute at the middle table. He saw Mick edge[⑥] gradually up to him and at his invitation sit down. Singer pointed to something on the menu and the waitress brought a Coca-Cola for her. Nobody but a freak like a deaf-mute, cut off from other people, would ask a right young girl to sit down to the table where he was drinking with another man.[⑦] Blount and Mick both kept their eyes on Singer. They talked, and the mute's expression changed as he watched them. It was a funny thing. The reason —was it in them or in him? He sat very still with his hands in his pockets, and because he did not speak it made him seem superior. What did that fellow think and realize? What did he know?

Twice during the evening Biff started to go over to the middle

---

① yawn：打哈欠

② snap：（使啪地）扣上或打开

③ streetcar：有轨电车

④ sunset：日落，傍晚

⑤ dragnet：拖网

⑥ edge：缓慢地移动

⑦ 参考译文：只有像聋哑人一样的怪物，与其他人隔绝的人，才会邀请一个年轻女孩一起坐到他跟另一个男人喝酒的桌上来。nobody but 意为“除了……没有其他人，只有”；table 后是由 where 引导的定语从句修饰地点。

table, but each time he checked[1] himself. After they were gone he still wondered what it was about this mute—and in the early dawn when he lay in bed he turned over questions and solutions in his mind without satisfaction. The puzzle had taken root in him. It worried him in the back of his mind and left him uneasy. There was something wrong.

① check：克制，抑制

3

MANY TIMES Doctor Copeland talked to Mr. Singer. Truly he was not like other white men. He was a wise man, and he understood the strong, true purpose in a way that other white men could not. He listened, and in his face there was something gentle and Jewish, the knowledge of one who belongs to a race that is oppressed.① On one occasion② he took Mr. Singer with him on his rounds. He led him through cold and narrow passages smelling of dirt and sickness and fried fatback③. He showed him a successful skin graft made on the face of a woman patient who had been severely burned. He treated a syphilitic④ child and pointed out to Mr. Singer the scaling⑤ eruption on the palms of the hand, the dull, opaque⑥ surface of the eye, the sloping upper front incisors⑦. They visited two-room shacks that housed as many as twelve or fourteen persons. In a room where the fire burned low and orange on the hearth they were helpless while an old man strangled with pneumonia⑧. Mr. Singer walked behind him and watched and understood. He gave nickels to the children, and because of his quietness and decorum he did not disturb the patients as

---

① 参考译文：他懂得倾听，脸上有种温和的东西，像犹太人，他理解一个属于受压迫民族的人。（oppressed：受压制的，受压迫的）

② occasion：机会；场合

③ fatback：肥肉；脂肪

④ syphilitic：感染梅毒的

⑤ scaling：鳞屑

⑥ opaque：不透明的

⑦ incisor：门齿；切牙

⑧ pneumonia：肺炎

would have another visitor.

The days were chilly[1] and treacherous[2]. In the town there was an outbreak of influenza[3] so that Dr. Copeland was busy most of the hours of the day and night. He drove through the Negro sections of the town in the high Dodge automobile he had used for the past nine years. He kept the isinglass[4] curtains snapped to the windows to cut off the draughts[5], and tight around his neck he wore his gray wool shawl. During this time he did not see Portia or William or Highboy, but often he thought of them. Once when he was away Portia came to see him and left a note and borrowed half a sack of meal.

There came a night when he was so exhausted that, although there were other calls to make, he drank hot milk and went to bed. He was cold and feverish[6] so that at first he could not rest. Then it seemed that he had only begun to sleep when a voice called him. He got up wearily and, still in his long flannel[7] nightshirt, he opened the front door. It was Portia.

'The Lord Jesus help us, Father,' she said.

Doctor Copeland stood shivering with his nightshirt drawn close around his waist. He held his hand to his throat and looked at her and waited.

'It about our Willie. He been a bad boy and done got hisself in mighty bad trouble. And us got to do something.'

Doctor Copeland walked from the hall with rigid steps. He stopped in the bedroom for his bathrobe, shawl, and slippers and went back to the kitchen. Portia was waiting for him there. The kitchen was lifeless and cold.

'All right. What has he done? What is it?'

---

① chilly：寒冷的
② treacherous：有潜在危险的
③ influenza：流行性感冒（同 flu）
④ isinglass：明胶；鱼胶
⑤ draught：穿堂风，冷风
⑥ feverish：发烧的，发热的
⑦ flannel：法兰绒的

'Just wait a minute. Just let me find brain room so I can study it all out and tell it to you plain.'

He crushed some sheets of newspaper lying on the hearth and picked up a few sticks of kindling.

'Let me make the fire,' Portia said. 'You just sit down at the table, and soon as this here stove is hot us going to have a cup of coffee. Then maybe it all won't seem so bad.'

'There is not any coffee. I used the last of it yesterday.'

When he said this Portia began to cry. Savagely[①] she stuffed paper and wood into the stove and lighted it with a trembling hand. 'This here the way it is,' she said. 'Willie and Highboy were messing around tonight at a place where they got no business being. You know how I feels like I always got to keep my Willie and my Highboy close to me? Well, if I'd been there none of this trouble would of come about. But I were at the Ladies' Meeting at the church and them boys got restless. They went down to Madame Reba's Palace of Sweet Pleasure. And Father, this is sure one bad, wicked place. They got a man sells tickets on the bug—but they also got these strutting, bad-blood, tail-shaking nigger gals and these here red satin[②] curtains and—'

'Daughter,' said Doctor Copeland irritably[③]. He pressed his hands to the side of his head. 'I know the place. Get to the point.'

'Love Jones were there—and she is one bad colored gal. Willie he drunk liquor[④] and shimmied[⑤] around with her until first thing you know he were in a fight. He were in a fight with this boy named Junebug—over Love. And for a while they fights there with their hands and then this Junebug got out his knife. Our Willie didn't have no knife, so he commenced to bellow and run around the parlor[⑥].

---

① savagely：野蛮地；残忍地
② satin：绸缎做的
③ irritably：性急地；暴躁地
④ liquor：酒，含酒精饮料
⑤ shimmy：摇动，振动
⑥ parlor：客厅；会客室

Then finally Highboy found Willie a razor and he backed up[①] and nearbout cut this Junebug's head off.'

Doctor Copeland drew his shawl closer around him. 'Is he dead?'

'That boy too mean to die. He in the hospital, but he going to be out and making trouble again before long.'

'And William?'

'The police come in and taken him to the jail in the Black Maria. He still locked up.'

'And he did not get hurt?'

'Oh, he got a busted[②] eye and a little chunk cut out his behind. But it won't bother him none. What I can't understand is how come he would be messing around with that Love. She at least ten shades blacker than I is and she the ugliest nigger I ever seen. She walk like she have an egg between her legs and don't want to break it. She ain't even clean. And here Willie done cut the buck like this over her.'

Doctor Copeland leaned closer to the stove and groaned. He coughed and his face stiffened. He held his paper handkerchief to his mouth and it became spotted with blood. The dark skin of his face took on[③] a greenish pallor[④].

'Course Highboy come and tell me soon as it all happened. Understand, my Highboy didn't have nothing to do with these here bad gals[⑤]. He were just keeping Willie company. He so grieved[⑥] about Willie he been sitting out on the street curb in front of the jail ever since.' The fire-colored tears rolled down Portia's face. 'You know how us three has always been. Us haves our own plan and nothing ever went wrong with it before. Even money hasn't bothered us none. Highboy he pay the rent and I buys the food—and Willie

---

① back up：倒退，后退
② busted：破了的；坏了的
③ take on：呈现
④ pallor：苍白（尤指脸色）
⑤ gal：姑娘
⑥ grieved：悲伤的

he takes care of Saturday Night. Us has always been like three-piece twinses.'

At last it was morning. The mill whistles blew for the first shift. The sun came out[①] and brightened the clean saucepans[②] hanging on the wall above the stove. They sat for a long time. Portia pulled at the rings on her ears until her lobes[③] were irritated and purplish red[④]. Doctor Copeland still held his head in his hands.

'Seem to me,' Portia said finally, 'if us can just get a lot of white peoples to write letters about Willie it might help out some. I already been to see Mr. Brannon. He written exactly what I told him to. He were at his café after it all happened like he is ever night. So I just went in there and explained how it was. I taken the letter home with me. I done put it in the Bible so I won't lose it or dirty it'

'What did the letter say?'

'Mr. Brannon he wrote just hike I asked him to. The letter tell about how Willie has been working for Mr. Brannon going on three year. It tell how Willie is one fine upstanding colored boy and how he hasn't ever been in no trouble before now.[⑤] It tell how he always had plenty chances to take things in the café if he were like some other type of colored boy and how—'

'Pshaw!' said Doctor Copeland. 'All that is no good.'

'Us just can't sit around and wait. With Willie locked up in the jail. My Willie, who is such a sweet boy even if he did do wrong tonight. Us just can't sit around and wait.'

'We will have to. That is the only thing we can do.'

'Well, I know I ain't.'

Portia got up from the chair. Her eyes roved distractedly[⑥] around

---

① come out：（太阳、星星或月亮）出来

② saucepan：炖锅；深平底锅

③ lobe：耳垂

④ purplish red：紫红色

⑤ 参考译文：（信上还）说威利是个正直的黑人男孩，以前从来没惹过麻烦。（upstanding：正直的）

⑥ distractedly：心烦意乱地

the room as though searching for something. Then abruptly she went toward the front door.

'Wait a minute,' said Doctor Copeland. 'Where do you intend to[1] go now?'

'I got to work. I sure got to keep my job. I sure have to stay on with Mrs. Kelly and get my pay ever week.'

'I want to go to the jail,' said Doctor Copeland. 'Maybe I can see William.'

'I going to drop by[2] the jail[3] on my way to work. I got to send Highboy off to his work, too—else he liable to sit there grieving about Willie all the morning.'

Doctor Copeland dressed hurriedly and joined Portia in the hall. They went out into the cool, blue autumn morning. The men at the jail were rude to them and they were able to find out very little. Doctor Copeland then went to consult[4] a lawyer with whom he had had dealings before. The following days were long and full of worried thoughts. At the end of three weeks the trial for William was held and he was convicted of assault with a deadly weapon.[5] He was sentenced to nine months of hard labor and sent immediately to a prison in the northern part of the state.

Even now the strong true purpose was always in him, but he had no time in which to think on it. He went from one house to another and the work was unending. Very early in the morning he drove off in the automobile, and then at eleven o'clock the patients came to the office. After the sharp autumn air outside there would be a hot, stale[6] odor in the house that made him cough. The benches in the hall

---

① intend to do sth：打算做某事，表示计划或打算去做某件事情。

② drop by：顺道拜访

③ jail：监狱

④ consult：请教；咨询

⑤ 参考译文：到了第三周，威廉的案子开庭了。他被认定犯持致命武器伤人罪。（be convicted of：被认定为……罪名；assault：攻击，袭击；weapon：武器，兵器）

⑥ stale：陈腐的；不新鲜的

were always full of sick and patient Negroes who waited for him, and sometimes even the front porch and his bedroom would be crowded. All the day and frequently half the night there was work. Because of the tiredness in him he wanted sometimes to lie down on the floor and beat with his fists and cry. If he could rest he might get well. He had tuberculosis[①] of the lungs, and he measured his temperature four times a day and had an X-ray once a month. But he could not rest. For there was another thing bigger than the tiredness—and this was the strong true purpose.

He would think of this purpose until sometimes, after a long day and night of work, he would become blank so that he would forget for a minute just what the purpose was. And then it would come to him again and he would be restless and eager to take on a new task. But the words often stuck in his mouth, and his voice now was hoarse[②] and not loud as it had been before. He pushed the words into the sick and patient faces of the Negroes who were his people.

Often he talked to Mr. Singer. With him he spoke of chemistry and the enigma[③] of the universe. Of the infinitesimal sperm and the cleavage of the ripened egg. Of the complex million-fold division of the cells. Of the mystery of living matter and the simplicity[④] of death. And also he spoke with him of race.

'My people were brought from the great plains, and the dark, green jungles[⑤],' he said once to Mr. Singer. 'On the long chained journeys to the coast they died by the thousands. Only the strong survived. Chained in the foul ships that brought them here they died again. Only the hardy Negroes with will could live. Beaten and chained and sold on the block, the least of these strong ones perished again. And finally through the bitter years the strongest of my people

---

① tuberculosis：肺结核；结核病
② hoarse：嘶哑的
③ enigma：谜，不可思议的东西
④ simplicity：简单（性），简易（性）
⑤ jungle：丛林；雨林

are still here. Their sons and daughters, their grandsons and great-grandsons.'

'I come to borrow and I come to ask a favor,' Portia said.

Doctor Copeland was alone in his kitchen when she walked through the hall and stood in the doorway to tell him this. Two weeks had passed since William had been sent away①. Portia was changed. Her hair was not oiled and combed as usual, her eyes were bloodshot as though she had partaken of strong drink.② Her cheeks were hollow, and with her sorrowful, honey-colored face she truly resembled③ her mother now.

'You know them nice white plates and cups you have?'

'You may have them and keep them.'

'No, I only wants to borrow. And also I come here to ask a favor of you.'

'Anything you wish,' said Doctor Copeland.

Portia sat down across the table from her father. First I suppose I better explain. Yesdiddy I got this here message from Grandpapa saying they all coming in tomorrow and spend the night and part of Sunday with us. Course they been mighty worried about Willie, and Grandpapa feel like us all ought to get together again. He right, too. I sure do want to see our kinfolks again. I been mighty homesick④ since Willie been gone.'

'You may have the plates and anything else you can find around here,' Doctor Copeland said. 'But hold up your shoulders, Daughter. Your carriage is bad.'

'It going to be a real reunion⑤. You know this is the first time Grandpapa have spent the night in town for twenty years. He haven't

---

① send away：送走（sent 为 send 的过去分词，此处为被动语态。）

② 参考译文：她的头发不再抹油，也不像往常梳得那么整洁，她两眼充血，好像喝了烈性酒一样。（partake of：吃，喝，例：I like to partake of the feast, but not to share the company. 我喜欢享用那次丰盛大餐，但是不喜欢和那些人待在一起。）

③ resemble：像，与……相似

④ homesick：想家的；思乡的

⑤ reunion：重聚；（班级或学校的）同学会，同窗会

ever slept outside of his own home except two times in his whole life. And anyway he kind of nervous at night. All during the dark he have to get up and drink water and be sure the childrens is covered up and all right. I a little worried about if Grandpapa will be comfortable here.'

'Anything of mine you think you will need—'

'Course Lee Jackson bringing them in,' said Portia. 'And with Lee Jackson it going to take them all day to get here. I not expecting them till around supper-time. Course Grandpapa always so patient with Lee Jackson he wouldn't make him hurry none.'

'My soul! Is that old mule[①] still alive? He must be fully eighteen years old.'

'He even older than that. Grandpapa been working him now for twenty years. He done had that mule so long he always say it just like Lee Jackson is one of his blood kin. He understand and love Lee Jackson like he do his own grandchildrens. I never seen a human who know so good what a animal is thinking as Grandpapa. He haves a close feeling for everthing that walks and eats.'

'Twenty years is a long time to work a mule.'

'It sure is. Now Lee Jackson is right feeble. But Grandpapa sure do take good care of him. When they plows out in the hot sun Lee Jackson haves a great big straw hat on his head just like Grandpapa—with holes cut for his ears.[②] That mule's straw hat is a real joke, and Lee Jackson won't budge a step when he going to plow without that hat is on his head.'

Doctor Copeland took down[③] the white china dishes from the shelf and began to wrap[④] them in a newspaper. 'Have you enough pots and pans to cook all the food you will need?'

---

① mule：骡，骡子

② 参考译文：他们在外面炽热的太阳底下犁地时，李・杰克逊像外公一样头上也戴着顶宽大的草帽——有两个洞可以露出耳朵。（straw：稻草的）

③ take down：取下

④ wrap：包，裹，包装

'Plenty,' Portia said. 'I not going to any special trouble. Granpapa, he Mr. Thoughtful hisself—and he always bring in something to help out when the fambly[①] come to dinner. I only going to have plenty meal and cabbage and two pounds of nice mullet[②].'

'Sounds good.'

Portia laced her nervous yellow fingers together[③]. 'There one thing I haven't told you yet. A surprise. Buddy going to be here as well as Hamilton. Buddy just come back from Mobile. He helping out on the farm now.'

'It has been five years since I last saw Karl Marx.'

'And that just what I come to ask you about,' said Portia. 'You remember when I walked in the door I told you I come to borrow and to ask a favor[④].'

Doctor Copeland cracked the points of his fingers. 'Yes.'

'Well, I come to see if I can't get you to be there tomorrow at the reunion[⑤]. All your childrens but Willie going to be there. Seem to me like you ought to join us. I sure will be glad if you come.'

Hamilton and Karl Marx and Portia—and William. Doctor Copeland removed his spectacles and pressed his fingers against his eyelids. For a minute he saw the four of them very plainly as they were a long time ago. Then he looked up and straightened his glasses on his nose. Thank you,' he said. 'I will come.'

That night he sat alone by the stove in the dark room and remembered. He thought back to the time of his childhood. His mother had been born a slave, and after freedom she was a washerwoman[⑥]. His father was a preacher[⑦], who had once known John Brown. They had taught him, and out of the two or three dollars

---

① fambly：方言，即 family。
② mullet：鲱鱼；鲻鱼
③ lace...together：把……交叉在一起
④ ask a favor：寻求帮助
⑤ reunion：聚会，团聚
⑥ washerwoman：洗衣女工，洗衣妇
⑦ preacher：牧师；传教士

they had earned each week they saved.[①] When he was seventeen years old they had sent him north with eighty dollars hidden in his shoe. He had worked in a blacksmith's shop and as a waiter and as a bellboy in a hotel. And all the while he studied and read and went to school. His father died and his mother did not live long without him. After ten years of struggle he was a doctor and he knew his mission and he came South again.

He married and made a home. He went endlessly from house to house and spoke the mission[②] and the truth. The hopeless suffering of his people made in him a madness, a wild and evil[③] feeling of destruction. At times he drank strong liquor and beat his head against the floor. In his heart there was a savage violence, and once he grasped the poker from the hearth and struck down his wife. She took Hamilton, Karl Marx, William, and Portia with her to her father's home. He wrestled[④] in his spirit and fought down the evil blackness. But Daisy did not come back to him. And eight years later when she died his sons were not children any more and they did not return to him. He was left an old man in an empty house.[⑤]

Promptly at five o'clock the next afternoon he arrived at the house where Portia and Highboy lived. They resided in the part of town called Sugar Hill, and the house was a narrow cottage with a porch and two rooms. From inside there was a babble[⑥] of mixed voices. Doctor Copeland approached stiffly[⑦] and stood in the doorway holding his shabby felt hat in his hand.

The room was crowded and at first he was not noticed. He

---

① 参考译文：他们教他学知识，他们每周赚两三块钱，省吃俭用。本句为并列句，主结构为 They had taught him, and they saved，而 out of the two or three dollars they had earned each week 相当于插入语，给 save 定义了一个范围，即"从每周赚的两三块钱里省吃俭用"。

② mission：使命，任务

③ evil：邪恶的

④ wrestle：努力解决，艰难对付

⑤ 参考译文：他成了一位老人，独自住在一幢空荡荡的房子里。

⑥ babble：含糊不清地说；喋喋不休

⑦ stiffly：生硬地；顽固地

sought the faces of Karl Marx and Hamilton. Besides them there was Grandpapa and two children who sat together on the floor. He was still looking into the faces of his sons when Portia perceived him standing in the door.

'Here Father,' she said.

The voices stopped. Grandpapa turned around in his chair. He was thin and bent and very wrinkled. He was wearing the same greenish-black suit that he had worn thirty years before at his daughter's wedding. Across his vest there was a tarnished① brass watch chain②. Karl Marx and Hamilton looked at each other, then down at the floor, and finally at their father.

'Benedict Mady—' said the old man. 'Been a long time. A real long time.'

'Ain't it, though!' Portia said. 'This here the first reunion us is all had in many a year. Highboy, you get a chair from the kitchen. Father, here Buddy and Hamilton.'

Doctor Copeland shook hands with his sons. They were both tall and strong and awkward③. Against their blue shirts and overalls their skin had the same rich brown color as did Portia's. They did not look him in the eye, and in their faces there was neither love nor hate.

It sure is a pity everybody couldn't come—Aunt Sara and Jim and all the rest,' said Highboy. 'But this here is a real pleasure to us.'

'Wagon too full,' said one of the children. 'Us had to walk a long piece 'cause the wagon too full anyways.'

Grandpapa scratched his ear with a matchstick. 'Somebody got to stay home.'

Nervously Portia licked④ her dark, thin lips. 'It our Willie I thinking about. He were always a big one for any kind of party or to-do. My mind just won't stay off our Willie.'

---

① tarnished：失去光泽的
② watch chain：表链
③ awkward：局促不安的
④ lick：舔

Through the room there was a quiet murmur[①] of agreement. The old man leaned back in his chair and waggled[②] his head up and down. 'Portia, Hon, supposing you reads to us a little while. The word of God sure do mean a lot in a time of trouble.'

Portia took up the Bible from the table in the center of the room. 'What part you want to hear now, Grandpapa?'

'It all the book of the Holy Lord. Just any place your eye fall on will do.'

Portia read from the Book of Luke. She read slowly, tracing the words with her long, limp finger. The room was still. Doctor Copeland sat on the edge of the group, cracking his knuckles, his eyes wandering from one point to another. The room was very small, the air close and stuffy. The four walls were cluttered[③] with calendars and crudely painted advertisements from magazines. On the mantel there was a vase of red paper roses. The fire on the hearth burned slowly and the wavering light from the oil lamp made shadows on the wall. Portia read with such slow rhythm that the words slept in Doctor Copeland's ears and he was drowsy. Karl Marx lay sprawled[④] upon the floor beside the children. Hamilton and Highboy dozed[⑤]. Only the old man seemed to study the meaning of the words.

Portia finished the chapter[⑥] and closed the book.

'I done pondered[⑦] over this thing a many a time.' said Grandpapa.

The people in the room came out of their drowsiness.'What? ' asked Portia.

'It this way. You recall them parts about Jesus raising the dead and curing the sick? '

'Course we does, sir,' said Highboy deferentially.

---

① murmur：低语；低语声
② waggle：摆动；来回摇动
③ cluttered：杂乱的
④ sprawled：四肢伸开的
⑤ doze：打瞌睡
⑥ chapter：章，回
⑦ ponder：仔细考虑

'Many a day when I be plowing or working,' Grandpapa said slowly, 'I done thought and reasoned about the time when Jesus going to descend again to this earth. Cause I done always wanted it so much it seem to me like it will be while I am living. I done studied about it many a time. And this here the way I done planned it. I reason I will get to stand before Jesus with all my childrens and grandchildrens[①] and great-grandchildrens and kinfolks and friends and I say to him, "Jesus Christ, us is all sad colored peoples." And then he will place His holy hand upon our heads and straightway us will be white as cotton. That the plan and reasoning that been in my heart a many and a many a time.'

A hush[②] fell on the room. Doctor Copeland jerked the cuff[③] of his sleeves and cleared his throat. His pulse beat too fast and his throat was tight Sitting in the corner of the room he felt isolated and angry and alone.

'Has any of you ever had a sign from Heaven?' asked Grandpapa.

'I has, sir,' said Highboy. 'Once when I were sick with the pneumonia I seen God's face looking out the fireplace at me. It were a large white man's face with a white beard and blue eyes.'

'I seen a ghost,' said one of the children—the girl.

'Once I seen—' began the little boy.

Grandpapa held up his hand. 'You childrens hush. You. Celia—and you, Whitman—it now the time for you to listen but not be heard,' he said. 'Only one time has I had a real sign.' And this here the way it come about. It were in the summer of last year, and hot. I were trying to dig up[④] the roots of that big oak stump[⑤] near the hogpen[⑥] and when I leaned down a kind of catch, a misery, come suddenly in

---

① grandchildrens：孙辈（复数形式），正确表达为 grandchildren，此处为作者表现这些贫民区不地道的英语而故意为之，前文也有提及，本书大量类似句法错误均为作者故意的表现手法。

② hush：寂静

③ cuff：袖口

④ dig up：挖出；掘起

⑤ stump：树桩

⑥ hogpen：猪圈

the small of my back. I straightened up and then all around went dark. I were holding my hand to my back and looking up at the sky when suddenly I seen this little angel. It were a little white girl angel—look to me about the size of a field pea[①]—with yellow hair and a white robe. Just flying around near the sun. After that I come in the house and prayed. I studied the Bible for three days before I went out in the field again.'

Doctor Copeland felt the old evil anger in him. The words rose inchoately[②] to his throat and he could not speak them. They would listen to the old man. Yet to words of reason they would not attend. These are my people, he tried to tell himself—but because he was dumb this thought did not help him now. He sat tense and sullen.

'It a queer thing,' said Grandpapa suddenly. 'Benedict Mady, you a fine doctor. How come I get them miseries sometime in the small of my back after I been digging and planting for a good while? How come that misery[③] bother me?'

'How old are you now?'

'I somewhere between seventy and eighty year old.'

The old man loved medicine and treatment. Always when he used to come in with his family to see Daisy he would have himself examined and take home medicine and salves for the whole group of them. But when Daisy left him the old man did not come anymore and he had to content himself with purges[④] and kidney[⑤] pills[⑥] advertised in the newspapers. Now the old man was looking at him with timid[⑦] eagerness.

'Drink plenty of water,' said Doctor Copeland. 'And rest as much as you can.'

---

① field pea：田园豌豆，一种常见的豌豆品种，通常在田地里种植。
② inchoately：初步地
③ misery：痛苦，悲惨；不幸
④ purge：泻药
⑤ kidney：肾脏
⑥ pill：药丸（kidney pill 指“肾丸”）
⑦ timid：羞怯的，胆小的

Portia went into the kitchen to prepare the supper. Warm smells began to fill the room. There was quiet, idle talking, but Doctor Copeland did not listen or speak. Now and then he looked at Karl Marx or Hamilton. Karl Marx talked about Joe Louis. Hamilton spoke mostly of the hail that had ruined some of the crops. When they caught their father's eye they grinned and shuffled their feet on the floor. He kept staring at them with angry misery.

Doctor Copeland clamped his teeth down hard. He had thought so much about Hamilton and Karl Marx and William and Portia, about the real true purpose he had had for them, that the sight of their faces made a black swollen feeling in him.① If once he could tell it all to them, from the far away beginning until this very night, the telling would ease the sharp ache in his heart. But they would not listen or understand.

He hardened himself so that each muscle in his body was rigid② and strained③. He did not listen or look at anything around him. He sat in a corner like a man who is blind and dumb. Soon they went into the supper table and the old man said grace. But Doctor Copeland did not eat. When Highboy brought out a pint, bottle of gin, and they laughed and passed the bottle from mouth to mouth, he refused that also. He sat in rigid silence, and at last he picked up his hat and left the house without a farewell④. If he could not speak the whole long truth no other word would come to him.

He lay tense and wakeful throughout the night. Then the next day was Sunday. He made half a dozen calls, and in the middle of the morning he went to Mr. Singer's room. The visit blunted the feeling of loneliness in him so that when he said goodbye he was at peace

---

① 参考译文：他一直想着汉密尔顿、卡尔·马克思、威廉和波西娅，想着他赋予他们的真正使命。他想得太多了，以至于一看到他们的面孔，他的心里便会涌上一种阴郁的感觉。本句在翻译中，将主结构 He had thought so much 放在这些人名之后再陈述“他想得太多了”，衔接更加自然。

② rigid：僵化的

③ strained：紧张的

④ farewell：告别，辞别

with himself once more.

However, before he was out of the house this peace had left him. An accident occurred. As he started down the stairs he saw a white man carrying a large paper sack and he drew close to the banisters so that they could pass each other. But the white man was running up the steps two at a time, without looking, and they collided with such force that Doctor Copeland was left sick and breathless.

'Christ! I didn't see you.'

Doctor Copeland looked at him closely but made no answer. He had seen this white man once before. He remembered the stunted, brutal-looking body and the huge, awkward hands. Then with sudden clinical[①] interest he observed the white man's face, for in his eyes he saw a strange, fixed, and withdrawn[②] look of madness.

'Sorry,' said the white man.

Doctor Copeland put his hand on the banister[③] and passed on.

---

① clinical：临床的；诊所的

② withdrawn：沉默寡言的；与世隔绝的

③ banister：（楼梯的）栏杆，扶手

4

'WHO WAS that?' Jake Blount asked. 'Who was the tall, thin colored man that just come out of here?'

The small room was very neat[①]. The sun lighted a bowl of purple grapes on the table. Singer sat with his chair tilted[②] back and his hands in his pockets, looking out of the window.

'I bumped into him on the steps and he gave me this look—why, I never had anybody to look at me so dirty.'[③]

Jake put the sack of ales[④] down on the table. He realized with a shock that Singer did not know he was in the room. He walked over[⑤] to the window and touched Singer on the shoulder.

'I didn't mean to bump into him. He had no cause to act like that.'

Jake shivered. Although the sun was bright there was a chill in the room. Singer held up his forefinger and went into the hall. When he returned he brought with him a scuttle[⑥] of coal and some kindling. Jake watched him kneel before the hearth[⑦]. Neatly he broke the sticks of kindling over his knee and arranged them on the foundation

---

① neat：整洁的

② tilt：使倾斜

③ 参考译文：我在楼梯上跟他撞在一起，他用那副眼神看着我——哎呀，从来没有人那么恶狠狠地看着我。本句为不定式短语作后置定语。（bump into：无意中碰到；dirty：恶狠狠地）

④ ale：麦芽啤酒

⑤ walk over：走过去

⑥ scuttle：煤框

⑦ hearth：灶台；炉边

of paper. He put the coal on according to a system. At first the fire would not draw. The flames quivered[①] weakly and were smothered by a black roll of smoke. Singer covered the grate with a double sheet of newspapers. The draught gave the fire new life. In the room there was a roaring sound. The paper glowed and was sucked inward. A crackling orange sheet of flame filled the grate.

The first morning ale had a fine mellow[②] taste. Jake gulped his share down quickly and wiped his mouth with the back of his hand.

'There was this lady I knew a long time ago,' he said. 'You sort of remind me of her, Miss Clara. She had a little farm in Texas. And made pralines[③] to sell in the cities. She was a tall, big, fine-looking lady. Wore those long, baggy sweaters and clodhopper shoes and a man's hat. Her husband was dead when I knew her. But what I'm getting at is this: If it hadn't been for her I might never have known. I might have gone on through life like the millions of others who don't know. I would have just been a preacher or a linthead or a salesman. My whole life might have been wasted.'

Jake shook his head wonderingly[④].

'To understand you got to know what went before. You see, I lived in Gastonia when I was a youngun[⑤]. I was a knock-kneed little runt, too small to put in the mill. I worked as pin boy in a bowling joint and got meals for pay. Then I heard a smart, quick boy could make thirty cents a day stringing tobacco[⑥] not very far from there. So I went and made that thirty cents a day. That was when I was ten years old. I just left my folks. I didn't write. They were glad I was gone. You understand how those things are. And besides, nobody could read a letter but my sister.'

---

① quiver：颤抖
② mellow：芳醇的
③ praline：胡桃糖
④ wonderingly：惊讶地；觉得奇怪地
⑤ youngun：（非正式）年轻人；小孩（同 young'un）
⑥ tobacco：烟草，烟叶

He waved his hand in the air as though brushing something from his face. 'But I mean this. My first belief was Jesus. There was this fellow working in the same shed with me. He had a tabernacle① and preached every night. I went and listened and I got this faith. My mind was on Jesus all day long. In my spare time I studied the Bible and prayed. Then one night I took a hammer and laid my hand on the table. I was angry and I drove the nail all the way through. My hand was nailed to the table and I looked at it and the fingers fluttered② and turned blue.'

Jake held out his palm and pointed to the ragged③, dead-white scar in the center.

'I wanted to be an evangelist④. I meant to travel around the country preaching and holding revivals. In the meantime I moved around from one place to another, and when I was nearly twenty I got to Texas. I worked in a pecan⑤ grove near where Miss Clara lived. I got to know her and at night sometimes I would go to her house. She talked to me. Understand, I didn't begin to know all at once. That's not the way it happens to any of us. It was gradual. I began to read. I would work just so I could put aside enough money to knock off for a while and study. It was like being born a second time. Just us who know can understand what it means. We have opened our eyes and have seen. We're like people from way off yonder somewhere.'

Singer agreed with him. The room was comfortable in a homey way. Singer brought out from the closet the tin box in which he kept crackers and fruit and cheese.⑥ He selected an orange and peeled it

---

① tabernacle：神龛

② flutter：飘动

③ ragged：衣衫褴褛的

④ evangelist：福音传道者

⑤ pecan：美洲山核桃（树）

⑥ 参考译文：辛格从壁橱里拿出一个铁盒子，里面放着饼干、水果和奶酪。本句 in which 引导定语从句修饰 tin box，同时将 bring out 的宾语 tin box 后置，即置于 from the closet 后，便于定语从句表达。（tin box：铁盒）

slowly. He pulled off shreds of pith① until the fruit was transparent② in the sun. He sectioned the orange and divided the plugs between them. Jake ate two sections at a time and with a loud whoosh spat the seeds into the fire. Singer ate his share slowly and deposited his seeds neatly in the palm of one hand. They opened two more ales.

'And how many of us are there in this country? Maybe ten thousand. Maybe twenty thousand. Maybe a lot more. I been to a lot of places but I never met but a few of us. But say a man does know. He sees the world as it is and he looks back thousands of years to see how it all come about.③ He watched the slow agglutination④ of capital and power and he sees its pinnacle today. He sees America as a crazy house. He sees how men have to rob their brothers in order to live. He sees children starving and women working sixty hours a week to get to eat. He sees a whole damn army of unemployed⑤ and billions of dollars and thousands of miles of land wasted. He sees war coming. He sees how when people suffer just so much they get mean and ugly and something dies in them. But the main thing he sees is that the whole system of the world is built on a lie. And although it's as plain as the shining sun—the don't-knows⑥ have lived with that lie so long they just can't see it.'

The red corded vein in Jake's forehead swelled angrily. He grasped the scuttle on the hearth and rattled an avalanche of coal on the fire. His foot had gone to sleep, and he stamped it so hard that the floor shook.

'I been all over this place. I walk around. I talk. I try to explain to them. But what good does it do? Lord God!'

---

① pith：精髓；核心
② transparent：透明的
③ 参考译文：他看到了这个世界的本质，回顾几千年前，明白这一切是怎么发生的。本句 come 应为第三人称单数形式 comes。（come about：发生）
④ agglutination：凝集；胶合
⑤ unemployed：失业的
⑥ don't-know：（合成词）不知道的人

He gazed into the fire, and a flush[①] from the ale and heat deepened the color of his face. The sleepy tingling[②] in his foot spread up his leg. He drowsed and saw the colors of the fire, the tints of green and blue and burning yellow. 'You're the only one,' he said dreamily.'The only one.'

He was a stranger no longer. By now he knew every street, every alley, every fence[③] in all the sprawling[④] slums of the town. He still worked at the Sunny Dixie. During the fall the show moved from one vacant lot to another, staying always within the fringes of the city limit, until at last it had encircled the town.[⑤] The locations were changed but the settings were alike—a strip of wasteland[⑥] bordered by rows of rotted shacks, and somewhere near a mill, a cotton gin, or a bottling plant. The crowd was the same, for the most part factory workers and Negroes. The show was gaudy[⑦] with colored lights in the evening. The wooden horses of the flying-jinny revolved in the circle to the mechanical music. The swings whirled[⑧], the rail around the penny[⑨] throwing game was always crowded. From the two booths were sold drinks and bloody brown hamburgers and cotton candy.

He had been hired as a machinist[⑩], but gradually the range of his duties widened[⑪]. His coarse, bawling voice called out through the noise, and continually he was lounging from one place on the show grounds to another. Sweat stood out on his forehead and often his mustache was soaked with beer. On Saturday his job was to keep the people in order. His squat, hard body pushed through the crowd with

---

① flush：脸红，皮肤发红

② tingling：麻刺感

③ fence：栅栏

④ sprawling：蔓延的，杂乱延伸的

⑤ 参考译文：秋天，游乐场从一块空地搬到另一块空地，但总是在城市的边缘。最后，游乐场转遍了小镇的每一个地方。（vacant lot：空地；encircle：环绕）

⑥ wasteland：荒地；未开垦地

⑦ gaudy：华而不实的；俗丽的

⑧ whirl：旋转，回旋

⑨ penny：（美）分；便士

⑩ machinist：机械工；机械师

⑪ widen：扩展；扩宽

savage energy. Only his eyes did not share the violence of the rest of him. Wide gazing beneath his massive scowling forehead, they had a withdrawn and distracted appearance.

He reached home between twelve and one in the morning. The house where he lived was squared into four rooms and the rent was a dollar fifty per person. There was a privy in the back and a hydrant on the stoop. In his room the walls and floor had a wet, sour smell. Sooty, cheap lace curtains hung at the window. He kept his good suit in his bag and hung his overalls on a nail. The room had no heat and no electricity. However, a street light shone outside the window and made a pale greenish reflection inside. He never lighted the oil lamp by his bed unless he wanted to read. The acrid① smell of burning oil in the cold room nauseated② him.

If he stayed at home he restlessly walked the floor. He sat on the edge of the unmade bed and gnawed savagely at the broken, dirty ends of his fingernails. The sharp taste of grime lingered in his mouth.③ The loneliness in him was so keen that he was filled with terror. Usually he had a pint of bootleg white lightning. He drank the raw liquor and by daylight he was warm and relaxed. At five o'clock the whistles from the mills blew for the first shift. The whistles made lost, eerie④ echoes, and he could never sleep until after they had sounded.

But usually he did not stay at home. He went out into the narrow, empty streets. In the first dark hours of the morning the sky was black and the stars hard and bright. Sometimes the mills were running. From the yellow-lighted buildings came the racket⑤ of the machines. He waited at the gates for the early shift. Young girls in sweaters and print dresses came out into the dark street. The men

---

① acrid：（气味）辛辣的，刺鼻的

② nauseate：使厌恶；使恶心；使作呕

③ 参考译文：他坐在凌乱的床边狠命啃着残破肮脏的手指甲，污垢的刺激味道在嘴巴里久留不去。（unmade：尚未做好的，形容床未铺好，凌乱的；gnaw：啃咬；savagely：野蛮地；grime：尘垢，污垢）

④ eerie：可怕的

⑤ racket：吵闹，喧闹

came out carrying their dinner pails. Some of them always went to a streetcar café for Coca-Cola or coffee before going home, and Jake went with them. Inside the noisy mill the men could hear plainly[①] every word that was spoken, but for the first hour outside they were deaf.

In the streetcar Jake drank Coca-Cola with whiskey added. He talked. The winter dawn was white and smoky and cold. He looked with drunken urgency into the drawn, yellow faces of the men. Often he was laughed at, and when this happened he held his stunted body very straight and spoke scornfully in words of many syllables[②]. He stuck his little finger out from his glass and haughtily[③] twisted his mustache. And if he was still laughed at he sometimes fought. He swung his big brown fists with crazed violence and sobbed aloud.

After such mornings he returned to the show with relief. It eased him to push through the crowds of people. The noise, the rank stinks, the shouldering contact of human flesh soothed his jangled[④] nerves.

Because of the blue laws in the town the show closed for the Sabbath. On Sunday he got up early in the morning and took from the suitcase his serge[⑤] suit. He went to the main street. First he dropped into the New York Café and bought a sack of ales. Then he went to Singer's room. Although he knew many people in the town by name or face, the mute was his only friend. They would idle in the quiet room and drink the ales. He would talk, and the words created themselves from the dark mornings spent in the streets or in his room alone.[⑥] The words were formed[⑦] and spoken with relief.

---

① plainly：明白地

② syllable：音节

③ haughtily：傲慢地；骄傲地

④ jangled：烦躁不安的，紧张的

⑤ serge：哔叽；一种结实的羊毛布

⑥ 参考译文：他总是一直说话，在大街上或房间里独自度过的那些阴沉沉的清晨，他总有很多话要说。spent in the streets or hi his room alone 为过去分词作后置定语修饰 mornings，表被动。

⑦ form：使成形

The fire had died down. Singer was playing a game of fools with himself at the table. Jake had been asleep. He awoke with a nervous quiver. He raised his head and turned to Singer.'Yeah,' he said as though in answer to a sudden question. 'Some of us are Communists. But not all of us—. Myself, I'm not a member of the Communist Party. Because in the first place I never knew but one of them. You can bum around[①] for years and not meet Communists. Around here there's no office where you can go up and say you want to join—and if there is I never heard of it. And you just don't take off for[②] New York and join. As I say I never knew but one—and he was a seedy[③] little teetotaler whose breath stunk. We had a fight. Not that I hold that against the Communists. The main fact is I don't think so much of Stalin and Russia. I hate every damn country and government there is. But even so maybe I ought to joined up with the Communists first place. I'm not certain one way or the other. What do you think?'

Singer wrinkled his forehead and considered. He reached for his silver pencil and wrote on his pad of paper that he didn't know.

'But there's this. You see, we just can't settle down after knowing, but we got to act. And some of us go nuts. There's too much to do and you don't know where to start. It makes you crazy. Even me—I've done things that when I look back at them they don't seem rational[④]. Once I started an organization myself.[⑤] I picked out[⑥] twenty lintheads and talked to them until I thought they knew. Our motto was one word: Action. Huh! We meant to start riots[⑦]—stir

---

① bum around：闲荡，流浪

② take off (for)：离开（去某地）

③ seedy：破烂的

④ rational：合理的；理性的

⑤ 参考译文：即便是我——我做了很多事，再回过头去看时，这些事似乎都很不理性。我自己曾经建立过一个组织。本句原文并不是很正确的句子表达，正确表达应为：Even me—I've done things that don't seem rational when I look back at them. Once I started an organization myself. that 引导的定语从句修饰 things，并在从句中作主语。此处仍为作者故意表达，表现文中角色语言素养不高的地域特点。

⑥ pick out：挑选出

⑦ riot：骚乱，暴动

up all the big trouble we could. Our ultimate[①] goal was freedom—but a real freedom, a great freedom made possible only by the sense of justice of the human soul. Our motto, "Action," signified the razing of capitalism[②]. In the constitution (drawn up by myself) certain statutes dealt with the swapping of our motto from "Action" to "Freedom" as soon as our work was through.'

Jake sharpened the end of a match and picked a troublesome cavity in a tooth. After a moment he continued:

'Then when the constitution[③] was all written down and the first followers well organized—then I went out on a hitch-hiking tour to organize component[④] units of the society. Within three months I came back, and what do you reckon I found? What was the first heroic[⑤] action? Had their righteous[⑥] fury overcome planned action so that they had gone ahead without me? Was it destruction, murder, revolution?'

Jake leaned forward in his chair. After a pause he said somberly:

'My friend, they had stole the fifty-seven dollars and thirty cents from the treasury[⑦] to buy uniform caps and free Saturday suppers. I caught them sitting around the conference table, rolling the bones, their caps on their heads, and a ham and a gallon of gin in easy reach.'

A timid smile from Singer followed Jake's outburst of laughter. After a while the smile on Singer's face grew strained and faded. Jake still laughed. The vein in his forehead swelled, his face was dusky red. He laughed too long.

Singer looked up at the clock and indicated[⑧] the time—half-past twelve. He took his watch, his silver pencil and pad, his cigarettes and

---

① ultimate：最终的；根本的
② capitalism：资本主义
③ constitution：宪法；体制
④ component：组成部分；成分
⑤ heroic：英雄的；英勇的
⑥ righteous：正义的；正直的；公正的
⑦ treasury：国库，金库；财政部
⑧ indicate：指示，指出

matches from the mantel and distributed them among his pockets. It was dinner-time.

But Jake still laughed. There was something maniacal in the sound of his laughter. He walked about the room, jingling the change in his pockets. His long, powerful arms swung tense and awkward. He began to name over parts of his coming meal. When he spoke of food his face was fierce with gusto. With each word he raised his upper lip like a ravenous animal.

'Roast beef with gravy. Rice. And cabbage and light bread. And a big hunk of apple pie. I'm famished. Oh, Johnny, I can hear the Yankees coming. And speaking of meals, my friend, did I ever tell you about Mr. Clark Patterson, the gentleman who owns the Sunny Dixie Show? He's so fat he hasn't seen his privates for twenty years, and all day he sits in his trailer playing solitaire① and smoking reefers②. He orders his meals from a short-order joint nearby and every day he breaks his fast with—'

Jake stepped back so that Singer could leave the room. He always hung back at doorways when he was with the mute. He always followed and expected Singer to lead. As they descended the stairs he continued to talk with nervous volubility③. He kept his brown, wide eyes on Singer's face.

The afternoon was soft and mild. They stayed indoors. Jake had brought back with them a quart of④ whiskey. He sat brooding and silent on the foot of the bed, leaning now and then to fill his glass from the bottle on the floor.⑤ Singer was at his table by the window playing a game of chess. Jake had relaxed somewhat⑥. He watched the

① solitaire：单人纸牌游戏
② reefer：大麻卷烟
③ volubility：流利；健谈
④ a quart of：一夸脱的
⑤ 参考译文：他坐在床头苦思冥想，一言不发，不时倾斜一下身子拿起地下的酒瓶，给自己的杯子里倒满酒。（brood：沉思；now and then：偶尔，不时）
⑥ somewhat：有点，稍微

game of his friend and felt the mild, quiet afternoon merge[1] with the darkness of evening. The firelight made dark, silent waves on the walls of the room.

But at night the tension[2] came in him again. Singer had put away his chess men and they sat facing each other. Nervousness made Jake's lips twitch raggedly and he drank to soothe himself. A backwash of restlessness and desire overcame him. He drank down the whiskey and began to talk again to Singer. The words swelled with him and gushed[3] from his mouth. He walked from the window to the bed and back again—again and again. And at last the deluge of swollen words took shape and he delivered them to the mute with drunken emphasis[4]:

'The things they have done to us! The truths they have turned into lies. The ideals they have fouled and made vile. Take Jesus. He was one of us. He knew. When He said that it is harder for a camel to pass through the eye of a needle than for a rich man to enter the kingdom of God—he damn well meant just what he said.[5] But look what the Church has done to Jesus during the last two thousand years. What they have made of him. How they have turned every word He spoke for their own vile[6] ends. Jesus would be framed and in jail if He was living today. Jesus would be one who really knows. Me and Jesus would sit across the table and I would look at Him and He would look at me and we would both know that the other knew. Me and Jesus and Karl Marx could all sit at a table and—

---

① merge：合并；融合

② tension：紧张，不安

③ gush：涌出；迸出

④ 参考译文：终于，那些千言万语汇成洪流，他带着醉醺醺的强调语气一并将它们倾吐给哑巴。(deluge of sth.：涌现的……，例如 a deluge of thoughts 意为"层出不穷的想法"；emphasis：强调）

⑤ 参考译文：耶稣说，骆驼要想穿过针眼，比富人要想进入上帝的王国还要难——他说的是真的。本句原文引用有误，《马太福音》原文为：It is easier for a camel to go through the eye of a needle than for someone who is rich to enter the kingdom of God. 即"骆驼穿过针眼比富人进天国都要容易"，这是耶稣对富人的针砭。

⑥ vile：卑鄙的；邪恶的

'And look what has happened to our freedom. The men who fought the American Revolution were no more like these D.A.R. dames than I'm a pot-bellied, perfumed Pekingese dog. They meant what they said about freedom. They fought a real revolution. They fought so that this could be a country where every man would be free and equal. Huh! And that meant every man was equal in the sight of Nature—with an equal chance. This didn't mean that twenty per cent of the people were free to rob the other eighty per cent of[①] the means[②] to live. This didn't mean for one rich man to sweat the piss out of ten thousand poor men so that he can get richer. This didn't mean the tyrants were free to get this country in such a fix that millions of people are ready to do anything—cheat, lie, or whack off their right arm—just to work for three squares and a flop.[③] They have made the word freedom a blasphemy[④]. You hear me? They have made the word freedom stink like a skunk to all who know.'

The vein[⑤] in Jake's forehead throbbed[⑥] wildly. His mouth worked convulsively[⑦]. Singer sat up, alarmed, Jake tried to speak again and the words choked in his mouth. A shudder passed through his body. He sat down in the chair and pressed his trembling lips with his fingers. Then he said huskily[⑧]:

'It's this way, Singer. Being mad is no good. Nothing we can do is any good. That's the way it seems to me. All we can do is go around telling the truth. And as soon as enough of the don't-knows have learned the truth then there won't be any use for fighting.[⑨] The

---

① rob sb. of...：抢劫某人某物

② means：方法，手段（means to live 意为"谋生手段"，即"生计"）

③ 参考译文：这也不意味着暴君们可以任意让这个国家陷入困境当中，让数以百万计的人们可以为了混口饭吃、有个地方睡觉便为所欲为——欺诈、撒谎、打掉自己的右臂。（tyrant：暴君；fix：困境；whack off：用力敲掉；square：餐食；flop：廉价旅馆，便宜栖身处）

④ blasphemy：亵渎神明；轻视上帝或神祇

⑤ vein：血管

⑥ throb：（有规律地）抽动；（有节奏地）跳动

⑦ convulsively：痉挛性地

⑧ huskily：嘎声地，沙哑地

⑨ 参考译文：如果哪一天，有足够多的不知道的人明白了这个真理，便用不着斗争了。（as soon as：一……就……，例：I told you as soon as I knew the news. 我一知道消息就告诉你了。）

only thing for us to do is let them know. All that's needed. But how? Huh?'

The fire shadows lapped[①] against the walls. The dark, shadowy waves rose higher and the room took on motion. The room rose and fell and all balance was gone. Alone Jake felt himself sink downward, slowly in wavelike[②] motions downward into a shadowed ocean. In helplessness and terror he strained his eyes, but he could see nothing except the dark and scarlet waves that roared hungrily over him.[③] Then at last he made out the thing which he sought. The mute's face was faint[④] and very far away. Jake closed his eyes.

The next morning he awoke very late. Singer had been gone for hours. There was bread, cheese, an orange, and a pot of coffee on the table. When he had finished his breakfast it was time for work. He walked somberly[⑤], his head bent, across the town toward his room. When he reached the neighborhood where he lived he passed through a certain narrow street that was flanked on one side by a smoke-blackened brick warehouse[⑥]. On the wall of this building there was something that vaguely distracted him. He started to walk on, and then his attention was suddenly held. On the wall a message was written in bright red chalk, the letters drawn thickly and curiously formed:

Ye shall eat the flesh of the mighty, and drink the blood of the princes of the earth.[⑦]

He read the message twice and looked anxiously up and down

---

① lap：轻拍（lap against 意为"拍打，轻拍"，此处将炉火的影子拟人化，指炉火的影子笼罩房间。）

② wavelike：波状的；波浪般的

③ 参考译文：他感到无助和恐惧，使劲睁着眼睛，但除了朝他拼命怒号的暗红色波浪，他什么都看不见。

④ faint：模糊的

⑤ somberly：阴沉地，忧郁地

⑥ warehouse：仓库

⑦ 参考译文：你必吃勇士的肉，喝地上首领的血。出自《以西结书》39:18，描写了屠杀歌革与玛各大军的血腥画面。

the street. No one was in sight[①]. After a few minutes of puzzled deliberation[②] he took from his pocket a thick red pencil and wrote carefully beneath the inscription:

Whoever wrote the above meet me here tomorrow at noon.

Wednesday, November 29. Or the next day.

At twelve o'clock the next day he waited before the wall.'Now and then[③] he walked impatiently to the corner to look up and down the streets. No one came. After an hour he had to leave for the show.

The next day he waited, also.

Then on Friday there was a long, slow winter rain. The wall was sodden[④] and the messages streaked[⑤] so that no word could be read. The rain continued, gray and bitter and cold.

---

① in sight：在视野中，被看到，例：We came in sight of the library. 我们来到可以看见图书馆的地方。

② deliberation：考虑

③ now and then：偶尔，时不时地

④ sodden：浸透的；浑身湿透的

⑤ streaked：被染花的（streak 的过去分词），此处为被动语态独立结构，中间省略谓语were。

5

'Mick,' Bubber said. 'I come to believe we all gonna[1] drown.'

It was true that it like to never quit raining. Mrs. Wells rode them back and forth to school in her car, and every afternoon they had to stay on the front porch or in the house. She and Bubber played Parcheesi and Old Maid and shot marbles on the living-room rug[2]. It was nearing along toward Christmas time and Bubber began to talk about the Little Lord Jesus and the red bicycle he wanted Santa Claus to bring him. The rain was silver on the windowpanes[3] and the sky was wet and cold and gray. The river rose so high that some of the factory people had to move out of their houses. Then when it looked like the rain would keep on and on forever it suddenly stopped. They woke up one morning and the bright sun was shining. By afternoon the weather was almost warm as summer. Mick came home late from school and Bubber and Ralph and Spareribs were on the front sidewalk. The kids looked hot and sticky[4] and their winter clothes had a sour smell. Bubber had his slingshot[5] and a pocketful[6] of rocks. Ralph sat up in his wagon, his hat crooked[7] on his head, and he was

---

① gonna：（美）将要（等于 going to)
② rug：小地毯
③ windowpane：窗玻璃
④ sticky：（皮肤因热而）黏湿的
⑤ slingshot：弹弓
⑥ pocketful：一袋之量；满袋
⑦ crook：弯曲

fretful. Spareribs had his new rifle[①] with him. The sky was a wonderful blue.

'We waited for you a long time, Mick,' Bubber said. 'Where you been?'

She jumped up the front steps three at a time and threw her sweater toward the hat rack. 'Practicing on the piano in the gym.'

Every afternoon she stayed after school for an hour to play. The gym was crowded and noisy because the girls' team had basketball games. Twice today she was hit on the head with the ball. But getting a chance to sit at a piano was worth any amount of knocks and trouble. She would arrange bunches of notes together until the sound came that she wanted. It was easier than she had thought. After the first two or three hours she figured out some sets of chords in the bass that would fit in with the main tune her right hand was playing.[②] She could pick out almost any piece now. And she made up new music too. That was better than just copying tunes. When her hands hunted out these beautiful new sounds it was the best feeling she had ever known.

She wanted to learn how to read music already written down. Delores Brown had taken music lessons for five years. She paid Delores the fifty cents a week she got for lunch money to give her lessons. This made her very hungry all through the day. Delores played a good many fast, runny pieces—but Delores did not know how to answer all the questions she wanted to know. Delores only taught her about the different scales[③], the major and minor chords[④], the values of the notes, and such beginning rules as those.

Mick slammed[⑤] the door of the kitchen stove. 'This all we got to

---

① rifle：步枪，来复枪

② 参考译文：试了两三个小时后，她在低音区摸索出了几组和弦，可以搭配右手弹奏的主旋律。原文为 that 引导的定语从句修饰“和弦”。（set：套；系列）

③ scale：音阶

④ chord：和弦，和音

⑤ slam：砰地关上

eat?'

'Honey, it the best I can do for you,' Portia said.

Just cornpones and margarine[①]. As she ate she drank a glass of water to help wash down[②] the swallows.

'Quit acting so greedy. Nobody going to snatch[③] it out your hand.'

The kids still hung around[④] in front of the house. Bubber had put his slingshot in his pocket and now he played with the rifle[⑤]. Spareribs was ten years old and his father had died the month before and this had been his father's gun[⑥]. All the smaller kids loved to handle that rifle. Every few minutes Bubber would haul the gun up to his shoulder. He took aim and made a loud pow sound.

'Don't monkey with[⑦] the trigger,' said Spareribs. I got the gun loaded.'

Mick finished the cornbread and looked around for something to do. Harry Minowitz was sitting on his front porch banisters with the newspaper. She was glad to see him. For a joke she threw up her arm and hollered to him, 'Heil!'

But Harry didn't take it as a joke. He went into his front hall and shut the door. It was easy to hurt his feelings. She was sorry, because lately she and Harry had been right good friends. They had always played in the same gang when they were kids, but in the last three years he had been at Vocational while she was still in grammar school. Also he worked at part-time jobs. He grew up very suddenly and quit hanging around the back and front yards with kids. Sometimes she could see him reading the paper in his bedroom or undressing

---

① margarine：人造黄油；人造奶油

② wash down：冲洗，文中指“冲服”。

③ snatch：夺去

④ hung around：闲荡（hang around 的过去式）

⑤ rifle：步枪；来复枪

⑥ gun：枪支

⑦ monkey with：瞎弄，乱搞，例：Don't monkey with my stuff without permission. 未经许可不要乱动我的东西。

late at night. In mathematics and history he was the smartest boy at Vocational. Often, now that she was in high school too, they would meet each other on the way home and walk together. They were in the same shop class, and once the teacher made them partners to assemble[①] a motor. He read books and kept up with the newspapers every day. World politics[②] were all the time on his mind. He talked slow, and sweat stood out on his forehead when he was very serious about something. And now she had made him mad with her.

'I wonder has Harry still got his gold piece,' Spareribs said.

'What gold piece?'

'When a Jew boy is born they put a gold piece in the bank for him. That's what Jews do.'

'Shucks. You got it mixed up[③],' she said. 'It's Catholics you're thinking about. Catholics[④] buy a pistol for a baby soon as it's born. Some day the Catholics mean to start a war and kill everybody else.'

'Nuns give me a funny feeling,' Spareribs said. 'It scares me when I see one on the street.'

She sat down on the steps and laid her head on her knees. She went into the inside room. With her it was like there was two places—the inside room and the outside room. School and the family and the things that happened every day were in the outside room. Mister Singer was in both rooms. Foreign countries and plans and music were in the inside room. The songs she thought about were there. And the symphony. When she was by herself in this inside room the music she had heard that night after the party would come back to her. This symphony grew slow like a big flower in her mind. During the day sometimes, or when she had just waked up in the morning, a new part

① assemble：组装；装配
② politics：政治，政治学
③ mixed up：混淆不清的
④ Catholic：天主教徒

of the symphony would suddenly come to her.[1] Then she would have to go into the inside room and listen to it many times and try to join it into the parts of the symphony she remembered. The inside room was a very private place. She could be in the middle of a house full of people and still feel like she was locked up[2] by herself.

Spareribs stuck his dirty hand up to her eyes because she had been staring off at space. She slapped him.

'What is a nun?' Bubber asked.

'A Catholic lady,' Spareribs said. 'A Catholic lady with a big black dress that comes up over her head.'

She was tired of hanging around with the kids. She would go to the library and look at pictures in the National Geographic. Photographs of all the foreign places in the world. Paris, France. And big ice glaciers[3]. And the wild jungles[4] in Africa.

'You kids see that Ralph don't get out in the street,' she said.

Bubber rested the big rifle on his shoulder. 'Bring me a story back with you.'

It was like that kid had been born knowing how to read. He was only in the second grade but he loved to read stories by himself—and he never asked anybody else to read to him.'What kind you want this time?'

'Pick out some stories with something to eat in them. I like that one a whole lot about them German kids going out in the forest and coming to this house made out of all different kinds of candy and the witch.[5] I like a story with something to eat in it.'

'I'll look for one,' said Mick.

---

① 参考译文：白天有些时候，或者清晨刚醒来时，她脑子里会突然想起这首交响乐的一个新部分。本句是对音乐家产生灵感方式的一个具体描写。

② lock up：锁定，锁起来

③ glacier：冰川

④ jungle：丛林；雨林

⑤ 参考译文：我特别喜欢那种德国孩子的故事，他们到森林里去，碰到一所房子，全都是各种各样的糖果做的，还有巫婆。本句原文表达较累赘，故在译文中也出现较像日常对话的表达"那种……"，配合人物的表达特点。(a whole lot：很，非常；witch：巫婆，女巫)

'But I'm getting kinda[1] tired of candy,' Bubber said. 'See if you can't bring me a story with something like a barbecue sandwich in it. But if you can't find none of them I'd like a cowboy story.'

She was ready to leave when suddenly she stopped and stared. The kids stared too. They all stood still and looked at Baby Wilson coming down the steps of her house across the street.

'Ain't Baby cute!' said Bubber softly.

Maybe it was the sudden hot, sunny day after all those rainy weeks. Maybe it was because their dark winter clothes were ugly to them on an afternoon like this one. Anyway Baby looked like a fairy[2] or something in the picture show. She had on her last year's soiree costume—with a little pink-gauze skirt that stuck out short and stiff, a pink body waist, pink dancing shoes, and even a little pink pocketbook.[3] With her yellow hair she was all pink and white and gold—and so small and clean that it almost hurt to watch her. She prissed across the street in a cute way, but would not turn her face toward them.

'Come over here,' said Bubber. 'Lemme look at your little pink pocketbook—'

Baby passed them along the edge of the street with her head held to one side. She had made up her mind not to speak to them.

There was a strip of[4] grass between the sidewalk and the street, and when Baby reached it she stood still for a second and then turned a handspring[5].

'Don't pay no mind to her,' said Spareribs. 'She always tries to show off. She's going down to Mister Brannon's café to get candy. He's her uncle and she gets it free.'

---

① kinda：有点（相当于 kind of）

② fairy：仙女；小精灵

③ 参考译文：她穿着去年的晚会礼服——一条小小的粉色纱裙，微微朝外翘着，很挺括，一条粉色腰带，粉色舞鞋，甚至还拿了一个粉色小皮夹。本句其实是 have...on，但为了在破折号后面带上“晚会礼服”的同位语，原文表达调整为 have on...。

④ a strip of：一条

⑤ handspring：翻筋斗；前手翻腾越

Bubber rested the end of the rifle on the ground. The big gun was too heavy for him. As he watched Baby walk off[①] down the street he kept pulling the straggly bangs of his hair. 'That sure is a cute little pink pocketbook,' he said.

'Her Mama always talks about how talented she is,' said Spareribs. 'She thinks she's gonna get Baby in the movies.'

It was too late to go look at the National Geographic. Supper was almost ready. Ralph tuned up to cry and she took him off the wagon and put him on the ground. Now it was December, and to a kid Bubber's age that was a long time from summer. All last summer Baby had come out in that pink soiree[②] costume and danced in the middle of the street. At first the kids would flock around and watch her, but soon they got tired of it. Bubber was the only one who would watch her as she came out to dance. He would sit on the curb and yell to her when he saw a car coming. He had watched Baby do her soiree dance a hundred times—but summer had been gone for three months and now it seemed new to him again.

'I sure do wish I had a costume,' Bubber said.

'What kind do you want?'

'A real cool costume. A real pretty one made out of all different colors. Like a butterfly. That's what I want for Christmas. That and a bicycle!'

'Sissy,' said Spareribs.

Bubber hauled[③] the big rifle up to his shoulder again and took aim at[④] a house across the street. 'I'd dance around in my costume if I had one. I'd wear it every day to school.'

Mick sat on the front steps and kept her eyes on Ralph. Bubber wasn't a sissy[⑤] like Spareribs said. He just loved pretty things. She'd

---

① walk off：离开
② soiree：（法）晚会；社交聚会；黄昏时的聚会
③ haul：（用力）拖，举起
④ take aim at：瞄准
⑤ sissy：胆小鬼；胆小无用的男子

better not let old Spareribs get away with that.[1]

'A person's got to fight for every single thing they get,' she said slowly. 'And I've noticed a lot of times that the farther down a kid comes in the family the better the kid really is. Younger kids are always the toughest[2]. I'm pretty hard 'cause I've a lot of them on top of me. Bubber—he looks sick, and likes pretty things, but he's got guts underneath that. If all this is true Ralph sure ought to be a real strong one when he's old enough to get around. Even though he's just seventeen months old I can read something hard and tough in that Ralph's face already.'

Ralph looked around because he knew he was being talked about. Spareribs sat down on the ground and grabbed[3] Ralph's hat off his head and shook it in his face to tease him.

'All right!' Mick said. 'You know what I'll do to you if you start him to cry. You just better watch out.'

Everything was quiet. The sun was behind the roofs of the houses and the sky in the west was purple and pink. On the next block there was the sound of kids skating. Bubber leaned up against a tree and he seemed to be dreaming about something. The smell of supper came out of the house and it would be time to eat soon.

'Look it,' Bubber said suddenly. 'Here comes Baby again. She sure is pretty in the pink costume.'

Baby walked toward them slowly. She had been given a prize box of popcorn[4] candy and was reaching in the box for the prize. She walked in that same prissy[5], dainty[6] way. You could tell that she knew they were all looking at her.

'Please, Baby—' Bubber said when she started to pass them.

---

① 参考译文：斯波尔瑞巴斯居然这么说，她饶不了他。此处 had better 是一种推测，表示“应该，可能”。（get away with：逃脱惩罚）

② toughest：最坚强的；最坚韧的

③ grab：攫取；强夺

④ popcorn：爆米花，爆玉米花

⑤ prissy：为小事挂虑的；谨小慎微的

⑥ dainty：讲究的

'Lemme see your little pink pocketbook and touch your pink costume.'

Baby started humming[①] a song to herself and did not listen. She passed by without letting Bubber play with her. She only ducked her head and grinned at him a little.

Bubber still had the big rifle up to his shoulder. He made a loud pow sound and pretended like he had shot. Then he called to Baby again—in a soft, sad voice like he was calling a little kitty. 'Please, Baby—come here, Baby—'

He was too quick for Mick to stop him. She had just seen his hand on the trigger[②] when there was the terrible ping[③] of the gun. Baby crumpled down to the sidewalk. It was like she was nailed to the steps and couldn't move or scream. Spareribs had his arm up over his head.

Bubber was the only one that didn't realize. 'Get up, Baby,' he hollered. 'I ain't mad with you.'

It all happened in a second. The three of them reached Baby at the same time. She lay crumpled down on the dirty sidewalk. Her skirt was over her head, showing her pink panties and her little white legs. Her hands were open—in one there was the prize from the candy and in the other the pocketbook. There was blood all over her hair ribbon and the top of her yellow curls[④]. She was shot in the head and her face was turned down toward the ground.

So much happened in a second. Bubber screamed and dropped the gun and ran. She stood with her hands up to her face and screamed too. Then there were many people. Her Dad was the first to get there. He carried Baby into the house.

'She's dead,' said Spareribs. 'She's shot through the eyes. I seen her face.'

---

① hum：哼唱（humming 为动名词形式）
② trigger：（枪械等的）扳机
③ ping：乒乓的声响，砰的声响
④ curl：卷发

Mick walked up and down the sidewalk, and her tongue stuck in her mouth when she tried to ask was Baby killed.① Mrs. Wilson came running down the block from the beauty parlor where she worked. She went into the house and came back out again. She walked up and down in the street, crying and pulling a ring on and off her finger.② Then the ambulance③ came and the doctor went in to Baby. Mick followed him. Baby was lying on the bed in the front room. The house was quiet as a church.

Baby looked like a pretty little doll on the bed. Except for④ the blood she did not seem hurt. The doctor bent over and looked at her head. After he finished they took Baby out on a stretcher⑤. Mrs. Wilson and her Dad got into the ambulance with her.

The house was still quiet. Everybody had forgotten about Bubber. He was nowhere around. An hour passed. Her Mama and Hazel and Etta and all the boarders⑥ waited in the front room. Mister Singer stood in the doorway.

After a long time her Dad came home. He said Baby wouldn't die but that her skull was fractured⑦. He asked for Bubber. Nobody knew where he was. It was dark outside. They called Bubber in the back yard and in the street. They sent Spareribs and some other boys out to hunt for him. It looked like Bubber had gone clear out of⑧ the neighborhood. Harry went around to a house where they thought he might be.

Her Dad walked up and down the front porch. 'I never have

---

① 参考译文：米克在人行道上来回走着，她想问问巴比是不是死了，舌头却像卡在了嘴里一样。本句表达出米克此时内心的忐忑。

② 参考译文：她在街上来回走着，大哭着，把手指上的戒指摘下来又戴上。本句原文为动名词短语作主补说明威尔逊太太的状态，形容其紧张焦急的情绪。

③ ambulance：急救车，救护车

④ except for：除了……以外，要不是，例：I answered all the questions except for the first one. 除了第一道题，我全都答上了。

⑤ stretcher：担架

⑥ boarder：寄宿者

⑦ fracture：破裂，粉碎

⑧ go clear out of：彻底离开

whipped[1] any of my kids yet,' he kept saying. 'I never believed in it. But I'm sure going to lay it onto that kid as soon as I get my hands on him.'

Mick sat on the banisters and watched down the dark street. 'I can manage Bubber. Once he comes back I can take care of him all right.'

'You go out and hunt for him. You can find him better than anybody else.'

As soon as her Dad said that she suddenly knew where Bubber was. In the back yard there was a big oak and in the summer they had built a tree house. They had hauled[2] a big box up in this oak[3], and Bubber used to love to sit up in the tree house by himself. Mick left the family and the boarders on the front porch and walked back through the alley of the dark yard.

She stood for a minute by the trunk of the tree. 'Bubber—,' she said quietly. 'It's Mick.'

He didn't answer, but she knew he was there. It was like she could smell him. She swung upon the lowest branch and climbed slowly. She was really mad with that kid and would have to teach him a lesson. When she reached the tree house she spoke to him again—and still there wasn't any answer. She climbed into the big box and felt around the edges[4]. At last she touched him. He was scrounged up in a corner and his legs were trembling[5]. He had been holding his breath, and when she touched him the sobs and the breath came out all at once.

'I—I didn't mean Baby to fall. She was just so little and cute—seemed to me like I just had to take a pop at her.'

Mick sat down on the floor of the tree house. 'Baby's dead,' she

---

① whip：鞭打
② haul：拖，拉
③ oak：橡树
④ edge：边缘；边界
⑤ tremble：发抖，战栗

said. 'They got a lot of people hunting for you.'

Bubber quit crying. He was very quiet.

'You know what Dad's doing in the house?'

It was like she could hear Bubber listening.

'You know Warden Lawes—you heard him over the radio. And you know Sing Sing[①]. Well, our Dad's writing a letter to Warden Lawes for him to be a little bit kind to you when they catch you and send you to Sing Sing.'

The words were so awful-sounding in the dark that a shiver[②] came over her. She could feel Bubber trembling.

'They got little electric chairs there—just your size. And when they turn on the juice you just fry up[③] like a piece of burnt bacon[④]. Then you go to Hell.'

Bubber was squeezed up in the corner and there was not a sound from him. She climbed over the edge of the box to get down. 'You better stay up here because they got policemen guarding[⑤] the yard. Maybe in a few days I can bring you something to eat.'

Mick leaned against the trunk of the oak tree. That would teach Bubber all right. She had always managed him and she knew more about that kid than anybody else. Once, about a year or two ago, he was always wanting to stop off[⑥] behind bushes and pee and play with himself awhile. She had caught on to that pretty quick. She gave him a good slap[⑦] every time it happened and in three days he was cured. Afterwards he never even peed normal like other kids—he held his hands behind him. She always had to nurse that Bubber and she could always manage him. In a little while she would go back up to the tree

---

① Sing Sing：纽约州新新监狱（纽约州的一座监狱，1825—1828 年建于哈德逊河的奥西宁村，曾以严厉的纪律而臭名昭著，官方名奥西宁教养所。）

② shiver：颤抖，哆嗦

③ fry up：把食物煎热一下

④ bacon：咸肉；腌肉；熏猪肉

⑤ guard：保卫；看守

⑥ stop off：逗留，例：Go straight home at once; don't stop off anywhere. 立刻回家，别在任何地方逗留。

⑦ slap：掌击

house and bring him in. After this he would never want to pick up a gun again in all his life.

There was still this dead feeling in the house. The boarders all sat on the front porch without talking or rocking in the chairs. Her Dad and her Mama were in the front room. Her Dad drank beer out of a bottle and walked up and down the floor. Baby was going to get well all right, so this worry was not about her. And nobody seemed to be anxious about Bubber. It was something else.

'That Bubber!' said Etta.

'I'm shamed to go out of the house after this,' Hazel said.

Etta and Hazel went into the middle room and closed the door. Bill was in his room at the back. She didn't want to talk with them. She stood around in the front hall and thought it over by herself.

Her Dad's footsteps stopped. 'It was deliberate①,' he said. 'It's not like the kid was just fooling with the gun and it went off by accident. Everybody who saw it said he took deliberate aim.'

'I wonder when we'll hear from Mrs. Wilson,' her Mama said.

'We'll hear plenty, all right!'

'I reckon we will.'

Now that the sun was down the night was cold again like November. The people came in from the front porch and sat in the living-room—but nobody lighted a fire. Mick's sweater was hanging on the hat rack②, so she put it on and stood with her shoulders bent over③ to keep warm. She thought about Bubber sitting out④ in the cold, dark tree house. He had really believed every word she said. But he sure deserved to worry some. He had nearly killed that Baby.

'Mick, can't you think of some place where Bubber might be?' her Dad asked.

---

① deliberate：故意的，蓄意的

② hat rack：帽架

③ bent over：弯腰，俯身（bent 为 bend 过去分词）

④ sit out：坐在户外

'He's in the neighborhood, I reckon[①].'

Her Dad walked up and down with the empty beer bottle in his hand. He walked like a blind man and there was sweat on his face. 'The poor kid's scared to come home. If we could find him I'd feel better. I've never laid a hand on Bubber. He oughtn't be scared of me.'

She would wait until an hour and a half was gone. By that time he would be plenty sorry for what he did. She always could manage that Bubber and make him learn.

After a while there was a big excitement in the house. Her Dad telephoned again to the hospital to see how Baby was, and in a few minutes Mrs. Wilson called back. She said she wanted to have a talk with them and would come to the house.

Her Dad still walked up and down the front room like a blind man. He drank three more bottles of beer. 'The way it all happened she can sue my britches off.[②] All she could get would be the house outside of the mortgage[③]. But the way it happened we don't have any comeback[④] at all.'

Suddenly Mick thought about something. Maybe they would really try Bubber in court and put him in a children's jail[⑤]. Maybe Mrs. Wilson would send him to reform school. Maybe they would really do something terrible to Bubber. She wanted to go out to the tree house right away and sit with him and tell him not to worry. Bubber was always so thin and little and smart. She would kill anybody that tried to send that kid out of the family. She wanted to kiss him and bite him because she loved him so much.

But she couldn't miss anything. Mrs. Wilson would be there in a few minutes and she had to know what was going on. Then she

---

① reckon：估计，猜想

② 参考译文：发生这样的事，她完全可以去告我，让我连裤子都赔掉。(sue：控告，sue sth. off 表示控告某人后，让某人付出……代价)

③ mortgage：抵押；抵押贷款额

④ comeback：(对批评迅速作出的)反驳，回应

⑤ put sb. in jail：把某人送进监狱

would run out and tell Bubber that all the things she said were lies. And he would really have learned the lesson he had coming to him.

A ten-cent taxicab drove up to the sidewalk. Everybody waited on the front porch, very quiet and scared. Mrs. Wilson got out of the taxi with Mister Brannon. She could hear her Dad grinding[①] his teeth together in a nervous way as they came up the steps. They went into the front room and she followed along after them and stood in the doorway. Etta and Hazel and Bill and the boarders kept out of it.

'I've come to talk over all this with you,' Mrs. Wilson said.

The front room looked tacky[②] and dirty and she saw Mister Brannon notice everything. The mashed celluloid[③] doll and the beads[④] and junk Ralph played with were scattered[⑤] on the floor. There was beer on her Dad's workbench[⑥], and the pillows on the bed where her Dad and Mama slept were right gray.

Mrs. Wilson kept pulling the wedding ring on and off her finger. By the side of her Mister Brannon was very calm. He sat with his legs crossed. His jaws were blue-black and he looked like a gangster[⑦] in the movies. He had always had this grudge[⑧] against her. He always spoke to her in this rough voice different from the way he talked to other people. Was it because he knew about the time she and Bubber swiped a pack of chewing gum[⑨] off his counter? She hated him.

'It all boils down to[⑩] this,' said Mrs. Wilson. 'Your kid shot my baby in the head on purpose.'

Mick stepped into the middle of the room. 'No, he didn't,' she

① grind teeth：磨牙，此处使用现在分词 grinding 表示"听见他的爸爸"正在磨牙。
② tacky：俗气的
③ celluloid doll：赛璐珞洋娃娃
④ bead：珠子
⑤ scattered：分散的；散乱的
⑥ workbench：工作台
⑦ gangster：歹徒，流氓；恶棍
⑧ grudge：怨恨
⑨ chewing gum：口香糖，泡泡糖
⑩ boil down to：（情况或问题）归根结底，例：Most crimes boil down to want of money. 大部分犯罪都可以归结到对金钱的欲望。

said. 'I was right there. Bubber had been aiming that gun at me and Ralph and everything around there. He just happened to aim it at Baby and his finger slipped. I was right there.'

Mister Brannon rubbed his nose and looked at her in a sad way. She sure did hate him.

'I know how you all feel—so I want to come to the point right now.'

Mick's Mama rattled a bunch of keys and her Dad sat very still with his big hands hanging over his knees.

'Bubber didn't have it in his mind beforehand,' Mick said. 'He just—'

Mrs. Wilson jabbed[①] the ring on and off her finger. 'Wait a minute. I know how everything is. I could bring it to court and sue for every cent you own.'

Her Dad didn't have any expression on his face. 'I tell you one thing,' he said. 'We don't have much to sue for. All we got is—'

'Just listen to me,' said Mrs. Wilson. 'I haven't come here with any lawyer to sue you. Bartholomew—Mister Brannon—and I talked it over when we came and we just about agree on the main points. In the first place, I want to do the fair, honest thing—and in the second place, I don't want Baby's name mixed up in no common lawsuit[②] at her age.'

There was not a sound and everybody in the room sat stiff in their chairs. Only Mister Brannon halfway smiled at Mick, but she squinted[③] her eyes back at him in a tough way.

Mrs. Wilson was very nervous and her hand shook when she lighted a cigarette. 'I don't want to have to sue you or anything like that. All I want is for you to be fair. I'm not asking you to pay for all the suffering and crying Baby went through with until they gave her

① jab：（用……）戳，刺
② lawsuit：诉讼（尤指非刑事案件）
③ squint：眯眼看

something to sleep.[1] There's not any pay that would make up for that. And I'm not asking you to pay for the damage this will do to her career and the plans we had made.[2] She's going to have to wear a bandage for several months. She won't get to dance in the soirée—maybe there'll even be a little bald place on her head.'

Mrs. Wilson and her Dad looked at each other like they was hypnotized[3]. Then Mrs. Wilson reached around to her pocketbook and took out a slip of paper.

'The things you got to pay are just the actual price of what it will cost us in money. There's Baby's private room in the hospital and a private nurse until she can come home. There's the operating room and the doctor's bill[4]—and for once I intend the doctor to be paid right away. Also, they shaved all Baby's hair off and you got to pay me for the permanent wave[5] I took her to Atlanta to get—so when her hair grows back natural she can have another one. And there's the price of her costume and other little extra bills like that. I'll write all the items down just as soon as I know what they'll be. I'm trying to be just as fair and honest as I can, and you'll have to pay the total when I bring it to you.'

Her Mama smoothed her dress over her knees and took a quick, short breath. 'Seems to me like the children's ward would be a lot better than a private room. When Mick had penumonia[6]—'

'I said a private room.'

Mister Brannon held out his white, stumpy[7] hands and balanced

---

① 参考译文：他们给巴比吃了什么东西（才）让她睡过去之前，她经历了那么多折磨，哭了那么久，我不是要让你们为这些付出代价。本文原文包含一个定语从句修饰 suffering and crying，同时含一个时间状语从句表示巴比吃了什么东西后才睡过去。

② 参考译文：这会影响她的事业，会影响我们的计划，我也不是要让你们为这些付出代价。本句原文为定语从句修饰 damage，而定语从句中又有 career 和 plans 并列，plans 后又由定语从句修饰，阅读时需分解。

③ hypnotize：对……施催眠术

④ bill：账单

⑤ permanent wave：烫发

⑥ penumonia：肺炎

⑦ stumpy：粗短的

them like they was on scales. 'Maybe in a day or two Baby can move into a double room with some other kid.'

Mrs. Wilson spoke hard-boiled[①]. 'You heard what I said. Long as your kid shot my Baby she certainly ought to have every advantage until she gets well.'

'You're in your rights,' her Dad said. 'God knows we don't have anything now—but maybe I can scrape it up. I realize you're not trying to take advantage of[②] us and I appreciate it. We'll do what we can.'

She wanted to stay and hear everything that they said, but Bubber was on her mind.[③] When she thought of him sitting up in the dark, cold tree house thinking about Sing Sing she felt uneasy. She went out of the room and down the hall toward the back door. The wind was blowing and the yard was very dark except for the yellow square that came from the light in the kitchen. When she looked back she saw Portia sitting at the table with her long, thin hands up on her face, very still. The yard was lonesome[④] and the wind made quick, scary[⑤] shadows and a mourning kind of sound in the darkness.

She stood under the oak tree. Then just as she started to reach for the first limb[⑥] a terrible notion came over her. It came to her all of a sudden that Bubber was gone. She called him and he did not answer. She climbed quick and quiet as a cat.

'Say! Bubber!'

Without feeling in the box she knew he wasn't there. To make sure she got into the box and felt in all the corners. The kid was gone. He must have started down the minute she left. He was running away

---

① hard-boiled：不懂感情的，不流露感情的

② take advantage of：利用，例：We shall take advantage of every second to finish the work on time. 要想准时完成工作，我们要利用好每分每秒。

③ 参考译文：她想待在这里，听听他们还会说些什么，但她满脑子都是巴伯。（on one's mind：挂在心上，使人担心）

④ lonesome：寂寞的；人迹稀少的

⑤ scary：恐怖的

⑥ limb：分支；（树的）大枝，主枝

for sure now, and with a smart kid like Bubber it was no telling where they'd catch him.[1]

She scrambled down the tree and ran to the front porch. Mrs. Wilson was leaving and they had all come out to the front steps with her.

'Dad!' she said. 'We got to do something about Bubber. He's run away. I'm sure he left our block. We all got to get out and hunt him.'

Nobody knew where to go or how to begin. Her Dad walked up and down the street, looking in all the alleys[2]. Mister Brannon telephoned for a ten-cent taxi for Mrs. Wilson and then stayed to help with the hunt. Mister Singer sat on the banisters of the porch and he was the only person who kept calm. They all waited for Mick to plan out the best places to look for Bubber. But the town was so big and the little kid so smart that she couldn't think what to do.

Maybe he had gone to Portia's house over in Sugar Hill. She went back into the kitchen where Portia was sitting at the table with her hands up to her face.

'I got this sudden notion he went down to your house. Help us hunt him.'

'How come[3] I didn't think of that! I bet a nickel my little scared Bubber been staying in my home all the time.'

Mister Brannon had borrowed an automobile. He and Mister Singer and Mick's Dad got into the car with her and Portia. Nobody knew what Bubber was feeling except her. Nobody knew he had really run away[4] like he was escaping to save his life.

Portia's house was dark except for the checkered[5] moonlight

---

① 参考译文：现在他肯定跑了。像巴伯这么聪明的孩子，谁也不知道到哪里才能找到他。it was no telling... 表示“无法判断……”。

② alley：大街小巷

③ how come：为什么；怎么会。用于疑问句及反问句。

④ run away：逃跑

⑤ checkered：多变的；斑驳的

on the floor. As soon as they stepped inside they could tell there was nobody in the two rooms. Portia lighted the front lamp. The rooms had a colored smell, and they were crowded with cut-out pictures on the walls and the lace table covers and lace pillows on the bed. Bubber was not there.

'He been here,' Portia suddenly said. 'I can tell somebody been in here.'

Mister Singer found the pencil and piece of paper on the kitchen table. He read it quickly and then they all looked at it. The writing was round and scraggly① and the smart little kid hadn't misspelled② but one word. The note said:

Dear Portia,

I gone to Florada. Tell every body.

Yours truly,

Bubber Kelly

They stood around surprised and stumped. Her Dad looked out the doorway and picked his nose with his thumb in a worried way. They were all ready to pile in the car and ride toward the highway leading south.

'Wait a minute,' Mick said. 'Even if Bubber is seven years old he's got brains enough not to tell us where he's going if he wants to run away.③ That about Florida is just a trick④.'

'A trick?' her Dad said.

'Yeah. There only two places Bubber knows very much about. One is Florida and the other is Atlanta. Me and Bubber and Ralph have been on the Atlanta road many a time. He knows how to start

① scraggly：散乱的

② misspell：拼错

③ 参考译文：巴伯尽管只有七岁，但他很聪明，如果真要逃跑的话，他不会告诉我们他要跑到哪里去。本句原文使用 enough...not to 来表示巴伯信中说自己去佛罗里达的不可信。

④ trick：花招，诡计，骗局

there and that's where he's headed. He always talks about what he's going to do when he gets a chance to go to Atlanta.'

They went out to the automobile again. She was ready to climb into the back seat when Portia pinched[①] her on the elbow[②]. 'You know what Bubber done?' she said in a quiet voice. 'Don't you tell nobody else, but my Bubber done also taken my gold earrings off my dresser[③]. I never thought my Bubber would have done such a thing to me.'

Mister Brannon started the automobile. They rode slow, looking up and down the streets for Bubber, headed toward the Atlanta road.

It was true that[④] in Bubber there was a tough, mean[⑤] streak[⑥]. He was acting different today than he had ever acted before. Up until now he was always a quiet little kid who never really done anything mean. When anybody's feelings were hurt it always made him ashamed and nervous. Then how come he could do all the things he had done today?

They drove very slow out the Atlanta road. They passed the last line of houses and came to the dark fields and woods. All along they had stopped to ask if anyone had seen Bubber. 'Has a little barefooted[⑦] kid in corduroy knickers been by this way?' But even after they had gone about ten miles nobody had seen or noticed him. The wind came in cold and strong from the open windows and it was late at night. They rode[⑧] a little farther and then went back toward town. Her Dad and Mister Brannon wanted to look up all the children in the second grade, but she made them turn around and go back on the

---

① pinch：捏，拧

② elbow：肘部

③ dresser：梳妆台

④ It is true that：确实……，例：It is true that I am lucky enough to meet a good tutor. 我能遇见一位好导师，确实是幸运的。

⑤ mean：吝啬的；刻薄的

⑥ streak：（尤指不好的）性格特征

⑦ barefooted：光着脚的（等于 barefoot）

⑧ ride：搭乘

Atlanta road again. All the while she remembered[1] the words she had said to Bubber. About Baby being dead and Sing Sing and Warden Lawes. About the small electric chairs that were just his size, and Hell. In the dark the words had sounded terrible.

They rode very slow for about half a mile out of town, and then suddenly she saw Bubber. The lights of the car showed him up in front of them very plain. It was funny. He was walking along the edge of the road and he had his thumb[2] out trying to get a ride. Portia's butcher knife was stuck in his belt, and on the wide, dark road he looked so small that it was like he was five years old instead of seven.

They stopped the automobile and he ran to get in. He couldn't see who they were, and his face had the squint-eyed look it always had when he took aim with a marble[3]. Her Dad held him by the collar. He hit with his fists[4] and kicked. Then he had the butcher knife in his hand. Their Dad yanked[5] it away from him just in time. He fought like a little tiger in a trap[6], but finally they got him into the car. Their Dad held him in his lap on the way home and Bubber sat very stiff, not leaning against anything.

They had to drag him into the house, and all the neighbors and the boarders were out to see the commotion. They dragged him into the front room and when he was there he backed off into a corner, holding his fists very tight and with his squinted eyes looking from one person to the other like he was ready to fight the whole crowd.[7]

He hadn't said one word since they came into the house until he began to scream: 'Mick done it! I didn't do it Mick done it!'

There were never any kind of yells like the ones Bubber made. The veins in his neck stood out and his fists were hard as little rocks.

---

① remember：记得
② thumb：拇指
③ marble：大理石
④ fist：拳头
⑤ yank：猛地一拉
⑥ trap:（捕捉动物的）陷阱
⑦ 参考译文：他们把他拖进前屋，到了屋里，他退缩到角落里，紧攥着拳头，眯起眼睛，挨个儿看着屋里的人，好像随时要对抗整个人群。（squinted：斜视的）

'You can't get me! Nobody can get me!' he kept yelling.

Mick shook him by the shoulder. She told him the things she had said were stories. He finally knew what she was saying but he wouldn't hush[1]. It looked like nothing could stop that screaming.

'I hate everybody! I hate everybody!'

They all just stood around. Mister Brannon rubbed his nose and looked down at the floor. Then finally he went out very quietly. Mister Singer was the only one who seemed to know what it was all about. Maybe this was because he didn't hear that awful noise. His face was still calm, and whenever Bubber looked at him he seemed to get quieter. Mister Singer was different from any other man, and at times like this it would be better if other people would let him manage. He had more sense and he knew things that ordinary[2] people couldn't know. He just looked at Bubber, and after a while the kid quieted down[3] enough so that their Dad could get him to bed.

In the bed he lay on his face and cried. He cried with long, big sobs that made him tremble all over. He cried for an hour and nobody in the three rooms could sleep. Bill moved to the living-room sofa and Mick got into bed with Bubber. He wouldn't let her touch him or snug up to him. Then after another hour of crying and hiccoughing he went to sleep.

She was awake a long time. In the dark she put her arms around him and held him very close. She touched him all over and kissed him everywhere. He was so soft and little and there was this salty, boy smell about him.[4] The love she felt was so hard that she had to squeeze him to her until her arms were tired. In her mind she thought about Bubber and music together. It was like she could never do anything good enough for him. She would never hit him or even

① hush：安静，停止说话

② ordinary：普通的

③ quiet down：安静下来

④ 参考译文：他那么柔软，那么小，身上散发着男孩子的那种咸味。

tease[1] him again. She slept all night with her arms around his head. Then in the morning when she woke up he was gone.

But after that night there was not much of a chance for her to tease him any more—her or anybody else. After he shot Baby the kid was not ever like little Bubber again. He always kept his mouth shut and he didn't fool around with anybody. Most of the time he just sat in the back yard or in the coal house by himself. It got closer and closer toward Christmas time. She really wanted a piano, but naturally[2] she didn't say anything about that. She told everybody she wanted a Micky Mouse watch. When they asked Bubber what he wanted from Santa Claus he said he didn't want anything. He hid his marbles and jack-knife[3] and wouldn't let anyone touch his story books.

After that night nobody called him Bubber any more. The big kids in the neighborhood started calling him Baby-Killer Kelly. But he didn't speak much to any person and nothing seemed to bother him. The family called him by his real name—George. At first Mick couldn't stop calling him Bubber and she didn't want to stop. But it was funny how after about a week she just naturally called him George like the others did. But he was a different kid—George—going around by himself always like a person much older and with nobody, not even her, knowing what was really in his mind.[4]

She slept with him on Christmas Eve night. He lay in the dark without talking. 'Quit acting so peculiar[5],' she said to him. 'Less talk about the wise men and the way the children in Holland put out their wooden shoes instead of hanging up their stockings.'

George wouldn't answer. He went to sleep.

---

① tease：取笑；戏弄

② naturally：自然地

③ jack-knife：折叠刀

④ 参考译文：但这个孩子——乔治——变了，他总是独来独往，老气横秋的样子，没有人知道他脑子里在想什么，即便是她，也是如此。本句原文插入表达较多，拆分理解后再整合即可。

⑤ peculiar：奇怪的，不寻常的

She got up at four o'clock in the morning and waked everybody in the family. Their Dad built a fire in the front room and then let them go into the Christmas tree and see what they got. George had an Indian suit and Ralph a rubber doll. The rest of the family just got clothes. She looked all through her stocking for the Mickey Mouse watch but it wasn't there. Her presents were a pair of brown Oxford shoes and a box of cherry candy. While it was still dark she and George went out on the sidewalk and cracked nigger-toes and shot firecrackers① and ate up the whole two-layer box of cherry② candy. And by the time it was daylight they were sick to the stomach and tired out. She lay down③ on the sofa. She shut her eyes and went into the inside room.

---

① firecrackers：鞭炮，爆竹（firecracker 的复数）

② cherry：樱桃

③ lie down：躺下

6

AT eight o'clock doctor Copeland sat at his desk, studying a sheaf of papers by the bleak morning light from the window. Beside him the tree, a thick-fringed cedar[①], rose up dark and green to the ceiling[②]. Since the first year he began to practice he had given an annual party on Christmas Day, and now all was in readiness.[③] Rows of benches and chairs lined the walls of the front rooms. Throughout[④] the house there was the sweet spiced odor of newly baked cake and steaming coffee. In the office with him Portia sat on a bench against the wall, her hands cupped[⑤] beneath her chin[⑥], her body bent almost double.

'Father, you been scrooched over the desk since five o'clock. You got no business to be up. You ought to stayed in bed until time for the to-do.'

Doctor Copeland moistened[⑦] his thick lips with his tongue. So much was on his mind that he had no attention to give to Portia. Her presence fretted[⑧] him.

At last he turned to her irritably. 'Why do you sit there moping?'

'I just got worries,' she said. 'For one thing, I worried about our

---

① cedar：雪松；香柏；西洋杉木

② ceiling：天花板

③ 参考译文：自执业第一年起，他每年圣诞节都会办一次聚会，现在一切准备就绪。（in readiness：准备就绪）

④ throughout：自始至终；遍及

⑤ cup：（双手）捧，窝成杯状托住

⑥ chin：下巴

⑦ moisten：弄湿

⑧ fret：（使）焦躁

Willie.'

'William?'

'You see he been writing me regular ever Sunday. The letter will get here on Monday or Tuesday. But last week he didn't write. Course I not really anxious. Willie—he always so good-natured and sweet I know he going to be all right. He been transferred[1] from the prison to the chain gang and they going to work up somewhere north of Atlanta. Two weeks ago he wrote this here letter to say they going to attend a church service today, and he done asked me to send him his suit of clothes and his red tie.'

'Is that all William said?'

'He written that this Mr. B. F. Mason is at the prison, too. And that he run into Buster Johnson—he a boy Willie used to know. And also he done asked me to please send him his harp because he can't be happy without he got his harp[2] to play on. I done sent everthing. Also a checker set and a white-iced cake. But I sure hope I hears from him in the next few days.'

Doctor Copeland's eyes glowed with fever and he could not rest his hands. 'Daughter, we shall have to discuss this later. It is getting late and I must finish here. You go back to the kitchen and see that all is ready.'

Portia stood up and tried to make her face bright and happy. 'What you done decided about that five-dollar prize[3]?'

'As yet I have been unable to decide just what is the wisest course,' he said carefully.

A certain friend of his, a Negro pharmacist, gave an award of five dollars every year to the high-school student who wrote the

① transfer：转移
② harp：竖琴
③ prize：奖品，奖励

best essay on a given subject.[1] The pharmacist always made Doctor Copeland sole[2] judge of the papers and the winner was announced[3] at the Christmas party. The subject of the composition this year was 'My Ambition: How I Can Better the Position of the Negro Race in Society. 'There was only one essay worthy of real consideration. Yet this paper was so childish[4] and ill-advised that it would hardly be prudent to confer upon it the award. Doctor Copeland put on his glasses and re-read the essay with deep concentration.

This is my ambition[5]. First I wish to attend Tuskegee College but I do not wish to be a man like Booker Washington[6] or Doctor Carver[7]. Then when I deem that my education is complete I wish to start off being a fine lawyer like the one who defended the Scottsboro Boys[8]. I would only take cases for colored people against white people. Every day our people are made in every way and by every means to feel that they are inferior[9]. This is not so. We are a Rising Race. And we cannot sweat beneath the white man's burdens for long. We cannot always sow where others reap.

I want to be like Moses, who led the children of Israel from the land of the oppressors[10]. I want to get up a Secret Organization of Colored Leaders and Scholars. All colored people will organize under

---

① 参考译文：他的一个朋友是位黑人药剂师，每年都会提供五块钱的奖金，奖励命题作文中写得最好的高中生。本句原文主语为双重所有格结构，并跟随同位语进行补充说明；而宾语student后跟随定语从句。（given：给定的）

② sole：唯一的

③ announce：宣布，公布

④ childish：幼稚的，孩子气的

⑤ ambition：野心，抱负

⑥ Booker Washington：布克·华盛顿，美国政治家、教育家和作家，1890年到1915年间美国黑人历史上的重要人物之一，曾任阿拉巴马州塔斯基吉学院（现塔斯基吉大学）校长。

⑦ Doctor Carver：卡弗博士，全名乔治·华盛顿·卡弗，美国教育家、农业化学家、植物学家。他于1896年获得硕士学位后，应布克·华盛顿之邀，前往阿拉巴马州塔斯基吉学院主持新设立的农业系。

⑧ Scottsboro Boys：斯科茨伯勒男孩（案件），1931年3月，9名黑人男孩经过亚拉巴马州被控强奸了两名搭乘同列货车的白人女孩。这一事件是美国民权运动的一大前兆，并导致了美国最高法院两个里程碑式的裁决，从而加强了所有美国人的基本权利，即“平等的法律保护”。

⑨ inferior：下等的

⑩ oppressor：压制者，压迫者

the direction of these picked leaders and prepare for revolt[1]*. Other nations in the world who are interested in the plight of our race and who would like to see the United States divided would come to our aid.*[2] *All colored people will organize and there will be a revolution, and at the close colored people will take up all the territory*[3] *east of the Mississippi and south of the Potomac. I shall set up a mighty country under the control of the Organization of Colored Leaders and Scholars. No white person will be allowed a passport—and if they get into the country they will have no legal rights.*

I hate the whole white race and will work always so that the colored race can achieve revenge[4] *for all their sufferings. That is my ambition.*

Doctor Copeland felt the fever warm in his veins. The ticking of the clock on his desk was loud and the sound jarred his nerves. How could he give the award to a boy with such wild notions as this? What should he decide?

The other essays were without any firm content at all. The young people would not think. They wrote only about their ambitions and omitted the last part of the tide altogether. Only one point was of some significance. Nine out of the lot of twenty-five began with the sentence, 'I do not want to be a servant[5].' After that they wished to fly airplanes, or be prizefighters[6], or preachers or dancers. One girl's sole ambition was to be kind to the poor.

The writer of the essay that troubled him was Lancy Davis. He had known the identity of the author before he turned the last sheet over and saw the signature. Already he had some trouble with Lancy.

---

① revolt：反抗；起义

② 参考译文：世界上的其他国家，如果他们关注我们民族的困境，愿意看到美国分裂，那么他们就会来帮助我们。（plight：困境；come to one's aid：帮助某人）

③ territory：领土，领域

④ revenge：报复，报仇

⑤ servant：仆人，佣人；雇工

⑥ prizefighter：职业拳击手

His older sister had gone out to work as a servant when she was eleven years old and she had been raped by her employer, a white man past middle age. Then a year or so later he had received an emergency[①] call to attend Lancy.

Doctor Copeland went to the filing case in his bedroom where he kept notes on all of his patients. He took out the card marked 'Mrs. Dan Davis and Family' and glanced through the notations until he reached Lancy's name. The date was four years ago. The entries on him were written with more care than the others and in ink: 'thirteen years old—past puberty[②]. Unsuccessful attempt self-emasculation. Oversexed and hyperthyroid[③]. Wept boisterously[④] during two visits, though little pain. Voluble—very glad to See Lucy Davis—mother washerwoman. Intelligent talk through paranoiac[⑤]. Environment fair with one exception[⑥] and well worth watching and all possible help. Keep contact. Fee: $1 (?)'

'It is a difficult decision to make this year,' he said to Portia.'But I suppose I will have to confer the award on Lancy Davis.'

'If you done decide, then—come tell me about some of these here presents.'

The gifts to be distributed at the party were in the kitchen. There were paper sacks of groceries[⑦] and clothing, all marked with a red Christmas card. Anyone who cared to come was invited to the party, but those who meant to attend had stopped by the house and written (or had asked a friend to write) their names in a guest book kept on the table in the hall for that purpose.[⑧] The sacks were piled on the

① emergency：紧急情况；突发事件
② puberty：青春期
③ hyperthyroid：甲状腺机能亢进的
④ boisterously：吵闹地；喧闹地
⑤ paranoiac：偏执狂患者；妄想狂者
⑥ exception：例外
⑦ grocery：杂货
⑧ 参考译文：愿意来的人都接到邀请参加聚会，但想来参加聚会的客人之前已经来过这里，在走廊桌子上专门的会客簿上写下了（或请朋友代写）自己的名字。（stop by：顺便访问；for that purpose：专用的）

floor. There were about forty of them, each one depending in size on the need of the receiver. Some gifts were only small packages of nuts or raisins and others were boxes almost too heavy for a man to lift. The kitchen was crowded with good things. Doctor Copeland stood in the doorway and his nostrils① quivered with pride.

'I think you done right well this year. Folks certainly have been kindly.'

'Pshaw!' he said. This is not a hundredth part of what is needed.'

'Now, there you go, Father! I know good and well you just as pleased as you can be. But you don't want to show it. You got to find something to grumble② about. Here we haves about four pecks of peas, twenty sacks of meal about fifteen pounds of side meat, mullet, six dozen eggs, plenty grits, jars of tomatoes and peaches. Apples and two dozen oranges. Also garments③. And two mattresses④ and four blankets. I call this something!'

'A drop in the bucket.'

Portia pointed to a large box in the corner. These here—what you intend to do with them?'

The box contained nothing but junk—a headless doll, some duty lace, a rabbit skin. Doctor Copeland scrutinized each article. 'Do not throw them away. There is use for everything. These are the gifts from our guests who have nothing better to contribute. I will find some purpose for them later.'

'Then suppose you look over these here boxes and sacks so I can commence to tie them up. There ain't going to be room here in the kitchen. Time they all pile in⑤ for the refreshments⑥. I just going to put these here presents out on the back steps and in the yard.'

---

① nostril：鼻孔

② grumble：抱怨；嘟囔

③ garment：服装，衣着

④ mattress：床垫

⑤ pile in：挤进，挤入

⑥ refreshment：小食，点心

The morning sun had risen. The day would be bright and cold. In the kitchen there were rich, sweet odors. A dishpan of coffee was on the stove and iced cakes filled a shelf in the cupboard.

'And none of this comes from white people. All from colored.'

'No,' said Doctor Copeland. 'That is not wholly true. Mr. Singer contributed a check for twelve dollars to be used for coal. And I have invited him to be present today.'

'Holy Jesus!' Portia said. 'Twelve dollars!'

'I felt that it was proper to ask him. He is not like other people of the Caucasian race.'

'You right,' Portia said. 'But I keep thinking about my Willie. I sure do wish he could enjoy this here party today. And I sure do wish I could get a letter from him. It just prey on my mind. But here! Us got to quit this here talking and get ready. It mighty near time for the party to come.'

Time enough remained. Doctor Copeland washed and clothed himself carefully. For a while he tried to rehearse what he would say when the people had all come.① But expectation and restlessness would not let him concentrate②. Then at ten o'clock the first guests arrived and within half an hour they were all assembled.

'Joyful Christmas to you!' said John Roberts, the postman. He moved happily about the crowded room, one shoulder held higher than the other, mopping his face with a white silk handkerchief.

'Many happy returns of the day!'

The front of the house was thronged. Guests were blocked at the door and they formed groups on the front porch and in the yard. There was no pushing or rudeness; the turmoil③ was orderly. Friends called out to each other and strangers were introduced and clasped

① 参考译文：有一阵子，他想练习一下人们都来了之后他要说的话。（rehearse：排练，预演）

② concentrate：集中；全神贯注

③ turmoil：混乱，骚动

hands.[①] Children and young people clotted[②] together and moved back toward the kitchen.

'Christmas gift!'

Doctor Copeland stood in the center of the front room by the tree. He was dizzy. He shook hands and answered salutations[③] with confusion[④]. Personal gifts, some tied elaborately with ribbons and others wrapped in newspapers, were thrust[⑤] into his hands. He could find no place to put them. The air thickened and voices grew louder. Faces whirled about him so that he could recognize no one. His composure[⑥] returned to him gradually. He found space to lay aside the presents in his arms. The dizziness[⑦] lessened, the room cleared. He settled his spectacles and began to look around him.

'Merry Christmas! Merry Christmas!'

There was Marshall Nicolls, the pharmacist, in a long-tailed coat, conversing with his son-in-law who worked on a garbage truck. The preacher from the Most Holy Ascension Church had come. And two deacons from other churches. Highboy, wearing a loud checked suit, moved sociably through the crowd. Husky young dandies[⑧] bowed to young women in long, bright-colored dresses. There were mothers with children and deliberate old men who spat into gaudy handkerchiefs. The room was warm and noisy.

Mr. Singer stood in the doorway. Many people stared at him. Doctor Copeland could not remember if he had welcomed him or not. The mute stood by himself. His face resembled[⑨] somewhat a

---

① 参考译文：朋友们彼此喊着名字，陌生人被介绍认识，然后握手。（introduce：介绍；clasp hands：紧紧地握手）

② clot：（血或乳脂）凝结成块，此处指人"聚集"。

③ salutation：称呼，问候

④ confusion：困惑

⑤ thrust：塞进（过去式及过去分词均为 thrust，文中为过去分词）

⑥ composure：镇静；沉着

⑦ dizziness：头晕；头昏眼花

⑧ dandy：好打扮的男子；花花公子

⑨ resemble：像，类似

picture of Spinoza[①]. A Jewish face. It was good to see him.

The doors and the windows were open. Draughts blew through the room so that the fire roared. The noises quieted. The seats were all filled and the young people sat in rows on the floor. The hall, the porch, even the yard were crowded with silent guests. The time had come for him to speak—and what was he to say? Panic tightened[②] his throat. The room waited. At a sign from John Roberts all sounds were hushed.

'My People,' began Doctor Copeland blankly[③]. There was a pause[④]. Then suddenly the words came to him.

'This is the nineteenth year that we have gathered together in this room to celebrate Christmas Day. When our people first heard of the birth of Jesus Christ it was a dark time. Our people were sold as slaves in this town on the courthouse[⑤] square. Since then we have heard and told the story of His life more times than we could remember. So today our story will be a different one.

'One hundred and twenty years ago another man was born in the country that is known as Germany—a country far across the Atlantic Ocean. This man understood as did Jesus. But his thoughts were not concerned with Heaven or the future of the dead. His mission was for the living. For the great masses of human beings who work and suffer and work until they die. For people who take in washing and work as cooks, who pick cotton and work at the hot dye vats of the factories.[⑥] His mission was for us, and the name of this man was Karl Marx.

'Karl Marx was a wise man. He studied and worked and

① Spinoza：斯宾诺莎（1632—1677），被称作"近代最伟大的犹太人和最伟大的哲学家"，近代西方哲学的三大理性主义者之一，与笛卡尔和莱布尼茨齐名。此处说辛格的脸宛若一张斯宾诺莎像，表现出科普兰医生眼中辛格的智慧形象。

② tighten：（使）变紧

③ blankly：茫然地；毫无表情地

④ pause：暂停

⑤ courthouse：法院

⑥ 参考译文：他的使命是为了活着的人，为了那些工作、受苦、工作一直到死的劳苦大众，为了那些以洗衣、做饭为工作的人们。本句原文用几个 for 小分句说明"使命"，翻译时则使用中文习惯的排比表达。（mass：民众）

understood the world around him. He said that the world was divided into two classes, the poor and the rich. For every rich man there were a thousand poor people who worked for this rich man to make him richer. He did not divide the world into Negroes or white people or Chinese—to Karl Marx it seemed that being one of the millions of poor people or one of the few rich was more important to a man than the color of his skin.① The life mission of Karl Marx was to make all human beings equal and to divide the great wealth of the world so that there would be no poor or rich and each person would have his share. This is one of the commandments② Karl Marx left to us: "From each according to his ability, to each according to his needs."'

A wrinkled③, yellow palm waved timidly from the hall. Were he the Mark in the Bible?'

Doctor Copeland explained. He spelled the two names and cited dates. 'Are there any more questions? I wish each one of you to feel free to start or enter into any discussion.'

'I presume Mr. Marx was a Christian church man?' asked the preacher.

'He believed in the holiness④ of the human spirit'

'Were he a white man?'

'Yes. But he did not think of himself as a white man. He said, "I consider nothing human as alien to myself." He thought of himself as a brother to all people.'

Doctor Copeland paused a moment longer. The faces around him were waiting.

'What is the value of any piece of property, of any merchandise⑤ we buy in a store? The value depends only on one thing—and that

---

① 参考译文：他没有把世界分成黑人、白人或中国人——对卡尔·马克思而言，一个人是成为数百万的穷人之一还是成为少数的富人之一，这似乎比他的肤色更重要。本句其实是描述马克思对资本的观点。

② commandment：戒律，法令

③ wrinkled：有皱纹的

④ holiness：神圣

⑤ merchandise：商品；货物

is the work it took to make or to raise this article. Why does a brick house cost more than a cabbage? Because the work of many men goes into the making of one brick house. There are the people who made the bricks and mortar and the people who cut down[①] the trees to make the planks used for the floor. There are the men who made the building of the brick house possible. There are the men who carried the materials to the ground where the house was to be built. There are the men who made the wheelbarrows[②] and trucks that carried the materials to this place. Then finally there are the workmen who built the house. A brick house involves the labor of many, many people—while any of us can raise a cabbage in his back yard. A brick house costs more than a cabbage because it takes more work to make. So when a man buys this brick house he is paying for the labor that went to make it. But who gets the money—the profit[③]? Not the many men who did the work—but the bosses who control them. And if you study this further you will find that these bosses have bosses above them and those bosses have bosses higher up—so that the real people who control all this work, which makes any article worth money, are very few.[④] Is this clear so far?'

'Us understand!'

But did they? He started all over and retold what he had said. This time there were questions.

'But don't clay for these here bricks cost money? And don't it take money to rent land and raise crops on?'

'That is a good point,' said Doctor Copeland. 'Land, clay, timber—those things are called natural resources. Man does not make these natural resources—man only develops them, only uses them for

---

① cut down：削减；砍倒

② wheelbarrow：独轮手推车

③ profit：利润；利益

④ 参考译文：你如果进一步仔细研究一下这件事，你会发现，老板上面又有老板，上面还有更大的老板——因此，劳动生产出有价值的物品，而控制这种劳动的人是极少数。本句原文中 so that 引导结果状语从句，而在该从句中又嵌套了两个定语从句，即限制性定语从句修饰 people，非限制性定语从句修饰 work。

work. Therefore should any one person or group of persons own these things? How can a man own ground and space and sunlight and rain for crops? How can a man say "this is mine" about those things and refuse to let others share them? Therefore Marx says that these natural resources should belong to everyone, not divided into little pieces but used by all the people according to their ability to work. It is like this. Say a man died and left his mule to his four sons. The sons would not wish to cut up the mule to four parts and each take his share. They would own and work the mule together. That is the way Marx says all of the natural resources should be owned—not by one group of rich people but by all the workers of the world as a whole.①

'We in this room have no private properties②. Perhaps one or two of us may own the homes we live in, or have a dollar or two set aside③—but we own nothing that does not contribute directly toward keeping us alive. All that we own is our bodies. And we sell our bodies every day we live. We sell them when we go out in the morning to our jobs and when we labor all day. We are forced to sell at any price, at any time, for any purpose. We are forced to sell our bodies so that we can eat and live. And the price which is given us for this is only enough so that we will have the strength to labor longer for the profits of others. Today we are not put up on the platforms④ and sold at the courthouse⑤ square. But we are forced to sell our strength, our time, our souls during almost every hour that we live. We have been freed from one kind of slavery⑥ only to be delivered into another. Is this freedom? Are we yet free men?'

A deep voice called out from the front yard. 'That the real truth! '

---

① 参考译文：按照马克思的观点，人们拥有自然资源也应该这样——不是归一群富人所有，而是全世界所有工人们作为一个整体去拥有它。本句原文中 Marx says 为定语从句作为插入语，表示是马克思提出的人们拥有自然资源的方式。

② property：所有物，财产

③ set aside：节省，存储

④ platform：平台；讲台

⑤ courthouse：法院

⑥ slavery：奴役；奴隶制度；奴隶身份

'That how things is!'

'And we are not alone in this slavery. There are millions of others throughout the world, of all colors and races and creeds[①]. This we must remember. There are many of our people who hate the poor of the white race, and they hate us. The people in this town living by the river who work in the mills. People who are almost as much in need as we are ourselves. This hatred is a great evil, and no good can ever come from it. We must remember the words of Karl Marx and see the truth according to his teachings. The injustice[②] of need must bring us all together and not separate us. We must remember that we all make the things of this earth of value because of our labor.[③] These main truths from Karl Marx we must keep in our hearts always and not forget.

'But my people! We in this room—we Negroes—have another mission that is for ourselves alone. Within us there is a strong, true purpose, and if we fail in this purpose we will be forever lost. Let us see, then, what is the nature of this special mission.

Doctor Copeland loosened the collar of his shirt, for in his throat there was a choked feeling. The grievous[④] love he felt within him was too much. He looked around him at the hushed guests. They waited. The groups of people in the yard and on the porch stood with the same quiet attention as did those in the room. A deaf old man leaned forward with his hand to his ear. A woman hushed a fretful baby with a pacifier[⑤]. Mr. Singer stood attentively in the doorway. Most of the young people sat on the floor. Among them was Lancy Davis. The boy's lips were nervous and pale. He clasped his knees very tightly with his arms, and his young face was sullen. All the eyes in the room

---

① creed：宗教信仰

② injustice：不公正；不讲道义

③ 参考译文：我们必须牢记，我们都是通过劳动在这个世界上制造着有价值的东西。（of value：有价值的）

④ grievous：剧烈的

⑤ pacifier：安抚奶嘴

watched, and in them there was hunger for truth.

'Today we are to confer[①] the five-dollar award upon the high-school student who wrote the best essay on the topic, "My Ambition: How I can Better the Position of the Negro Race in Society." This year the award goes to Lancy Davis.' Doctor Copeland took an envelope from his pocket. 'There is no need for me to tell you that the value of this award is not wholly in the sum of money it represents—but the sacred trust and faith that goes with it.[②]'

Lancy rose awkwardly[③] to his feet. His sullen lips trembled. He bowed and accepted the award. 'Do you wish me to read the essay I have written?'

'No,' said Doctor Copeland. 'But I wish you to come and talk with me sometime this week.'

'Yes, sir.' The room was quiet again.

'"I do not wish to be a servant!" That is the desire I have read over and over in these essays. Servant? Only one in a thousand of us is allowed to be a servant. We do not work! We do not serve!'

The laughter in the room was uneasy.

'Listen! One out of five of us labors to build roads, or to take care of the sanitation[④] of this city, or works in a sawmill[⑤] or on a farm. Another one out of the five is unable to get any work at all. But the other three out of this five—the greatest number of our people? Many of us cook for those who are incompetent[⑥] to prepare the food that they themselves eat. Many work a lifetime tending[⑦] flower gardens for the pleasure of one or two people. Many of us polish slick waxed

---

① confer：授予，给予

② 参考译文：我无须再告诉大家，这个奖项的价值不仅仅在于奖金的数目——而是其代表的神圣真理和信念。（sacred：神圣的）

③ awkwardly：笨拙地

④ sanitation：环境卫生

⑤ sawmill：锯木厂

⑥ incompetent：无能力的，不胜任的

⑦ tend：照料，照管

floors of fine houses.[①] Or we drive automobiles for rich people who are too lazy to drive themselves. We spend our lives doing thousands of jobs that are of no real use to anybody. We labor and all of our labor is wasted. Is that service? No, that is slavery.

We labor, but our labor is wasted. We are not allowed to serve. You students here this morning represent the fortunate few of our race. Most of our people are not allowed to go to school at all. For each one of you there are dozens of young people who can hardly write their names. We are denied the dignity of study and wisdom.

"From each according to his ability, to each according to his needs." All of us here know what it is to suffer for real need. That is a great injustice. But there is one injustice bitterer even than that—to be denied[②] the right to work according to one's ability. To labor a lifetime uselessly. To be denied the chance to serve. It is far better for the profits of our purse to be taken from us than to be robbed of the riches of our minds and souls.

Some of you young people here this morning may feel the need to be teachers or nurses or leaders of your race. But most of you will be denied. You will have to sell yourselves for a useless purpose in order to keep alive. You will be thrust back and defeated. The young chemist picks cotton. The young writer is unable to learn to read. The teacher is held in useless slavery at some ironing board. We have no representatives in government. We have no vote. In all of this great country we are the most oppressed[③] of all people. We cannot lift up our voices. Our tongues rot in our mouths from lack of use. Our hearts grow empty and lose strength for our purpose.

People of the Negro race! We bring with us all the riches of the human mind and soul. We offer the most precious of all gifts. And our

---

① 参考译文：很多人在豪华的房子里擦亮打过蜡的地板。本句原文 slick 实际是宾语 floor 的补语，但因 floor 受到修饰后较冗长，为避免头重脚轻，将 slick 调整到宾语前。（slick：光滑的；waxed：打过蜡的）

② deny：拒绝，否认

③ oppressed：受压迫的

offerings are held in scorn and contempt[①]. Our gifts are trampled[②] in the mud and made useless. We are put to labor more useless than the work of beasts. Negroes! We must arise and be whole again! We must be free!'

In the room there was a murmur. Hysteria mounted. Doctor Copeland choked and clenched[③] his fists. He felt as though he had swelled up to the size of a giant. The love in him made his chest a dynamo[④], and he wanted to shout so that his voice could be heard throughout the town. He wanted to fall upon the floor and call out in a giant voice. The room was full of moans and shouts.

'Save us!'

'Mighty Lord! Lead us from this wilderness[⑤] of death! '

'Hallelujah! Save us, Lord!'

He struggled for the control in him. He struggled and at last the discipline returned. He pushed down the shout in him and sought for the strong, true voice.

'Attention!' he called. 'We will save ourselves. But not by prayers of mourning. Not by indolence[⑥] or strong drink. Not by the pleasures of the body or by ignorance. Not by submission[⑦] and humbleness. But by pride. By dignity[⑧]. By becoming hard and strong. We must build strength for our real true purpose.'

He stopped abruptly and held himself very straight. 'Each year at this time we illustrate[⑨] in our small way the first commandment from Karl Marx. Every one of you at this gathering has brought in advance some gift. Many of you have denied yourselves comfort that the needs

---

① contempt：轻视，蔑视
② trample：踩，践踏
③ clench：紧握
④ dynamo：发电机（使胸膛变成发电机，即使胸膛充满力量的意思。）
⑤ wilderness：荒野
⑥ indolence：懒散
⑦ submission：服从；谦恭
⑧ dignity：尊严
⑨ illustrate：阐明

of others may be lessened[1]. Each of you has given according to his best ability, without thought to the value of the gift he will receive in return.[2] It is natural for us to share with each other. We have long realized that it is more blessed to give than to receive. The words of Karl Marx have always been known in our hearts: "From each according to his ability, to each according to his needs."

Doctor Copeland was silent a long time as though his words were complete. Then he spoke again:

'Our mission is to walk with strength and dignity through the days of our humiliation[3]. Our pride must be strong, for we know the value of the human mind and soul. We must teach our children. We must sacrifice so that they may earn the dignity of study and wisdom. For the time will come. The time will come when the riches in us will not be held in scorn and contempt.[4] The time will come when we will be allowed to serve. When we will labor and our labor will not be wasted. And our mission is to await this time with strength and faith.'

It was finished. Hands were clapped, feet were stamped upon the floor and en the hard winter ground outside. The odor of hot, strong coffee floated from the kitchen. John Roberts took charge of the presents, calling out the names written on the cards. Portia ladled the coffee from the dish-pan on the stove while Marshall Nicolls passed slices of cake. Doctor Copeland moved about among the guests, a little crowd always surrounding him.

Someone nagged[5] at his elbow: 'He the one your Buddy named for?' He answered yes. Lancy Davis followed him with questions; he answered yes to everything. The joy made him feel like a drunken

---

① lessen：减少

② 参考译文：你们每个人都尽了自己最大的能力，从来没想过将来会得到什么价值的礼物回报。（in return：作为回报）

③ humiliation：丢脸，耻辱

④ 参考译文：这个时刻终究会到来。我们心里的财富将不再被蔑视和嗤之以鼻。when 引导同位语从句修饰 time，表示……的时代终究会到来。（scorn：蔑视，轻视；contempt：嗤之以鼻的态度）

⑤ nag：使烦恼，此处表示有人碰了碰科普兰医生的胳膊。

man. To teach and exhort[1] and explain to his people—and to have them understand. That was the best of all. To speak the truth and be attended.

'Us certainly have had one fine time at this party.'

He stood in the vestibule[2] saying goodbye. Over and over he shook hands. He leaned heavily against the wall and only his eyes moved, for he was tired.

'I certainly do appreciate.[3]'

Mr. Singer was the last to leave. He was a truly good man. He was a white man of intellect and true knowledge. In him there was none of the mean insolence. When all had departed he was the last to remain. He waited and seemed to expect some final word.

Doctor Copeland held his hand to his throat because his larynx was sore. 'Teachers,' he said huskily. 'That is our greatest need. Leaders. Someone to unite and guide us.'

After the festivity the rooms had a bare, ruined look. The house was cold. Portia was washing the cups in the kitchen. The silver snow on the Christmas tree had been tracked[4] over the floors and two of the ornaments[5] were broken.

He was tired, but the joy and the fever would not let him rest. Beginning with the bedroom, he set to work to put the house in order. On the top of the filing case there was a loose card—the note on Lancy Davis. The words that he would say to him began to form in his mind, and he was restless[6] because he could not speak them now. The boy's sullen face was full of heart and he could not thrust it from his thoughts. He opened the top drawer of the file to replace the card, A, B, C—he thumbed through the letters nervously. Then his eye was

---

① exhort：忠告；劝诫

② vestibule：前厅；门廊

③ 参考译文：我当然明白。本句助动词 do 是对 appreciate 的强调，助动词 do/does/did 用于动词前表示对动作行为的强调。（appreciate：领会，理解）

④ track：跟踪，追踪

⑤ ornament：装饰品

⑥ restless：焦躁不安的

fixed on his own name: Copeland, Benedict Mady.

In the folder were several lung X-rays and a short case history. He held an X-ray up to the light. On the upper left lung there was a bright place like a calcified[①] star. And lower down a large clouded spot that duplicated[②] itself in the right lung farther up. Doctor Copeland quickly replaced the X-rays in the folder. Only the brief notes he had written on himself were still in his hand. The words stretched out large and scrawling[③] so that he could hardly read them. '1920—calcif. of lymph glands—very pronounced thickening of hili. Lesions arrested—duties resumed. 1937—lesion reopened—X-ray shows—[④]' He could not read the notes. At first he could not make out the words, and then when he read them clearly they made no reason. At the finish there were three words: 'Prognosis[⑤]: Don't know.'

The old black, violent feeling came in him again. He leaned down and wrenched[⑥] open a drawer at the bottom of the case. A jumbled[⑦] pile of letters. Notes from the Association for the Advancement of Colored People. A yellowed letter from Daisy. A note from Hamilton asking for a dollar and a half. What was he looking for? His hands rummaged[⑧] in the drawer and then at last he arose stiffly.

Time wasted. The past hour gone.

Portia peeled potatoes at the kitchen table. She was slumped over and her face was dolorous.

'Hold up your shoulders,' he said angrily. 'And cease moping. You mope and drool around until I cannot bear to look on you.'

---

① calcified：钙化的；石灰化的

② duplicate：复制；复印；（使）成倍增加

③ scrawl：马马虎虎（或潦草）地写

④ 参考译文：一九二〇年——淋巴结钙化——淋巴结明显增厚，病变已得到控制——功能恢复。一九三七年——病变复发——X 光片显示——。（lymph gland：淋巴腺，淋巴结；lesion：损伤，病变）

⑤ prognosis：（尤指对病人能否康复的）预后，预断

⑥ wrench：猛拉

⑦ jumbled：乱七八糟的

⑧ rummage：到处翻寻

‘I were just thinking about Willie,’ she said. ‘Course the letter is only three days due. But he got no business to worry me like this. He not that kind of a boy. And I got this queer feeling.’

‘Have patience, Daughter.’

‘I reckon I have to.’

‘There are a few calls I must make, but I will be back shortly.’

‘O.K.’

All will be well,’ he said.

Most of his joy was gone in the bright, cool noonday sun. The diseases of his patients lay scattered in his mind. An abscessed kidney. Spinal meningitis①. Pott’s disease. He lifted the crank of the automobile from the back seat. Usually he hailed some passing Negro from the street to crank the car for him. His people were always glad to help and serve. But today he fitted the crank and turned it vigorously② himself. He wiped the perspiration③ from his face with the sleeve of his overcoat and hurried to get beneath the wheel and on his way.

How much that he had said today was understood? How much would be of any value? He recalled the words he had used, and they seemed to fade and lose their strength. The words left unsaid were heavier on his heart. They rolled up to his lips and fretted④ them. <u>The faces of his suffering people moved in a swelling mass before his eyes.</u>⑤ And as he steered the automobile slowly down the street his heart turned with this angry, restless love.

---

① meningitis：脑膜炎

② vigorously：精神旺盛地，活泼地

③ perspiration：汗水

④ fret：使烦恼，使发愁

⑤ 参考译文：他眼前浮现出同胞们遭受苦难的面孔，这些面孔越来越多。本句原文主语为“面孔”，但在翻译中将主语变为人，即“他”（科普兰医生），而这些面孔以“肿胀的数量”出现（in a swelling mass），即翻译为这些面孔“越来越多。”

7

THE town had not known a winter as cold as this one for years[1]. Frost[2] formed on the windowpanes and whitened the roofs of houses. The winter afternoons glowed with a hazy lemon light and shadows were a delicate blue. A thin coat of ice crusted[3] the puddles[4] in the streets, and it was said on the day after Christmas that only ten miles to the north there was alight fall of snow.

A change came over Singer. Often he went out for the long walks that had occupied him during the months when Antonapoulos was first gone. These walks extended for miles in every direction and covered the whole of the town. He rambled through the dense neighborhoods along the river that were more squalid[5] than ever since the mills had been slack[6] this winter. In many eyes there was a look of somber loneliness. Now that people were forced to be idle, a certain restlessness could be felt. There was a fervid outbreak of new beliefs. A young man who had worked at the dye vats in a mill claimed suddenly that a great holy power had come in him.[7] He said it was his duty to deliver a new set of commandments from the Lord, The young man

① for years：好几年
② frost：严寒天气，冰冻；霜
③ crust：形成（或结成）硬皮（或硬壳）
④ puddle：（尤指雨水积成的）水坑
⑤ squalid：肮脏的
⑥ slack：懈怠
⑦ 参考译文：一个在工厂染缸处工作的年轻人突然宣布，他具有了一种伟大的神圣力量。（dye vat：染缸）

set up a tabernacle and hundreds of people came each night to roll on the ground and shake each other, for they believed that they were in the presence of something more than human.[①] There was murder, too. A woman who could not make enough to eat believed that a foreman had cheated on her work tokens and she stabbed[②] him in the throat. A family of Negroes moved into the end house on one of the most dismal streets, and this caused so much indignation that the house was burned and the black man beaten by his neighbors. But these were incidents. Nothing had really changed. The strike that was talked about never came off because they could not get together. All was the same as before. Even on the coldest nights the Sunny Dixie Show was open. The people dreamed and fought and slept as much as ever. And by habit they shortened their thoughts so that they would not wander out into the darkness beyond tomorrow.[③]

Singer walked through the scattered odorous parts of town where the Negroes crowded together. There was more gaiety[④] and violence here. Often the fine, sharp smell of gin lingered in the alleys. Warm, sleepy firelight colored the windows. Meetings were held in the churches almost every night. Comfortable little houses set off in plots[⑤] of brown grass—Singer walked in these parts also. Here the children were huskier and more friendly to strangers. He roamed[⑥] through the neighborhoods of the rich. There were houses very grand and old, with white columns[⑦] and intricate[⑧] fences of wrought iron. He walked past the big brick houses where automobiles honked in

① 参考译文：年轻人建起一个神龛，每天晚上都有成百上千人过来。他们在地上打滚，彼此摇晃，他们认为自己面对的是一个超人类的东西。本句原文为长句，为表达流畅，译文分割为两个分句。（in the presence of：在……面前，面对）

② stab：刺

③ 参考译文：出于习惯，他们简化了自己的思想，这样他们便不会迷失在明日之后的黑暗中了。（by habit：出于习惯）

④ gaiety：快乐；庆祝活动

⑤ plot：小块土地

⑥ roam：漫游，漫步

⑦ column：圆形支柱

⑧ intricate：复杂的

the driveways and where the plumes of smoke rolled lavishly from chimneys.[①] And out to the very edges of the roads that led from the town to general stores where fanners came on Saturday nights and sat around the stove. He wandered often about the four main business blocks that were brightly lighted and then through the black, deserted[②] alleys behind. There was no part of the town that Singer did not know. He watched the yellow squares of light reflect from a thousand windows. The winter nights were beautiful. The sky was a cold azure[③] and the stars were very bright.

Often it happened now that he would be spoken to and stopped during these walks. All kinds of people became acquainted with him. If the person who spoke to him was a stranger, Singer presented his card so that his silence would be understood. He came to be known through all the town. He walked with his shoulders very straight and kept his hands always stuffed[④] down into his pockets. His gray eyes seemed to take in everything around him, and in his face there was still the look of peace that is seen most often in those who are very wise or very sorrowful. He was always glad to stop with anyone wishing his company. For after all he was only walking and going nowhere.

Now it came about that various rumors started in the town concerning the mute. In the years before with Antonapoulos they had walked back and forth[⑤] to work, but except for this they were always alone together in their rooms. No one had bothered about them then—and if they were observed it was the big Greek on whom attention was focused. The Singer of those years was forgotten.

So the rumors about the mute were rich and varied. The Jews said that he was a Jew. The merchants along the main street claimed he

---

① 参考译文：他走过那些高大的砖房子，汽车在门前车道上鸣着喇叭，烟囱里不断地飘出一股股烟。本句原文由两个并列定语从句修饰“高大的砖房子”。（chimney：烟囱）

② deserted：荒芜的

③ azure：天蓝色

④ stuff：塞进（stuffed 为过去分词表被动）

⑤ back and forth：来回移动或交换，例：The children were running back and forth between the two trees. 孩子们在两棵树之间来回奔跑。

received a large legacy[①] and was a very rich man. It was whispered in one browbeaten textile union that the mute was an organizer for the C.I.O.[②] A lone Turk who had roamed into the town years ago and who languished with his family behind the little store where they sold linens claimed passionately to his wife that the mute was Turkish.[③] He said that when he spoke his language the mute understood. And as he claimed this his voice grew warm and he forgot to squabble[④] with his children and he was full of plans and activity. One old man from the country said that the mute had come from somewhere near his home and that the mute's father had the finest tobacco crop in all the country. All these things were said about him.

Antonapoulos! Within Singer there was always the memory of his friend. At night when he closed his eyes the Greek's face was there in the darkness—round and oily, with a wise and gentle smile. In his dreams they were always together.

It was more than a year now since his friend had gone away. This year seemed neither long nor short. Rather it was removed from the ordinary sense of time—as when one is drunk or half-asleep. Behind each hour there was always his friend. And this buried life with Antonapoulos changed and developed as did the happenings around him. During the first few months he had thought most of the terrible weeks before Antonapoulos was taken away—of the trouble that followed his illness, of the summons for arrest, and the misery in

---

① legacy：遗产

② 参考译文：一个被打压的纺织联盟里则有人背地里说，哑巴是美国产业组织委员会的组织者。（browbeat：威逼，恫吓）

③ 参考译文：好几年前，一个孤单的土耳其人流落到镇上，跟家人一起开了家小店，靠卖家庭日用织品艰难度日，他跟妻子情绪激昂地说哑巴是土耳其人。本句原文是一个多重的复合句，由两个 who 引导的并列定语从句修饰主语 Turk，第二个定语从句中，又由一个 where 引导的定语从句修饰 store；谓语 claim 后则跟随宾语从句。（passionately：热情地）

④ squabble：（为琐事）发生口角，大声争吵

trying to control the whims of his friend.[①] He thought of times in the past when he and Antonapoulos had been unhappy. There was one recollection[②], far in the past, that came back to him several times.

They never had no friends.[③] Sometimes they would meet other mutes—there were three of them with whom they became acquainted during the ten years. But something always happened. One moved to another state the week after they met him. Another was married and had six children and did not talk with his hands. But it was their relation with the third of these acquaintances that Singer remembered when his friend was gone.[④]

The mute's name was Carl. He was a sallow young man who worked in one of the mills. His eyes were pale yellow and his teeth so brittle[⑤] and transparent[⑥] that they seemed pale and yellow also. In his blue overalls[⑦] that hung limp over his skinny little body he was like a blue-and-yellow rag doll.

They invited him to dinner and arranged to meet him beforehand at the store where Antonapoulos worked. The Greek was still busy when they arrived. He was finishing a batch of caramel fudge in the cooking room at the back of the store. The fudge lay golden and glossy[⑧] over the long marble-topped table. The air was warm and rich with sweet smells. Antonapoulos seemed pleased to have Carl watch him as he glided[⑨] the knife down the warm candy and cut it into squares. He offered their new friend a corner of the fudge[⑩] on

---

① 参考译文：在最初几个月里，他经常想起安东纳普勒斯被带走之前那几个糟糕的星期——想起他生病之后的麻烦事，想起逮捕的传票，想起努力控制好友异想天开时所经历的痛苦。本句原文由多个并列的宾语组成，由介词 of 连接。（whim：突发的念头）

② recollection：回忆

③ 参考译文：他们没有朋友。此处有误，应为“They never had friends.”

④ 参考译文：但在好友离开之后，辛格记得最清楚的是与第三个哑巴熟人的关系。此处为 it was...that... 强调句，并嵌入 when 引导的时间状语从句。

⑤ brittle：易碎的，脆弱的

⑥ transparent：透明的

⑦ overalls：工装裤；工作裤（复数形式）

⑧ glossy：光滑的；有光泽的

⑨ glide：滑动

⑩ fudge：乳脂软糖

the edge of his greased knife, and showed him the trick that he always performed for anyone when he wished to be liked. He pointed to a vat of syrup boiling on the stove and fanned his face and squinted his eyes to show how hot it was. Then he wet his hand in a pot of cold water, plunged it into the boiling syrup, and swiftly put it back into the water again. His eyes bulged and he rolled out his tongue as though he were in great agony. He even wrung[①] his hand and hopped on one foot so that the building shook. Then he smiled suddenly and held out his hand to show that it was a joke and hit Carl on the shoulder.

It was a pale winter evening, and their breath clouded in the cold air as they walked with their arms interlocked down the street. Singer was in the middle and he left them on the sidewalk twice while he went into stores to shop. Carl and Antonapoulos carried the sacks of groceries, and Singer held to their arms tightly and smiled all the way home. Their rooms were cozy[②] and he moved happily about. making conversation with Carl. After the meal the two of them talked while Antonapoulous watched with a slow smile. Often the big Greek would lumber to the closet and pour out drinks of gin. Carl sat by the window, only drinking when Antonapoulos pushed the glass into his face, and then taking solemn[③] little sips. Singer could not ever remember his friend so cordial[④] to a stranger before, and he thought ahead with pleasure to the time when Carl would visit them often.

Midnight had passed when the thing happened that ruined the festive party. Antonapoulos returned from one of his trips to the closet and his face had a glowering look. He sat on his bed and began to stare repeatedly at their new friend with expressions of offense and great disgust[⑤]. Singer tried to make eager conversation to hide this strange

---

① wring：拧
② cozy：舒适的
③ solemn：严肃的；郑重的
④ cordial：热情友好的
⑤ disgust：厌恶，嫌恶

behavior, but the Greek was persistent. Carl huddled[1] in a chair, nursing his bony knees, fascinated and bewildered[2] by the grimaces of the big Greek. His face was flushed[3] and he swallowed timidly[4]. Singer could ignore the situation no longer, so at last he asked Antonapoulos if his stomach pained him or if he perhaps felt bad and wished to go to sleep. Antonapoulos shook his head. He pointed to Carl and began to make all the gestures of obscenity which he knew. The disgust on his face was terrible to see. Carl was small with fear. At last the big Greek ground his teeth and rose from his chair. Hurriedly Carl picked up his cap and left the room. Singer followed him down the stairs. He did not know how to explain his friend to this stranger. Carl stood hunched[5] in the doorway downstairs, limp[6], with his peaked cap[7] pulled down over his face. At last they shook hands and Carl went away.

Antonapoulos let him know that while they were not noticing, their guest had gone into the closet and drunk up all the gin. No amount of persuasion could convince Antonapoulos that it was he himself who had finished the bottle. The big Greek sat up in bed and his round face was dismal[8] and reproachful[9]. Large tears trickled slowly down to the neck of his undershirt and he could not be comforted. At last he went to sleep, but Singer was awake in the dark a long time. They never saw Carl again.

Then years later there was the time Antonapoulos took the rent money from the vase on the mantelpiece and spent it all on the slot machines. And the summer afternoon Antonapoulos went downstairs naked to get the paper. He suffered so from the summer

---

① huddle：挤成一团
② bewildered：困惑的
③ flushed：脸红的
④ timidly：羞怯地
⑤ hunch：弯腰驼背
⑥ limp：不直挺的，无精神的
⑦ peaked cap：尖顶帽，鸭舌帽
⑧ dismal：忧郁的
⑨ reproachful：（表情或话语）责备的；责怪的

heat. They bought an electric refrigerator on the installment plan, and Antonapoulos would suck the cubes of ice constantly and even let a few of them melt in bed with him as he slept. And the time Antonapoulos got drunk and threw a bowl of macaroni[①] in his face.

Those ugly memories wove through his thoughts during the first months like bad threads through a carpet. And then they were gone. All the times that they had been unhappy were forgotten. For as the year went on his thoughts of his friend spiraled[②] deeper until he dwelt only with the Antonapoulos whom he alone could know.

This was the friend to whom he told all that was in his heart. This was the Antonapoulos who no one knew was wise but him. As the year passed his friend seemed to grow larger in his mind, and his face looked out in a very grave and subtle way from the darkness at night. The memories of his friend changed in his mind so that he remembered nothing that was wrong or foolish—only the wise and good.

He saw Antonapoulos sitting in a large chair before him. He sat tranquil[③] and unmoving. His round face was inscrutable[④]. His mouth was wise and smiling. And his eyes were profound[⑤]. He watched the things that were said to him. And in his wisdom he understood.

This was the Antonapoulos who now was always in his thoughts. This was the friend to whom he wanted to tell things that had come about. For something had happened in this year. He had been left in an alien land. Alone. He had opened his eyes and around him there was much he could not understand. He was bewildered[⑥].

He watched the words shape on their lips.

---

① macaroni：通心粉；通心面条
② spiral：盘旋；螺旋形上升
③ tranquil：平静的
④ inscrutable：神秘的，难以理解的
⑤ profound：深邃的
⑥ bewilder：使困惑

We Negroes want a chance to be free at last. And freedom is only the right to contribute. We want to serve and to share, to labor and in turn consume that which is due to us. But you are the only white man I have ever encountered[1] who realizes this terrible need of my people.

You see, Mister Singer? I got this music in me all the time. I got to be a real musician. Maybe I don't know anything now, but I will when I'm twenty. See, Mister Singer? And then I mean to travel in a foreign country where there's snow.

Let's finish up the bottle. I want a small one. For we were thinking of freedom. That's the word like a worm in my brain. Yes? No? How much? How little? The word is a signal for piracy[2] and theft and cunning. We'll be free and the smartest will then be able to enslave the others. But! But there is another meaning to the word. Of all words this one is the most dangerous. We who know must be wary[3]. The word makes us feel good—in fact the word is a great ideal. But it's with this ideal that the spiders spin their ugliest webs for us.

The last one rubbed his nose. He did not come often and he did not say much. He asked questions.

The four people had been coming to his rooms now for more than seven months. They never came together—always alone. And invariably[4] he met them at the door with a cordial smile. The want for Antonapoulos was always with him—just as it had been the first months after his friend had gone—and it was better to be with any person than to be too long alone.[5] It was like the time years ago when he had made a pledge[6] to Antonapoulos (and even written it on a paper and tacked it on the wall above his bed)—a pledge that he would

---

① encounter：遇到；遭遇

② piracy：剽窃

③ wary：谨慎的

④ invariably：总是；不变地

⑤ 参考译文：对安东纳普勒斯的想念一直伴随着他——跟好友走后最初的那几个月一样——跟其他人在一起总比长时间一个人待着强得多。

⑥ pledge：保证，誓言

give up cigarettes, beer, and meat for one month. The first days had been very bad. He could not rest or be still. He visited Antonapoulos so much at the fruit store that Charles Parker was unpleasant to him. When he had finished all the engraving① on hand he would dawdle around the front of the store with the watchmaker and the salesgirl or wander out to some soda fountain② to drink a Coca-Cola. In those days being near any stranger was better than thinking alone about the cigarettes and beer and meat that he wanted.

At first he had not understood the four people at all. They talked and they talked—and as the months went on they talked more and more. He became so used to their lips that he understood each word they said. And then after a while he knew what each one of them would say before he began, because the meaning was always the same.

His hands were a torment③ to him. They would not rest. They twitched④ in his sleep, and sometimes he awoke to find them shaping the words in his dreams before his face. He did not like to look at his hands or to think about them. They were slender and brown and very strong. In the years before he had always tended them with care. In the winter he used oil to prevent⑤ chapping, and he kept the cuticles pushed down and his nails always filed to the shape of his finger-tips. He had loved to wash and tend his hands. But now he only scrubbed⑥ them roughly with a brush two times a day and stuffed them back into his pockets.

When he walked up and down the floor of his room he would crack the joints of his fingers and jerk at them until they ached. Or he would strike the palm of one hand with the fist of the other. And then

---

① engraving：雕刻
② fountain：喷泉，泉水
③ torment：痛苦，苦恼；痛苦的根源
④ twitch：（使）抽搐，痉挛
⑤ prevent：阻止，避免（prevent doing sth.：避免做某事）
⑥ scrub：擦洗，揉搓

sometimes when he was alone and his thoughts were with his friend his hands would begin to shape the words before he knew about it. Then when he realized he was like a man caught talking aloud to himself, it was almost as though he had done some moral wrong. The shame and the sorrow mixed together and he doubled his hands and put them behind him. But they would not let him rest.

Singer stood in the street before the house where he and Antonapoulos had lived. The late afternoon was smoky and gray. In the west there were streaks of cold yellow and rose. A ragged winter sparrow① flew in patterns against the smoky sky and at last came to light on② a gable③ of the house. The street was deserted.

His eyes were fixed on a window on the right side of the second story. This was then front room, and behind was the big kitchen where Antonapoulos had cooked all their meals. Through the lighted window he watched a woman move back and forth across the room. She was large and vague④ against the light and she wore an apron. A man sat with the evening newspaper in his hand. A child with a slice of bread came to the window and pressed his nose against the pane. Singer saw the room just as he had left it—with the large bed for Antonapoulos and the iron cot for himself, the big overstuffed⑤ sofa and the camp chair⑥. The broken sugar bowl used for an ash tray, the damp spot on the ceiling where the roof leaked, the laundry box in the corner. On late afternoons like this there would be no light in the kitchen except the glow from the oil-burners of the big stove. Antonapoulos always turned the wicks⑦ so that only a ragged fringe of gold and blue could be seen inside each burner. The room was warm

---

① sparrow：麻雀
② light on：停落于
③ gable：山墙，三角墙
④ vague：模糊的；含糊的；不明确的
⑤ overstuffed：垫得又软又厚的
⑥ camp chair：轻便折椅
⑦ wick：灯芯，烛心

and full of the good smells from the supper. Antonapoulos tasted the dishes with his wooden spoon and they drank glasses of red wine. On the linoleum[①] rug before the stove the flames from the burners made luminous reflections—five little golden lanterns. As the milky twilight grew darker these little lanterns were more intense, so that when at last the night had come they burned with vivid purity.[②] Supper was always ready by that time and they would turn on the light and draw their chairs to the table.

Singer looked down at the dark front door. He thought of them going out together in the morning and coming home at night. There was the broken place in the pavement where Antonapoulos had stumbled once and hurt his elbow. There was the mailbox where their bill from the light company came each month. He could feel the warm touch of his friend's arm against his fingers.

The street was dark now. He looked up at the window once more and he saw the strange woman and the man and the child in a group together. The emptiness spread in him. All was gone. Antonapoulos was away; he was not here to remember. The thoughts of his friend were somewhere else. Singer shut his eyes and tried to think of the asylum[③] and the room that Antonapoulos was in tonight. He remembered the narrow white beds and the old men playing slapjack in the corner. He held his eyes shut tight, but that room would not become clear in his mind. The emptiness was very deep inside him, and after a while he glanced up at the window once more and started down the dark sidewalk where they had walked together so many times.

It was Saturday night. The main street was thick with people. Shivering Negroes in overalls loitered[④] before the windows of the ten-

① linoleum：油布；油毯

② 参考译文：乳白色的暮色渐浓，这些小灯笼便愈发明显起来，夜晚终于降临的时候，它们便欢快地燃烧着，非常清晰。（milky：乳白色的；twilight：黄昏，暮色；purity：纯净；纯粹）

③ asylum：收容所

④ loiter：虚度；闲荡

cent store. Families stood in line before the ticket box of the movie and young boys and girls stared at the posters on display outside. The traffic from the automobiles was so dangerous that he had to wait a longtime before crossing the street.

He passed the fruit store. The fruits were beautiful inside the windows—bananas, oranges, alligator pears[①], bright little cumquats[②], and even a few pineapples. But Charles Parker waited on a customer inside. The face of Charles Parker was very ugly to him. Several times when Charles Parker was away he had entered the store and stood around a long while. He had even gone to the kitchen in the back where Antonapoulos made the candies. But he never went into the store while Charles Parker was inside. They had both taken care to avoid each other since that day when Antonapoulos left on the bus. When they met in the street they always turned away without nodding. Once when he had wanted to send his friend a jar of his favorite tupelo honey he had ordered it from Charles Parker by mail so as not to be obliged to meet him.

Singer stood before the window and watched the cousin of his friend wait on a group of customers. Business was always good on Saturday night. Antonapoulos sometimes had to work as late as ten o'clock. The big automatic popcorn popper was near the door. A clerk shoved in a measure of kernels and the corn whirled inside the case like giant flakes of snow. The smell from the store was warm and familiar. Peanut hulls were trampled[③] on the floor.

Singer passed on down the street. He had to weave his way carefully in the crowds to keep from being jostled[④]. The streets were strung with red and green electric lights because of the holidays. People stood in laughing groups with their arms about each other. Young fathers nursed cold and crying babies on their shoulders. A

---

① alligator pear：鳄梨（同 avocado）
② cumquat：金橘（同 kumquat）
③ trample：踩伤；践踏
④ jostle：推挤，撞

Salvation Army girl in her red-and-bluebonnet tinkled[1] a bell on the corner, and when she looked at Singer he felt obliged to drop a coin into the pot beside her. There were beggars, both Negro and white, who held out caps or crusty[2] hands. The neon advertisements cast an orange glow on the faces of the crowd.

He reached the corner where he and Antonapoulos had once seen a mad dog on an August afternoon. Then he passed the room above the Army and Navy Store where Antonapoulos had had his picture taken every pay-day[3]. He carried many of the photographs in his pocket now. He turned west toward the river. Once they had taken a picnic lunch and crossed the bridge and eaten in a field on the other side.

Singer walked along the main street for about an hour. In all the crowd he seemed the only one alone. At last he took out his watch and turned toward the house where he lived. Perhaps one of the people would come this evening to his room. He hoped so.

He mailed Antonapoulos a large box of presents for Christmas. Also he presented gifts to each of the four people and to Mrs. Kelly. For all of them together he had bought a radio and put it on the table by the window. Doctor Copeland did not notice the radio. Biff Brannon noticed it immediately and raised his eyebrows. Jake Blount kept it turned on all the time he was there, at the same station, and as he talked he seemed to be shouting above the music, for the veins stood out on his forehead.[4] Mick Kelly did not understand when she saw the radio. Her face was very red and she asked him over and over if it was really his and whether she could listen. She worked with a

① tinkle：发叮当（或清脆）声

② crusty：易怒的

③ pay-day：发薪日

④ 参考译文：杰克·布朗特只要在这里，便会一直开着收音机，总是听同一个台。他说话的时候，似乎在大声喊叫着好压过音乐声，额头上青筋暴突。本句原文由两个并列句组成，在第二个并列句中，含一个 as 引导的时间状语从句及 for 引导的原因状语从句。

dial for several minutes before she got it to the place that suited her. She sat leaning forward in her chair with her hands on her knees, her mouth open and a pulse① beating very fast in her temple②. She seemed to listen all over to whatever it was she heard. She sat there the whole afternoon, and when she grinned③ at him once her eyes were wet and she rubbed them with her fists. She asked him if she could come in and listen sometimes when he was at work and he nodded yes. So for the next few days whenever he opened the door he found her by the radio. Her hand raked through her short rumpled④ hair and there was a look in her face he had never seen before.

One night soon after Christmas all four of the people chanced to visit him at the same time. This had never happened before. Singer moved about the room with smiles and refreshments and did his best in the way of politeness to make his guests comfortable. But something was wrong.

Doctor Copeland would not sit down. He stood in the doorway, hat in hand, and only bowed coldly to the others. They looked at him as though they wondered why he was there. Jake Blount opened the beers he had brought with him and the foam spilled down on his shirtfront⑤. Mick Kelly listened to the music from the radio. Biff Brannon sat on the bed, his knees crossed, his eyes scanning⑥ the group before him and then becoming narrow and fixed.

Singer was bewildered. Always each of them had so much to say. Yet now that they were together they were silent. When they came in he had expected an outburst of some kind. In a vague way he had expected this to be the end of something. But in the room there was only a feeling of strain. His hands worked nervously as though they

① pulse：律动
② temple：太阳穴
③ grin：露齿而笑，咧着嘴笑
④ rumpled：凌乱的；弄皱的
⑤ shirtfront：衬衫的胸部；胸衣
⑥ scan：扫视，浏览

were pulling things unseen from the air and binding them together.

Jake Blount stood beside Doctor Copeland. 'I know your face. We ran into each other once before—on the steps outside.'

Doctor Copeland moved his tongue precisely as though he clipped out his words with scissors. 'I was not aware that we were acquainted,' he said. Then his stiff body seemed to shrink.① He stepped back until he was just outside the threshold of the room.

Biff Brannon smoked his cigarette composedly②. The smoke lay in thin layers across the room. He turned to Mick and when he looked at her a blush reddened his face. He half-closed his eyes and in a moment his face was bloodless once more. 'And how are you getting on you're your business now?'

'What business?' Mick asked suspiciously③.

'Just the business of living,' he said. 'School—and so forth.'

'O.K., I reckon,' she said.

Each one of them looked at Singer as though in expectation④. He was puzzled. He offered refreshments⑤ and smiled.

Jake rubbed his lips with the palm of his hand. He left off trying to make conversation with Doctor Copeland and sat down on the bed beside Biff. 'You know who it is that used to write those bloody warnings in red chalk on the fences and walls around the mills?'

'No,' Biff said. 'What bloody warnings?'

'Mostly from the Old Testament I been wondering about that for a long time.'

Each person addressed⑥ his words mainly to the mute. Their thoughts seemed to converge in⑦ him as the spokes⑧ of a wheel lead

---

① shrink：（使）缩小，减少
② composedly：镇定地
③ suspiciously：怀疑地
④ in expectation：期待中
⑤ refreshment：茶点，点心
⑥ address：向……讲话
⑦ converge in：汇聚，集中于
⑧ spoke：辐条

to the center hub.

'The cold has been very unusual,' Biff said finally. The other day I was looking through some old records and I found that in the year 1919 the thermometer① got down to ten degrees Fahrenheit②.'It was only sixteen degrees this morning, and that's the coldest since the big freeze that year.'

'There were icicles hanging off the roof of the coal house this morning,' Mick said.

'We didn't take in enough money last week to meet the payroll③,' Jake said.

They discussed the weather some more. Each one seemed to be waiting for the others to go. Then on an impulse④ they all rose to leave at the same time. Doctor Copeland went first and the others followed him immediately. When they were gone Singer stood alone in the room, and as he did not understand the situation he wanted to forget it. He decided to write to Antonapoulos that night.

The fact that Antonapoulos could not read did not prevent Singer from writing to him. He had always known that his friend was unable to make out the meaning of words on paper, but as the months went by he began to imagine that perhaps he had been mistaken, that perhaps Antonapoulos only kept his knowledge of letters a secret from everyone.⑤ Also, it was possible there might be a deaf-mute at the asylum who could read his letters and then explain them to his friend. He thought of several justifications⑥ for his letters, for he always felt

① thermometer：温度计

② Fahrenheit：华氏温度，符号 F，单位是℉，1724 年，德国人华伦海特制定了华氏温标。他把纯水的冰点温度定为 32 ℉，把标准大气压下水的沸点温度定为 212 ℉，中间分为 180 等份，每一等份代表 1 度，这就是华氏温标。摄氏温度 (C) 与华氏温度 (F) 的换算式是：C = 5 × (F-32)/9，F = 9 × C /5+32。

③ payroll：工资单；在册职工人数；工资名单；工资

④ impulse：冲动；刺激；神经冲动

⑤ 参考译文：他一直知道好友弄不懂纸面上那些词的意思，但几个月过去了，他开始想，也许自己弄错了，也许安东纳普勒斯只是不想让别人知道自己是识字的。(make out：理解)

⑥ justification：理由；辩护

a great need to write to his friend when he was bewildered or sad. Once written, however, these letters were never mailed. He cut out the comic strips[①] from the morning and evening papers and sent them to his friend each Sunday. And every month he mailed a postal money order. But the long letters he wrote to Antonapoulos accumulated[②] in his pockets until he would destroy them.

When the four people had gone, Singer slipped on his warm gray overcoat and his gray felt hat and left his room. He always wrote his letters at the store. Also, he had promised to deliver a certain piece of work the next morning, and he wanted to finish it now so that there would be no question of delay. The night was sharp and frosty. The moon was full and rimmed[③] with a golden light. The rooftops were black against the starlit[④] sky. As he walked he thought of ways to begin his letter, but he had already reached the store before the first sentence was clear in his mind. He let himself into the dark store with his key and switched on the front lights.

He worked at the very end of the store. A cloth curtain separated his place from the rest of the shop so that it was like a small private room. Besides his workbench and chair there was a heavy safe in the corner, a lavatory[⑤] with a greenish mirror, and shelves full of boxes and worn-out clocks. Singer rolled up the top of his bench and removed from its felt case the silver platter he had promised to have ready. Although the store was cold he took off his coat and turned up the blue-striped cuffs of his shirt so that they would not get in his way.

For a long time he worked at the monogram[⑥] in the center of the platter[⑦]. With delicate, concentrated strokes he guided the scriber on

① comic strip：连环漫画
② accumulate：积累；积聚
③ rim：形成边缘
④ starlit：星光照耀的
⑤ lavatory：厕所，盥洗室
⑥ monogram：花押字（常由姓名首字母组成，标在自己的衣服等物品上）
⑦ platter：大平盘

the silver.[1] As he worked his eyes had a curiously penetrating[2] look of hunger. He was thinking of his letter to his friend Antonapoulos. Midnight had passed before the work was finished. When he put the platter away his forehead was damp with excitement. He cleared his bench and began to write. He loved to shape words with a pen on paper and he formed the letters with as much care as if the paper had been a plate of silver.

My Only Friend:

I see from our magazine that the Society meets this year at a convention in Macon. They will have speakers and a four-course banquet. I imagine it. Remember we always planned to attend one of the conventions but we never did. I wish now that we had. I wish we were going to this one and I have imagined how it would be. But of course I could never go without you. They will come from many states and they will all be full of words and long dreams from the heart. There is also to be a special service at one of the churches and some kind of a contest with a gold medal for the prize.[3] *I write that I imagine all this. I both do and do not. My hands have been still so long that it is difficult to remember how it is. And when I imagine the convention I think of all the guests being like you, my Friend.*

I stood before our home the other day. Other people live in it now. Do you remember the big oak tree in front? The branches were cut back so as not to interfere[4] *with the telephone wires and the tree died. The limbs are rotten and there is a hollow place in the trunk. Also, the cat here at the store (the one you used to stroke and fondle) ate something poisonous and died. It was very sad.*

---

① 参考译文：他集中精力，用刻刀在银器上小心翼翼地移动着。

② penetrating：尖锐的；有洞察力的

③ 参考译文：在一个教堂里还会举办一次特别仪式，进行一种什么竞赛，获奖的人会得到一枚金牌。（service：仪式）

④ interfere：干涉，干扰

Singer held the pen poised above the paper. He sat for a long while, erect[①] and tense, without continuing the letter. Then he stood up and lighted himself a cigarette. The room was cold and the air had a sour stale odor—the mixed smells of kerosene[②] and silver polish and tobacco. He put on his overcoat and muffler[③] and began writing again with slow determination.

You remember the four people I told you about when I was there. I drew their pictures for you, the black man, the young girl, the one with the mustache, and the man who owns the New York Café. There are some things I should like to tell you about them but how to put them in words I am not sure.[④]

They are all very busy people. In fact they are so busy that it will be hard for you to picture them. I do not mean that they work at their jobs all day and night but that they have much business in their minds always that does not let them rest. They come up to my room and talk to me until I do not understand how a person can open and shut his or her mouth so much without being weary[⑤]*. (However, the New York Café owner is different—he is not just like the others. He has a very black beard so that he has to shave twice daily, and he owns one of these electric razors*[⑥]*. He watches. The others all have something they hate. And they all have something they love more than eating or sleeping or wine or friendly company. That is why they are always so busy.)*

The one with the mustache I think is crazy. Sometimes he speaks his words very clear like my teacher long ago at the school. Other

---

① erect：竖直的，直立的
② kerosene：煤油，火油
③ muffler：围巾
④ 参考译文：关于他们的一些事情，我想跟你说说，但不知道该怎么说出来。本句由 but 连接两个并列句，第一个句子由定语从句修饰 things，第二个句子则由一个倒装的宾语从句构成，其中 how to put them in words 为宾语，而 I am not sure 才是主谓结构，用于强调宾语成分。
⑤ weary：疲惫的
⑥ razor：剃刀；刮胡刀

times he speaks such a language that I cannot follow. Sometimes he is dressed in a plain suit, and the next time he will be black with dirt and smelling bad and in the overalls he wears to work. He will shake his fist and say ugly drunken words that I would not wish you to know about. He thinks he and I have a secret together but I do not know what it is. And let me write you something hard to believe. He can drink three pints of Happy Days whiskey and still talk and walk on his feet and not wish for the bed. You will not believe this but it is true.

I rent my room from the girl's mother for $16 per month. The girl used to dress in short trousers like a boy but now she wears a blue skirt and a blouse. She is not yet a young lady. I like her to come and see me. She comes all the time now that I have a radio for them. She likes music. I wish I knew what it is she hears. She knows I am deaf but she thinks I know about music.

The black man is sick with consumption[①] *but there is not a good hospital for him to go to here because he is black. He is a doctor and he works more than anyone I have ever seen. He does not talk like a black man at all. Other Negroes I find it hard to understand because their tongues do not move enough for the words. This black man frightens me sometimes. His eyes are hot and bright. He asked me to a party and I went. He has many books. However, he does not own any mystery books. He does not drink or eat meat or attend the movies.*

Yah Freedom and pirates. Yah Capital and Democrats, says the ugly one with the mustache. Then he contradicts[②] *himself and says, Freedom is the greatest of all ideals. I just got to get a chance, to write this music in me and be a musician. I got to have a chance, says the girl. We are not allowed to serve, says the black Doctor. That is the Godlike*[③] *need for my people. Aha, says the owner of the New York Café. He is a thoughtful*[④] *one.*

---

① consumption：肺痨
② contradict：反驳；否定；与……矛盾
③ Godlike：神圣的，庄严的
④ thoughtful：深思的

*That is the way they talk when they come to my room. Those words in their heart do not let them rest, so they are always very busy. Then you would think when they are together they would be like those of the Society who meet at the convention in Macon this week. But that is not so. They all came to my room at the same time today. They sat like they were from different cities. They were even rude, and you know how I have always said that to be rude and not attend to the feelings of others is wrong. So it was like that. I do not understand, so I write it to you because I think you will understand. I have queer*① *feelings. But I have written of this matter enough and I know you are weary of it. I am also.*

It has been five months and twenty-one days now. All of that time I have been alone without you. The only thing I can imagine is when I will be with you again. If I cannot come to you soon I do not know what.

Singer put his head down on the bench and rested. The smell and the feel of the slick wood against his cheek reminded him of his schooldays. His eyes closed and he felt sick. There was only the face of Antonapoulos in his mind, and his longing for② his friend was so sharp that he held his breath. After some time Singer sat up and reached for his pen.

*The gift I ordered for you did not come in time for the Christmas box. I expect it shortly. I believe you will like it and be amused*③*. I think of us always and remember everything. I long for the food you used to make. At the New York Café it is much worse than it used to be. I found a cooked fly in my soup not long ago. It was mixed with the vegetables and the noodles like letters. But that is nothing. The*

---

① queer：奇怪的，异常的
② longing for：对……的渴望
③ amused：逗笑的，开心的

way I need you is a loneliness I cannot bear. Soon I will come again. My vacation is not due for six months more but I think I can arrange it before then. I think I will have to. I am not meant to be alone and without you who understand.

Always,

JOHN SINGER

It was two o'clock in the morning before he was home again. The big, crowded house was in darkness, but he felt his way carefully up three flights[①] of stairs and did not stumble[②]. He took from his pockets the cards he carried about with him, his watch, and his fountain pen. Then he folded his clothes neatly over the back of his chair. His gray-flannel pajamas[③] were warm and soft. Almost as soon as he pulled the blankets to his chin he was asleep.

Out of the blackness of sleep a dream formed. There were dull[④] yellow lanterns lighting up a dark flight of stone steps. Antonapoulos kneeled at the top of these steps. He was naked and he fumbled with something that he held above his head and gazed at it as though in prayer. He himself knelt halfway down the steps. He was naked and cold and he could not take his eyes from Antonapoulos and the thing he held above him. Behind him on the ground he felt the one with the mustache and the girl and the black man and the last one. They knelt naked and he felt their eyes on him. And behind them there were uncounted crowds of kneeling people in the darkness. His own hands were huge windmills[⑤] and he stared fascinated at the unknown thing that Antonapoulos held. The yellow lanterns swayed to and fro[⑥] in the darkness and all else was motionless. Then suddenly there was

---

① flight：一段（台阶或楼梯）
② stumble：踌躇，蹒跚
③ pajamas：睡衣
④ dull：不明亮的
⑤ windmill：风车
⑥ to and fro：来回；往返；反复

a ferment[1]. In the upheaval[2] the steps collapsed and he felt himself falling downward. He awoke with a jerk. The early light whitened the window. He felt afraid.

Such a long time had passed that something might have happened to his friend. Because Antonapoulos did not write to him he would not know. Perhaps his friend had fallen and hurt himself. He felt such an urge to be with him once more that he would arrange it at any cost—and immediately.

In the post-office that morning he found a notice in his box that a package had come for him. It was the gift he had ordered for Christmas that did not arrive in time. The gift was a very fine one. He had bought it on the installment plan[3] to be paid for over a period of two years. The gift was a moving-picture machine for private use, with a half-dozen of the Mickey Mouse and Popeye comedies[4] that Antonapoulos enjoyed.

Singer was the last to reach the store that morning. He handed the jeweler[5] for whom he worked a formal written request for leave on Friday and Saturday. And although there were four weddings on hand that week, the jeweler nodded that he could go.

He did not let anyone know of the trip beforehand, but on leaving he tacked a note to his door saying that he would be absent for several days because of business. He traveled at night, and the train reached the place of his destination just as the red winter dawn was breaking.

In the afternoon, a little before time for the visiting hour[6], he went out to the asylum. His arms were loaded with the parts of the moving-picture machine and the basket of fruit he carried his

① ferment：动荡，骚乱
② upheaval：激变，剧变
③ installment plan：分期付款方式
④ comedy：喜剧
⑤ jeweler：珠宝商
⑥ visiting hour：（医院、监狱的）探视时间

friend. He went immediately to the ward[①] where he had visited Antonapoulos before.

The corridor, the door, the rows of beds were just as he remembered them. He stood at the threshold and looked eagerly for his friend. But he saw at once that though all the chairs were occupied, Antonapoulos was not there.

Singer put down his packages and wrote at the bottom of one of his cards, 'Where is Spiros Antonapoulos?' A nurse came into the room and he handed her the card. She did not understand. She shook her head and raised her shoulders. He went out into the corridor and handed the card to everyone he met. Nobody knew. There was such a panic in him that he began motioning with his hands. At last he met an intern in a white coat. He plucked at[②] the intern's elbow and gave him the card. The intern read it carefully and then guided him through several halls. They came to a small room where a young woman sat at a desk before some papers. She read the card and then looked through some files in a drawer.

Tears of nervousness and fear swam in Singer's eyes. The young woman began deliberately to write on a pad of paper, and he could not restrain himself from[③] twisting around to see immediately what was being written about his friend.

Mr. Antonapoulos has been transferred[④] to the infirmary[⑤]. He is ill with nephritis[⑥]. I will have someone show you the way.

On the way through the corridors he stopped to pick up the packages he had left at the door of the ward. The basket of fruit had

---

① ward：病房；保卫；监视

② pluck at：拉住，拽住

③ restrain onself from doing sth.：控制自己不去做某事，例：Most of smokers can not restrain themselves from smoking. 大多数吸烟者都无法控制自己不吸烟。（restrain：抑制）

④ transfer：转移

⑤ infirmary：医务室；医院

⑥ nephritis：肾炎

been stolen, but the other boxes were intact. He followed the intern out of the building and across a plot of grass to the infirmary.

Antonapoulos! When they reached the proper ward he saw him at the first glance. His bed was placed in the middle of the room and he was sitting propped with pillows. He wore a scarlet dressing-gown and green silk pajamas and a turquoise[1] ring. His skin was a pale yellow[2] color, his eyes very dreamy and dark. His black hair was touched at the temples with silver. He was knitting[3]. His fat fingers worked with the long ivory needles very slowly. At first he did not see his friend. Then when Singer stood before him he smiled serenely[4], without surprise, and held out his jeweled hand.

A feeling of shyness and restraint such as he had never known before came over Singer. He sat down by the bed and folded his hands on the edge of the counterpane[5]. His eyes did not leave the face of his friend and he was deathly pale. The splendor[6] of his friend's raiment startled him. On various occasions he had sent him each article of the outfit, but he had not imagined how they would look when all combined.[7] Antonapoulos was more enormous than he had remembered. The great pulpy folds of his abdomen showed beneath his silk pajamas. His head was immense against the white pillow. The placid composure of his face was so profound[8] that he seemed hardly to be aware that Singer was with him.

Singer raised Ms hands timidly[9] and began to speak. His strong, skilled fingers shaped the signs with loving precision. He spoke of the cold and of the long months alone. He mentioned old memories, the

---

① turquoise：蓝绿色的
② pale yellow：淡黄色
③ knit：编织
④ serenely：安详地
⑤ counterpane：床罩；床单
⑥ splendor：光彩；壮丽
⑦ 参考译文：这套衣服，他是分好几次、一件件给他寄过来的，但从没想过成套穿起来会是什么样子。本句原文 when 后跟随独立结构，即省略谓语 be。
⑧ profound：深邃的，深远的
⑨ timidly：羞怯地；胆小地

cat that had died, the store, the place where he lived. At each pause Antonapoulos nodded graciously[1]. He spoke of the four people and the long visits to his room. The eyes of his friend were moist[2] and dark, and in them he saw the little rectangled pictures of himself that he had watched a thousand times. The warm blood flowed back to his face and his hands quickened. He spoke at length of the black man and the one with the jerking mustache and the girl. The designs of his hands shaped faster and faster. Antonapoulos nodded with slow gravity. Eagerly Singer leaned closer and he breathed with long, deep breaths and in his eyes there were bright tears.

Then suddenly Antonapoulos made a slow circle in the air with his plump forefinger. His finger circled toward Singer and at last he poked his friend in the stomach. The big Greek's smile grew very broad and he stuck out his fat, pink tongue. Singer laughed and his hands shaped the words with wild speed. His shoulders shook with laughter and his head hung backward. Why he laughed he did not know. Antonapoulos rolled his eyes. Singer continued to laugh riotously[3] until his breath was gone and his fingers trembled. He grasped the arm of his friend and tried to steady himself. His laughs came slow and painfully like hiccoughs[4].

Antonapoulos was the first to compose himself. His fat little feet had untucked the cover at the bottom of the bed. His smile faded and he kicked contemptuously at the blanket. Singer hastened to put things right, but Antonapoulos frowned and held up his finger regally[5] to a nurse who was passing through the ward. When she had straightened the bed to his liking the big Greek inclined his head so deliberately that the gesture seemed one of benediction[6] rather than a simple nod

---

① graciously：和蔼地
② moist：潮润的，微湿的
③ riotously：暴乱地；骚动地；放纵地
④ hiccough：打嗝
⑤ regally：像帝王地，威严地
⑥ benediction：恩赐

of thanks. Then he turned gravely to his friend again.

As Singer talked he did not realize how the time had passed. Only when a nurse brought Antonapoulos his supper on a tray did he realize that it was late. The lights in the ward were turned on and outside the windows it was almost dark. The other patients had trays of supper before them also. They had put down their work (some of them wove baskets, others did leatherwork or knitted) and they were eating listlessly[①]. Besides Antonapoulos they all seemed very sick and colorless. Most of them needed a haircut and they wore seedy gray nightshirts slit down the back. They stared at the two mutes with wonder.

Antonapoulos lifted the cover from his dish and inspected[②] the food carefully. There was fish and some vegetables. He picked up the fish and held it to the light in the palm of his hand for a thorough examination. Then he ate with relish[③]. During supper he began to point out the various people in the room. He pointed to one man in the corner and made faces of disgust. The man snarled[④] at him. He pointed to a young boy and smiled and nodded and waved his plump hand. Singer was too happy to feel embarrassment. He picked up the packages from the floor and laid them on the bed to distract his friend. Antonapoulos took off the wrappings, but the machine did not interest him at all. He turned back to his supper.

Singer handed the nurse a note explaining about the movie. She called an intern and then they brought in a doctor. As the three of them consulted they looked curiously at Singer. The news reached the patients and they propped up on their elbows excitedly. Only Antonapoulos was not disturbed.

Singer had practiced with the movie beforehand. He set up the screen so that it could be watched by all the patients. Then he worked

---

① listlessly：无精打采地
② inspect：检查；调查
③ with relish：津津有味地
④ snarl：咆哮，吼叫

with the projector[①] and the film. The nurse took out the supper trays and the lights in the ward were turned off. A Mickey Mouse comedy flashed[②] on the screen.

Singer watched his friend. At first Antonapoulos was startled. He heaved himself up for a better view and would have risen from the bed if the nurse had not restrained him. Then he watched with a beaming smile. Singer could see the other patients calling out to each other and laughing. Nurses and orderlies[③] came in from the hall and the whole ward was in commotion. When the *Mickey Mouse*[④] was finished Singer put on a *Popeye*[⑤] film. Then at the conclusion of this film he felt that the entertainment had lasted long enough for the first time. He switched on[⑥] the light and the ward settled down again. As the intern put the machine under his friend's bed he saw Antonapoulos slyly cut his eyes across the ward to be certain that each person realized that the machine was his.

Singer began to talk with his hands again. He knew that he would soon be asked to leave, but the thoughts he had stored in his mind were too big to be said in a short time. He talked with frantic haste. In the ward there was an old man whose head shook with palsy[⑦] and who picked feebly at his eyebrows. He envied the old man because he lived with Antonapoulos day after day. Singer would have exchanged places with him joyfully.

His friend fumbled for something in his bosom. It was the little brass cross that he had always worn. The dirty string had been replaced by a red ribbon. Singer thought of the dream and he told that, also,

---

① projector：投影仪；放映机；探照灯

② flash：闪现，此处指“播映”。

③ orderly：看护人，护理员

④ *Mickey Mouse*：迪士尼电影《米老鼠》。

⑤ *Popeye*：《大力水手》，是美国 1980 年罗伯特·奥特曼执导的电影，由罗宾·威廉姆斯主演，1980 年上映。故事讲述的是一个水手奇迹般的际遇。

⑥ switch on：打开

⑦ palsy：麻痹，麻痹状态；中风

to his friend. In his haste[①] the signs sometimes became blurred[②] and he had to shake his hands and begin all over. Antonapoulos watched him with his dark, drowsy eyes. Sitting motionless in his bright, rich garments he seemed like some wise king from a legend.

The interne in charge of the ward allowed Singer to stay for an hour past the visiting time. Then at last he held out his thin, hairy wrist and showed him his watch. The patients were settled for sleep. Singer's hand faltered[③]. He grasped his friend by the arm and looked intently into his eyes as he used to do each morning when they parted for work. Finally Singer backed himself out of the room. At the doorway his hands signed a broken farewell and then clenched into fists.

During the moonlit[④] January nights Singer continued to walk about the streets of the town each evening when he was not engaged[⑤]. The rumors about him grew bolder. An old Negro woman told hundreds of people that he knew the ways of spirits come back from the dead. A certain piece-worker claimed that he had worked with the mute at another mill somewhere else in the state—and the tales he told were unique. The rich thought that he was rich and the poor considered him a poor man like themselves. And as there was no way to disprove these rumors they grew marvelous[⑥] and very real. Each man described the mute as he wished him to be.

---

① in one's haste：在某人匆忙之中
② blurred：模糊不清的；记不清的
③ falter：颤抖
④ moonlit：月光照耀的
⑤ engaged：忙碌的
⑥ marvelous：非凡的；令人惊异的

8

WHY?

The Question flowed through Biff always, unnoticed, like the blood in his veins. He thought of people and of objects and of ideas and the question was in him. Midnight, the dark morning, noon. Hitler and the rumors of war. The price of loin[①] of pork and the tax on beer. Especially he meditated on the puzzle of the mute. Why, for instance, did Singer go away on the train and, when he was asked where he had been, pretend that he did not understand the question?[②] And why did everyone persist in[③] thinking the mute was exactly as they wanted him to be—when most likely it was all a very queer mistake? Singer sat at the middle table three times a day. He ate what was put before him—except cabbage and oysters[④]. In the battling tumult[⑤] of voices he alone was silent. He liked best little green soft butter beans and he stacked them in a neat pile on the prongs[⑥] of his fork. And sopped their gravy with his biscuits.

Biff thought also of death. A curious incident occurred. One day

---

① loin：腰；腰肉

② 参考译文：比如，辛格为什么会坐火车离开。而当问他去了哪里时，他为什么会假装听不懂？本句原文含插入语，加大了理解困难，但实际上先去掉插入语看主干就会发现，这句话问的是辛格为什么假装听不懂别人问他去哪里的问题。

③ persist in doing：坚持做某事，例：If you persist in doing exercise every day, you will see the results. 如果你坚持每天锻炼，你会看到效果。

④ oyster：牡蛎，蚝

⑤ tumult：骚动；骚乱

⑥ prong：尖头叉子

while rummaging[①] through the bathroom closet he found a bottle of Agua Florida that he had overlooked when taking Lucile the rest of Alice's cosmetics. Meditatively he held the bottle of perfume in his hands. It was four months now since her death—and each month seemed as long and full of leisure as a year. He seldom thought of her.

Biff uncorked the bottle. He stood shirtless before the mirror and dabbled some of the perfume on his dark, hairy armpits. The scent made him stiffen. He exchanged a deadly secret glance with himself in the mirror and stood motionless. He was stunned by the memories brought to him with the perfume, not because of their clarity, but because they gathered together the whole long span of years and were complete.[②] Biff rubbed his nose and looked sideways at himself. The boundary[③] of death. He felt in him each minute that he had lived with her. And now their life together was whole as only the past can be whole. Abruptly Biff turned away.

The bedroom was done over. His entirely now. Before it had been tacky and flossy and drab. There were always stockings and pink rayon[④] knickers with holes in them hung on a string across the room to dry. The iron bed had been flaked and rusty, decked with soiled lace boudoir pillows. A bony mouser from downstairs would arch its back and rub mournfully[⑤] against the slop jar.

All of this he had changed. He traded the iron bed for a studio couch. There was a thick red rug on the floor, and he had bought a beautiful cloth of Chinese blue to hang on the side of the wall where the cracks were worst. He had unsealed[⑥] the fireplace and kept it laid with pine logs. Over the mantel was a small photograph of Baby and

---

① rummage：翻找

② 参考译文：香水一下子带回了那些记忆，让他惊诧，并非因为这些记忆很清晰，而是因为这些记忆将所有那些漫长的岁月都汇集起来，完整地呈现出来。（stun：使震惊，stunned 在文中为过去分词，用于被动语态。）

③ boundary：边界

④ rayon：人造丝；人造纤维

⑤ mournfully：悲哀地

⑥ unseal：启封

a colored picture of a little boy in velvet holding a ball in his hands. A glassed case in the corner held the curios he had collected—specimens of butterflies, a rare arrowhead①, a curious rock shaped like a human profile. Blue-silk cushions were on the studio couch, and he had borrowed Lucile's sewing-machine② to make deep red curtains for the windows. He loved the room. It was both luxurious and sedate. On the table there was a little Japanese pagoda③ with glass pendants④ that tinkled with strange musical tones in a draught⑤.

In this room nothing reminded him of her. But often he would uncork the bottle of Agua Florida and touch the stopper to the lobes of his ears or to his wrists. The smell mingled with his slow ruminations. The sense of the past grew in him. Memories built themselves with almost architectural order. In a box where he stored souvenirs he came across old pictures taken before their marriage. Alice sitting in a field of daisies. Alice with him in a canoe on the river. Also among the souvenirs⑥ there was a large bone hairpin⑦ that had belonged to his mother. As a little boy he had loved to watch her comb and knot her long black hair. He had thought that hairpins were curved as they were to copy the shape of a lady and he would sometimes play with them like dolls. At that time he had a cigar box full of scraps. He loved the feel and colors of beautiful cloth and he would sit with his scraps for hours under the kitchen table. But when he was six his mother took the scraps away from him. She was a tall, strong woman with a sense of duty like a man. She had loved him best. Even now he sometimes dreamed of her. And her worn gold wedding ring stayed on his finger always.

Along with the Agua Florida he found in the closet a bottle of

---

① arrowhead：箭头；箭头状物
② sewing-machine：缝纫机
③ pagoda：（南亚或东亚的）佛塔
④ pendant：垂饰，坠饰
⑤ draught：气流，风
⑥ souvenir：纪念品，纪念物
⑦ hairpin：发簪

lemon rinse Alice had always used for her hair. One day he tried it on himself. The lemon made his dark, white-streaked hair seem fluffy[①] and thick. He liked it. He discarded the oil he had used to guard against baldness and rinsed with the lemon preparation regularly.[②] Certain whims that he had ridiculed in Alice were now his own. Why?

Every morning Louis, the colored boy downstairs, brought him a cup of coffee to drink in bed. Often he sat propped on the pillows for an hour before he got up and dressed. He smoked a cigar and watched the patterns the sunlight made on the wall. Deep in meditation[③] he ran his forefinger between his long, crooked toes. He remembered.

Then from noon until five in the morning he worked downstairs. And all day Sunday. The business was losing money. There were many slack hours. Still at meal-times the place was usually full and he saw hundreds of acquaintances every day as he stood guard behind the cash register.

'What do you stand and think about all the time?' Jake Blount asked him. 'You look like a Jew in Germany.'

'I am an eighth part Jew,' Biff said. 'My Mother's grandfather was a Jew from Amsterdam. But all the rest of my folks that I know about were Scotch-Irish.'

It was Sunday morning. Customers lolled[④] at the tables and there were the smell of tobacco and the rustle[⑤] of newspaper. Some men in a corner booth shot dice[⑥], but the game was a quiet one.

'Where's Singer?' Biff asked. 'Won't you be going up to his place this morning?'

Blount's face turned dark and sullen. He jerked his head forward.

---

① fluffy：蓬松的

② 参考译文：他扔掉了那瓶预防脱发的头油，经常用那瓶柠檬洗发水洗头。（discard：丢弃；baldness：光秃，脱发；preparation：用作食品、药品或化妆品的配制品，制剂）

③ meditation：冥想；沉思，深思；静坐

④ loll：懒洋洋地倚靠

⑤ rustle：发出沙沙声

⑥ dice：骰子；色子（shoot dice：指“掷骰子”。）

Had they quarreled—but how could a dummy quarrel? No, for this had happened before. Blount hung around sometimes and acted as though he were having an argument with himself. But pretty soon he would go—he always did—and the two of them would come in together, Blount talking.

'You live a fine life. Just standing behind a cash register. Just standing with your hand open.'

Biff did not take offense. He leaned his weight on his elbows and narrowed① his eyes. 'Let's me and you have a serious talk. What is it you want anyway?'

Blount smacked his hands down on the counter. They were warm and meaty and rough.'Beer. And one of them little packages of cheese crackers② with peanut butter in the inside.'

'That's not what I meant,' Biff said. 'But well come around to it later.'

The man was a puzzle. He was always changing. He still drank like a crazy fish, but liquor did not drag him down as it did some men. The rims of his eyes were often red, and he had a nervous trick of looking back startled over his shoulder. His head was heavy and huge on his thin neck. He was the sort of fellow that kids laughed at and dogs wanted to bite. Yet when he was laughed at it cut him to the quick—he got rough and loud like a sort of clown.③ And he was always suspecting that somebody was laughing.

Biff shook his head thoughtfully. 'Come,' he said.'What makes you stick with that show? You can find something better than that. I could give you a part-time job here.'

'Christamighty! I wouldn't park myself behind that cash box if you was to give me the whole damn place, lock, stock, and barrel.

---

① narrow：使变狭窄

② cracker：咸饼干

③ 参考译文：然而，当别人嘲笑时，他又很容易受伤——他发脾气，大声叫嚷，像个小丑。（to the quick：触及要害；触及痛处；clown：小丑）

'There he was. It was irritating[1]. He could never have friends or even get along with people.

Talk sense,' Biff said. 'Be serious.'

A customer had come up with his check and he made change. The place was still quiet. Blount was restless. Biff felt him drawing away. He wanted to hold him. He reached for two A-1 cigars on the shelf behind the counter and offered Blount a smoke. Warily his mind dismissed one question after another, and then finally he asked:

'If you could choose the time in history you could have lived, what era would you choose? '

Blount licked his mustache with his broad, wet tongue. 'If you had to choose between being a stiff and never asking another question, which would you take? '

'Sure enough,' Biff insisted. 'Think it over.'

He cocked[2] his head to one side and peered down over his long nose. This was a matter he liked to hear others talk about. Ancient Greece was his. Walking in sandals[3] on the edge of the blue Aegean. The loose robes girdled[4] at the waist. Children. The marble baths and the contemplations in the temples.

'Maybe with the Incas. In Peru.'

Biff's eyes scanned over him, stripping him naked. He saw Blount burned a rich, red brown by the sun, his face smooth and hairless, with a bracelet of gold and precious stones on his forearm. When he closed his eyes the man was a good Inca[5]. But when he looked at him again the picture fell away. It was the nervous mustache that did not belong to his face, the way he jerked his shoulder, the Adam's apple on his thin neck, the bagginess of his trousers. And it was more than that.

'Or maybe around 1775.'

---

① irritating：气人的；使愤怒的
② cock：使歪斜
③ sandals：凉鞋；拖鞋（使用复数形式）
④ girdle：围绕
⑤ Inca：印加；印加人

'That was a good time to be living,' Biff agreed.

Blount shuffled his feet self-consciously[①]. His face was rough and unhappy. He was ready to leave. Biff was alert to detain him. 'Tell me—why did you ever come to this town anyway? ' He knew immediately that the question had not been a politic[②] one and he was disappointed with himself. Yet it was queer how the man could land up in a place like this.

'It's the God's truth I don't know.'

They stood quietly for a moment, both leaning on the counter. The game of dice in the corner was finished. The first dinner order, a Long Island duck special, had been served to the fellow who managed the A&P. store. The radio was turned halfway between a church sermon[③] and a swing band[④].

Blount leaned over suddenly and smelled Biff's face.

'Perfume? '

'Shaving lotion[⑤],' Biff said composedly.

He could not keep Blount longer. The fellow was ready to go. He would come in with Singer later. It was always like this. He wanted to draw Blount out completely so that he could understand certain questions concerning him. But Blount would never really talk—only to the mute. It was a most peculiar[⑥] thing.

'Thanks for the cigar,' Blount said. 'See you later.'

'So long.'

Biff watched Blount walk to the door with his rolling, sailor-like gait. Then he took up the duties before him. He looked over the display in the window. The day's menu had been pasted on the glass and a special dinner with all the trimmings[⑦] was laid out to attract

---

① self-consciously：自觉地；不自然地

② politic：（行动）明智的

③ sermon：训诫；启示

④ swing band：摇滚乐队

⑤ shaving lotion：剃毛润肤乳

⑥ peculiar：特殊的；独特的

⑦ trimming：（主菜之外的）配菜

customers. It looked bad. Right nasty. The gravy from the duck had run into the cranberry[①] sauce and a fly, was stuck in the dessert.

'Hey, Louis!' he called. 'Take this stuff out of the window. And bring me that red pottery bowl and some fruit.'

He arranged[②] the fruits with an eye for color and design. At last the decoration pleased him. He visited the kitchen and had a talk with the cook. He lifted the lids of the pots and sniffed[③] the food inside, but without heart for the matter. Alice always had done this part. He disliked it. His nose sharpened when he saw the greasy sink with its scum[④] of food bits at the bottom. He wrote down the menus and the orders for the next day. He was glad to leave the kitchen and take his stand by the cash register again.

Lucile and Baby came for Sunday dinner. The little kid was not so good now. The bandage was still on her head and the doctor said it could not come off until next month. The binding of gauze in place of the yellow curls made her head look naked.

'Say hello to Uncle Biff, Hon,' Lucile prompted.

Baby bridled fretfully.'Hello to Unca Biff Hon,' she sassed.

She put up a struggle when Lucile tried to take off her Sunday coat.'Now you just behave yourself,' Lucile kept saying. 'You got to take it off or you'll catch pneumonia when we go out again. Now you just behave yourself.'

Biff took the situation in charge. He soothed Baby with a ball of candy gum and eased the coat from her shoulders. Her dress had lost its set in the struggle with Lucile. He straightened it so that the yoke[⑤] was in line across her chest. He retied[⑥] her sash and crushed the bow to just the right shape with his fingers. Then he patted Baby on her

---

① cranberry：蔓越橘
② arrange：安排；计划；准备
③ sniff：嗅；闻
④ scum：浮渣；泡沫
⑤ yoke：上衣抵肩；裙（或裤）腰
⑥ retie：重新系

little behind. 'We got some strawberry ice cream today,' he said.

'Bartholomew, you'd make a mighty good mother.'

'Thanks,' Biff said. 'That's a compliment[①].'

'We just been to Sunday School and church. Baby, say the verse from the Bible you learned for your Uncle Biff.'

The kid hung back and pouted[②]. 'Jesus wept,' she said finally. The scorn that she put in the two words made it sound like a terrible thing.

'Want to see Louis?' Biff asked. 'He's back in the kitchen.'

'I wanna see Willie. I wanna hear me play the harp.'

'Now, Baby, you're just trying yourself,' Lucile said impatiently 'You know good and well that Willie's not here. Willie was sent off to the penitentiary[③].'

'But Louis,' Biff said. 'He can play the harp, too. Go tell him to get the ice cream ready and play you a tune.'

Baby went toward the kitchen, dragging one heel on the floor. Lucile laid her hat on the counter. There were tears in her eyes. 'You know I always said this: If a child is kept clean and well cared for and pretty then that child will usually be sweet and smart. But if a child's dirty and ugly then you can't expect anything much. What I'm trying to get at is that Baby is so shamed over losing her hair and that bandage on her head that it just seems like it makes her cut the buck all the time.[④] She won't practice her elocution[⑤]—she won't do a thing. She feels so bad I just can't manage her.'

'If you'd quit picking with her so much she'd be all right.'

At last he settled them in a booth[⑥] by the window. Lucile had a

---

① compliment：称赞，赞美

② pout：噘嘴；生气

③ penitentiary：监狱

④ 参考译文：我想说的是，巴比没了头发，头上还缠着绷带，她觉得很丢人，这好像让她对什么都失去了兴趣。本句原文仍然是对地方英语的体现，cut the buck 本意为“不负众望，干得出色”，但此处根据上下文完全不可能是这个意思，而是“失去兴致”的意思。

⑤ elocution：朗诵法

⑥ booth：（隔开的）小间

special and there was a breast of chicken cut up fine, cream of wheat, and carrots for Baby. She played with her food and spilled milk on her little frock. He sat with them until the rush started. Then he had to be on his feet to keep things going smoothly.

People eating. The wide-open mouths with the food pushed in. What was it? The line he had read not long ago. Life was only a matter of intake and alimentation and reproduction.[①] The place was crowded. There was a swing band on the radio.

Then the two he was waiting for came in. Singer entered the door first, very straight and swank in his tailored[②] Sunday suit. Blount followed along just behind his elbow. There was something about the way they walked that struck him. They sat at their table, and Blount talked and ate with gusto while Singer watched politely. When the meal was finished they stopped by the cash register for a few minutes. Then as they went out he noticed again there was something about their walking together that made him pause and question himself. What could it be? The suddenness with which the memory opened up deep down in his mind was a shock.[③] The big deaf mute moron whom Singer used to walk with sometimes on the way to work. The sloppy Greek who made candy for Charles Parker. The Greek always walked ahead and Singer followed. He had never noticed them much because they never came into the place. But why had he not remembered this? Of all times he had wondered about the mute to neglect such an angle. See everything in the landscape except the three waltzing[④] elephants. But did it matter after all?

Biff narrowed his eyes. How Singer had been before was not important. The thing that mattered was the way Blount and Mick

---

① 参考译文：生命就是摄入、吸收营养和繁殖。（intake：食物、饮料、空气等的摄入；alimentation：营养）

② tailored：定制的，裁缝做的

③ 参考译文：他脑海深处的记忆之门猛然打开了，让他大为震惊。本句原文主结构为“The suddenness was a shock.”，定语从句修饰 suddenness，表示“突然”的所在。

④ waltzing：跳华尔兹舞的

made of him a sort of home-made God. Owing to the fact he was a mute they were able to give him all the qualities they wanted him to have. Yes. But how could such a strange thing come about? And why?

A one-armed man came in and Biff treated him to a whiskey on the house. But he did not feel like talking to anyone. Sunday dinner was a family meal. Men who drank beer by themselves on weeknights brought their wives and little kids with them on Sunday. The highchair they kept in the back was often needed. It was two-thirty and though many tables were occupied the meal was almost over. Biff had been on his feet for the past four hours and was tired. He used to stand for fourteen or sixteen hours and not notice any effects at all. But now he had aged. Considerably. There was no doubt about it. Or maybe matured was the word. Not aged—certainly not-yet. The waves of sound in the room swelled and subsided① against his ears. Matured. His eyes smarted② and it was as though some fever in him made everything too bright and sharp.

He called to one of the waitresses: 'Take over for me will you, please? I'm going out.'

The street was empty because of Sunday. The sun shone bright and clear, without warmth. Biff held the collar③ of his coat close to his neck. Alone in the street he felt out of pocket. The wind blew cold from the river. He should turn back and stay in the restaurant where he belonged. He had no business going to the place where he was headed. For the past four Sundays he had done this. He had walked in the neighborhood where he might see Mick. And there was something about it that was not quite right. Yes. Wrong.

He walked slowly down the sidewalk opposite the house where she lived. Last Sunday she had been reading the funny papers on the front steps. But this time as he glanced swiftly toward the house he

---

① subside：平息；减弱
② smart：（身体部位）感到刺痛
③ collar：衣领

saw she was not there. But tilted the brim of his felt hat down over his eyes. Perhaps she would come into the place later. Often on Sunday after supper she came for a hot cocoa and stopped for a while at the table where Singer was sitting. On Sunday she wore a different outfit from the blue skirt and sweater she wore on other days. Her Sunday dress was wine-colored silk with a dingy lace[①] collar. Once she had had on stockings—with runs in them. Always he wanted to set her up to something, to give to her. And not only a sundae or some sweet to eat—but something real. That was all he wanted for himself—to give to her. Biff's mouth hardened. He had done nothing wrong but in him he felt a strange guilt. Why? The dark guilt in all men, unreckoned and without a name.[②]

On the way home Biff found a penny lying half concealed by rubbish in the gutter[③]. Thriftily he picked it up, cleaned the coin with his handkerchief, and dropped it into the black pocket purse, he carried. It was four o'clock when he reached the restaurant. Business was stagnant[④]. There was not a single customer in the place.

Business picked up around five. The boy he had recently hired to work part time showed up early. The boy's name was Harry Minowitz. He lived in the same neighborhood with Mick and Baby. Eleven applicants[⑤] had answered the ad in the paper, but Harry seemed to be best bet. He was well developed for his age, and neat. Biff had noticed the boy's teeth while talking to him during the interview. Teeth were always a good indication. His were large and very clean and white. Harry wore glasses, but that would not matter in the work. His mother made ten dollars a week sewing for a tailor down the street, and Harry was an only child.

'Well,' Biff said. 'You've been with me a week, Harry. Think

---

① lace：花边
② 参考译文：所有男人心里的那种阴暗的罪恶感，莫名其妙，说不清楚。
③ gutter：排水沟
④ stagnant：停滞的，不景气的
⑤ applicant：申请人，应征人

you're going to like it?'

'Sure, sir. Sure I like it.'

Biff turned the ring on his finger. 'Let's see. What time do you get off from school?'

'Three o'clock, sir.'

'Well, that gives you a couple of hours for study and recreation[1]. Then here from six to ten. Does that leave you enough time for plenty of sleep? '

'Plenty. I don't need near that much.'

'You need about nine and a half hours at your age, son. Pure, wholesome[2] sleep.'

He felt suddenly embarrassed. Maybe Harry would think it was none of his business. Which it wasn't anyway. He started to turn aside and then thought of something.

'You go to Vocational[3]?'

Harry nodded and rubbed his glasses on his shirtsleeve[4].

'Let's see. I know a lot of girls and boys there. Alva Richards—I know his father. And Maggie Henry. And a kid named Mick Kelly—' He felt as though his ears had caught afire. He knew himself to be a fool. He wanted to turn and walk away and yet he only stood there, smiling and mashing his nose with his thumb. 'You know her?' he asked faintly.

'Sure, I live right next door to her. But in school I'm a senior while she's a freshman.'

Biff stored this meager[5] information neatly in his mind to be thought over later when he was alone. 'Business will be quiet here for a while,' he said hurriedly. 'I'll leave it with you. By now you know how to handle things. Just watch any customers drinking beer and

---

① recreation：娱乐，消遣
② wholesome：有益健康的
③ vocational：职业的，职业技术的
④ shirtsleeve：衬衣袖子
⑤ meager：数量很少的

remember how many they've drunk so you won't have to ask them and depend on what they say. Take your time making change and keep track of what goes on.'

Biff shut himself in his room downstairs. This was the place where he kept his files. The room had only one small window and looked out on the side alley, and the air was musty and cold. Huge stacks of newspapers rose up to the ceiling. A home-made filing case covered one wall. Near the door there was an old-fashioned rocking-chair and a small table laid with a pair of shears, a dictionary, and a mandolin.[①] Because of the piles of newspaper it was impossible to take more than two steps in any direction. Biff rocked himself in the chair and languidly[②] plucked the strings of the mandolin. His eyes closed and he began to sing in a doleful voice:

I went to the animal fair.
The birds and the beasts were there,
And the old baboon by the light of the moon
Was combing his auburn hair.

He finished with a chord from the strings and the last sounds shivered to silence in the cold air.

To adopt a couple of little children. A boy and a girl. About three or four years old so they would always feel like he was their own father. Their Dad. Our Father. The little girl like Mick(or Baby?) at that age. Round cheeks and gray eyes and flaxen[③] hair. And the clothes he would make for her—pink crêpe de Chine frocks with dainty smocking at the yoke and sleeves. Silk socks and white buckskin

---

① 参考译文：门口旁边放着一把老式摇椅，还有一张小桌子，上面有一把大剪刀、一本字典，还有一把曼陀林。（old-fashioned：老式的；shear：大剪刀；mandolin：曼陀林，一种琵琶乐器）

② languidly：疲倦地；不感兴趣地

③ flaxen：淡黄色的；亚麻的；亚麻色的

shoes. And a little red-velvet coat and cap and muff[①] for winter. The boy was dark and black-haired. The little boy walked behind him and copied the things he did. In the summer the three of them would go to a cottage on the Gulf and he would dress the children in their sun suits and guide them carefully into the green, shallow waves. And then they would bloom as he grew old. Our Father. And they would come to him with questions and he would answer them.

Why not?

Biff took up his mandolin again. '*Tum*-ti-*tim*-ti-*tee*, ti-*tee*, the *wedd*-ing of the painted *doll*' The mandolin mocked the refrain. He sang through all the verses and wagged his foot to the time. Then he played 'K-K-K-Katie,' and 'Love's Old Sweet Song.' These pieces were like the Agua Florida in the way they made him remember. Everything. Through the first year when he was happy and when she seemed happy even too. And when the bed came down with them twice in three months. And he didn't know that all the time her brain was busy with how she could save a nickel or squeeze out an extra dime. And then him with Rio and the girls at her place. Gyp and Madeline and Lou. And then later when suddenly he lost it. When he could lie with a woman no longer. Motherogod! So that at first it seemed everything was gone.

Lucile always understood the whole setup. She knew the kind of woman Alice was. Maybe she knew about him, too. Lucile would urge them to get a divorce[②]. And she did all a person could to try to straighten out their messes.

Biff winced[③] suddenly. He jerked his hands from the strings of the mandolin so that a phrase of music was chopped off. He sat tense in his chair. Then suddenly he laughed quietly to himself. What had made him come across this? Ah, Lordy Lordy Lord! It was the day

---

① muff：暖手筒，皮手筒；保暖套

② get a divorce：离婚

③ wince：畏缩，退避

of his twenty-ninth birthday, and Lucile had asked him to drop by[①] her apartment when he finished with an appointment at the dentist's. He expected from this some little remembrance[②]—a plate of cherry tarts or a good shirt. She met him at the door and blindfolded his eyes before he entered. Then she said she would be back in a second. In the silent room he listened to her footsteps and when she had reached the kitchen he broke wind. He stood in the room with his eyes blindfolded[③] and pooted. Then all at once he knew with horror he was not alone. There was a titter[④] and soon great rolling whoops[⑤] of laughter deafened[⑥] him. At that minute Lucile came back and undid his eyes. She held a caramel cake on a platter[⑦]. The room was full of people. Leroy and that bunch and Alice, of course. He wanted to crawl up the wall. He stood there with his bare face hanging out, burning hot all over. They kidded[⑧] him and the next hour was almost as bad as the death of his mother—the way he took it. Later that night he drank a quart of whiskey. And for weeks after—Motherogod!

Biff chuckled[⑨] coldly. He plucked a few chords on his mandolin and started a rollicking cowboy song. His voice was a mellow tenor and he closed his eyes as he sang. The room was almost dark. The damp chill penetrated to his bones so that his legs ached with rheumatism[⑩].

At last he put away his mandolin and rocked slowly in. the darkness. Death. Sometimes he could almost feel it in the room with him. He rocked to and fro[⑪] in the chair. What did he understand?

---

① drop by：顺道拜访，例：I'll drop by your sister on my way home if I have time. 如果我有时间，在回家路上我会顺便来看你姐姐。

② remembrance：回想，回忆；纪念品；记忆力

③ blindfold：蒙住眼睛

④ titter：窃笑，嗤笑

⑤ whoops：（非正式）（险些出事故或小失误时说）哎呀

⑥ deafen：使变聋

⑦ platter 大浅盘

⑧ kid：戏弄

⑨ chuckle：咯咯地笑，轻声笑

⑩ rheumatism：风湿病

⑪ to and fro：来回地

Nothing. Where was he headed? Nowhere. What did he want? To know. What? A meaning. Why? A riddle.

Broken pictures lay like a scattered jigsaw puzzle in his head. Alice soaping in the bathtub. Mussolini's mug. Mick pulling the baby in a wagon. A roast turkey on display. Blount's mouth. The face of Singer. He felt himself waiting. The room was completely dark. From the kitchen he could hear Louis singing.

Biff stood up and touched the arm of his chair to still its rocking. When he opened the door the hall outside was very warm and bright. He remembered that perhaps Mick would come. He straightened his clothes and smoothed back his hair. A warmth and liveliness returned to him. The restaurant was in a hubbub①. Beer rounds and Sunday supper had begun. He smiled genially② to young Harry and settled himself behind the cash register. He took in the room with a glance like a lasso③. The place was crowded and humming④ with noise. The bowl of fruit in the window was a genteel, artistic display. He watched the door and continued to examine the room with a practiced eye. He was alert and intently waiting. Singer came finally and wrote with his silver pencil that he wanted only soup and whiskey as he had a cold. But Mick did not come.

---

① in a hubbub：形容声音吵闹杂乱，沸沸扬扬

② genially：亲切地

③ lasso：套索

④ hum：嗡嗡作响

9

SHE NEVER even had a nickel to herself any more. They were that poor. Money was the main thing. All the time it was money, money, money. They had to pay through the nose① for Baby Wilson's private room and private nurse. But even that was just one bill. By the time one thing was paid for something else always would crop up.② They owed around two hundred dollars that had to be paid right away. They lost the house. Their Dad got a hundred dollars out of the deal and let the bank take over the mortgage. Then he borrowed another fifty dollars and Mister Singer went on the note with him. Afterward they had to worry about rent every month instead of taxes. They were mighty near as poor as factory folks. Only nobody could look down on them.

Bill had a job in a bottling plant and made ten dollars a week. Hazel worked as a helper in a beauty parlor for eight dollars. Etta sold tickets at a movie for five dollars. Each of them paid half of what they earned for their keep. Then the house had six boarders at five dollars a head. And Mister Singer, who paid his rent very prompt③. With what their Dad picked up it all came to about two hundred dollars a

---

① pay through the nose：支付过高或过度的金额，无论是以金钱还是其他方式。例：I had to pay through the nose for that concert ticket. 我不得不为那张音乐会门票支付过高的价格。

② 参考译文：付完一笔钱，另一件需要付钱的事情便又出现了。本句原文看似一个句子结构中出现了两个谓语动词，比较费解。但细读发现，by the time 引导时间状语从句，something else always would crop up 则是主结构。（crop up：突然出现）

③ prompt：及时的；准时的

month—and out of that they had to feed the six boarders pretty good and feed the family and pay rent for the whole house and keep up the payments on the furniture.[①]

George and her didn't get any lunch money now. She had to stop the music lessons. Portia saved the leftovers[②] from the dinner for her and George to eat after school. All the time they had their meals in the kitchen. Whether Bill and Hazel and Etta sat with the boarders or ate in the kitchen depended on how much food there was. In the kitchen they had grits and grease and side meat and coffee for breakfast. For supper they had the same thing along with whatever could be spared from the dining-room. The big kids griped whenever they had to eat in the kitchen. And sometimes she and George were downright[③] hungry for two or three days.

But this was in the outside room. It had nothing to do with music and foreign countries and the plans she made. The winter was cold. Frost was on the windowpanes. At night the fire in the living-room crackled very warm. All the family sat by the fire with the boarders, so she had the middle bedroom to herself. She wore two sweaters and a pair of Bill's outgrown corduroy pants. Excitement kept her warm. She would bring out her private box from under the bed and sit on the floor to work.

In the big box there were the pictures she had painted at the government free art class. She had taken them out of Bill's room. Also in the box she kept three mystery books her Dad had given her, a compact, a box of watch parts, a rhinestone[④] necklace, a hammer[⑤], and some notebooks. One notebook was marked on the top with red crayon—PRIVATE. KEEP OUT.PRIVATE—and tied with a string.

---

① 参考译文：他爸爸能拿到手的，一个月总共大约二百块——而用这些钱，他们得给六位房客提供较好的伙食，养活全家人，付整个房子的房租，续交买家具的钱。

② leftover：遗留；剩余物

③ downright：（坏事或令人不快之事）彻头彻尾地

④ rhinestone：人造钻石；莱茵石（一种假钻石）

⑤ hammer：锤子

She had worked on music in this notebook all the winter. She quit studying school lessons at night so she could have more time to spend on music. Mostly she had written just little tunes—songs without any words and without even any bass① notes to them. They were very short. But even if the tunes were only half a page long she gave them names and drew her initials underneath them. Nothing in this book was a real piece or a composition②. They were just songs in her mind she wanted to remember. She named them how they reminded her—'Africa' and 'A Big Fight' and 'The Snowstorm.'

She couldn't write the music just like it sounded in her mind. She had to thin it down to only a few notes; otherwise she got too mixed up to go further. There was so much she didn't know about how to write music. But maybe after she learned how to write these simple tunes fairly quick she could begin to put down the whole music in her mind.

In January she began a certain very wonderful piece called 'This Thing I Want, I Know Not What' It was a beautiful and marvelous③ song—very slow and soft. At first she had started to write a poem along with it, but she couldn't think of ideas to fit the music. Also it was hard to get a word for the third line to rhyme with what. This new song made her feel sad and excited and happy all at once. Music beautiful as this was hard to work on. Any song was hard to write. Something she could hum in two minutes meant a whole week's work before it was down in the notebook—after she had figured up the scale and the time and every note.④

She had to concentrate hard and sing it many times. Her voice was always hoarse⑤. Her Dad said this was because she had bawled

---

① bass：低音的

② composition：作曲

③ marvelous：非凡的，令人惊异的

④ 参考译文：她用不了两分钟就可以哼完的东西，要想写在笔记本上，却意味着要埋头苦干整整一个星期——还不算她要弄明白音阶、时间和每一个音符。本句表现了音乐家“台上一分钟，台下十年功”的背后付出。（figure up：把……总加起来；scale：音阶）

⑤ hoarse：嘶哑的

so much when she was a baby. Her Dad would have to getup and walk with her every night when she was Ralph's age. The only thing would hush her, he always said, was for him to beat the coal scuttle with a poker and sing 'Dixie.'

She lay on her stomach on the cold floor and thought. Later on—when she was twenty—she would be a great world-famous composer. She would have a whole symphony orchestra and conduct all of her music herself. She would stand up on the platform[①] in front of the big crowds of people. To conduct the orchestra she would wear either a real man's evening suit or else a red dress spangled with rhinestones. The curtains of the stage would be red velvet and M.K. would be printed on them in gold. Mister Singer would be there, and afterward they would go out and eat fried chicken. He would admire her and count her as his very best friend. George would bring up big wreaths of flowers to the stage. It would be in New York City or else in a foreign country. Famous people would point at her—Carole Lombard and Arturo Toscanini and Admiral Byrd.

And she could play the Beethoven symphony any time she wanted to. It was a queer thing about this music she had heard last autumn. The symphony stayed inside her always and grew little by little. The reason was this: the whole symphony was in her mind. It had to be. She had heard every note, and somewhere in the back of her mind the whole of the music was still there just as it had been played. But she could do nothing to bring it all out again. Except wait and be ready for the times when suddenly a new part came to her. Wait for it to grow like leaves grow slowly on the branches of a spring oak tree.

In the inside room, along with music, there was Mister Singer. Every afternoon as soon as she finished playing on the piano in the gym she walked down the main street past the store where he worked.

---

① platform：平台

From the front window she couldn't see Mister Singer. He worked in the back, behind a curtain. But she looked at the store where he stayed every day and saw the people he knew. Then every night she waited on the front porch for him to come home. Sometimes she followed him upstairs. She sat on the bed and watched him put away his hat and undo[①] the button on his collar and brush his hair. For some reason it was like they had a secret together. Or like they waited to tell each other things that had never been said before.

He was the only person in the inside room. A long time ago there had been others. She thought back and remembered how it was before he came. She remembered a girl way back in the sixth grade named Celeste. This girl had straight blonde hair and a turned-up nose[②] and freckles[③]. She wore a red-wool jumper with a white blouse. She walked pigeon-toed[④]. Every day she brought an orange for little recess[⑤] and a blue tin box of lunch for big recess. Other kids would gobble the food they had brought at little recess and then were hungry later—but not Celeste.[⑥] She pulled off the crusts of her sandwiches and ate only the soft middle part. Always she had a stuffed hard-boiled egg and she would hold it in her hand, mashing[⑦] the yellow with her thumb so that the print of her finger was left there.

Celeste never talked to her and she never talked to Celeste. Although that was what she wanted more than anything else. At night she would lie awake and think about Celeste. She would plan that they were best friends and think about the time when Celeste could come home with her to eat supper and spend the night. But that never happened. The way she felt about Celeste would never let her go

---

① undo：解开
② turned-up nose：朝天鼻（等于 upturned nose）
③ freckle：雀斑
④ pigeon-toed：内八字脚的；足内翻的
⑤ recess：课间休息
⑥ 参考译文：其他孩子趁小课间就把带的食物狼吞虎咽吃掉了，然后便饥肠辘辘——但西莱斯特不会这样。（gobble：狼吞虎咽）
⑦ mash：捣碎；磨碎

up and make friends with her like she would any other person. After a year Celeste moved to another part of town and went to another school.

Then there was a boy called Buck. He was big and had pimples[①] on his face. When she stood by him in line to march in at eight-thirty he smelled bad—like his britches needed airing. Buck did a nose-dive at the principal once and was suspended[②]. When he laughed he lifted his upper lip and shook all over. She thought about him like she had thought about Celeste. Then there was the lady who sold lottery tickets[③] for a turkey raffle. And Miss Anglin, who taught the seventh grade. And Carole Lombard in the movies. All of them.

But with Mister Singer there was a difference. The way she felt about him came on her slowly, and she could not think back and realize just how it happened. The other people had been ordinary, but Mister Singer was not The first day he rang the doorbell to ask about a room she had looked a long time into his face. She had opened the door and read over the card he handed her. Then she called her Mama and went back in the kitchen to tell Portia and Bubber about him. She followed him and her Mama up the stairs and watched him poke the mattress on the bed and roll up[④] the shades[⑤] to see if they worked. The day he moved she sat on the front porch banisters and watched him get out of the ten-cent taxi with his suitcase and his chessboard[⑥]. Then later she listened to him thump around in his room and imagined about him. The rest came in a gradual way. So that now there was this secret feeling between them. She talked to him more than she had ever talked to a person before. And if he could have talked he would have told her many things. It was like he was some kind of a great

---

① pimple：丘疹，面疱
② suspend：使暂时停职（或停学等）（此处过去分词 suspended 用于被动语态）
③ lottery ticket：彩票
④ roll up：卷起
⑤ shade：遮光窗帘；百叶窗
⑥ chessboard：棋盘

teacher, only because he was a mute he did not teach. In the bed at night she planned about how she was an orphan and lived with Mister Singer—just the two of them in a foreign house where in the winter it would snow. Maybe in a little Switzerland town with the high glaciers and the mountains all around. Where rocks were on top of all the houses and the roofs were steep and pointed. Or in France where the people carried home bread from the store without its being wrapped. Or in the foreign country of Norway by the gray winter ocean.

In the morning the first thing she would think of him. Along with music. When she put on her dress she wondered where she would see him that day. She used some of Etta's perfume or a drop of vanilla① so that if she met him in the hall she would smell good. She went to school late so she could see him come down the stairs on his way to work. And in the afternoon and night she never left the house if he was there.

Each new thing she learned about him was important. He kept his toothbrush and toothpaste in a glass on his table. So instead of leaving her toothbrush on the bathroom shelf she kept it in a glass, also. He didn't like cabbage. Harry, who worked for Mister Brannon, mentioned that to her. Now she couldn't eat cabbage either. When she learned new facts about him, or when she said something to him and he wrote a few words with his silver pencil, she had to be off by herself for a long time to think it over. When she was with him the main thought in her mind was to store up everything so that later she could live it over and remember.

But in the inside room with music and Mister Singer was not all. Many things happened in the outside room. She fell down the stairs and broke off one of her front teeth. Miss Minner gave her two bad cards in English. She lost a quarter② in a vacant lot③, and although she

---

① vanilla：香子兰，香草

② quarter：（美国和加拿大的）二十五分硬币

③ vacant lot：空地

and George hunted for three days they never found it.

This happened:

One afternoon she was studying for an English test out on the back steps. Harry began to chop wood over on his side of the fence and she hollered[①] to him. He came and diagrammed[②] a few sentences for her. His eyes were quick behind his horn-rimmed[③] glasses. After he explained the English to her he stood up and jerked his hands in and out the pockets of his lumberjack[④]. Harry was always full of energy, nervous, and he had to be talking or doing something every minute.

'You see, there's just two things nowadays,' he said.

He liked to surprise people and sometimes she didn't know how to answer him.

'It's the truth, there's just two things ahead nowadays.'

'What?'

'Militant[⑤] Democracy or Fascism.'

'Don't you like Republicans?'

'Shucks[⑥],' Harry said. 'That's not what I mean.'

He had explained all about the Fascists one afternoon. He told how the Nazis made little Jew children get down on their hands and knees and eat grass from the ground. He told about how he planned to assassinate[⑦] Hitler. He had it all worked out thoroughly[⑧]. He told about how there wasn't any justice or freedom hi Fascism. He said the newspapers wrote deliberate lies and people didn't know what was going on in the world. The Nazis were terrible—everybody knew that. She plotted with him to kill Hitler. It would be better to have four or five people in the conspiracy[⑨] so that if one missed him the

---

① holler：发牢骚；叫喊
② diagram：以图表示
③ horn rimmed：角质框的
④ lumberjack：短夹克衫
⑤ militant：好战的
⑥ shucks：唉，糟了（表示窘迫或失望）
⑦ assassinate：暗杀；行刺
⑧ thoroughly：彻底地，完全地
⑨ conspiracy：阴谋；共谋

others could bump him off[①] just the same. And even if they died they would all be heroes. To be a hero was almost like being a great musician.

'Either one or the other. And although I don't believe in war I'm ready to fight for what I know is right'

'Me too,' she said. 'I'd like to fight the Fascists. I could dress up like a boy and nobody could ever tell. Cut my hair off and all.'

It was a bright winter afternoon. The sky was blue-green and the branches of the oak trees in the back yard were black and bare against this color. The sun was warm. The day made her feel full of energy. Music was in her mind. Just to be doing something she picked up a ten-penny[②] nail and drove it into the steps with a few good wallops[③]. Their Dad heard the sound of the hammer and came out in his bathrobe to stand around awhile. Under the tree there were two carpenter's horses, and little Ralph was busy putting a rock on top of one and then carrying it over to the other one. Back and forth. He walked with his hands out to balance himself. He was bowlegged[④] and his diapers[⑤] dragged down to his knees. George was shooting marbles. Because he needed a haircut his face looked thin. Some of his permanent teeth had already come—but they were small and blue like he had been eating blackberries. He drew a line for taw[⑥] and lay on his stomach to take aim for the first hole. When their Dad went back to his watch work he carried Ralph with him. And after a while George went off into the alley by himself. Since he shot Baby he wouldn't buddy with a single person.

'I got to go,' Harry said. 'I got to be at work before six.'

'You like it at the café? Do you get good things to eat free?'

---

① bump off：干掉，谋杀
② ten-penny：（钉子）三英寸长的
③ wallop：（非正式）痛打，重击
④ bowlegged：弯脚的
⑤ diaper：（美）尿布
⑥ taw：石弹；射石弹者站立的基线

'Sure. And all kinds of folks come in the place. I like it better than any job I ever had. It pays more.'

'I hate Mister Brannon,' Mick said. It was true that even though he never said anything mean to her he always spoke in a rough, funny way. He must have known all along about the pack of chewing-gum she and George swiped[①] that time. And then why would he ask her how her business was coming along—like he did up in Mister Singer's room? Maybe he thought they took things regular. And they didn't. They certainly did not. Only once a little water-color set from the ten-cent store. And a nickel pencil-sharpener.

'I can't stand[②] Mister Brarmon.'

'He's all right,' Harry said. 'Sometimes he seems a right queer kind of person, but he's not crabby[③]. When you get to know him.'

'One thing I've thought about,' Mick said. 'A boy has a better advantage like that than a girl. I mean a boy can usually get some part-time job that don't take him out of school and leaves him time for other things. But there's not jobs like that for girls. When a girl wants a job she has to quit school and work full time. I'd sure like to earn a couple of bucks a week like you do, but there's just not any way.'

Harry sat on the steps and untied his shoestrings[④]. He pulled at them until one broke. 'A man comes to the café named Mr. Blount. Mr. Jake Blount. I like to listen to him. I learn a lot from the things he says when he drinks beer. He's given me some new ideas.'

'I know him good. He comes here every Sunday.'

Harry unlaced[⑤] his shoe and pulled the broken string to even lengths so he could tie it in a bow[⑥] again. 'Listen'—he rubbed his glasses on his lumberjack in a nervous way—'You needn't mention to

---

① swipe：偷窃
② stand：忍受，容忍
③ crabby：易怒的；脾气坏的
④ shoestring：鞋带
⑤ unlace：解开带子
⑥ bow：蝴蝶结

him what I said. I mean I doubt if he would remember me. He don't talk to me. He just talks to Mr. Singer. He might think it was funny if you—you know what I mean.'

'O.K.' She read between the words that he had a crush on Mister Blount and she knew how he felt. 'I wouldn't mention it.'

Dark came on. The moon, white like milk, showed in the blue sky and the air was cold. She could hear Ralph and George and Portia in the kitchen. The fire in the stove made the kitchen window a warm orange. There was the smell of smoke and supper.

'You know this is something I never have told anybody,' he said. 'I hate to realize about it myself.'

'What?'

'You remember when you first began to read the newspapers and think about the things you read?'

'Sure.'

'I used to be a Fascist. I used to think I was. It was this way. You know all the pictures of the people our age in Europe marching and singing songs and keeping step together. I used to think that was wonderful. All of them pledged[①] to each other and with one leader. All of them with the same ideals and marching in step together. I didn't worry much about what was happening to the Jewish minorities[②] because I didn't want to think about it. And because at the time I didn't want to think like I was Jewish. You see, I didn't know. I just looked at the pictures and read what it said underneath and didn't understand. I never knew what an awful thing it was. I thought I was a Fascist. Of course later on I found out different.'

His voice was bitter against himself and kept changing from a man's voice to a young boy's.

'Well, you didn't realize then—' she said.

---

① pledge：保证；抵押；给予

② minority：少数

'It was a terrible transgression[1]. A moral wrong.'

That was the way he was. Everything was either very right or very wrong—with no middle way. It was wrong for anyone under twenty to touch beer or wine or smoke a cigarette. It was a terrible sin[2] for a person to cheat on a test, but not a sin to copy homework. It was a moral wrong for girls to wear lipstick or sun-backed dresses. It was a terrible sin to buy anything with a German or Japanese label, no matter if it cost only a nickel.

She remembered Harry back to the time when they were kids. Once his eyes got crossed and stayed crossed for a year. He would sit out on his front steps with his hands between his knees and watch everything. Very quiet and cross-eyed. He skipped[3] two grades in grammar school and when he was eleven he was ready for Vocational. But at Vocational when they read about the Jew in *Ivanhoe*[4] the other kids would look around at Harry and he would come home and cry. So his mother took him out of school. He stayed out for a whole year. He grew taller and very fat. Every time she climbed the fence she would see him making himself something to eat in his kitchen. They both played around on the block, and sometimes they would wrestle[5]. When she was a kid she liked to fight with boys—real fights but just in play. She used a combination jujitsu and boxing. Sometimes he got her down and sometimes she got him. Harry never was very rough with anybody. When little kids ever broke any toy they would come to him and he always took the time to fix it. He could fix anything. The ladies on the block got him to fix their electric lights or sewing-machines when something went wrong. Then when he was thirteen he started back at Vocational and began to study hard. He

---

① transgression：犯罪

② sin：罪恶；罪孽

③ skip：跳过（正常的步骤）

④ *Ivanhoe*：《艾凡赫》，英国作家沃尔特·司各特创作的长篇历史小说。司各特是较早对反犹主义进行揭露的少数作家之一，在《艾凡赫》中他再现了那个时代犹太人普遍面临的困境，还通过塑造栩栩如生的人物映衬出他对犹太人宽容、人道主义的态度。

⑤ wrestle：摔跤；搏斗

threw papers and worked on Saturdays and read. For a long time she didn't see much of him—until after that party she gave. He was very changed.

'Like this,' Harry said. 'It used to be I had some big ambition for myself all the time. A great engineer or a great doctor or lawyer. But now I don't have it that way. All I can think about is what happens in the world now. About Fascism and the terrible things in Europe—and on the other hand Democracy. I mean I can't think and work on what I mean to be in life because I think too much about this other. I dream about killing Hitler every night And I wake up in the dark very thirsty and scared of something—I don't know what.'

She looked at Harry's face and a deep, serious feeling made her sad. His hair hung over his forehead. His upper lip was thin and tight, but the lower one was thick and it trembled. Harry didn't look old enough to be fifteen. With the darkness a cold wind came. The wind sang up in the oak trees on the block and banged the blinds against the side of the house. Down the street Mrs. Wells was calling Sucker home. The dark late afternoon made the sadness heavy inside her. I want a piano—I want to take music lessons, she said to herself. She looked at Harry and he was lacing his thin fingers together in different shapes. There was a warm boy smell about him.

What was it made her act like she suddenly did? Maybe it was remembering the times when they were younger. Maybe it was because the sadness made her feel queer. But anyway all of a sudden she gave Harry a push that nearly knocked him off the steps. 'S.O.B. to your Grandmother,' she hollered to him. Then she ran. That was what kids used to say in the neighborhood when they picked a fight Harry stood up and looked surprised. He settled his glasses on his nose and watched her for a second. Then he ran back to the alley[1].

The cold air made her strong as Samson. When she laughed there

---

① alley：小巷，小路，小径

was a short, quick echo. She butted[①] Harry with her shoulder and he got a holt on her. They wrestled hard and laughed. She was the tallest but his hands were strong. He didn't fight good enough and she got him on the ground. Then suddenly he stopped moving and she stopped too. His breathing was warm on her neck and he was very still. She felt his ribs[②] against her knees and his hard breathing as she sat on him. They got up together. They did not laugh any more and the alley was very quiet. As they walked across the dark back yard for some reason she felt funny. There was nothing to feel queer[③] about, but suddenly it had just happened. She gave him a little push and he pushed her back. Then she laughed again and felt all right.

'So long,' Harry said. He was too old to climb the fence[④], so he ran through the side alley to the front of his house.

'Gosh it's hot!' she said. 'I could smother[⑤] in here.'

Portia was warming her supper in the stove. Ralph banged his spoon on his high-chair tray[⑥]. George's dirty little hand pushed up his grits[⑦] with a piece of bread and his eyes were squinted in a faraway look. She helped herself to white meat and gravy[⑧] and grits and a few raisins and mixed them up together on her plate. She ate three bites of them. She ate until all the grits were gone but still she wasn't full.

She had thought about Mister Singer all the day, and as soon as supper was over she went upstairs. But when she reached the third floor she saw that his door was open and his room dark. This gave her an empty feeling.

Downstairs she couldn't sit still and study for the English test. It

---

① butt：对接的
② rib：肋骨
③ feel queer：感到头晕，不适
④ fence：栅栏；围墙
⑤ smother：窒息
⑥ tray：托盘
⑦ grit：（美国南部吃的）粗玉米粉，玉米渣
⑧ gravy：肉汁

was like she was so strong she couldn't sit on a chair in a room the same as other people. It was like she could knock down all the walls of the house and then march through the streets big as a giant.

Finally she got out her private box from under the bed. She lay on her stomach and looked over the notebook. There were about twenty songs now, but she didn't feel satisfied with them. If she could write a symphony! For a whole orchestra—how did you write that? Sometimes several instruments played one note, so the staff would have to be very large. She drew five lines across a big sheet of test paper—the lines about an inch apart. When a note was for violin or cello or flute she would write the name of the instrument to show. And when they all played the same note together she would draw a circle around them. At the top of the page she wrote SYMPHONY in large letters[①]. And under that MICK KELLY. Then she couldn't go any further.

If she could only have music lessons!

If only she could have a real piano!

A long time passed before she could get started. The tunes were in her mind but she couldn't figure how to write them. It looked like this was the hardest play in the world. But she kept on figuring until Etta and Hazel came into the room and got into bed and said she had to turn the light off because it was eleven o'clock.

---

① in large letter：（写成）大写字母

10

FOR six weeks Portia had waited to hear from William. Every evening she would come to the house and ask Doctor Copeland the same question: 'You seen anybody who gotten a letter from Willie yet?' And every night he was obliged[1] to tell her that he had heard nothing.

At last she asked the question no more. She would come into the hall and look at him without a word. She drank. Her blouse was often half unbuttoned[2] and her shoestrings loose.

February came. The weather turned milder, then hot. The sun glared down with hard brilliance. Birds sang in the bare trees and children played out of doors barefoot and naked to the waist. The nights were torrid[3] as in midsummer. Then after a few days winter was upon the town again. The mild skies darkened. A chill rain fell and the air turned dank and bitterly cold. In the town the Negroes suffered badly. Supplies of fuel had been exhausted and there was a struggle everywhere for warmth. An epidemic[4] of pneumonia[5] raged through the wet, narrow streets, and for a week Doctor Copeland slept at odd hours[6], fully clothed. Still no word came from William.

---

① be obliged to do sth.：被迫做某事

② unbuttoned：纽扣解开的

③ torrid：晒热的，酷热的

④ epidemic：流行的

⑤ pneumonia：肺炎

⑥ at odd hours：偶尔，极少时间，例：These days my parents are so busy that I can see them at odd hours. 这些日子，我的父母很忙，只有偶尔能见到他们。

Portia had written four times and Doctor Copeland twice.

During most of the day and night he had no time to think. But occasionally he found a chance to rest for a moment at home. He would drink a pot of coffee by the kitchen stove and a deep uneasiness would come in him. Five of his patients had died. And one of these was Augustus Benedict Mady Lewis, the little deaf-mute. He had been asked to speak at the burial service[①], but as it was his rule not to attend funerals he was unable to accept this invitation. The five patients had not been lost because of any negligence on his part. The blame was in the long years of want which lay behind. The diets of cornbread[②] and sowbelly[③] and syrup[④], the crowding of four and five persons to a single room. The death of poverty. He brooded on this and drank coffee to stay awake. Often he held his hand to his chin, for recently a slight tremor in the nerves of his neck made his head nod unsteadily when he was tired.[⑤]

Then during the fourth week of February Portia came to the house. It was only six o'clock in the morning and he was sitting by the fire in the kitchen, warming a pan of milk for breakfast. She was badly intoxicated[⑥]. He smelled the keen, sweetish odor of gin and his nostrils widened with disgust. He did not look at her but busied himself with his breakfast. He crumpled some bread in a bowl and poured over it hot milk. He prepared coffee and laid the table.

Then when he was seated before his breakfast he looked at Portia sternly. 'Have you had your morning meal?'

'I not going to eat breakfast,' she said.

'You will need it. If you intend to get to work today;'

'I not going to work.'

---

① burial service：葬礼（同 funeral）

② cornbread：玉米面包（等于 corn bread）

③ sowbelly：腌猪肉

④ syrup：糖浆

⑤ 参考译文：他经常用手托着下巴，因为最近，只要他一累，脖子上的神经便会微微颤抖，让他不由自主地点头。（for 在句中为连词，表原因，连接原因状语从句。）

⑥ intoxicated：醉酒的

A dread came in him. He did not wish to question her further. He kept his eyes on his bowl of milk and drank from a spoon that was unsteady in his hand. When he had finished he looked up at the wall above her head. 'Are you tongue-tied?'

'I going to tell you. You going to hear about it. Just as soon as I able to say it I going to tell you.'

Portia sat motionless in the chair, her eyes moving slowly from one corner of the wall to the other. Her arms hung down limp and her legs were twisted[①] loosely about each other. When he turned from her he had for a moment a perilous sense of ease and freedom, which was more acute because he knew that soon it was to be shattered.[②] He mended the fire and warmed his hands. Then he rolled a cigarette. The kitchen was in a state of spotless[③] order and cleanliness. The saucepans on the wall glowed with the light of the stove and behind each one there was a round, black shadow.

'It about Willie.'

'I know.' He rolled the cigarette gingerly[④] between his palms. His eyes glanced recklessly about him, greedy for the last sweet pleasures.

'Once I mentioned to you this here Buster Johnson were at the prison with Willie. Us knowed him before. He were sent home yestiddy.'

'So?'

'Buster been crippled for life[⑤].'

His head quavered. He pressed his hand to his chin to steady himself, but the obstinate trembling was difficult to control.

'Last night these here friends come round to my house and say

---

① twisted：扭曲的

② 参考译文：他从她身上移开视线的时候，有一瞬间感到一种危险的轻松和自由，这种感觉很强烈，因为他知道它很快就要土崩瓦解了。（perilous：危险的）

③ spotless：无可挑剔的

④ gingerly：谨慎的

⑤ for life：终身

that Buster were home and had something to tell me about Willie. I run all the way and this here is what he said.

"'Yes.'

'There were three of them. Willie and Buster and this other boy. They were friends. Then this here trouble come up.' Portia halted①. She wet her finger with her tongue and then moistened her dry lips with her finger. 'It were something to do with the way this here white guard picked on them all the time. They were out on roadwork② one day and Buster he sassed③ back and then the other boy he try to run off in the woods. They taken all three of them. They taken all three of them to the camp and put them in this here ice-cold room.'

He said yes again. But his head quavered④ and the word sounded like a rattle in his throat.

'It were about six weeks ago,' Portia said. 'You remember that cold spell then. They put Willie and them boys in this room like ice.'

Portia spoke in a low voice, and she neither paused between words nor did the grief⑤ in her face soften. It was like a low song. She spoke and he could not understand. The sounds were distinct in his ear but they had no shape or meaning. It was as though his head were the prow of a boat and the sounds were water that broke on him and then flowed past. He felt he had to look behind to find the words already said.

'...and their feets swolled up and they lay there and struggle on the floor and holler out⑥. And nobody come. They hollered there for three days and three nights and nobody come.'

'I am deaf,' said Doctor Copeland. 'I cannot understand.'

'They put our Willie and them boys in this here ice-cold room.

---

① halt：停顿
② roadwork：道路施工
③ sass：跟……顶嘴
④ quaver：颤抖
⑤ grief：悲痛；忧伤；不幸
⑥ holler out：突然呼喊，大叫

There were a rope hanging down from the ceiling. They taken their shoes off and tied their bare feets to this rope. Willie and them boys lay there with their backs on the floor and their feets in the air. And their feets swolled up and they struggle on the floor and holler out. It were ice-cold in the room and their feets froze. Their feets swolled up and they hollered for three nights and three days. And nobody come.'

Doctor Copeland pressed[①] his head with his hands, but still the steady trembling would not stop. 'I cannot hear what you say.'

'Then at last they come to get them. They quickly taken Willie and them boys to the sick ward and their legs were all swolled and froze[②]. Gangrene. They sawed off both our Willie's feet. Buster Johnson lost one foot and the other boy got well. But our Willie—he crippled[③] for life now. Both his feet sawed off.'

The words were finished and Portia leaned over and struck her head upon the table. She did not cry or moan, but she struck her head again and again on the hard-scrubbed top of the table. The bowl and spoon rattled and he removed them to the sink. The words were scattered in his mind, but he did not try to assemble them.[④] He scalded[⑤] the bowl and spoon and washed out the dishtowel. He picked up something from the floor and put it somewhere.

'Crippled?' he asked. 'William?'

Portia knocked her head on the table and the blows had a rhythm like the slow beat of a drum and his heart took up this rhythm also. Quietly the words came alive and fitted to the meaning and he understood.

'When will they send him home?'

Portia leaned her drooping[⑥] head on her arm. 'Buster don't

---

① pressed：挤，推

② swolled and froze：文中应使用 swell 和 freeze 的过去分词，即 swollen 和 frozen。

③ cripple：（使）残疾，（使）伤残

④ 参考译文：那些话在他脑子里散乱一片，但他并没有想要把它们拼接到一起。（assemble：使集合，使聚集）

⑤ scald：烫洗

⑥ drooping：下垂的；无力的

know that. Soon afterward they separate all three of them in different places. They sent Buster to another camp. Since Willie only haves a few more months he think he liable to be home soon now.'

They drank coffee and sat for a long time, looking into each other's eyes. His cup rattled against his teeth. She poured her coffee into a saucer and some of it dripped down on her lap.

'William—' Doctor Copeland said. As he pronounced the name his teeth bit deeply into his tongue and he moved his jaw with pain. They sat for a long while. Portia held his hand. The bleak morning light made the windows gray. Outside it was still raining.

'If I means to get to work I better go on now,' Portia said.

He followed her through the hall and stopped at the hatrack to put on his coat and shawl. The open door let in a gust of wet, cold air. Highboy sat out on the street curb with a wet newspaper over his head for protection. Along the sidewalk there was a fence. Portia leaned against this as she walked. Doctor Copeland followed a few paces after her and his hands, also, touched boards of the fence to steady himself. Highboy trailed① behind them.

He waited for the black, terrible anger as though for some beast out of the night. But it did not come to him. His bowels seemed weighted with lead, and he walked slowly and lingered against fences and the cold, wet walls of buildings by the way. Descent into the depths until at last there was no further chasm below. He touched the solid② bottom of despair and there took ease.

In this he knew a certain strong and holy gladness. The persecuted③ laugh, and the black slave sings to his outraged④ soul beneath the whip. A song was in him now—although it was not music but only the feeling of a song. And the sodden heaviness of peace weighted down his limbs so that it was only with the strong, true

---

① trail：尾随，追踪
② solid：固体；立方体
③ persecute：（尤指宗教或政治信仰的）迫害（the persecuted 指“受迫害的人”。）
④ outraged：义愤填膺的；愤慨的

purpose that he moved.[①] Why did he go onward? Why did he not rest here upon the bottom of utmost humiliation and for a while take his content?

But he went onward.

'Uncle,' said Mick. 'You think some hot coffee would make you feel better?'

Doctor Copeland looked into her face but gave no sign that he heard. They had crossed the town and come at last to the alley behind the Kellys' house. Portia had entered first and then he followed. Highboy remained on the steps outside. Mick and her two little brothers were already in the kitchen. Portia told of William. Doctor Copeland did not listen to the words but her voice had a rhythm[②]—a start, a middle, and an end. Then when she was finished she began all over. Others came into the room to hear.

Doctor Copeland sat on a stool in the corner. His coat and shawl[③] steamed[④] over the back of a chair by the stove. He held his hat on his knees and his long, dark hands moved nervously around the worn brim. The yellow insides of his hands were so moist that occasionally he wiped them with a handkerchief. His head trembled, and all of his muscles were stiff with the effort to make it be still.[⑤]

Mr. Singer came into the room. Doctor Copeland raised up his face to him. 'Have you heard of this?' he asked. Mr. Singer nodded. In his eyes there was no horror or pity or hate. Of all those who knew, his eyes alone did not express these reactions. For he alone understood this thing.

Mick whispered to Portia, 'What's your father's name?'

---

① 参考译文：一种平和的沉重负担压得他四肢动弹不得，他只有凭借那种坚强的真正使命感才能向前挪动。本句原文 so that 引导的结果状语从句中还包含了一个强调句结构 it was...that...。

② rhythm：节奏，韵律

③ shawl：披肩，围巾

④ steam：散发蒸汽，冒热气

⑤ 参考译文：他的头颤抖着，全身肌肉僵硬，拼命要让头部停止抖动。（still：静止的，不动的）

'He named Benedict Mady Copeland.'

Mick leaned over close to Doctor Copeland and shouted in his face as though he were deaf. 'Benedict, don't you think some hot coffee would make you feel a little better?'

Doctor Copeland started.

'Quit that hollering,' Portia said. 'He can hear well as you can.'

'Oh,' said Mick. She emptied[①] the grounds from the pot and put the coffee on the stove to boil again.

The mute still lingered in the doorway. Doctor Copeland still looked into his face. 'You heard?'

'What'll they do to those prison guards?' Mick asked.

'Honey, I just don't know,' Portia said. 'I just don't know.'

'I'd do something. I'd sure do something about it.'

'Nothing us could do would make no difference. Best thing us can do is keep our mouth shut.'

'They ought to be treated just like they did Willie and them. Worse. I wish I could round up[②] some people and kill those men myself.'

'That ain't no Christian way to talk,' Portia said. 'Lls can just rest back and know they going to be chopped up[③] with pitchforks[④] and fried everlasting[⑤] by Satan.'

'Anyway Willie can still play his harp.'

'With both feets sawed off that about all he can do.'

The house was full of noise and unrest[⑥]. In the room above the kitchen someone was moving furniture about. The dining-room was crowded with boarders. Mrs. Kelly hurried back and forth from the breakfast table to the kitchen. Mr. Kelly wandered about in a baggy[⑦]

---

① empty：清场
② round up：使集拢
③ chop up：切细；割断
④ pitchfork：干草叉；长柄草耙
⑤ everlasting：永恒的；接连不断的
⑥ unrest：不安
⑦ baggy：袋状的，膨胀的

pair of trousers and a bathrobe. The young Kelly children ate greedily[①] in the kitchen. Doors banged and voices could be heard in all parts of the house.

Mick handed Doctor Copeland a cup of coffee mixed with watery milk. The milk gave the drink a gray-blue sheen. Some of the coffee had sloshed[②] over into the saucer, so first he dried the saucer and the rim of the cup with his handkerchief. He had not wanted coffee at all.

'I wish I could kill them,' Mick said.

The house quieted. The people in the dining-room went out to work. Mick and George left for school and the baby was shut into one of the front rooms. Mrs. Kelly wrapped a towel around her head and took a broom[③] with her upstairs.

The mute still stood in the doorway. Doctor Copeland gazed up into his face. 'You know of this?' he asked again. The words did not sound—they choked[④] in his throat—but his eyes asked the question all the same. Then the mute was gone. Doctor Copeland and Portia were alone. He sat for some time on the stool in the corner. At last he rose to go.

'You sit back down, Father. Us going to stay together this morning. I going to fry some fish and have egg-bread and potatoes for the dinner. You stay on here, and then I means to[⑤] serve you a good hot meal.'

'You know I have calls[⑥].'

'Less us just this one day. Please, Father. I feels like I going to really bust loose. Besides, I don't want you messing around in the streets by yourself.'

---

① greedily：贪婪地，贪食地

② slosh：搅动

③ broom：扫帚

④ choke：卡住；说不出话

⑤ mean to do sth.：打算做某事，表示有意愿或计划去做某事。（句中 means 应为 mean，误加 -s。）

⑥ call：短暂拜访，访问（此处 calls 为复数，指“巡诊”。）

He hesitated and felt the collar of his overcoat. It was very damp[①]. 'Daughter, I am sorry. You know I have visits[②].'

Portia held his shawl over the stove until the wool was hot. She buttoned his coat and turned up the collar about his neck. He cleared his throat and spat into one of the squares of paper that he carried with him in his pocket Then he burned the paper in the stove. On the way out he stopped and spoke to Highboy on the steps. He suggested that Highboy stay with Portia if he could arrange to get leave from work.

The air was piercing and cold. From the low, dark skies the drizzling[③] rain fell steadily. The rain had seeped into the garbage cans and in the alley there was the rank[④] odor of wet refuse[⑤]. As he walked he balanced himself with the help of a fence and kept his dark eyes on the ground.

He made all the strictly[⑥] necessary visits. Then he attended to office patients from noon until two o'clock. Afterward he sat at his desk with his fists clenched tight. But it was useless to try to cogitate on this thing.

He wished never again to see a human face. Yet at the same time he could not sit alone in the empty room. He put on his overcoat and went out again into the wet, cold street. In his pocket were several prescriptions to be left at the pharmacy[⑦]. But he did not wish to speak with Marshall Nicolls. He went into the store and laid the prescriptions[⑧] upon the counter. The pharmacist[⑨] turned from the powders he was measuring and held out both his hands. His thick lips worked soundlessly for a moment before he gained his poise[⑩].

---

① damp：潮湿的
② visit：拜访，访问，就诊（此处 visits 复数同上文 calls，都表示"巡诊"。）
③ drizzling：毛毛细雨的
④ rank：讨厌的；恶臭的
⑤ refuse：垃圾；废弃物
⑥ strictly：完全地；确切地
⑦ pharmacy：药房；配药学，药剂学；制药业
⑧ prescription：医药处方，药方
⑨ pharmacist：药剂师
⑩ gain one's poise：保持平衡（poise：平衡）

'Doctor,' he said formally. 'You must be aware that I and all our colleagues and the members of my lodge and church—we have your sorrow uppermost in our minds and wish to extend to you our deepest sympathy.'

Doctor Copeland turned shortly and left without a word. That was too little. Something more was needed. The strong, true purpose, the will to justice. He walked stiffly, his arms held close to his sides, toward the main street. He cogitated[①] without success. He could think of no white person of power in all the town who was both brave and just. He thought of every lawyer, every judge, every public official with whose name he was familiar—but the thought of each one of these white men was bitter in his heart. At last he decided on the judge of the Superior Court. When he reached the courthouse he did not hesitate but entered quickly, determined to see the judge that afternoon.

The wide front hall was empty except for a few idlers who lounged in the doorways leading to the offices on either side. He did not know where he could find the judge's office, so he wandered uncertainly through the building, looking at the placards on the doors. At last he came to a narrow passage. Halfway through this corridor three white men stood talking together and blocked the way. He drew close to the wall to pass, but one of them turned to stop him.

'What you want?'

'Will you please tell me where the judge's office is located?'

The white man jerked his thumb toward the end of the passage. Doctor Copeland recognized him as a deputy sheriff[②]. They had seen each other dozens of times but the deputy did not remember him. All white people looked similar to Negroes but Negroes took care to differentiate[③] between them. On the other hand, all Negroes looked

---

① cogitate：仔细考虑；谋划

② deputy sheriff：县副治安官

③ differentiate：区分，区别

similar to white men but white men did not usually bother to fix the face of a Negro in their minds. So the white man said, 'What you want, Reverend?'

The familiar joking title nettled[①] him. 'I am not a minister,' he said, 'I am a physician, a medical doctor. My name is Benedict Mady Copeland and I wish to see the judge immediately on urgent business.' The deputy was like other white men in that a clearly enunciated[②] speech maddened him. 'Is that so?' he mocked[③]. He winked at his friends. Then I am the deputy sheriff and my name is Mister Wilson and I tell you the judge is busy. Come back some other day.'

'It is imperative[④] that I see the judge,' Doctor Copeland said. 'I will wait.'

There was a bench at the entrance of the passage and he sat down. The three white men continued to talk, but he knew that the sheriff watched him. He was determined not to leave. More than half an hour passed. Several white men went freely back and forth through the corridor. He knew that the deputy was watching him and he sat rigid[⑤], his hands pressed between his knees. His sense of prudence[⑥] told him to go away and return later in the afternoon when the sheriff was not there. All of his life he had been circumspect[⑦] in his dealings with such people. But now something in him would not let him withdraw.

'Come here, you!' the deputy said finally.

His head trembled, and when he arose he was not steady on his feet. 'Yes?'

What you say you wanted to see the judge about?'

'I did not say,' said Doctor Copeland. 'I merely said that my

---

① nettle：惹怒，使恼火
② enunciated：发音清晰的
③ mock：嘲笑
④ imperative：必要的
⑤ rigid：僵硬的
⑥ prudence：审慎
⑦ circumspect：小心谨慎的

business with him was urgent.'

'You can't stand up straight. You been drinking liquor, haven't you? I smell it on your breath.'

'That is a lie,' said Doctor Copeland slowly. I have not—'

The sheriff struck him on the face. He fell against the wall. Two white men grasped him by the arm and dragged him down the steps to the main floor. He did not resist.

'That's the trouble with this country,' the sheriff said. These damn biggity niggers like him.'

He spoke no word and let them do with him as they would. He waited for the terrible anger and felt it arise in him. Rage made him weak, so that he stumbled①. They put him into the wagon② with two men as guards. They took him to the station and then to the jail. It was only when they entered③ the jail that the strength of his rage came to him. He broke loose suddenly from their grasp. In a corner he was surrounded. They struck him on the head and shoulders with their clubs. A glorious④ strength was in him and he heard himself laughing aloud as he fought. He sobbed and laughed at the same time. He kicked wildly with his feet. He fought with his fists and even struck at them with his head. Then he was clutched fast so that he could not move. They dragged him foot by foot through the hall of the jail. The door to a cell was opened. Someone behind kicked him in the groin⑤ and he fell to his knees on the floor.

In the cramped⑥ cubicle⑦ there were five other prisoners—three Negroes and two white men. One of the white men was very old and drunk. He sat on the floor and scratched himself. The other

---

① stumble：绊脚，绊跌；跌跌撞撞地走
② wagon：（一般由马拉的）四轮运货车（此处为囚车）
③ enter：进入
④ glorious：光荣的；辉煌的；极好的
⑤ groin：腹股沟，大腿根儿
⑥ cramped：狭窄的
⑦ cubicle：小卧室，小隔间

white prisoner was a boy not more than fifteen years of age. The three Negroes were young. As Doctor Copeland lay on the bunk looking up into their faces he recognized one of them.

'How come you here?' the young man asked. 'Ain't you Doctor Copeland?'

He said yes.

'My name Dary White. You taken out my sister's tonsils[①] last year.'

The icy cell was permeated with a rotten odor. A pail[②] brimming[③] with urine was in a corner. Cockroaches crawled upon the walls. He closed his eyes and immediately he must have slept, for when he looked up again the small barred window was black and a bright light burned in the hall. Four empty tin plates were on the floor. His dinner of cabbage and cornbread was beside him.

He sat on the bunk and sneezed violently[④] several times. When he breathed the phlegm[⑤] rattled in his chest. After a while the young white boy began to sneeze also. Doctor Copeland ran out of squares of paper and had to use sheets from a notebook in his pocket. The white boy leaned over the pail in the corner or simply let the water run from his nose onto the front of his shirt. His eyes were dilated, his clear cheeks flushed. He huddled on the edge of a bunk and groaned.

Soon they were led out to the lavatory[⑥], and on their return they prepared for sleep. There were six men to occupy four bunks. The old man lay snoring[⑦] on the floor. Dary and another boy squeezed into a bunk together.

The hours were long. The light in the hall burned his eyes and the odor in the cell made every breath a discomfort. He could not

① tonsil：扁桃体
② pail：桶
③ brimming：满溢的
④ violently：激烈地
⑤ phlegm：痰
⑥ lavatory：厕所；盥洗室
⑦ snoring：打鼾（snore 的现在分词形式）

keep warm. His teeth chattered and he shook with a hard chill. He sat up with the dirty blanket wrapped around him and swayed① to and fro. Twice he reached over to cover the white boy, who muttered② and threw out his arms in sleep. He swayed, his head in his hands, and from his throat there came a singing moan. He could not think of William. Nor could he even cogitate upon the strong, true purpose and draw strength from that. He could only feel the misery in him.

Then the tide of his fever turned. A warmth spread through him. He lay back, and it seemed he sank down into a place warm and red and full of comfort.

The next morning the sun came out. The strange Southern winter was at its end. Doctor Copeland was released. A little group waited outside the jail for him. Mr. Singer was there. Portia and Highboy and Marshall Nicolls were present also. Their faces were confused and he could not see them clearly. The sun was very bright.

'Father, don't you know that ain't no way to help our Willie? Messing around at a white folks' courthouse? Best thing us can do is keep our mouth shut and wait.'

Her loud voice echoed③ wearily in his ears. They climbed into a ten-cent taxicab, and then he was home and his face pressed into the fresh white pillow.

---

① sway：摇摆

② mutter：咕哝；抱怨地说

③ echo：回响，发出回声

11

MICK COULD not sleep all night. Etta was sick, so she had to sleep in the living-room. The sofa was too narrow and short. She had nightmares about Willie. Nearly a month had gone by since Portia had told about what they had done to him—but still she couldn't forget it. Twice in the night she had these bad dreams and woke up on the floor. A bump① came out on her forehead. Then at six o'clock she heard Bill go to the kitchen and fix his breakfast. It was daylight, but the shades were down so that the room was half-dark. She felt queer waking up in the living-room. She didn't like it. The sheet② was twisted around her, half on the sofa and half on the floor. The pillow was in the middle of the room. She got up and opened the door to the hall. Nobody was on the stairs. She ran in her nightgown③ to the back room.

'Move over, George.'

The kid lay in the very center of the bed. The night had been warm and he was naked as a jay bird. His fists were shut tight, and even in sleep his eyes were squinted④ like he was thinking about something very hard to figure out. His mouth was open and there was a little wet spot on the pillow. She pushed him.

'Wait—' he said in his sleep.

---

① bump：肿块；隆起

② sheet：薄片，纸张；薄板；床单

③ nightgown：睡衣

④ squinted：眯眼的，斜视的

'Move over on your side.'

'Wait—Lemme just finish this here dream—this here—'

She hauled him over where he belonged and lay down[1] close to him. When she opened her eyes again it was late, because the sun shone in through the back window. George was gone. From the yard she heard kids' voices and the sound of water running. Etta and Hazel were talking in the middle room. As she dressed a sudden notion came to her. She listened at the door but it was hard to hear what they said. She jerked the door open quick to surprise them.

They were reading a movie magazine. Etta was still in bed. She had her hand halfway over the picture of an actor. 'From here up don't you think he favors that boy who used to date with—'

'How you feel this morning, Etta?' Mick asked. She looked down under the bed and her private[2] box was still in the exact place where she had left it.

'A lot you care,' Etta said.

'You needn't try to pick a fight[3].'

Etta's face was peaked[4]. There was a terrible pain in her stomach and her ovary was diseased. It had something to do with being unwell. The doctor said they would have to cut out her ovary[5] right away. But their Dad said they would have to wait. There wasn't any money.

'How do you expect me to act, anyway?' Mick said. 'I ask you a polite question and then you start to nag at me. I feel like I ought to be sorry for you because you're sick, but you won't let me be decent. Therefore I naturally get mad.' She pushed back the bangs of her hair and looked close into the mirror. 'Boy! See this bump I got! I bet my head's broke. Twice I fell out last night and it seemed to me like I

---

① lay down：放下；制定；铺设；主张

② private：私人的，私有的

③ pick a fight：寻衅打架，例：Your colleagues may want to pick a fight, but if you're sincere enough you will be able to make friends with them. 你的同事可能会想挑事儿，但如果你足够真诚，就可以和他们交朋友。

④ peaked：苍白的，消瘦的

⑤ ovary：卵巢

hit that table by the sofa. I can't sleep in the living-room. That sofa cramps[①] me so much I can't stay in it'

'Hush that talking so loud,' Hazel said.

Mick knelt down on the floor and pulled out the big box. She looked carefully at the string that was tied around it. 'Say, have either of you fooled with[②] this?'

'Shoot!' Etta said. 'What would we want to mess with your junk for?'

'You just better not. I'd kill anybody that tried to mess with my private things.'

'Listen to that,' Hazel said. 'Mick Kelly, I think you're the most selfish person I've ever known. You don't care a thing in the world about anybody but—'

'Aw, poot[③]!' She slammed[④] the door. She hated both of them. That was a terrible thing to think, but it was true.

Her Dad was in the kitchen with Portia. He had on his bathrobe and was drinking a cup of coffee. The whites of his eyes were red and his cup rattled against his saucer[⑤]. He walked round and round the kitchen table.

'What time is it? Has Mister Singer gone yet?'

'He been gone, Hon,' Portia said. 'It near about ten o'clock.'

'Ten o'clock! Golly! I never have slept that late before.'

'What you keep in that big hatbox you tote[⑥] around with you?'

Mick reached into the stove and brought out half a dozen biscuits. 'Ask me no questions and I'll tell you no lies. A bad end comes to a person who pries.'

'If there's a little extra milk I think I'll just have it poured over

---

① cramp：束缚；阻碍
② fool with：玩弄，乱摆弄
③ poot：（美国俚语）放屁
④ slam：（使）砰地关上
⑤ saucer：茶碟，茶托，碟状物
⑥ tote：手提；携带

some crumbled[①] bread,' her Dad said. 'Grave yard soup. Maybe that will help settle my stomach.'

Mick split open the biscuits and put slices of fried white meat inside them. She sat down on the back steps to eat her breakfast. The morning was warm and bright. Spare-ribs and Sucker were playing with George in the back yard. Sucker wore his sun suit and the other two kids had taken off all their clothes except their shorts. They were scooting each other with the hose. The stream of water sparkled[②] bright in the sun. The wind blew out sprays of it like mist and in this mist there were the colors of the rainbow. A line of clothes flapped[③] in the wind—white sheets, Ralph's blue dress, a red blouse and nightgowns—wet and fresh and blowing out in different shapes. The day was almost like summer-time. Fuzzy little yellow jackets buzzed around the honeysuckle on the alley fence.

'Watch me hold it up over my head!' George hollered. 'Watch how the water runs down.'

She was too full of energy to sit still. George had filled a meal sack with dirt and hung it to a limb of the tree for a punching bag[④]. She began to hit this. Puck! Pock! She hit it in time to the song that had been in her mind when she woke up. George had mixed a sharp rock in the dirt and it bruised her knuckles.

'Aoow! You skeeted[⑤] the water right in my ear. It's busted my eardrum. I can't even hear.'

'Gimme[⑥] here. Let me skeet some.'

Sprays of the water blew into her face, and once the kids turned the hose[⑦] on her legs. She was afraid her box would get wet, so she carried it with her through the alley to the front porch. Harry was

---

① crumbled：破碎的
② sparkle：（使）闪耀；（使）发光
③ flap：飘动；挥动
④ punching bag：练习拳击用的吊袋（相当于 punchbag）
⑤ skeet：喷液体
⑥ gimme：正确表达为 give me。
⑦ hose：软管；长筒袜

sitting on his steps reading the newspaper. She opened her box and got out the notebook. But it was hard to settle her mind on the song she wanted to write down. Harry was looking over[①] in her direction and she could not think.

She and Harry had talked about so many things lately. Nearly every day they walked home from school together. They talked about God. Sometimes she would wake up in the night and shiver[②] over what they had said. Harry was a Pantheist[③]. That was a religion, the same as Baptist or Catholic or Jew. Harry believed that after you were dead and buried you changed to plants and fire and dirt and clouds and water.[④] It took thousands of years and then finally you were a part of all the world. He said he thought that was better than being one single angel. Anyhow it was better than nothing.

Harry threw the newspaper into his hall and then came over. 'It's hot like summer,' he said. 'And only March.'

'Yeah. I wish we could go swimming.'

'We would if there was any place.'

'There's not any place. Except that country club pool.'

'I sure would like to do something—to get out and go somewhere.'

'Me too,' she said, 'Wait! I know one place. It's out in the country about fifteen miles. It's a deep, wide creek in the woods. The Girl Scouts have a camp there in the summertime. Mrs. Wells took me and George and Pete and Sucker swimming there one time last year.'

'If you want to I can get bicycles and we can go tomorrow. I have a holiday one Sunday a month.'

'Well ride out and take a picnic dinner,' Mick said.

'O.K. I'll borrow the bikes.'

It was time for him to go to work. She watched him walk down

---

① look over：检查，察看

② shiver：（因寒冷或害怕而）颤抖，哆嗦

③ Pantheist：泛神论者

④ 参考译文：哈里相信，人死了被埋葬之后，会变成植物、火、尘土、云彩和水。

the street. He swung his arms. Halfway down the block there was a bay tree with low branches. Harry took a running jump, caught a limb, and chinned[①] himself. A happy feeling came in her because it was true they were real good friends. Also he was handsome. Tomorrow she would borrow Hazel's blue necklace and wear the silk dress. And for dinner they would take jelly sandwiches and Nehi. Maybe Harry would bring something queer, because they ate orthodox Jew[②]. She watched him until he turned the corner. It was true that he had grown to be a very good-looking fellow.

Harry in the country was different from Harry sitting on the back steps reading the newspapers and thinking about Hitler. They left early in the morning. The wheels he borrowed were the kind for boys—with a bar between the legs. They strapped[③] the lunches and bathing-suits to the fenders[④] and were gone before nine o'clock. The morning was hot and sunny. Within an hour they were far out of town on a red clay[⑤] road. The fields were bright and green and the sharp smell of pine trees was in the air. Harry talked in a very excited way. The warm wind blew into their faces. Her mouth was very dry and she was hungry.

'See that house up on the hill there? Less us stop and get some water.'

'No, we better wait. Well water[⑥] gives you typhoid[⑦].'

'I already had typhoid. I had pneumonia and a broken leg and a infected foot.'

'I remember.'

---

① chin：引体向上

② orthodox Jew：正统派犹太人，是 19 世纪兴起的犹太教教派，最严格地恪守传统信仰和律法礼仪的犹太教徒。认为成文律法和口传律法都是上帝启示犹太民族，与之立约的见证，为犹太人对上帝承担义务的律法准绳。

③ strap：用带子系

④ fender：（车辆）挡泥板；防撞垫

⑤ clay：黏土；泥土

⑥ well water：井水，此处 well 意为"井"。

⑦ typhoid：伤寒

'Yeah,' Mick said. 'Me and Bill stayed in the front room when we had typhoid fever and Pete Wells would run past on the sidewalk holding his nose and looking up at the window. Bill was very embarrassed. All my hair came out so I was bald-headed[①].'

'I bet we're at least ten miles from town. We've been riding an hour and a half—fast riding, too.'

'I sure am thirsty,' Mick said. 'And hungry. What you got in that sack for lunch?'

'Cold liver pudding and chicken salad sandwiches and pie.'

That's a good picnic dinner. 'She was ashamed of what she had brought.' I got two hard-boiled eggs—already stuffed—with separate little packages of salt and pepper. And sandwiches—blackberry jelly with butter. Everything wrapped in oil paper. And paper napkins.'

'I didn't intend for you to bring anything,' Harry said. 'My Mother fixed lunch for both of us. I asked you out here and all. We'll come to a store soon and get cold drinks.'

They rode half an hour longer before they finally came to the filling-station[②] store. Harry propped up[③] the bicycles and she went in ahead of him. After the bright glare the store seemed dark. The shelves were stacked with slabs of white meat, cans of oil, and sacks of meal. Flies buzzed[④] over a big, sticky jar of loose candy on the counter.

'What kind of drinks you got?' Harry asked.

The store man started to name them over. Mick opened the icebox and looked inside. Her hands felt good in the cold water. 'I want a chocolate Nehi. You got any of them? '

'Ditto,' Harry said. 'Make it two.'

'No, wait a minute. Here's some ice-cold beer. I want a bottle of beer if you can treat as high as that.'

---

① bald-headed：秃头的

② filling-station：汽车加油站（等于 gas station）

③ prop up：支撑，支持

④ buzz：发嗡嗡声

Harry ordered one for himself, also. He thought it was a sin[①] for anybody under twenty to drink beer—but maybe he just suddenly wanted to be a sport[②]. After the first swallow he made a bitter face. They sat on the steps in front of the store. Mick's legs were so tired that the muscles in them jumped. She wiped the neck of the bottle with her hand and took a long, cold pull. Across the road there was a big empty field of grass, and beyond that a fringe of pine woods. The trees were every color of green—from a bright yellow-green to a dark color that was almost black. The sky was hot blue.

'I like beer,' she said. 'I used to sop bread down in the drops our Dad left. I like to lick salt out my hand while I drink. This is the second bottle to myself I've ever had.'

'The first swallow was sour. But the rest tastes good.'

The storeman[③] said it was twelve miles from town. They had four more miles to go. Harry paid him and they were out in the hot sun again. Harry was talking loud and he kept laughing without any reason.

'Gosh, the beer along with this hot sun makes me dizzy[④]. But I sure do feel good,' he said.

'I can't wait to get in swimming.'

There was sand in the road and they had to throw all their weight on the pedals to keep from bogging.[⑤] Harry's shirt was stuck to his back with sweat. He still kept talking. The road changed to red clay and the sand was behind them. There was a slow colored song in her mind—one Portia's brother used to play on his harp. She pedaled[⑥] in time to it.

Then finally they reached the place she had been looking

① sin：（违背宗教或道德的）罪，罪恶

② be a sport：大方一点（用于向人求助时），此处指 Harry 对自己喝酒的放纵。

③ storeman：零售店店主

④ dizzy：头晕目眩的

⑤ 参考译文：路上有沙子，他们只能把全身重量都压在脚踏板上，免得陷进去。（pedal：踏板；bog：陷入）

⑥ pedal：踩（自行车）踏板

for. 'This is it! See that sign that says PRIVATE? We got to climb the bob-wire fence and then take that path there—see!'

The woods were very quiet. Slick pine needles covered the ground. Within a few minutes they had reached the creek[①]. The water was brown and swift. Cool. There was no sound except from the water and a breeze singing high up in the pine trees. It was like the deep, quiet woods made them timid, and they walked softly along the bank beside the creek.

'Don't it look pretty.'

Harry laughed. 'What makes you whisper? Listen here!' He clapped his hand over his mouth and gave a long Indian whoop[②] that echoed back at them. 'Come on. Let's jump in the water and cool off.'

'Aren't you hungry?'

'O.K. Then we'll eat first. We'll eat half the lunch now and half later on when we come out.'

She unwrapped the jelly sandwiches. When they were finished Harry balled the papers neatly and stuffed them into a hollow tree stump. Then he took his shorts and went down the path. She shucked off[③] her clothes behind a bush and struggled into Hazel's bathing-suit The suit was too small and cut her between the legs.

'You ready?' Harry hollered.

She heard a splash in the water and when she reached the bank Harry was already swimming. 'Don't dive yet until I find out if there are any stumps or shallow places,' he said. She just looked at his head bobbing[④] in the water. She had never intended to dive, anyway. She couldn't even swim. She had been in swimming only a few times in her life—and then she always wore water-wings[⑤] or stayed out of parts

① creek：小溪；小湾
② whoop：大叫；呐喊
③ shuck off：脱去
④ bob：（使在水中）上下快速移动，摆动
⑤ water-wing：浮水圈

that were over her head. But it would be sissy to tell Harry. She was embarrassed. All of a sudden she told a tale:

'I don't dive[①] any more. I used to dive, high dive, all the time. But once I busted[②] my head open, so I can't dive any more.' She thought for a minute. 'It was a double jack-knife dive I was doing. And when I came up there was blood all in the water. But I didn't think anything about it and just began to do swimming tricks. These people were hollering at me. Then I found out where all this blood in the water was coming from. And I never have swam good since.'

Harry scrambled up[③] the bank. 'Gosh! I never heard about that.'

She meant to add on to[④] the tale to make it sound more reasonable, but instead she just looked at Harry. His skin was light brown and the water made it shining. There were hairs on his chest and legs. In the tight trunks he seemed very naked. Without his glasses his face was wider and more handsome. His eyes were wet and blue. He was looking at her and it was like suddenly they got embarrassed.

'The water's about ten feet deep except over on the other bank, and there it's shallow.'

'Less us get going. I bet that cold water feels good.'

She wasn't scared. She felt the same as if she had got caught at the top of a very high tree and there was nothing to do but just climb down the best way she could—a dead-calm feeling.[⑤] She edged off the bank and was in ice-cold water. She held to a root until it broke in her hands and then she began to swim. Once she choked and went under, but she kept going and didn't lose any face. She swam and reached the other side of the bank where she could touch bottom. Then she felt good. She smacked[⑥] the water with her fists and called out crazy

---

① dive：潜水
② bust：弄坏，打碎；打破
③ scramble up：爬上
④ add on to：增加，添加
⑤ 参考译文：她觉得自己就像困在了一棵很高的大树树顶，她别无选择，只能小心翼翼地爬下来——一种死一般平静的感觉。
⑥ smack：强力打进

words to make echoes.

'Watch here!'

Harry shimmied up[①] a tall, thin little tree. The trunk was limber and when he reached the top it swayed down with him. He dropped into the water.

'Me too! Watch me do it!'

'That's a sapling[②].'

She was as good a climber as anybody on the block. She copied exactly what he had done and hit the water with a hard smack. She could swim, too. Now she could swim O.K.

They played follow the leader and ran up and down the bank and jumped in the cold brown water. They hollered and jumped and climbed. They played around for maybe two hours. Then they were standing on the bank and they both looked at each other and there didn't seem to be anything new to do. Suddenly she said:

'Have you ever swam naked?'

The woods was very quiet and for a minute he did not answer. He was cold. His titties had turned hard and purple. His lips were purple and his teeth chattered[③]. 'I—I don't think so.'

This excitement was in her, and she said something she didn't mean to say. 'I would if you would. I dare you to.'

Harry slicked[④] back the dark, wet bangs[⑤] of his hair. 'O.K.'

They both took off their bathing-suits. Harry had his back to her. He stumbled and his ears were red. Then they turned toward each other. Maybe it was half an hour they stood there—maybe not more man a minute.

Harry pulled a leaf from a tree and tore it to pieces. 'We better get dressed.'

---

① shimmy up：攀爬

② sapling：树苗

③ chatter：唠叨；喋喋不休

④ slick：使（头发）打扮整洁

⑤ bang：刘海（bangs）

All through the picnic dinner neither of them spoke. They spread the dinner on the ground. Harry divided everything in half. There was the hot, sleepy feeling of a summer afternoon. In the deep woods they could hear no sound except the slow flowing of the water and the songbirds[①]. Harry held his stuffed egg and mashed[②] the yellow with his thumb. What did that make her remember? She heard herself breathe.

Then he looked up over her shoulder. 'Listen here. I think you're so pretty, Mick. I never did think so before. I don't mean I thought you were very ugly—I just mean that—'

She threw a pine cone in the water. 'Maybe we better start back if we want to be home before dark.'

'No,' he said. 'Let's lie down. Just for a minute.'

He brought handfuls of pine needles and leaves and gray moss[③]. She sucked[④] her knee and watched him. Her fists were tight and it was like she was tense all over.

'Now we can sleep and be fresh for the trip home.'

They lay on the soft bed and looked up at the dark-green pine clumps[⑤] against the sky. A bird sang a sad, clear song she had never heard before. One high note like an oboe[⑥]—and then it sank down five tones and called again. The song was sad as a question without words.

'I love that bird,' Harry said. 'I think it's a vireo.'

'I wish we was at the ocean. On the beach and watching the ships far out on the water. You went to the beach one summer—exactly what is it like?'

His voice was rough and low. Well—there are the waves.

---

① songbird：鸣禽
② mash：捣碎
③ moss：苔藓；泥沼
④ suck：吸，吮
⑤ clump：(树或植物的)丛，此处 pine clumps(松树丛)。
⑥ oboe：双簧管

Sometimes blue and sometimes green, and in the bright sun they look glassy. And on the sand you can pick up these little shells. Like the kind we brought back in a cigar box. And over the water are these white gulls. We were at the Gulf of Mexico—these cool bay breezes[①] blew all the time and there it's never baking hot like it is here. Always—'

'Snow,' Mick said. 'That's what I want to see. Cold, white drifts of snow like in pictures. Blizzards. White, cold snow that keeps falling soft and falls on and on and on through all the winter. Snow like in Alaska.'

They both turned at the same time. They were close against each other. She felt him trembling and her fists were tight enough to crack[②]. 'Oh, God,' he kept saying over and over. It was like her head was broke off from her body and thrown away[③]. And her eyes looked up straight into the blinding[④] sun while she counted something in her mind. And then this was the way.

This was how it was.

They pushed the wheels slowly along the road. Harry's head hung down and his shoulders were bent. Their shadows were long and black on the dusty road, for it was late afternoon.

'Listen here,' he said.

'Yeah.'

'We got to understand this. We got to. Do you—any?'

'I don't know. I reckon not.'

'Listen here. We got to do something. Let's sit down.'

They dropped the bicycles and sat by a ditch[⑤] beside the road. They sat far apart from each other. The late sun burned down on their

---

① breeze：微风
② crack：破裂，裂开
③ throw away：扔掉，丢弃
④ blinding：使人炫目的
⑤ ditch：沟渠，壕沟

heads and there were brown, crumbly[①] ant beds all around them.

'We got to understand this,' Harry said.

He cried. He sat very still and the tears rolled down[②] his white face. She could not think about the thing that made him cry. An ant stung her on the ankle and she picked it up in her fingers and looked at it very close.

'It's this way,' he said. 'I never had even kissed a girl before.'

'Me neither. I never kissed any boy. Out of the family.'

'That's all I used to think about—was to kiss this certain girl. I used to plan about it during school and dream about it at night. And then once she gave me a date. And I could tell she meant for me to kiss her. And I just looked at her in the dark and I couldn't. That was all I had thought about—to kiss her—and when the time came I couldn't.'

She dug a hole in the ground with her finger and buried the dead ant.

It was all my fault. Adultery is a terrible sin any way you look at it. And you were two years younger than me and just a kid.'

'No, I wasn't. I wasn't any kid. But now I wish I was, though.'

'Listen here. If you think we ought to we can get married—secretly or any other way.'

Mick shook her head. 'I didn't like that. I never will marry with any boy.'

'I never will marry either. I know that and I'm not just saying so—it's true.'

His face scared her. His nose quivered and his bottom lip was mottled[③] and bloody where he had bitten it. His eyes were bright and wet and scowling[④]. His face was whiter than any face she could remember. She turned her head from him. Things would be better if

---

① crumbly：脆的；易碎的

② roll down：滚下

③ mottled：（颜色）斑驳的

④ scowling：愁眉不展的；闷闷不乐的

only he would just quit talking. Her eyes looked slowly around her—at the streaked red-and-white clay of the ditch, at a broken whiskey bottle, at a pine tree across from them with a sign advertising for a man for county sheriff.① She wanted to sit quiet for a long time and not think and not say a word.

'I'm leaving town. I'm a good mechanic② and I can get a job some other place. If I stayed home Mother could read this in my eyes.'

'Tell me. Can you look at me and see the difference?'

Harry watched her face a long time and nodded that he could. Then he said:

'There's just one more thing. In a month or two I'll send you my address and you write and tell me for sure whether you're all right.'

'How you mean?' she asked slowly.

He explained to her. 'All you need to write is "O.K." and then TO know.'

They were walking home again, pushing the wheels. Their shadows stretched out③ giant-sized on the road. Harry was bent over like an old beggar and kept wiping his nose on his sleeve. For a minute there was a bright, golden glow over everything before the sun sank down behind the trees and their shadows were gone on the road before them.④ She felt very old, and it was like something was heavy inside her. She was a grown person now, whether she wanted to be or not.

They had walked the sixteen miles and were in the dark alley at home. She could see the yellow light from their kitchen. Harry's house was dark—his mother had not come home. She worked for a tailor in a shop on a side street. Sometimes even on Sunday. When

---

① 参考译文：她慢慢环顾四周——望着水沟里的红白相间的黏土，望着一个碎掉的威士忌瓶子，望着他们对面的一棵松树，上面挂了个牌子，为一个竞选乡村治安官的男人做宣传。（ditch：水沟；sheriff：州长）

② mechanic：机械工，机修工

③ stretch out：伸出；伸展

④ 参考译文：有一瞬间，一切都闪耀着明亮金黄的光芒，然后太阳落到了树木背后，她们眼前路上的影子消失了。（此句中 before 引导的时间状语从句表示事件发生的先后顺序。）

you looked through the window you could see her bending over the machine in the back or pushing a long needle through the heavy pieces of goods. She never looked up while you watched her. And at night she cooked these orthodox dishes for Harry and her.

'Listen here—' he said.

She waited in the dark, but he did not finish. They shook hands with each other and Harry walked up the dark alley between the houses. When he reached the sidewalk he turned and looked back over his shoulder. A light shone on his face and it was white and hard. Then he was gone.

'This here is a riddle,' George said.

'I listening.'

'Two Indians was walking on a trail. The one in front was the son of the one behind but the one behind was not his father. What kin was they?'

'Less see. His stepfather.'

George grinned at Portia with his little square, blue teeth.

'His uncle, then.'

'You can't guess. It was his mother. The trick is that you don't think about a Indian being a lady.'

She stood outside the room and watched them. The doorway framed① the kitchen like a picture. Inside it was homey② and clean. Only the light by the sink was turned on and there were shadows in the room. Bill and Hazel played black-jack at the table with matches for money. Hazel felt the braids③ of her hair with her plump, pink fingers while Bill sucked in his cheeks and dealt the cards in a very serious way. At the sink Portia was drying the dishes with a clean checked④ towel. She looked thin and her skin was golden yellow, her

---

① frame：给……做框
② homey：舒适的
③ braid：辫子
④ checked：格子花纹的

greased[1] black hair slicked neat[2]. Ralph sat quietly on the floor and George was trying a little harness on him made out of old Christmas tinsel[3].

'This here is another riddle, Portia. If the hand of a clock points to half-past two—'

She went into the room. It was like she had expected them to move back when they saw her and stand around in a circle and look. But they just glanced at her. She sat down at the table and waited.

'Here you come traipsing in after everbody done finished supper. Seem to me like I never will get off from work.'

Nobody noticed her. She ate a big plateful of cabbage and salmon and finished off with junket[4]. It was her Mama she was thinking about. The door opened and her Mama came in and told Portia that Miss Brown had said she found a bedbug[5] in her room. To get out the gasoline.

'Quit frowning[6] like that, Mick. You're coming to the age where you ought to fix up and try to look the best you can. And hold on—don't barge[7] out like that when I speak with you—I mean you to give Ralph a good sponge bath before he goes to bed. Clean his nose and ears good.'

Ralph's soft hair was sticky with oatmeal[8]. She wiped it with a dishrag[9] and rinsed[10] his face and hands at the sink. Bill and Hazel finished their game. Bill's long fingernails scraped on the table as he took up the matches. George carried Ralph off to bed. She and Portia were alone in the kitchen.

---

① greased：加过润滑脂的
② neat：整洁的
③ tinsel：金属箔；俗丽的东西
④ junket：乳冻甜食
⑤ bedbug：臭虫；床虱
⑥ frown：皱眉头
⑦ barge：蓄意冲撞
⑧ oatmeal：燕麦粥；燕麦片
⑨ dishrag：抹布；洗碟用布
⑩ rinse：（用清水）冲洗

'Listen! Look at me. Do you notice anything different?'

'Sure I notice, Hon.'

Portia put on her red hat and changed her shoes.

'Well—?'

'Just you take a little grease and rub it on your face. Your nose already done peeled[①] very bad. They say grease is the best thing for bad sunburn.'

She stood by herself in the dark back yard, breaking off[②] pieces of bark from the oak tree with her fingernails. It was almost worse, this way. Maybe she would feel better if they could look at her and tell. If they knew.

Her Dad called her from the back steps. 'Mick! Oh, Mick!'

'Yes, sir.'

'The telephone.'

George crowded up close and tried to listen in, but she pushed him away. Mrs. Minowitz talked very loud and excited.

'My Harry should be home by now. You know where he is? '

'No, ma'am.'

'He said you two would ride out on bicycles. Where should he be now? You know where he is?'

'No, ma'am,' Mick said again.

---

① peel：脱皮，剥落
② break off：折断

12

NOW THAT the days were hot again the Sunny Dixie Show was always crowded. The March wind quieted. Trees were thick with their foliage① of ocherous green. The sky was a cloudless② blue and the rays of the sun grew stronger. The air was sultry③. Jake Blount hated this weather. He thought dizzily of the long, burning summer months ahead. He did not feel well. Recently a headache had begun to trouble him constantly. He had gained weight so that his stomach developed a little pouch. He had to leave the top button of his trousers undone. He knew that this was alcoholic fat, but he kept on drinking. Liquor helped the ache in his head. He had only to take one small glass to make it better. Nowadays one glass was the same to him as a quart. It was not the liquor of the moment that gave him the kick—but the reaction of the first swallow to all the alcohol which had saturated his blood during these last months.④ A spoonful of beer would help the throbbing in his head, but a quart of whiskey could not make him drunk.

He cut out liquor entirely. For several days he drank only water and Orange Crush. The pain was like a crawling worm in his head.

---

① foliage：植物

② cloudless：无云的

③ sultry：闷热的；狂暴的

④ 参考译文：让他兴奋的不是当时的酒——而是第一口酒下肚后，引发了过去几个月中储存在他血液中的所有酒精的反应。本句原文是强调句与定语从句并存的复合句。（saturate：使饱和，使充满）

He worked wearily during the long afternoons and evenings. He could not sleep and it was agony to try to read. The damp, sour stink in his room infuriated[①] him. He lay restless in the bed and when at last he fell asleep daylight had come.

A dream haunted him. It had first come to him four months ago. He would awake with terror—but the strange point was that never could he remember the contents of this dream. Only the feeling remained when his eyes were opened. Each time his fears at awakening were so identical that he did not doubt but what these dreams were the same. He was used to dreams, the grotesque[②] nightmares of drink that led him down into a madman's region of disorder, but always the morning light scattered the effects of these wild dreams and he forgot them.

This blank, stealthy dream was of a different nature. He awoke and could remember nothing. But there was a sense of menace[③] that lingered in him long after. Then he awoke one morning with the old fear but with a faint remembrance of the darkness behind him. He had been walking among a crowd of people and in his arms he carried something. That was all he could be sure about. Had he stolen? Had he been trying to save some possession? Was he being hunted by all these people around him? He did not think so. The more he studied this simple dream the less he could understand. Then for some time afterward the dream did not return.

He met the writer of signs whose chalked message he had seen the past November. From the first day of their meeting the old man clung to[④] him like an evil genius[⑤]. His name was Simms and he preached on the sidewalks. The winter cold had kept him indoors, but in the spring he was out on the streets all day. His white hair was soft

---

① infuriate：激怒

② grotesque：怪诞的，奇怪的

③ sense of menace：恐怖氛围（menace：威胁，恐吓）

④ cling to：紧跟不放（clung 为 cling 过去式，表示“抓紧”）

⑤ evil genius：邪恶天才

and ragged on his neck and he carried around with him a woman's big silk pocketbook full of chalk and Jesus ads. His eyes were bright and crazy. Simms tried to convert him.

'Child of adversity①, I smell the sinful stink of beer on thy breath. And you smoke cigarettes. If the Lord had wanted us to smoke cigarettes He would have said so in His Book. The mark of Satan is on thy brow. I see it. Repent. Let me show you the light.'

Jake rolled up his eyes and made a slow pious② sign in the air. Then he opened his oil-stained hand. 'I reveal this only to you,' he said in a low stage voice. Simms looked down at the scar in his palm. Jake leaned closer and whispered: 'And there's the other sign. The sign you know. For I was born with them.'

Simms backed against the fence. With a womanish③ gesture he lifted a lock of silver hair from his forehead and smoothed it back on his head. Nervously his tongue licked the corners of his mouth. Jake laughed.

'Blasphemer!' Simms screamed. 'God will get you. You and all your crew. God remembers the scoffers④. He watches after me. God watches everybody but He watches me the most. Like He did Moses. God tells me things in the night. God will get you.'

He took Simms down to a corner store for Coca-Colas and peanut-butter⑤ crackers. Simms began to work on him again. When he left for the show Simms ran along behind him.

'Come to this corner tonight at seven o'clock. Jesus has a message just for you.'

The first days of April were windy and warm. White clouds trailed across the blue sky. In the wind there was the smell of the river and also the fresher smell of fields beyond the town. The show was

---

① adversity：逆境，厄运
② pious：虔诚的
③ womanish：女子气的
④ scoffer：嘲笑者
⑤ peanut-butter：花生酱

crowded every day from four in the afternoon until midnight. The crowd was a tough one. With the new spring he felt an undertone of trouble.

One night he was working on the machinery of the swings when suddenly he was roused from thought by the sounds of angry voices.[1] Quickly he pushed through the crowd until he saw a white girl fighting with a colored girl by the ticket booth of the flying-jinny. He wrenched[2] them apart, but still they struggled to get at each other. The crowd took sides and there was a bedlam[3] of noise. The white girl was a hunchback. She held something tight in her hand.

'I seen you,' the colored girl yelled. 'I ghy beat that hunch off your back, too.'

'Hush your mouth, you black nigger!'

'Low-down factory tag. I done paid my money and I ghy ride. White man, you make her give me back my ticket.'

'Black nigger slut!'

Jake looked from one to the other. The crowd pressed close. There were mumbled[4] opinions on every side.

'I seen Lurie drop her ticket and I watched this here white lady pick it up. That the truth,' a colored boy said.

'No nigger going to put her hands on no white girl while—.'

'You quit that pushing me. I ready to hit back even if your skin do be white.'

Roughly Jake pushed into the thick[5] of the crowd. 'All right!' he yelled. 'Move on—break it up. Every damn one of you.' There was something about the size of his fists that made the people drift sullenly away. Jake turned back to the two girls.

---

① 参考译文：一天晚上，他正在检修秋千的机械装置，突然被一阵愤怒的声音惊得回过神来。（when 引导的时间状语从句表示某事发生的时候另一件事也发生了。）

② wrench：猛扭（wrench…+*adj.*：猛地使……处于某种状态，例：He wrenched the door open. 他猛地把门拉开了。）

③ bedlam：混乱，骚乱

④ mumbled：说话含糊的

⑤ thick：最密集处，中心处

'This here the way it is,' said the colored girl. 'I bet I one of the few peoples here who done saved over fifty cents till Friday night. I done ironed double this week. I done paid a good nickel for that ticket she holding. And now I means to ride.'

Jake settled the trouble quickly. He let the hunchback[①] keep the disputed ticket and issued another one to the colored girl. For the rest of that evening there were no more quarrels. But Jake moved alertly through the crowd. He was troubled and uneasy.

In addition to himself there were five other employees at the show—two men to operate[②] the swings and take tickets and three girls to manage the booths. This did not count Patterson. The show-owner spent most of his time playing cards with himself in his trailer. His eyes were dull, with the pupils shrunken, and the skin of his neck hung in yellow, pulpy folds.[③] During the past few months Jake had had two raises in pay. At midnight it was his job to report to Patterson and hand over the takings of the evening. Sometimes Patterson did not notice him until he had been in the trailer for several minutes; he would be staring at the cards, sunk in a stupor[④]. The air of the trailer was heavy with the stinks of food and reefers. Patterson held his hand over his stomach as though protecting it from something. He always checked over the accounts very thoroughly.

Jake and the two operators had a squabble[⑤]. These men were both former doffers at one of the mills. At first he had tried to talk to them and help them to see the truth. Once he invited them to a pool room for a drink. But they were so dumb[⑥] he couldn't help them. Soon after this he overheard the conversation between them that caused the trouble. It was an early Sunday morning, almost two

---

① hunchback：驼背

② operate：操作

③ 参考译文：他眼神迟钝，瞳孔缩着，脖子上的皮肤堆成层层黄色的褶皱，软软的。本文原文为典型的 with 伴随结构，后跟随独立主格结构。（pupil：瞳孔；shrunken：皱缩的）

④ stupor：（尤指由于醉酒、吸毒或震动而出现的）神志不清，恍惚，麻痹状态

⑤ squabble：争吵，口角

⑥ dumb：愚蠢而恼人的

o'clock, and he had been checking the accounts with Patterson. When he stepped out of the trailer the grounds seemed empty. The moon was bright. He was thinking of Singer and the free day ahead. Then as he passed by the swings he heard someone speak his name. The two operators had finished work and were smoking together. Jake listened.

'If there's anything I hate worse than a nigger it's a Red.'

'He tickles me. I don't pay him no mind. The way he struts around. I never seen such a sawed-off runt. How tall is he, you reckon?'

'Around five foot But he thinks he got to tell everybody so much. He oughta be in jail. That's where. The Red Bolshevik.'

'He just tickles me. I can't look at him without laughing.'

'He needn't act biggity with me.'

Jake watched them follow the path toward Weavers Lane. His first thought was to rush out and confront them, but a certain shrinking held him back. For several days he fumed① in silence. Then one night after work he followed the two men for several blocks and as they turned a corner he cut in front of them.

'I heard you,' he said breathlessly. 'It so happened I heard every word you said last Saturday night. Sure I'm a Red. At least I reckon I am. But what are you?' They stood beneath a street light. The two men stepped back from him. The neighborhood was deserted. 'You pasty-faced②, shrunk-gutted, ricket-ridden little rats! I could reach out and choke your stringy③ necks—one to each hand. Runt or no, I could lay you on this sidewalk where they'd have to scrape you up with shovels.④'

The two men looked at each other, cowed⑤, and tried to walk

① fume：十分恼火

② pasty-faced：脸色苍白的

③ stringy：多筋的

④ 参考译文：别管是不是小矮子，我可以把你们打倒在人行道上，到时候得用铲子才能把你们铲起来。

⑤ cow：威胁，恐吓

on. But Jake would not let them pass. He kept step with them, walking backward, a furious[①] sneer[②] on his face.

'All I got to say is this: In the future I suggest you come to me whenever you feel the need to make remarks about my height, weight, accent, demeanor, or ideology[③]. And that last is not what I take a leak with either—case you don't know. We will discuss it together.'

Afterward Jake treated the two men with angry contempt[④]. Behind his back they jeered at him. One afternoon he found that the engine of the swings had been deliberately damaged and he had to work three hours overtime to fix it. Always he felt someone was laughing at him. Each time he heard the girls talking together he drew himself up straight and laughed carelessly aloud to himself as though thinking of some private joke.

The warm southwest winds from the Gulf of Mexico were heavy with the smells of spring. The days grew longer and the sun was bright. The lazy warmth depressed him. He began to drink again. As soon as work was done he went home and lay down on his bed. Sometimes he stayed there, fully clothed and inert[⑤], for twelve or thirteen hours. The restlessness that had caused him to sob and bite his nails only a few months before seemed to have gone. And yet beneath his inertia Jake felt the old tension[⑥]. Of all the places he had been this was the loneliest town of all. Or it would be without Singer. Only he and Singer understood the truth. He knew and could not get the don't-knows to see. It was like trying to fight darkness or heat or a stink in the air. He stared morosely out of his window. A stunted, smoked-blackened tree at the corner had put out new leaves of a bilious green[⑦]. The sky was always a deep, hard blue. The mosquitoes

---

① furious：激烈的；猛烈的
② sneer：嘲笑，冷笑
③ ideology：意识形态；思想意识
④ contempt：轻视，蔑视；耻辱
⑤ inert：惰性的；呆滞的
⑥ tension：紧张，不安
⑦ bilious green：胆绿色，又指绿得扎眼。

from a fetid stream that ran through this part of the town buzzed in the room.

He caught the itch. He mixed some sulphur and hog fat and greased his body every morning. He clawed himself raw[①] and it seemed that the itching[②] would never be soothed. One night he broke loose. He had been sitting alone for many hours. He had mixed gin and whiskey and was very drunk. It was almost morning. He leaned out of the window and looked at the dark silent street. He thought of all the people around him. Sleeping. The don't-knows. Suddenly he bawled out in a loud voice: 'This is the truth! You bastards don't know anything. You don't know. You don't know!'

The street awoke angrily. Lamps were lighted and sleepy curses were called to him. The men who lived in the house rattled furiously[③] on his door. The girls from a cat-house across the street stuck their heads out of the windows.

'You dumb dumb dumb dumb bastards. You dumb dumb dumb dumb—'

'Shuddup! Shuddup!'

The fellows in the hall were pushing against the door: 'You drunk bull! You'll be a sight dumber when we get through with you.'

'How many out there?' Jake roared. He banged an empty bottle on the windowsill[④]. 'Come on, everybody. Come one, come all. I'll settle you three at a time.'

'That's right, Honey,' a whore called.

The door was giving way. Jake jumped from the window and ran through a side alley. 'Hee-haw! Hee-haw!' he yelled drunkenly[⑤]. He was barefooted and shirtless. An hour later he stumbled[⑥] into Singer's

---

① raw：刺痛的
② itching：痒
③ furiously：猛烈地；狂暴地
④ windowsill：窗台；窗沿
⑤ drunkenly：醉醺醺地
⑥ stumble：绊脚，绊跌；跌跌撞撞地走

room. He sprawled[①] on the floor and laughed himself to sleep.

On an April morning he found the body of a man who had been murdered. A young Negro. Jake found him in a ditch about thirty yards from the showgrounds. The Negro's throat had been slashed so that the head was rolled back at a crazy angle. The sun shone hot on his open, glassy eyes and flies hovered[②] over the dried blood that covered his chest. The dead man held a red-and-yellow cane with a tassel like the ones sold at the hamburger booth at the show. Jake stared gloomily down at the body for some time. Then he called the police. No clues were found. Two days later the family of the dead man claimed his body at the morgue[③].

At the Sunny Dixie there were frequent fights and quarrels. Sometimes two friends would come to the show arm in arm, laughing and drinking—and before they left they would be struggling together in a panting[④] rage. Jake was always alert. Beneath the gaudy gaiety of the show, the bright lights, and the lazy laughter, he felt something sullen and dangerous.

Through these dazed, disjointed weeks Simms nagged his footsteps constantly. The old man liked to come with a soapbox and a Bible and take a stand in the middle of the crowd to preach. He talked of the second coming of Christ. He said that the Day of Judgment would be October 2, 1951. He would point out certain drunks and scream at them in his raw, worn voice. Excitement made his mouth fill with water so that his words had a wet, gurgling[⑤] sound. Once he had slipped in and set up his stand no arguments could make him budge. He made Jake a present of a Gideon Bible, and told him to pray on his knees for one hour each night and to hurl away every glass of beer or cigarette that was offered him.

---

① sprawl：伸开四肢坐（或躺）
② hover：盘旋，翱翔；徘徊
③ morgue：陈尸所
④ panting：气喘吁吁的
⑤ gurgle：发汩汩声；（婴儿）咯咯作声

They quarreled over walls and fences. Jake had begun to carry chalk in his pockets, also. He wrote brief sentences. He tried to word them so that a passerby[1] would stop and ponder over the meaning. So that a man would wonder. So that a man would think. Also, he wrote short pamphlets and distributed them in the streets.

If it had not been for Singer, Jake knew that he would have left the town. Only on Sunday, when he was with his friend, did he feel at peace. Sometimes they would go for a walk together or play chess—but more often they spent the day quietly in Singer's room. If he wished to talk Singer was always attentive. If he sat morosely[2] through the day the mute understood his feelings and was not surprised. It seemed to him that only Singer could help him now.

Then one Sunday when he climbed the stairs he saw that Singer's door was open. The room was empty. He sat alone for more than two hours. At last he heard Singer's footsteps on the stairs.

'I was wondering about you. Where you been?'

Singer smiled. He brushed off his hat with a handkerchief and put it away. Then deliberately he took his silver pencil from his pocket and leaned over the mantelpiece[3] to write a note.

'What you mean?' Jake asked when he read what the mute had written. 'Whose legs are cut off?'

Singer took back the note and wrote a few additional[4] sentences.

'Huh!' Jake said. That don't surprise me.'

He brooded[5] over the piece of paper and then crumpled[6] it in his hand. The listlessness of the past month was gone and he was tense and uneasy. 'Huh!' he said again.

Singer put on a pot of coffee and got out his chessboard. Jake

---

① passerby：行人，过路人
② morosely：愁眉苦脸地；忧郁地
③ mantelpiece：壁炉架；壁炉台
④ additional：附加的，额外的
⑤ brood：沉思
⑥ crumple：弄皱

tore[1] the note to pieces and rolled the fragments[2] between his sweating palms.

'But something can be done about this,' he said after a while. 'You know it?'

Singer nodded uncertainly.

'I want to see the boy and hear the whole story. When can you take me around there?'

Singer deliberated. Then he wrote on a pad of paper, 'Tonight.'

Jake held his hand to his mouth and began to walk restlessly around the room. 'We can do something.'

---

① tear：撕开

② fragment：碎片

13

JAKE and Singer waited on the front porch. When they pushed the doorbell there was no sound of a ring in the darkened house. Jake knocked impatiently and pressed his nose against the screen door. Beside him Singer stood wooden and smiling, with two spots of color on his cheeks, for they had drunk a bottle of gin together. The evening was quiet and dark. Jake watched a yellow light shaft softly through the hall. And Portia opened the door for them.

'I certainly trust you not been waiting long. So many folks been coming that us thought it wise to unlatch the bell. You gentlemens[①] just let me take you hats—Father been mighty sick.'

Jake tiptoed heavily behind Singer down the bare, narrow hall. At the threshold[②] of the kitchen he stopped short The room was crowded and hot. A fire burned in the small wood stove and the windows were closed tight. Smoke mingled with a certain Negro smell. The glow from the stove was the only light in the room. The dark voices he had heard back in the hall were silent.

'These here are two white gentlemens come to inquire about Father,' Portia said. 'I think maybe he be able to see you but I better go on in first and prepare him.'

Jake fingered his thick lower lip. On the end of his nose there

---

① gentlemens：绅士（gentleman 的复数形式应为 gentlemen，此处为表现文中主人公的蹩脚英语。）

② threshold：入口；门槛

was a latticed[1] impression from the front screen door. 'That's not it,' he said. 'I come to talk with your brother.'

The Negroes in the room were standing. Singer motioned to them to be seated again. Two grizzled[2] old men sat down on a bench by the stove. A loose-limbed mulatto lounged against the window. On a camp cot in a corner was a boy without legs whose trousers were folded and pinned[3] beneath his stumpy thighs.

'Good evening,' Jake said awkwardly. 'Your name Copeland?'

The boy put his hands over the stumps of his legs and shrank[4] back close to the wall. 'My name Willie.'

'Honey, don't you worry none,' said Portia. 'This here is Mr. Singer that you heard Father speak about. And this other white gentleman is Mr. Blount and he a very close friend of Mr. Singer. They just kindly come to inquire about us in our trouble.' She turned to Jake and motioned to the three other people in the room. This other boy leaning on the window is my brother too. Named Buddy. And these here over by the stove is two dear friends of my Father. Named Mr. Marshall Nicolls and Mr. John Roberts. I think it a good idea to understand who all is in a room with you.'

'Thanks,' Jake said. He turned to Willie again. 'I just want you to tell me about it so I can get it straight in my mind.'

'This the way it is,' Willie said. 'I feel like my feets is still hurting. I got this here terrible misery down in my toes. Yet the hurt in my feets is down where my feets should be if they were on my l-l-legs.[5] And not where my feets is now. It a hard thing to understand. My feets hurt me so bad all the time and I don't know where they is. They never given them back to me. They s-somewhere more than a hundred m-miles from here.'

---

① latticed：装有格子的；制成格状的
② grizzled：头发斑白的
③ pin：用针别住
④ shrink：收缩；缩小
⑤ 参考译文：但如果两只脚还在腿上的话，这种疼痛会一直传到原来长脚的地方。

'I mean about how it all happened,' Jake said.

Uneasily Willie looked up at his sister. 'I don't remember—very good.'

'Course you remember, Honey. You done already told us over and over.'

'Well—' The boy's voice was timid and sullen. Us were all out on the road and this here Buster say something to the guard. The w-white man taken a stick to him. Then this other boy he tries to run off[1]. And I follow him. It all come about so quick I don't remember good just how it were. Then they taken us back to the camp and—'

'I know the rest,' Jake said. 'But give me the names and addresses of the other two boys. And tell me the names of the guards.'

'Listen here, white man. It seem to me like you meaning to get me into trouble.'

'Trouble!' Jake said rudely. 'What in the name of Christ do you think you're in now?'

'Less us quiet down,' Portia said nervously. 'This here the way it is, Mr. Blount. They done let Willie off at the camp before his time were served. But they done also impressed it on him not to—I believe you understand what us means. Naturally Willie he scared. Naturally us means to be careful—cause that the best thing us can do. We already got enough trouble as is.'

'What happened to the guards?'

' Them w-white men were fired. That what they told me.'

'And where are your friends now?'

'What friends?'

'Why, the other two boys.'

They n-not my friends,' Willie said. 'Us all has had a big falling out[2].'

'How you mean?'

---

① run off：逃跑；印出；流掉；进行决赛

② falling out：吵架，争吵

Portia pulled her earrings so that the lobes① of her ears stretched out like rubber. 'This here what Willie means. You see, during them three days when they hurt so bad they commenced② to quarrel. Willie don't ever want to see any of them again. That one thing Father and Willie done argued about already. This here Buster—'

'Buster got a wooden leg,' said the boy by the window. I seen him on the street today.'

'This here Buster don't have no folks and it were Father's idea to have him move on in with us. Father want to round up all the boys together. How he reckons③ us can feed them I sure don't know.'

'That ain't a good idea. And besides us was never very good friends anyway.' Willie felt the stumps④ of his legs with his dark, strong hands. 'I just wish I knowed where my f-f-feets are. That the main thing worries me. The doctor never given them back to me. I sure do wish I knowed where they are.'

Jake looked around him with dazed⑤, gin-clouded eyes. Everything seemed unclear and strange. The heat in the kitchen dizzied him so that voices echoed in his ears. The smoke choked him. The light hanging from the ceiling was turned on but, as the bulb was wrapped in newspaper to dim⑥ its strength, most of the light came from between the chinks⑦ of the hot stove. There was a red glow on all the dark faces around him. He felt uneasy and alone. Singer had left the room to visit Portia's father. Jake wanted him to come back so that they could leave. He walked awkwardly across the floor and sat down on the bench between Marshall Nicolls and John Roberts.

'Where is Portia's father?' he asked.

'Doctor Copeland is in the front room, sir,' said Roberts.

---

① lobe：耳垂
② commence：开始
③ reckon：认为
④ stump：残余部分；假肢
⑤ dazed：茫然的
⑥ dim：使暗淡
⑦ chink：裂缝

'Is he a doctor?'

'Yes, sir. He is a medical doctor.'

There was a scuffle[①] on the steps outside and the backdoor opened. A warm, fresh breeze lightened the heavy air. First a tall boy dressed in a linen suit and gilded[②] shoes entered the room with a sack in his arms. Behind him came a young boy of about seventeen.

'Hey, Highboy. Hey there, Lancy,' Willie said. 'What you all brought me? '

Highboy bowed elaborately[③] to Jake and placed on the table two fruit jars of wine. Lancy put beside them a plate covered with a fresh white napkin.

'This here wine is a present from the Society,' Highboy said. 'And Lancy's mother sent some peach puffs.'

'How is the Doctor, Miss Portia?' Lancy asked.

'Honey, he been mighty sick these days. What worries me is he so strong. It a bad sign when a person sick as he is suddenly come to be so strong.' Portia turned to Jake. 'Don't you think it a bad sign, Mr. Blount?'

Jake stared at her dazedly. 'I don't know.'

Lancy glanced sullenly at Jake and pulled down the cuffs of his outgrown shirt. 'Give the Doctor my family's regards.'

'Us certainly do appreciate this,' Portia said. 'Father was speaking of you just the other day. He haves a book he wants to give you. Wait just one minute while I get it and rinse out[④] this plate to return to your Mother. This were certainly a kindly thing for her to do.'

Marshall Nicolls leaned toward Jake and seemed about to speak to him. The old man wore a pair of pin-striped[⑤] trousers and a

---

① scuffle：（短时间与某人的）小扭打，冲突
② gilded：镀金的，装饰的
③ elaborately：精巧地
④ rinse out：冲洗，漂洗
⑤ pin-striped：有条纹的

morning coat with a flower in the buttonhole[①]. He cleared his throat and said: 'Pardon me, sir—but unavoidably[②] we overheard[③] a part of your conversation with William regarding the trouble he is now in. Inevitably[④] we have considered what is the best course to take.'

'You one of his relatives or the preacher in his church?'

'No, I am a pharmacist. And John Roberts on your left is employed in the postal department of the government.'

'A postman,' repeated John Roberts.

'With your permission—' Marshall Nicolls took a yellow silk handkerchief from his pocket and gingerly blew his nose. 'Naturally we have discussed this matter extensively.' And without doubt as members of the colored race here in this free country of America we are anxious to do our part toward extending amicable relationships.[⑤]'

We wish always to do the right thing,' said John Roberts.

'And it behooves us to strive with care and not endanger this amicable relationship already established.[⑥] Then by gradual means a better condition will come about.'

Jake turned from one to the other. 'I don't seem to follow you.' The heat was suffocating him. He wanted to get out. A film seemed to have settled over his eyeballs so that all the faces around him were blurred.

Across the room Willie was playing his harp. Buddy and Highboy were listening. The music was dark and sad. When the song was finished Willie polished his harp on the front of his shirt. 'I so hungry and thirsty the slobber in my mouth done wet out the tune. I certainly will be glad to taste some of that boogie-woogie. To have something

---

① buttonhole：扣眼；钮孔

② unavoidably：不可避免地；不得已地

③ overhear：偶尔听到；无意中听到

④ inevitably：不可避免地；必然地

⑤ 参考译文：无疑，作为在美国这个自由国度里的黑人种族的一员，我们急切地想要作出努力，希望发展我们的友好关系。（without doubt：毫无疑问地；amicable：友好的）

⑥ 参考译文：我们理应小心抗争，不要危及已经建立起来的友好关系。句中 It behooves sb. to do sth. 意为“某人有必要做某事”。（behoove：理应，有必要；endanger：危及，使遭到危险；established：已确立的）

good to drink is the only thing m-made me forget this misery. If I just knowed where my f-feets are now and could drink a glass of gin ever night I wouldn't mind so much.'

'Don't fret, Hon. You going to have something,' Portia said. 'Mr. Blount, would you care to take a peach puff and a glass of wine?'

'Thanks,' Jake said. 'That would be good.'

Quickly Portia laid a cloth on the table and set down one plate and a fork. She poured a large tumblerful of the wine. 'You just make yourself comfortable here. And if you don't mind I going to serve the others.'

The fruit jars were passed from mouth to mouth. Before Highboy passed a jar to Willie he borrowed Portia's lipstick and drew a red line to set the boundary① of the drink. There were gurgling noises and laughter. Jake finished his puff and carried his glass back with him to his place between the two old men. The home-made wine was rich and strong as brandy②. Willie started a low dolorous③ tune on his harp. Portia snapped her fingers and shuffled around the room.

Jake turned to Marshall Nicolls. 'You say Portia's father is a doctor?'

'Yes, sir. Yes, indeed. A skilled doctor.'

'What's the matter with him? '

The two Negroes glanced warily at each other.

'He were in an accident,' said John Roberts.

'What kind of an accident? '

'A bad one. A deplorable④ one.'

Marshall Nicolls folded and unfolded⑤ his silk handkerchief. 'As we were remarking a while ago, it is important not to impair

---

① boundary：边界；范围；分界线
② brandy：白兰地酒
③ dolorous：忧伤的；悲痛的
④ deplorable：悲惨的；恶劣的
⑤ unfold：展开

these amicable relations but to promote them in all ways earnestly[①] possible. We members of the colored race must strive in all ways to uplift[②] our citizens. The Doctor in yonder has strived in every way. But sometimes it has seemed to me like he had not recognized fully enough certain elements of the different races and the situation.[③]'

Impatiently Jake gulped down[④] the last swallows of his wine. 'Christ' sake, man, speak out plain, because I can't understand a thing you say.'

Marshall Nicolls and John Roberts exchanged a hurt look. Across the room Willie still sat playing music. His lips crawled over the square holes of the harmonica like fat, puckered[⑤] caterpillars[⑥]. His shoulders were broad and strong. The stumps of his thighs jerked in time to the music. Highboy danced while Buddy and Portia clapped out the rhythm.

Jake stood up, and once on his feet he realized that he was drunk. He staggered and then glanced vindictively around him, but no one seemed to have noticed. 'Where's Singer?' he asked Portia thickly.

The music stopped. 'Why, Mr. Blount, I thought you knowed he was gone. While you were sitting at the table with your peach puff[⑦] he come to the doorway and held out his watch to show it were time for him to go. You looked straight at him and shaken your head. I thought you knowed that.'

'Maybe I was thinking about something else.' He turned to Willie and said angrily to him:'I never did even get to tell you what I come here for, I didn't come to ask you to do anything. All I wanted—all I wanted was this. You and the other boys were to testify

---

① earnestly：认真地；诚挚地

② uplift：振奋，鼓舞

③ 参考译文：但有时候，我觉得他没有完全认清不同种族中的一些特定因素，没有认清局势。

④ gulp down：狼吞虎咽地吃

⑤ puckered：起皱的

⑥ caterpillar：毛毛虫

⑦ peach puff：桃酥

what happened and I was to explain why. Why is the only important thing—not what. I would have pushed you all around in a wagon and you would have told your story and afterward I would have explained why. And maybe it might have meant something. Maybe it—'

He felt they were laughing at him. Confusion caused him to forget what he had meant to say. The room was full of dark, strange faces and the air was too thick to breathe. He saw a door and staggered across to it. He was in a dark closet smelling of medicine. Then his hand was turning another doorknob[1].

He stood on the threshold of a small white room furnished only with an iron bed, a cabinet, and two chairs. On the bed lay the terrible Negro he had met on the stairs at Singer's house. His face was very black against the white, stiff pillows. The dark eyes were hot with hatred but the heavy, bluish[2] lips were composed. His face was motionless as a black mask except for the slow, wide flutters[3] of his nostrils with each breath.

'Get out,' the Negro said.

'Wait—' Jake said helplessly. 'Why do you say that?'

'This is my house.'

Jake could not draw his eyes away from the Negro's terrible face. 'But why?'

'You are a white man and a stranger.'

Jake did not leave. He walked with cumbersome[4] caution to one of the straight white chairs and seated himself. The Negro moved his hands on the counterpane[5]. His black eyes glittered with fever. Jake watched him. They waited. In the room there was a feeling tense as conspiracy or as the deadly quiet before an explosion[6].

---

① doorknob：门把手
② bluish：带蓝色的；有点蓝的
③ flutter：振动，颤动
④ cumbersome：笨拙的
⑤ counterpane：床罩，床单
⑥ explosion：爆炸

It was long past midnight. The warm, dark air of the spring morning swirled the blue layers of smoke in the room. On the floor were crumpled balls of paper and a half-empty bottle of gin. Scattered ashes were gray on the counterpane. Doctor Copeland pressed his head tensely into the pillow. He had removed his dressing-gown and the sleeves of his white cotton nightshirt were rolled to the elbow. Jake leaned forward in his chair. His tie was loosened and the collar of his shirt had wilted with sweat Through the hours there had grown between them a long, exhausting[①] dialogue. And now a pause had come.

'So the time is ready for—' Jake began.

But Doctor Copeland interrupted him. 'Now it is perhaps necessary that we—' he murmured huskily. They halted. Each looked into the eyes of the other and waited. 'I beg your pardon,' Doctor Copeland said.

'Sorry,' said Jake. 'Go on.'

'No, you continue.'

'Well—' Jake said. 'I won't say what I started to say. Instead we'll have one last word about the South. The strangled South. The wasted South, The slavish South.'

'And the Negro people.'

To steady himself Jake swallowed a long, burning draught from the bottle on the floor beside him. Then deliberately he walked to the cabinet[②] and picked up a small, cheap globe of the world that served as a paperweight[③]. Slowly he turned the sphere in his hands. 'All I can say is this: The world is full of meanness[④] and evil. Huh! Three fourths

① exhausting：使人筋疲力尽的；使耗尽的
② cabinet：展览艺术品的小陈列室
③ paperweight：书镇，压纸器
④ meanness：卑鄙，刻薄

of this globe is in a state of war or oppression[①]. The liars and fiends[②] are united and the men who know are isolated and without defense. But! But if you was to ask me to point out the most uncivilized[③] area on the face of this globe I would point here—'

'Watch sharp,' said Doctor Copeland. 'You're out in the ocean.'

Jake turned the globe again and pressed his blunt[④], grimy[⑤] thumb on a carefully selected spot.'Here. These thirteen states. I know what I'm talking about. I read books and I go around. I been in every damn one of these thirteen states. I've worked in every one. And the reason I think like I do is this: We live in the richest country in the world. There's plenty and to spare for no man, woman, or child to be in want.[⑥] And in addition to this our country was founded on what should have been a great, true principle—the freedom, equality, and rights of each individual. Huh! And what has come of that start? There are corporations worth billions of dollars—and hundreds of thousands of people who don't get to eat. And here in these thirteen states the exploitation of human beings is so that—that it's a thing you got to take in with your own eyes. In my life I seen things that would make a man go crazy. At least one third of all Southerners live and die no better off than the lowest peasant in any European Fascist state. The average wage of a worker on a tenant farm[⑦] is only seventy-three dollars per year. And mind you, that's the average! The wages of sharecroppers[⑧] run from thirty-five to ninety dollars per person. And thirty-five dollars a year means just about ten cents for a full day's

---

① oppression：压迫

② fiend：魔鬼

③ uncivilized：未开化的，不文明的

④ blunt：钝的

⑤ grimy：肮脏的，污秽的

⑥ 参考译文：（我们的国家）物产丰富，却不肯分给那些一无所有的男人、女人和孩子。（spare：抽出，分让；in want：在贫困中）

⑦ tenant farm：租佃农场

⑧ sharecropper：（美）收益分成的佃农

work. Everywhere there's pellagra[1] and hookworm[2] and anemia[3]. And just plain, pure starvation. But!' Jake nibbled[4] his lips with the knuckles of his dirty fist. Sweat stood out on his forehead. 'But!' he repeated. Those are only the evils you can see and touch. The other things are worse. I'm talking about the way that the truth has been hidden from the people. The things they have been told so they can't see the truth. The poisonous lies. So they aren't allowed to know.'

'And the Negro,' said Doctor Copeland. 'To understand what is happening to us you have to—'

Jake interrupted him savagely. 'Who owns the South? Corporations in the North own three fourths of all the South. They say the old cow grazes all over—in the south, the west, the north, and the east. But she's milked in just one place. Her old teats swing over just one spot when she's full. She grazes everywhere and is milked in New York. Take our cotton mills, our pulp mills, our harness factories, our mattress factories. The North owns them. And what happens?' Jake's mustache quivered angrily. 'Here's an example. Locale, a mill village according to the great paternal[5] system of American industry. Absentee ownership. In the village is one huge brick mill and maybe four or five hundred shanties[6]. The houses aren't fit for human beings to live in. Moreover, the houses were built to be nothing but slums in the first place. These shanties are nothing but two or maybe three rooms and a privy[7]—built with far less forethought than barns to house cattle. Built with far less attention to needs than sties for pigs. For under this system pigs are valuable and men are not. You can't make pork chops and sausage[8] out of skinny little mill kids. You can't

---

① pellagra：（皮肤）糙皮病；玉蜀黍疹，陪拉格拉病
② hookworm：钩虫（寄生于人或动物肠道）；钩虫病
③ anemia：贫血；贫血症
④ nibble：轻咬
⑤ paternal：父系的
⑥ shanty：棚屋，简陋小屋
⑦ privy：厕所
⑧ sausage：香肠；腊肠

sell but half the people these days. But a pig—'

'Hold on!' said Doctor Copeland. 'You are getting off on a tangent[1]. And besides, you are giving no attention to the very separate question of the Negro. I cannot get a word in edgeways. We have been over all this before, bat it is impossible to see the full situation without including us Negroes.'

'Back to our mill village,' Jake said. 'A young linthead begins working at the fine wage of eight or ten dollars a weeks at such times as he can get himself employed. He marries. After the first child the woman must work in the mill also. Their combined wages come to say eighteen dollars a week when they both got work. Huh! They pay a fourth of this for the shack the mill provides them. They buy food and clothes at a company-owned or dominated store. The store overcharges[2] on every item. With three or four younguns they are held down the same as if they had on chains. That is the whole principle of serfdom[3]. Yet here in America we call ourselves free. And the funny thing is that this has been drilled into the heads of sharecroppers and lintheads and all the rest so hard that they really believe it. But it's taken a hell of a lot of lies to keep them from knowing.'

'There is only one way out—' said Doctor Copeland.

'Two ways. And only two ways. Once there was a time when this country was expanding. Every man thought he had a chance. Huh! But that period has gone—and gone for good. Less than a hundred corporations have swallowed all but a few leavings. These industries have already sucked the blood and softened the bones of the people. The old days of expansion are gone. The whole system of capitalistic democracy is rotten and corrupt. There remains only two roads ahead. One: Fascism. Two: reform of the most revolutionary

---

① on a tangent：跑题，转移话题
② overcharge：对……要价过高
③ serfdom：农奴境遇；农奴身份

and permanent kind.'

'And the Negro. Do not forget the Negro. So far as I and my people are concerned the South is Fascist now and always has been.'

'Yeah.'

'The Nazis rob the Jews of their legal, economic, and cultural life. Here the Negro has always been deprived of these. And if wholesale[①] and dramatic robbery of money and goods has not taken place here as in Germany, it is simply because the Negro has never been allowed to accrue[②] wealth in the first place[③].'

'That's the system,' Jake said.

'The Jew and the Negro,' said Doctor Copeland bitterly. 'The history of my people will be commensurate with the interminable[④] history of the Jew—only bloodier and more violent. Like a certain species of sea gull. If you capture one of the birds and tie a red string of twine around his leg the rest of the flock will peck[⑤] him to death.'

Doctor Copeland took off his spectacles and rebound a wire around a broken hinge. Then he polished the lenses on his nightshirt. His hand shook with agitation[⑥]. 'Mr. Singer is a Jew.'

'No, you're wrong there.'

'But I am positive that he is. The name, Singer. I recognized his race the first time I saw him. From his eyes. Besides, he told me so.'

'Why, he couldn't have,' Jake insisted. 'He's pure Anglo-Saxon if I ever saw it. Irish and Anglo-Saxon.'

'But—'

'I'm certain. Absolutely.'

'Very well,' said Doctor Copeland. 'We will not quarrel.'

Outside the dark air had cooled so that there was a chill in the

---

① wholesale：批发；经营批发业
② accrue：获得；积累
③ in the first place：首先，起初
④ interminable：冗长的；无止尽的
⑤ peck：啄
⑥ agitation：搅动；煽动

room. It was almost dawn. The early morning sky was deep, silky blue and the moon had turned from silver to white. All was still. The only sound was the clear, lonely song of a spring bird in the darkness outside. Though a faint[①] breeze blew in from the window the air in the room was sour and close. There was a feeling both of tenseness and exhaustion. Doctor Copeland leaned forward from the pillow. His eyes were bloodshot and his hands clutched[②] the counterpane. The neck of his nightshirt had slipped down over his bony shoulder. Jake's heels were balanced on the rungs of his chair and his giant hands folded between his knees in a waiting and childlike[③] attitude. Deep black circles were beneath his eyes, his hair was unkempt. They looked at each other and waited. As the silence grew longer the tenseness between them became more strained[④].

At last Doctor Copeland cleared his throat and said: 'I am certain you did not come here for nothing. I am sure we have not discussed these subjects all through the night to no purpose[⑤]. We have talked of everything now except the most vital subject of all—the way out[⑥]. What must be done.'

They still watched each other and waited. In the face of each there was expectation. Doctor Copeland sat bolt upright[⑦] against the pillows. Jake rested his chin in his hand and leaned forward. The pause continued. And then hesitantly[⑧] they began to speak at the same time.

'Excuse me,' Jake said. 'Go ahead.'

'No, you. You started first.'

'Go on.'

'Pshaw!' said Doctor Copeland. 'Continue.'

---

① faint：微弱的

② clutch：抓紧

③ childlike：天真烂漫的

④ strained：紧张的；勉强的

⑤ to no purpose：漫无目的地；毫无效果地，例：His parents searched him to no purpose. 他的父母漫无目的地搜寻他的下落。

⑥ the way out：出路；解决办法

⑦ bolt upright：（身体）笔直

⑧ hesitantly：迟疑地

Jake stared at him with clouded, mystical[①] eyes. 'It's this way. This is how I see it. The only solution is for the people to know. Once they know the truth they can be oppressed no longer. Once just half of them know the whole fight is won.'

'Yes, once they understand the workings of this society. But how do you propose to tell them? '

'Listen,' Jake said. 'Think about chain letters. If one person sends a letter to ten people and then each of the ten people sends letters to ten more—you get it?' He faltered. 'Not that I write letters, but the idea is the same. I just go around telling. And if in one town I can show the truth to just ten of the don't-knows, then I feel like some good has been done. See? '

Doctor Copeland looked at Jake in surprise. Then he snorted[②]. 'Do not be childish! You cannot just go about talking. Chain letters indeed! Knows and don't-knows! '

Jake's lips trembled and his brow lowered with quick anger. 'O.K. What have you got to offer?'

'I will say first that I used to feel somewhat as you do on this question. But I have learned what a mistake that attitude is. For half a century I thought it wise to be patient.'

'I didn't say be patient.'

'In the face of brutality[③] I was prudent[④]. Before injustice I held my peace. I sacrificed the things in hand for the good of the hypothetical whole.[⑤] I believed in the tongue instead of the fist. As an armor against oppression I taught patience and faith in the human soul. I know now how wrong I was. I have been a traitor to myself and to my people. All that is rot. Now is the time to act and to act quickly.

---

① mystical：神秘的
② snort：轻蔑或愤怒地发出哼声
③ brutality：暴行
④ prudent：谨慎的
⑤ 参考译文：我牺牲掉拥有的东西，去换取假想中的整体利益。（in hand：在手头，在控制中；hypothetical：假设的）

Fight cunning with cunning and might with might[①].'

'But how?' Jake asked. 'How? '

'Why, by getting out and doing things. By calling crowds of people together and getting them to demonstrate.'

'Huh! That last phrase gives you away—"getting them to demonstrate[②]." What good will it do if you get them to demonstrate against a thing if they don't-know. You're trying to stuff the hog by way of his ass.'

'Such vulgar expressions annoy me,' Doctor Copeland said prudishly[③].

'For Christ' sake! I don't care if they annoy you or not.'

Doctor Copeland held up his hand. 'Let us not get so overheated[④],' he said. 'Let us attempt to see eye to eye[⑤] with each other.'

'Suits me. I don't want to fight with you.'

They were silent. Doctor Copeland moved his eyes from one corner of the ceiling to the other. Several times he wet his lips to speak and each time the word remained half-formed and silent in his mouth. Then at last he said: 'My advice to you is this. Do not attempt to stand alone.'

'But—'

'But, nothing,' said Doctor Copeland didactically[⑥]. 'The most fatal thing a man can do is try to stand alone.'

'I see what you're getting at.'

Doctor Copeland pulled the neck of his nightshirt up over his bony shoulder and held it gathered tight to his throat. 'You believe in

---

① 参考译文：以牙还牙，以眼还眼。

② demonstrate：游行，示威

③ prudishly：过分拘谨地

④ overheated：过于热情的；过于兴奋的

⑤ see eye to eye with each other：意见一致，达成共识，例：We don't always see eye to eye on everything, but we respect each other's opinions. 我们并不总是在所有事情上意见一致，但我们尊重彼此的观点。

⑥ didactically：教训地，教诲地

the struggle of my people for their human rights?'

The Doctor's agitation and his mild and husky[①] question made Jake's eyes brim suddenly with tears. A quick, swollen rush of love caused him to grasp the black, bony hand on the counterpane and hold it fast. 'Sure,' he said.

'The extremity of our need?'

'Yes.'

'The lack of justice? The bitter inequality?'

Doctor Copeland coughed and spat into one of the squares of paper which he kept beneath his pillow. 'I have a program. It is a very simple, concentrated plan. I mean to focus on only one objective. In August of this year I plan to lead more than one thousand Negroes in this county on a march[②]. A march to Washington. All of us together in one solid body. If you will look in the cabinet yonder[③] you will see a stack of letters which I have written this week and will deliver personally.' Doctor Copeland slid his nervous hands up and down the sides of the narrow bed.'You remember what I said to you a short while ago? You will recall that my only advice to you was: Do not attempt to stand alone.'

'I get it,' Jake said.

But once you enter this it must be all. First and foremost. Your work now and forever. You must give of your whole self without stint, without hope of personal return, without rest or hope of rest.[④]'

'For the rights of the Negro in the South.'

'In the South and here in this very county. And it must be either all or nothing. Either yes or no.'

Doctor Copeland leaned back on the pillow. Only his eyes

---

① husky：声音沙哑的

② march：游行示威（lead...on a march：带领……游行示威）

③ yonder：（过时语言或方言中的）那里；那边

④ 参考译文：但你一旦参与其中，必须要全情投入，这是最重要的。你要从一而终地干下去，必须毫无保留地奉献自己的全部，不求个人回报，永不停歇，也不祈望停歇。本句原文均为小短句，译文也应相应使用短小词语句子，表达出其中的节奏感。（first and foremost：首先，首要的是）

seemed alive. They burned in his face like red coals. The fever made his cheekbones a ghastly[①] purple. Jake scowled and pressed his knuckles to his soft, wide, trembling mouth. Color rushed to his face. Outside the first pale light of morning had come. The electric bulb suspended[②] from the ceiling burned with ugly sharpness in the dawn.

Jake rose to his feet and stood stiffly at the foot of the bed. He said flatly: 'No. That's not the right angle at all. I'm dead sure it's not. In the first place, you'd never get out of town. They'd break it up by saying it's a menace to public health—or some such trumped-up reason. They'd arrest you and nothing would come of it. But even if by some miracle you got to Washington it wouldn't do a bit of good. Why, the whole notion[③] is crazy.'

The sharp rattle of phlegm[④] sounded in Doctor Copeland's throat. His voice was harsh. 'As you are so quick to sneer[⑤] and condemn[⑥], what do you have to offer instead?'

'I didn't sneer,' Jake said. 'I only remarked that your plan is crazy. I come here tonight with an idea much better than that. I wanted your son, Willie, and the other two boys to let me push them around in a wagon. They were to tell what happened to them and afterward I was to tell why. In other words, I was to give a talk on the dialectics of capitalism[⑦]—and show up all of its lies. I would explain so that everyone would understand why those boys' legs were cut off. And make everyone who saw them know.'

'Pshaw! Double pshaw!' said Doctor Copeland furiously. I do not believe you have good sense. If I were a man who felt it worth my while to laugh I would surely laugh at that. Never have I had the

---

① ghastly：可怕的
② suspend：悬挂
③ notion：想法
④ phlegm：痰；黏液；黏液质
⑤ sneer：嘲笑，讥讽
⑥ condemn：谴责
⑦ capitalism：资本主义

opportunity to hear of such nonsense[①] firsthand.'

They stared at each other in bitter disappointment and anger. There was the rattle of a wagon in the street outside. Jake swallowed and bit his lips[②]. 'Huh!' he said finally. 'You're the only one who's crazy. You got everything exactly backward. The only way to solve the Negro problem under capitalism is to geld[③] every one of the fifteen million black men in these states.'

'So that is the kind of idea you harbor beneath your ranting[④] about justice.'

'I didn't say it should be done. I only said you couldn't see the forest for the trees.' Jake spoke with slow and painful care.'The work has to start at the bottom. The old traditions smashed and the new ones created. To forge a whole new pattern for the world. To make man a social creature for the first time, living in an orderly and controlled society where he is not forced to be unjust[⑤] in order to survive. A social tradition in which—'

Doctor Copeland clapped ironically[⑥]. 'Very good,' he said. 'But the cotton must be picked before the cloth is made. You and your crackpot[⑦] do-nothing theories can—'

'Hush! Who cares whether you and your thousand Negroes straggle up to that stinking cesspool of a place called Washington? What difference does it make? What do a few people matter—a few thousand people, black, white, good or bad? When the whole of our society is built on a foundation of black lies.'

'Everything!' Doctor Copeland panted. 'Everything! Everything!'

'Nothing!'

'The soul of the meanest and most evil of us on this earth is

---

① nonsense：胡说，废话
② bite one's lips：咬嘴唇
③ geld：阉割
④ ranting：吼闹
⑤ unjust：不公平的，不公正的；非正义的
⑥ ironically：讽刺地；说反话地
⑦ crackpot：古怪的，不切实际的

worth more in the sight of justice than—'

'Oh, the Hell with it!' Jake said. 'Balls!'

'Blasphemer!' screamed Doctor Copeland. 'Foul blasphemer!'

Jake shook the iron bars of the bed. The vein[①] in his forehead swelled to the point of bursting and his face was dark with rage. 'Short-sighted bigot[②]!'

'White—' Doctor Copeland's voice failed him. He struggled and no sound would come. At last he was able to bring forth a choked whisper: 'Fiend.'

The bright yellow morning was at the window. Doctor Copeland's head fell back on the pillow. His neck twisted at a broken angle, a fleck of bloody foam on his lips. Jake looked at him once before, sobbing with violence, he rushed headlong from the room.

---

① vein：血管

② short-sighted bigot：目光短浅的偏执狂，此处可译为：目光短浅，固执己见！

14

Now SHE could not stay in the inside room. She had to be around somebody all the time. Doing something every minute. And if she was by herself she counted or figured with numbers. She counted all the roses on the living-room wall-paper. She figured out the cubic[①] area of the whole house. She counted every blade of grass in the back yard and every leaf on a certain bush. Because if she did not have her mind on numbers this terrible afraidness came in her. She would be walking home from school on these May afternoons and suddenly she would have to think of something quick. A good thing—very good. Maybe she would think about a phrase of hurrying jazz music. Or that a bowl of jello[②] would be in the refrigerator when she got home. Or plan to smoke a cigarette behind the coal house. Maybe she would try to think a long way ahead to the time when she would go north and see snow, or even travel somewhere in a foreign land. But these thoughts about good things wouldn't last. The jello was gone in five minutes and the cigarette smoked. Then what was there after that? And the numbers mixed themselves up in her brain. And the snow and the foreign land were a long, long time away. Then what was there?

Just Mister Singer. She wanted to follow him everywhere. In the morning she would watch him go down the front steps to work

---

① cubic：立方体的，立方的
② jello：果子冻

and then follow along a half a block behind him. Every afternoon as soon as school was over she hung around at the corner near the store where he worked. At four o'clock he went out to drink a Coca-Cola. She watched him cross the street and go into the drugstore and finally come out again. She followed him home from work and sometimes even when he took walks. She always followed a long way behind him. And he did not know.

She would go up to see him in his room. First she scrubbed[①] her face and hands and put some vanilla on the front of her dress. She only went to visit him twice a week now, because she didn't want him to get tired of her. Most always he would be sitting over the queer, pretty chess game when she opened the door. And then she was with him.

'Mister Singer, have you ever lived in a place where it snowed in the winter-time?'

He tilted his chair back against the wall and nodded.

'In some different country than this one—in a foreign place?'

He nodded yes again and wrote on his pad with his silver pencil. Once he had traveled to Ontario, Canada—across the river from Detroit. Canada was so far up north that the white snow drifted up to the roofs of the houses.[②] That was where the Quints were and the St. Lawrence River. The people ran up and down the streets speaking French to each other. And far up in the north there were deep forests and white ice igloos[③]. The arctic region with the beautiful northern lights.

'When you was in Canada did you go out and get any fresh snow and eat it with cream and sugar? Once I read where it was mighty[④] good to eat that way.'

---

① scrub：擦洗；揉搓

② 参考译文：他曾经去过加拿大的安大略湖——从底特律过河。加拿大非常靠北，白皑皑的雪会飘落到房顶。（Ontario：安大略湖，北美五大湖之一；Detroit：底特律，美国一座城市）

③ igloo：冰屋

④ mighty：很；极；非常

He turned his head to one side because he didn't understand. She couldn't ask the question again because suddenly it sounded silly. She only looked at him and waited. A big, black shadow of his head was on the wall behind him. The electric fan cooled the thick, hot air. All was quiet. It was like they waited to tell each other things that had never been told before. What she had to say was terrible and afraid. But what he would tell her was so true that it would make everything all right. Maybe it was a thing that could not be spoken with words or writing. Maybe he would have to let her understand this in a different way. That was the feeling she had with him.

'I was just asking you about Canada—but it didn't amount to anything[①], Mister Singer.'

Downstairs in the home rooms there was plenty of trouble. Etta was still so sick that she couldn't sleep crowded three in a bed. The shades were drawn and the dark room smelled bad with a sick smell. Etta's job was gone, and that meant eight dollars less a week besides the doctor's bill. Then one day when Ralph was walking around in the kitchen he burned himself on the hot kitchen stove. The bandages made his hands itch and somebody had to watch him all the time else he would bust the blisters[②]. On George's birthday they had bought him a little red bike with a bell and a basket on the handlebars[③]. Everybody had chipped in[④] to give it to him. But when Etta lost her job they couldn't pay, and after two installments were past due the store sent a man out to take the wheel away.[⑤] George just watched the man roll the bike off the porch, and when he passed George kicked the back fender and then went into the coal house and shut the door.

It was money, money, money all the time. They owed to the

---

① it didn't amount to anything：表示不重要，没有意义。

② blister：水疱

③ handlebar：车把

④ chip in：凑钱，集资

⑤ 参考译文：但埃特丢了工作，他们付不起钱了，有两次未能按时分期付款，商店便派了个人过来，推走了自行车。（past due：逾期未付，指账单或款项已经过了支付截止日期，尚未支付。）

grocery and they owed the last payment on some furniture. And now since they had lost the house they owed money there too. The six rooms in the house were always taken, but nobody ever paid the rent on time.

For a while their Dad went over every day to hunt another job. He couldn't do carpenter work any more because it made him jittery[①] to be more than ten feet off the ground. He applied for many jobs but nobody would hire him. Then at last he got this notion.

'It's advertising, Mick,' he said. I've come to the conclusion that's all in the world the matter with my watch-repairing business right now. I got to sell myself. I got to get out and let people know I can fix watches, and fix them good and cheap. You just mark my words. I'm going to build up this business so I'll be able to make a good living for this family the rest of my life. Just by advertising.'

He brought home a dozen sheets of tin and some red paint. For the next week he was very busy. It seemed to him like this was a hell of a good idea. The signs were all over the floor of the front room. He got down on his hands and knees and took great care over the printing of each letter. As he worked he whistled[②] and wagged his head. He hadn't been so cheerful and glad in months. Every now and then he would have to dress in his good suit and go around the corner for a glass of beer to calm himself. On the signs at first he had:

Wilbur Kelly
Watch Repairing
Very Cheap and Expert.

'Mick, I want them to hit you right bang in the eye. To stand out wherever you see them.'[③]

---

① jittery：神经过敏的；战战兢兢的

② whistle：吹口哨

③ 参考译文：米克，我想让这几个词一下子抓人眼球，不管在哪里看到都能很醒目。

She helped him and he gave her three nickels. The signs were O.K. at first. Then he worked on them so much that they were ruined. He wanted to add more and more things—in the corners and at the top and bottom. Before he had finished the signs were plastered① all over with 'Very Cheap' and 'Come At Once' and 'You Give Me Any Watch And I Make It Run.'

'You tried to write so much in the signs that nobody will read anything,' she told him.

He brought home some more tin and left the designing up to her. She painted them very plain, with great big block letters and a picture of a clock. Soon he had a whole stack of them. A fellow he knew rode him out in the country where he could nail them to trees and fence posts. At both ends of the block he put up a sign with a black hand pointing toward the house. And over the front door there was another sign.

The day after this advertising was finished he waited in the front room dressed in a clean shirt and a tie. Nothing happened. The jeweler who gave him overflow② work to do at half price sent in a couple of clocks. That was all. He took it hard. He didn't go out to look for other jobs any more, but every minute he had to be busy around the house. He took down the doors and oiled the hinges③—whether they needed it or not. He mixed the margarine for Portia and scrubbed the floors upstairs. He worked out a contraption where the water from the icebox could be drained through the kitchen window.④ He carved some beautiful alphabet blocks for Ralph and invented a little needle-threader. Over the few watches that he had to work on he took great pains.

Mick still followed Mister Singer. But she didn't want to. It

---

① plaster：粘贴

② overflow：泛滥；挤不下或多余的

③ hinge：铰链；折页

④ 参考译文：他鼓捣出一个小装置，让冰箱里的水直接从厨房窗子里排走。（contraption：奇特的装置；icebox：冰箱）

was like there was something wrong about her following after him without his knowing. Two or three days she played hooky[①] from school. She walked behind him when he went to work and hung around on the corner near his store all day. When he ate his dinner at Mister Brannon's she went into the café and spent a nickel for a sack of peanuts. Then at night she followed him on these dark, long walks. She stayed on the opposite side of the street from him and about a block behind. When he stopped, she stopped also—and when he walked fast she ran to keep up with him. So long as she could see him and be near him she was right happy. But sometimes this queer feeling would come to her and she knew that she was doing wrong. So she tried hard to keep busy at home.

She and her Dad were alike in the way that now they always had to be fooling with something. She kept up with all that went on in the house and the neighborhood. Sparerib's big sister won fifty dollars at a movie bank night. Baby Wilson had the bandage off her head now, but her hair was cut short like a boy's. She couldn't dance in the soirée[②] this year, and when her mother took her to see it Baby began to yell and cut up during one of the dances. They had to drag her out of the Opera House. And on the sidewalk Mrs. Wilson had to whip[③] her to make her behave. And Mrs. Wilson cried, too. George hated Baby. He would hold his nose and stop up his ears when she passed by the house. Pete Wells ran away from home and was gone three weeks. He came back barefooted and very hungry. He bragged[④] about how he had gone all the way to New Orleans.

Because of Etta, Mick still slept in the living-room. The short sofa cramped[⑤] her so much that she had to make up sleep in study hall at school. Every other night Bill swapped with her and she slept with

---

① hooky：逃学；逃学者
② soiree：（法）晚会
③ whip：抽打
④ brag：吹牛
⑤ cramp：约束；束缚

George. Then a lucky break came for them. A fellow who had a room upstairs moved away. When after a week had gone by and nobody answered the ad in the paper, their Mama told Bill he could move up to the vacant room. Bill was very pleased to have a place entirely by himself away from the family. She moved in with George. He slept like a little warm kitty and breathed very quiet.

She knew the night-time again. But not the same as in the last summer when she walked in the dark by herself and listened to the music and made plans. She knew the night a different way now. In bed she lay awake. A queer afraidness came to her. It was like the ceiling was slowly pressing down toward her face. How would it be if the house fell apart①? Once their Dad had said the whole place ought to be condemned. Did he mean that maybe some night when they were asleep the walls would crack and the house collapse? Bury them under all the plaster and broken glass and smashed furniture? So that they could not move or breathe? She lay awake and her muscles were stiff. In the night there was creaking②. Was that somebody walking—somebody else awake besides her—Mister Singer?

She never thought about Harry. She had made up her mind to forget him and she did forget him. He wrote that he had a job with a garage in Birmingham. She answered with a card saying 'O.K.' as they had planned. He sent his mother three dollars every week. It seemed like a very long time had passed since they went to the woods together.

During the day she was busy in the outside room. But at night she was by herself in the dark and figuring was not enough. She wanted somebody. She tried to keep George awake. 'It sure is fun to stay awake and talk in the dark. Less us talk awhile together.'

He made a sleepy answer.

'See the stars out the window. If s a hard thing to realize that

① fell apart：崩溃；土崩瓦解（原形 fall apart）
② creak：（门、木地板等）嘎吱作响

every single one of those little stars is a planet as large as the earth.'

'How do they know that?'

'They just do. They got ways of measuring. That's science.'

'I don't believe in it'

She tried to egg him on to an argument so that he would get mad and stay awake. He just let her talk and didn't seem to pay attention. After a while he said:

'Look, Mick! You see that branch of the tree? Don't it look like a pilgrim① forefather lying down with a gun in his hand?'

'It sure does. That's exactly what it's like. And see over there on the bureau. Don't that bottle look like a funny man with a hat on?'

'Naw,' George said. 'It don't look a bit like one to me.'

She took a drink from a glass of water on the floor. 'Less me and you play a game—the name game. You can be It if you want to. Whichever you like. You can choose.'

He put his little fists up to his face and breathed in a quiet, even way because he was falling asleep.

'Wait, George!' she said. 'This'll be fun. I'm somebody beginning with an M. Guess who I am.'

George sighed and his voice was tired. 'Are you Harpo Marx?'

'No, I'm not even② in the movies.'

'I don't know.'

'Sure you do. My name begins with the letter M and I live in Italy. You ought to guess this.'

George turned over on his side and curled up③ in a ball. He did not answer.

'My name begins with an M but sometimes I'm called a f name beginning with D. In Italy. You can guess.'

The room was quiet and dark and George was asleep. She

---

① pilgrim：朝圣者；漫游者
② even：稳重的；温和的
③ curl up：蜷缩

pinched[1] him and twisted his ear. He groaned[2] but did not awake. She fitted in close to him and pressed her face against his hot little naked shoulder. He would sleep all through the night while she was figuring with decimals[3].

Was Mister Singer awake in his room upstairs? Did the ceiling creak because he was walking quietly up and down, drinking a cold orange crush and studying the chess men laid out on the table? Had ever he felt a terrible afraidness like this one? No. He had never done anything wrong. He had never done wrong and his heart was quiet in the night-time. Yet at the same time he would understand.

If only she could tell him about this, then it would be better. She thought of how she would begin to tell him. Mister Singer—I know this girl not any older than I am—Mister Singer, I don't know whether you understand a thing like this or not—Mister Singer. Mister Singer. She said his name over and over. She loved him better than anyone in the family, better even than George or her Dad. It was a different love. It was not like anything she had ever felt in her life before.

In the mornings she and George would dress together and talk. Sometimes she wanted very much to be close to George. He had grown taller and was pale and peaked[4]. His soft, reddish[5] hair lay raggedly over the tops of his little ears. His sharp eyes were always squinted so that his face had a strained[6] look. His permanent teeth[7] were coming in, but they were blue and far apart like his baby teeth had been. Often his jaw was crooked[8] because he had a habit of feeling out the sore new teeth with his tongue.

---

① pinch：捏；使苦恼
② groan：呻吟；抱怨
③ decimal：小数
④ peaked：苍白的，消瘦的
⑤ reddish：微红的；略带红色的
⑥ strained：紧张的；勉强的
⑦ permanent teeth：恒牙，人类在生长发育过程中，从6岁左右开始逐渐替换乳牙的牙齿，一直到成年后不再更换的牙齿。
⑧ crooked：弯曲的，歪的

'Listen here, George,' she said. 'Do you love me?'

'Sure. I love you O.K.'

It was a hot, sunny morning during the last week of school. George was dressed and he lay on the floor doing his number work. His dirty little fingers squeezed the pencil tight and he kept breaking the lead point. When he was finished she held him by the shoulders and looked hard into his face. 'I mean a lot. A whole lot.'

'Lemme go. Sure I love you. Ain't you my sister?'

'I know. But suppose I wasn't your sister. Would you love me then?'

George backed away. He had run out of shirts and wore a dirty pullover[①] sweater. His wrists were thin and blue-veined. The sleeves of the sweater had stretched[②] so that they hung loose and made his hands look very small.

'If you wasn't my sister then I might not know you. So I couldn't love you.'

'But if you did know me and I wasn't your sister.'

'But how do you know I would? You can't prove it.'

'Well, just take it for granted[③] and pretend.'

'I reckon I would like you all right. But I still say you can't prove—'

'Prove! You got that word on the brain. Prove and trick. Everything is either a trick or it's got to be proved. I can't stand you, George Kelly. I hate you.'

'O.K. Then I don't like you none either.'

He crawled down under the bed for something.

'What you want under there? You better leave my things alone. If I ever caught you meddling in my private box I'd bust your head against the side of the wall. I would. I'd stomp on your brains.'

---

① pullover：套领的

② stretch：有弹性

③ take it for granted：想当然，视为理所当然

George came out from under the bed with his spelling book. His dirty little paw[①] reached in a hole in the mattress where he hid his marbles. Nothing could faze[②] that kid. He took his time about choosing three brown agates[③] to take with him. 'Aw, shucks, Mick,' he answered her. George was too little and too tough. There wasn't any sense in loving him. He knew even less about things than she did.

School was out and she had passed every subject—some with A plus and some by the skin of her teeth. The days were long and hot. Finally she was able to work hard at music again. She began to write down pieces for the violin and piano. She wrote songs. Always music was in her mind. She listened to Mister Singer's radio and wandered around the house thinking about the programs she had heard.

'What ails[④] Mick?' Portia asked. 'What kind of cat is it got her tongue? She walk around and don't say a word. She not even greedy[⑤] like she used to be. She getting to be a regular[⑥] lady these days.'

It was as though in some way she was waiting—but what she waited for she did not know. The sun burned down glaring and white-hot in the streets. During the day she either worked hard at music or messed with kids. And waited. Sometimes she would look all around her quick and this panic would come in her. Then in late June there was a sudden happening so important that it changed everything.

That night they were all out on the porch. The twilight[⑦] was blurred[⑧] and soft. Supper was almost ready and the smell of cabbage floated to them from the open hall. All of them were together except Hazel, who had not come home from work, and Etta, who still lay sick in bed. Their Dad leaned back in a chair with his sock-feet on the

---

① paw:（动物的）爪子；（某人的）手
② faze：使狼狈，使慌乱
③ agate：玛瑙制工具；文中指玛瑙纹弹珠。
④ ail：困扰，使不适
⑤ greedy：贪吃的
⑥ regular：受约束的，此处 regular lady 指“淑女”。
⑦ twilight：黄昏，暮色
⑧ blurred：模糊不清的

banisters[①]. Bill was on the steps with the kids. Their Mama sat on the swing fanning herself with the newspaper. Across the street a girl new in the neighborhood skated up and down the sidewalk on one roller skate. The lights on the block were just beginning to be turned on, and far away a man was calling someone.

Then Hazel come home. Her high heels clopped up the steps and she leaned back lazily on the banisters. In the half-dark her fat, soft hands were very white as she felt the back of her braided hair. 'I sure do wish Etta was able to work,' she said. 'I found out about this job today.'

'What kind of a job?' asked their Dad. 'Anything I could do, or just for girls?'

'Just for a girl. A clerk down at Woolworth's is going to get married next week.'

'The ten-cent store—' Mick said.

'You interested?'

The question took her by surprise[②]. She had just been thinking about a sack of wintergreen[③] candy she had bought there the day before. She felt hot and tense. She rubbed her bangs up from her forehead and counted the first few stars.

Their Dad flipped his cigarette down to the sidewalk. 'No,' he said. 'We don't want Mick to take on too much responsibility at her age. Let her get her growth out. Her growth through with, anyway.'

'I agree with you,' Hazel said. 'I really do think it would be a mistake for Mick to have to work regular. I don't think it would be right.'

Bill put Ralph down from his lap and shuffled[④] his feet on the steps. 'Nobody ought to work until they're around sixteen. Mick should have two more years and finish at Vocational—if we can make

---

① banister：楼梯扶手；楼梯栏杆

② take sb. by surprise：使某人感到意外或措手不及

③ wintergreen：鹿蹄草，冬青树

④ shuffle：（笨拙或尴尬地）把脚动来动去

it.[1]'

'Even if we have to give up the house and move down in mill town,' their Mama said. 'I rather keep Mick at home for a while.'

For a minute she had been scared they would try to corner her into taking the job.[2] She would have said she would run away from home. But the way they took the attitude they did touched her. She felt excited. They were all talking about her—and in a kindly way. She was ashamed for the first scared feeling that had come to her. Of a sudden she loved all of the family and a tightness[3] came in her throat.

'About how much money is in it?' she asked.

'Ten dollars.'

'Ten dollars a week?'

'Sure,' Hazel said. 'Did you think it would be only ten a month?'

'Portia don't make but about that much.'

'Oh, colored people—' Hazel said.

Mick rubbed the top of her head with her fist. 'That's a whole lot of money. A good deal.'

'It's not to be grinned at,' Bill said. 'That's what I make.'

Mick's tongue was dry. She moved it around in her mouth to gather up spit[4] enough to talk. 'Ten dollars a week would buy about fifteen fried chickens. Or five pairs of shoes or five dresses. Or installments on a radio.' She thought about a piano, but she did not mention that aloud.

'It would tide us over,' their Mama said. 'But at the same time I rather keep Mick at home for awhile. Now, when Etta—'

'Wait!' She felt hot and reckless[5]. 'I want to take the job. I can hold it down. I know I can.'

---

① make it：成功或达到目标

② 参考译文：有一瞬间，她很害怕，担心他们会逼她接受这份工作。（corner：逼迫；逼……入绝境）

③ tightness：坚固

④ spit：唾液

⑤ reckless：鲁莽的

'Listen to little Mick,' Bill said.

Their Dad picked his teeth with a matchstick and took his feet down from the banisters[①]. 'Now, let's not rush into[②] anything. I rather Mick take her time and think this out. We can get along somehow without her working. I mean to increase my watch work by sixty per cent soon as—'

'I forgot,' Hazel said. 'I think there's a Christmas bonus every year.'

Mick frowned. 'But I wouldn't be working then. I'd be in school. I just want to work during vacation and then go back to school.'

'Sure,' Hazel said quickly.

'But tomorrow I'll go down with you and take the job if I can get it'

It was as though a great worry and tightness left the family. In the dark they began to laugh and talk. Their Dad did a trick for George with a matchstick[③] and a handkerchief. Then he gave the kid fifty cents to go down to the corner store for Coca-Colas to be drunk after supper. The smell of cabbage was stronger in the hall and pork chops were frying. Portia called. The boarders already waited at the table. Mick had supper in the dining-room. The cabbage leaves were limp and yellow on her plate and she couldn't eat. When she reached for the bread she knocked a pitcher of[④] iced tea over the table.

Then later she waited on the front porch by herself for Mister Singer to come home. In a desperate way she wanted to see him. The excitement of the hour before had died down and she was sick to the stomach. She was going to work in a ten-cent store and she did not want to work there. It was like she had been trapped into something. The job wouldn't be just for the summer—but for a long time, as long

---

① banister：（楼梯的）栏杆
② rush into：匆忙行动；仓促行事；草率决定
③ matchstick：火柴棍
④ a pitcher of：一壶

as she could see ahead. Once they were used to the money coming in it would be impossible to do without again.[1] That was the way things were. She stood in the dark and held tight to the banisters. A long time passed and Mister Singer still did not come. At eleven o'clock she went out to see if she could find him. But suddenly she got frightened in the dark and ran back home.

Then in the morning she bathed and dressed very careful. Hazel and Etta loaned[2] her the clothes to wear and primped[3] her to look nice. She wore Hazel's green silk dress and a green hat and high-heeled pumps with silk stockings. They fixed her face with rouge[4] and lipstick and plucked her eyebrows. She looked at least sixteen years old when they were finished.

It was too late to back down now. She was really grown and ready to earn her keep[5]. Yet if she would go to her Dad and tell him how she felt he would tell her to wait a year. And Hazel and Etta and Bill and their Mama, even now, would say that she didn't have to go. But she couldn't do it. She couldn't lose face like that. She went up to see Mister Singer. The words came all in a rush[6]:

'Listen—I believe I got this job. What do you think? Do you think it's a good idea? Do you think it's O.K. to drop out of school and work now? You think it's good?'

At first he did not understand. His gray eyes half-closed and he stood with his hands deep down in his pockets. There was the old feeling that they waited to tell each other things that had never been told before. The thing she had to say now was not much. But what he had to tell her would be right—and if he said the job sounded O.K.

---

① 参考译文：他们一旦习惯了这笔进账，再不干便不可能了。本句原文包含由 once 引导的条件状语从句，表达米克此时对未来的担忧及对这份工作的排斥。（do without：没有……也行，摒弃）

② loan：借；借给

③ primp：精心打扮；装饰

④ rouge：口红，胭脂

⑤ keep：生活必需品；生活费用

⑥ in a rush：匆忙地

then she would feel better about it. She repeated the words slowly and waited.

'You think it's good?'

Mister Singer considered. Then he nodded yes.

She got the job. The manager took her and Hazel back to a little office and talked with them. Afterward she couldn't remember how the manager looked or anything that had been said. But she was hired, and on the way out of the place she bought ten cents' worth of Chocolate and a little modeling[①] clay set for George. On June the fifth she was to start work. She stood for a long while before the window of Mister Singer's jewelry store. Then she hung around on the corner.

① modeling：制造模型的

15

THE TIME had come for Singer to go to Antonapoulos again. The journey was a long one. For, although the distance between them was something less than two hundred miles, the train meandered① to points far out of the way and stopped for long hours at certain stations during the night. Singer would leave the town in the afternoon and travel all through the night and until the early morning of the next day. As usual, he was ready far in advance. He planned to have a full week with his friend this visit. His clothes had been sent to the cleaner's, his hat blocked②, and his bags were in readiness. The gifts he would carry were wrapped in colored tissue paper—and in addition there was a deluxe③ basket of fruits done up in cellophane④ and a crate of late-shipped strawberries. On the morning before his departure Singer cleaned his room. In his ice box he found a bit of left-over goose liver and took it out to the alley for the neighborhood cat. On his door he tacked the same sign he had posted there before, stating that he would be absent for several days on business. During all these preparations he moved about leisurely with two vivid spots of color on his cheekbones. His face was very solemn.

Then at last the hour for departure was at hand⑤. He stood on

① meander：蜿蜒
② block：用模具使（帽等）成形
③ deluxe：高级的；豪华的
④ cellophane：玻璃纸
⑤ at hand：指某事物即将发生。

the platform, burdened with his suitcases and gifts, and watched the train roll in on the station tracks. He found himself a seat in the day coach and hoisted his luggage on the rack above his head. The car was crowded, for the most part with mothers and children. The green plush seats had a grimy smell. The windows of the car were dirty and rice thrown at some recent bridal pair lay scattered on the floor. Singer smiled cordially[①] to his fellow-travelers and leaned back in his seat. He closed his eyes. The lashes made a dark, curved fringe above the hollows of his cheeks. His right hand moved nervously inside his pocket.

For a while his thoughts lingered in the town he was leaving behind him. He saw Mick and Doctor Copeland and Jake Blount and Biff Brannon. The faces crowded in on him out of the darkness so that he felt smothered. He thought of the quarrel between Blount and the Negro. The nature of this quarrel was hopelessly confused in his mind—but each of them had on several occasions broken out into a bitter tirade against the other, the absent one. He had agreed with each of them in turn, though what it was they wanted him to sanction he did not know.[②] And Mick—her face was urgent and she said a good deal that he did not understand in the least. And then Biff Brannon at the New York Café. Brannon with his dark, iron-like jaw and his watchful eyes. And strangers who followed him about the streets and buttonholed him for unexplainable reasons. The Turk at the linen[③] shop who flung his hands up in his face and babbled with his tongue to make words the shape of which Singer had never imagined before. A certain mill foreman and an old black woman. A businessman on the main street and an urchin[④] who solicited[⑤] soldiers for a whorehouse[⑥]

① cordially：诚挚地

② 参考译文：他轮番同意他们的观点，尽管并不知道他们到底想让他认可什么。本句原文包含 though 引导的状语从句，从句中又包含一个宾语从句，且为了强调宾语部分，将从句前置。（in turn：轮流；sanction：认可，支持）

③ linen：亚麻的

④ urchin：（穿着破烂的）小脏孩

⑤ solicit：（妓女）拉客

⑥ whorehouse：妓院

near the river. Singer wriggled his shoulders uneasily. The train rocked with a smooth, easy motion. His head nodded to rest on his shoulder and for a short while he slept.

When he opened his eyes again the town was far behind him. The town was forgotten. Outside the dirty window there was the brilliant midsummer countryside. The sun slanted① in strong, bronze-colored② rays over the green fields of the new cotton. There were acres of tobacco, the plants heavy and green like some monstrous jungle weed. The orchards of peaches with the lush③ fruit weighting down the dwarfed④ trees. There were miles of pastures and tens of miles of wasted, washed-out land abandoned to the hardier weeds. The train cut through deep green pine forests where the ground was covered with the slick brown needles and the tops of the trees stretched up virgin and tall into the sky. And farther, a long way south of the town, the cypress swamps—with the gnarled⑤ roots of the trees writhing down into the brackish waters, where the gray, tattered moss trailed from the branches, where tropical water flowers blossomed in dankness and gloom. Then out again into the open beneath the sun and the indigo-blue sky.

Singer sat solemn and timid, his face turned fully toward the window. The great sweeps of space and the hard, elemental coloring almost blinded him. This kaleidoscopic⑥ variety of scene, this abundance of growth and color, seemed somehow connected with his friend. His thoughts were with Antonapoulos. The bliss of their reunion almost stifled him.⑦ His nose was pinched and he breathed with quick, short breaths through his slightly open mouth.

---

① slant：倾斜，斜照

② bronze-colored：青铜色的

③ lush：茂盛的

④ dwarfed：矮小的

⑤ gnarled：多节的；粗糙的

⑥ kaleidoscopic：千变万化的；万花筒似的

⑦ 参考译文：与他重逢的喜悦几乎令他喘不上气来。（bliss：极乐；stifle：使窒息，使喘不上气）

Antonapoulos would be glad to see him. He would enjoy the fresh fruits and the presents. By now he would be out of the sick ward and able to go on an excursion to the movies, and afterward to the hotel where they had eaten dinner on the first visit.[①] Singer had written many letters to Antonapoulos, but he had not posted them. He surrendered himself wholly to thoughts of his friend.

The half-year since he had last been with him seemed neither a long nor a short span of time. Behind each waking moment there had always been his friend. And this submerged[②] communion with Antonapoulos had grown and changed as though they were together in the flesh. Sometimes he thought of Antonapoulos with awe and self-abasement, sometimes with pride—always with love unchecked by criticism, freed of will. When he dreamed at night the face of his friend was always before him, massive and gentle. And in his waking thoughts they were eternally united.

The summer evening came slowly. The sun sank down behind a ragged line of trees in the distance and the sky paled. The twilight was languid[③] and soft. There was a white full moon, and low purple clouds lay over the horizon. The earth, the trees, the unpainted rural dwellings darkened slowly. At intervals[④] mild summer lightning quivered in the air. Singer watched all of this intently until at last the night had come, and his own face was reflected in the glass before him.

Children staggered up and down the aisle[⑤] of the car with dripping paper cups of water. An old man in overalls who had the seat before Singer drank whiskey from time to time from a Coca-Cola bottle. Between swallows he plugged the bottle carefully with a wad

① 参考译文：现在他应该出院了，可以跟他出去看电影，然后再去他初次探望时吃晚饭的那个旅馆。(go on an excursion to：到……去玩)

② submerged：水下的，在水中的

③ languid：懒洋洋的

④ at intervals：不时

⑤ aisle：通道，走道

of paper. A little girl on the right combed[①] her hair with a sticky red lollipop. Shoeboxes were opened and trays of supper were brought in from the dining-car. Singer did not eat. He leaned back in his seat and kept desultory[②] account of all that went on around him. At last the car settled down. Children lay on the broad plush[③] seats and slept, while men and women doubled up with their pillows and rested as best they could.

Singer did not sleep. He pressed his face close against the glass and strained to see into the night. The darkness was heavy and velvety. Sometimes there was a patch of moonlight or the flicker of a lantern from the window of some house along the way. From the moon he saw that the train had turned from its southward course and was headed toward the east. The eagerness[④] he felt was so keen that his nose was too pinched[⑤] to breathe through and his cheeks were scarlet. He sat there, his face pressed close against the cold, sooty glass of the window, through most of the long night journey.

The train was more than an hour late, and the fresh, bright summer morning was well under way when they arrived. Singer went immediately to the hotel, a very good hotel where he had made reservations[⑥] in advance. He unpacked his bags and arranged the presents he would take to Antonapoulos on the bed. From the menu the bellboy brought him he selected a luxurious breakfast—broiled bluefish, hominy, French toast, and hot black coffee. After breakfast he rested before the electric fan in his underwear. At noon he began to dress. He bathed and shaved and laid out fresh linen and his best seersucker[⑦] suit At three o'clock the hospital was open for visiting hours. It was Tuesday and the eighteenth of July.

---

① comb：梳头
② desultory：漫不经心的；散漫的
③ plush：长毛绒做的
④ eagerness：渴望；热心
⑤ pinched：压紧的，收缩的（指鼻塞）
⑥ make reservations：预订（房间、餐馆）
⑦ seersucker：泡泡纱；绉条纹薄织物

At the asylum he sought Antonapoulos first in the sick ward where he had been confined before. But at the doorway of the room he saw immediately that his friend was not there. Next he found his way through the corridors to the office where he had been taken the time before. He had his question already written on one of the cards he carried about with him. The person behind the desk was not the same as the one who had been there before. He was a young man, almost a boy, with a half-formed, immature face and a lank mop of hair. Singer handed him the card and stood quietly, his arms heaped① with packages, his weight resting on his heels.

The young man shook his head. He leaned over the desk and scribbled② loosely on a pad of paper. Singer read what he had written and the spots of color drained from his cheekbones instantly. He looked at the note a long time, his eyes cut sideways and his head bowed. For it was written there that Antonapoulos was dead.

On the way back to the hotel he was careful not to crush the fruit he had brought with him. He took the packages up to his room and then wandered down to the lobby③. Behind a potted palm tree there was a slot machine. He inserted a nickel but when he tried to pull the lever he found that the machine was jammed. Over this incident he made a great to-do. He cornered the clerk and furiously④ demonstrated what had happened. His face was deathly pale and he was so beside himself that tears rolled down the ridges of his nose. He flailed his hands and even stamped once with his long, narrow, elegantly shoed foot on the plush carpet. Nor was he satisfied when his coin was refunded, but insisted on checking out immediately. He packed his bag and was obliged to work energetically⑤ to make it close again. For in addition to the articles he had brought with him he

---

① heaped：堆得满满的
② scribble：乱画；潦草地书写
③ lobby：大厅；休息室
④ furiously：猛烈地；狂暴地
⑤ energetically：积极地；精力充沛地

carried away three towels, two cakes of soap, a pen and a bottle of ink, a roll of toilet paper, and a Holy Bible. He paid his bill and walked to the railway station to put his belongings in custody①. The train did not leave until nine in the evening and he had the empty afternoon before him.

This town was smaller than the one in which he lived. The business streets intersected to form the shape of a cross. The stores had a countrified② look; there were harnesses and sacks of feed in half of the display windows. Singer walked listlessly along the sidewalks. His throat felt swollen and he wanted to swallow but was unable to do so. To relieve this strangled feeling he bought a drink in one of the drugstores. He idled in the barber shop and purchased a few trifles③ at the ten-cent store. He looked no one full in the face and his head drooped down to one side like a sick animal's.

The afternoon was almost ended when a strange thing happened to Singer. He had been walking slowly and irregularly along the curb of the street. The sky was overcast and the air humid④. Singer did not raise his head, but as he passed the town pool room he caught a sidewise glance of something that disturbed him. He passed the pool room and then stopped in the middle of the street. Listlessly he retraced⑤ his steps and stood before the open door of the place. There were three mutes inside and they were talking with their hands together. All three of them were coatless. They wore bowler hats and bright ties. Each of them held a glass of beer in his left hand. There was a certain brotherly resemblance between them.

Singer went inside. For a moment he had trouble taking his hand from his pocket. Then clumsily he formed a word of greeting. He was clapped on the shoulder. A cold drink was ordered. They surrounded

---

① in custody：被拘留；被扣押
② countrified：带乡村风味的
③ trifle：琐事；鸡毛蒜皮的事
④ humid：潮湿的，湿热的
⑤ retrace：追溯

him and the fingers of their hands shot out like pistons[①] as they questioned him.

He told his own name and the name of the town where he lived. After that he could think of nothing else to tell about himself. He asked if they knew Spiros Antonapoulos. They did not know him. Singer stood with his hands dangling[②] loose. His head was still inclined to one side and his glance was oblique. He was so listless and cold that the three mutes in the bowler hats looked at him queerly. After a while they left him out of their conversation. And when they had paid for the rounds of beers and were ready to depart they did not suggest that he join them.

Although Singer had been adrift[③] on the streets for half a day he almost missed his train. It was not clear to him how this happened or how he had spent the hours before. He reached the station two minutes before the train pulled out, and barely had time to drag his luggage aboard and find a seat. The car he chose was almost empty. When he was settled he opened the crate[④] of strawberries and picked them over with finicky[⑤] care. The berries were of a giant size, large as walnuts and in full-blown ripeness[⑥]. The green leaves at the top of the rich-colored fruit were like tiny bouquets. Singer put a berry in his mouth and though the juice had a lush, wild sweetness there was already a subtle flavor of decay. He ate until his palate was dulled by the taste and then rewrapped the crate and placed it on the rack above him. At midnight he drew the window shade and lay down on the seat. He was curled in a ball, his coat pulled over his face and head. In this position he lay in a stupor[⑦] of half-sleep for about twelve hours. The conductor had to shake him when they arrived.

---

① piston：活塞
② dangling：摇晃（dangle 的现在分词形式）
③ adrift：漫无目的的
④ crate：一箱；一箱的量
⑤ finicky：过分讲究细节的
⑥ ripeness：成熟；老练；完成
⑦ stupor：恍惚

Singer left his luggage in the middle of the station floor. Then he walked to the shop. He greeted the jeweler for whom he worked with a listless turn of his head. When he went out again there was something heavy in his pocket. For a while he rambled with bent head along the streets. But the un refracted brilliance of the sun, the humid heat①, oppressed him. He returned to his room with swollen eyes and an aching head. After resting he drank a glass of iced coffee and smoked a cigarette. Then when he had washed the ash tray and the glass he brought out a pistol from his pocket and put a bullet in his chest.②

① humid heat：湿热

② 参考译文：然后，他洗干净烟灰缸和玻璃杯，从口袋里掏出一把手枪，把一颗子弹射进了自己的胸口。本句描写辛格自杀的情景，似乎轻描淡写一笔带过，但正是“重拿轻放”的手法表现了辛格此时内心的平静，甚至心如死灰。

Part Three

1

August 21, 1939

Morning

'I WILL not be hurried,' Doctor Copeland said. 'Just let me be. Kindly allow me to sithere[1] in peace a moment.'

'Father, us not trying to rush you. But it time now to get gone from here.'

Doctor Copeland rocked stubbornly, his gray shawl drawn close around his shoulders. Although the morning was warm and fresh, a small wood fire burned in the stove. The kitchen was bare of all furniture except the chair in which he sat. The other rooms were empty, too. Most of the furniture had been moved to Portia's house, and the rest was tied to the automobile outside. All was in readiness except his own mind. But how could he leave when there was neither beginning nor end, neither truth nor purpose in his thoughts? He put up his hand to steady his trembling head and continued to rock himself slowly in the creaking chair.

Behind the closed door he heard their voices:

'I done all I can. He determined to sit there till he good and ready to leave.'

'Buddy and me done wrapped the china plates and—'

① sithere：应为"sit here"。

'Us should have left before the dew dried,' said the old man. 'As is, night liable to catch us on the road.'

Their voices quieted. Footsteps echoed in the empty hallway and he could hear them no more. On the floor beside him was a cup and saucer. He filled it with coffee from the pot on the top of the stove. As he rocked he drank the coffee and warmed his fingers in the steam. This could not truly be the end. Other voices called wordless in his heart. The voice of Jesus and of John Brown. The voice of the great Spinoza and of Karl Marx. The calling voices of all those who had fought and to whom it had been vouchsafed① to complete their missions. The grief-bound voices of his people. And also the voice of the dead. Of the mute Singer, who was a righteous② white man of understanding. The voices of the weak and of the mighty. The rolling voice of his people growing always in strength and in power. The voice of the strong, true purpose. And in answer the words trembled on his lips—the words which are surely the root of all human grief—so that he almost said aloud: 'Almighty Host! Utmost power of the universe! I have done those things which I ought not to have done and left undone those things which I ought to have done. So this cannot truly be the end.'

He had first come into the house with her whom he loved. And Daisy was dressed in her bridal gown and wore a white lace veil③. Her skin was the beautiful color of dark honey and her laughter was sweet. At night he had shut himself in the bright room to study alone. He had tried to cogitate④ and to discipline⑤ himself to study. But with Daisy near him there was a strong desire in him that would not go away with study. So sometimes he surrendered to⑥ these feelings,

---

① vouchsafe：允诺；赐予
② righteous：正义的；正直的
③ veil：面纱
④ cogitate：仔细考虑；谋划
⑤ discipline：自我控制；严格要求（自己）
⑥ surrender to：投降，屈服于

and again he bit his lips and meditated with the books throughout the night. And then there were Hamilton and Karl Marx and William and Portia. All lost. No one remained.

And Madyben and Benny Mae. And Benedine Madine and Mady Copeland. Those who carried his name. And those whom he had exhorted. But out of the thousands of them where was there one to whom he could entrust[①] the mission and then take ease?

All of his life he had known it strongly. He had known the reason for his working and was sure in his heart because he knew each day what lay ahead of him. He would go with his bag from house to house, and on all things he would talk to them and patiently explain. And then in the night he would be happy in the knowledge that the day had been a day of purpose. And even without Daisy and Hamilton and Karl Marx and William and Portia he could sit by the stove alone and take joy from this knowledge. He would drink a pot of turnip-green liquor and eat a pone[②] of cornbread. A deep feeling of satisfaction would be in him because the day was good.

There were thousands of such times of satisfaction. But what had been their meaning? Out of all the years he could think of no work of lasting value.

After a while the door to the hall was opened and Portia came in. 'I reckon I going to have to dress you like a baby,' she said. 'Here your shoes and socks. Let me take off your bedroom shoes and put them on. We got to get gone from here pretty soon.'

'Why have you done this to me?' he asked bitterly[③].

'What I done to you now?'

'You know full well that I do not want to leave. You pressed me into saying yes when I was in no fit condition to make a decision. I wish to remain where I have always been, and you know it.'

---

① entrust：委托
② pone：玉米饼
③ bitterly：苦涩地，悲痛地

'Listen to you carry on!' Portia said angrily. 'You done grumbled[①] so much that I nearly worn out. You done fumed and fussed[②] so that I right shamed for you.'

'Pshaw! Say what you will. You only come before me like a gnat. I know what I wish and will not be pestered[③] into doing that which is wrong.'

Portia took off his bedroom shoes and unrolled a pair of clean black cotton socks. 'Father, less us quit this here argument. Us have all done the best we know how. It entirely the best plan for you to go out with Grandpapa and Hamilton and Buddy. They going to take good care of you and you going to get well.'

'No, I will not,' said Doctor Copeland. 'But I would have recovered here. I know it.'

'Who you think could pay the note on this here house? How you think us could feed you? Who you think could take care you here? '

'I have always managed, and I can manage yet.'

'You just trying to be contrary.'

'Pshaw! You come before me like a gnat. And I ignore you.'

'That certainly is a nice way to talk to me while I trying to put on your shoes and socks.'

'I am sorry. Forgive me, Daughter.'

'Course you sorry,' she said. 'Course we both sorry. Us can't afford to quarrel. And besides, once we get you settled on the farm you going to like it. They got the prettiest vegetable garden I ever seen. Make my mouth slobber[④] to think about it. And chickens and two breed[⑤] sows and eighteen peach trees. You just going to be crazy about it there. I sure do wish it was me could get a chance to go.'

---

① grumble：抱怨，嘟囔
② fuss：无事自扰
③ pester：纠缠
④ slobber：流口水
⑤ breed：品种

'I wish so, too.'

'How come you so determined to grieve?'

'I just feel that I have failed,' he said.

'How you mean you done failed?'

'I do not know. Just leave me be, Daughter. Just let me sit here in peace a moment.'

'O.K. But us got to get gone from here pretty soon.'

He would be silent. He would sit quietly and rock in the chair until the sense of order was in him once more. His head trembled and his backbone ached.

'I certainly hope this,' Portia said. 'I certainly hope that when I dead and gone as many peoples grieves① for me as grieves for Mr. Singer. I sure would like to know I were going to have as sad a funeral as he had and as many peoples—'

'Hush!' said Doctor Copeland roughly. 'You talk too much.'

But truly with the death of that white man a dark sorrow had lain down in his heart. He had talked to him as to no other white man and had trusted him. And the mystery of his suicide had left him baffled② and without support. There was neither beginning nor end to this sorrow. Nor understanding. Always he would return in his thoughts to this white man who was not insolent③ or scornful④ but who was just. And how can the dead be truly dead when they still live in the souls of those who are left behind? But of all this he must not think. He must thrust it from him now.

For it was discipline he needed. During the past month the black, terrible feelings had arisen⑤ again to wrestle with his spirit. There was the hatred that for days had truly let him down into the regions of death. After the quarrel with Mr. Blount, the midnight visitor, there

---

① grieve：悲痛，哀悼
② baffled：困惑的
③ insolent：无礼的；傲慢的
④ scornful：轻蔑的
⑤ arise：出现

had been in him a murderous darkness. Yet now he could not clearly recall those issues which were the cause of their dispute. And then the different anger that came in him when he looked on the stumps of Willie's legs. The warring[①] love and hatred—love for his people and hatred for the oppressors of his people—that left him exhausted and sick in spirit[②].

'Daughter,' he said. 'Get me my watch and coat. I am going.'

He pushed himself up with the arms of the chair. The floor seemed a far way from his face and after the long time in bed his legs were very weak. For a moment he felt he would fall. He walked dizzily across the bare room and stood leaning against the side of the doorway. He coughed and took from his pocket one of the squares of paper to hold over his mouth.

'Here your coat,' Portia said. 'But it so hot outside you not going to need it.'

He walked for the last time through the empty house. The blinds were closed and in the darkened rooms there was the smell of dust. He rested against the wall of the vestibule[③] and then went outside. The morning was bright and warm. Many friends had come to say goodbye the night before and in the very early morning—but now only the family was congregated[④] on the porch. The wagon and the automobile were parked out in the street.

'Well, Benedict Mady,' the old man said. 'I reckon you ghy[⑤] be a little bit homesick these first few days. But won't be long.'

'I do not have any home. So why should I be homesick?'

Portia wet her lips nervously and said: 'He coming back whenever he get good and ready. Buddy will be glad to ride him to town in the car. Buddy just love to drive.'

---

① warring：冲突的；矛盾的
② in spirit：在精神上
③ vestibule：前厅；门廊
④ congregate：聚集
⑤ ghy：应为 gonna。

The automobile was loaded. Boxes of books were tied to the running-board[①]. The back seat was crowded with two chairs and the filing case. His office desk, legs in the air, had been fastened to the top. But although the car was weighted down the wagon was almost empty. The mule stood patiently, a brick tied to his reins[②].

'Karl Marx,' Doctor Copeland said. 'Look sharp. Go over the house and make sure that nothing is left. Bring the cup I left on the floor and my rocking-chair.'

'Less us get started. I anxious to be home by dinnertime,' Hamilton said.

At last they were ready. Highboy cranked[③] the automobile. Karl Marx sat at the wheel and Portia, Highboy, and William were crowded together on the back seat.

'Father, suppose you set on Highboy's lap. I believe you be more comfortable than scrouged up here with us and all this furniture.'

'No, it is too crowded. I would rather ride in the wagon.'

'But you not used to the wagon,' Karl Marx said. 'It going to be very bumpy and the trip liable to take all day.'

'That does not matter. I have ridden in many a wagon before this.'

'Tell Hamilton to come with us. I sure he rather ride in the automobile.'

Grandpapa had driven the wagon into town the day before. They brought with them a load of produce, peaches and cabbages and turnips[④], for Hamilton to sell in town. All except a sack of peaches had been marketed.

'Well, Benedict Mady, I see you riding home with me,' the old man said.

Doctor Copeland climbed into the back of the wagon. He was

① running-board：踏板
② rein：缰绳
③ crank：用曲柄转动（或启动）
④ turnip：红萝卜；大头菜

weary as though his bones were made of lead. His head trembled and a sudden spasm[①] of nausea[②] made him lie down flat on the rough boards.

'I right glad you coming,' Grandpapa said. 'You understand I always had deep respect for scholars. Deep respect I able to overlook and forget a good many things if a man be a scholar. I very glad to have a scholar like you in the fambly[③] again.'

The wheels of the wagon creaked. They were on the way. 'I will return soon,' Doctor Copeland said. 'After only a month or two I will return.'

'Hamilton he a right good scholar. I think he favors you some. He do all my figuring on paper for me and he read the newspapers. And Whitman I think he may be a scholar. Right now he able to read the Bible to me. And do number work. Small a child as he is. I always had a deep respect for scholars.'

The motion of the wagon jolted his back. He looked up at the branches overhead, and then when there was no shade he covered his face with a handkerchief to shield[④] his eyes from the sun. It was not possible that this could be the end. Always he had felt in him the strong, true purpose. For forty years his mission was his life and his life was his mission. And yet all remained to be done and nothing was completed.

'Yes, Benedict Mady, I right glad to have you with us again. I been waiting to ask you about this peculiar[⑤] feeling in my right foot. A queer feeling like my foot gone to sleep. I taken and rubbed it with liniment[⑥]. I hoping you will find me a good treatment.'

'I will do what I can.'

---

① spasm：痉挛；抽搐
② nausea：恶心；晕船
③ fambly：应该为 family。
④ shield：遮蔽
⑤ peculiar：特殊的
⑥ liniment：擦剂

'Yes, I glad to have you. I believe in all kinfolks sticking together—blood kin and marriage kin.[①] I believe in all us struggling along and helping each other out, and some day us will have a reward in the Beyond.'

'Pshaw!' Doctor Copeland said bitterly. 'I believe in justice now.'

'What that you say you believe in? You speak so hoarse I ain't able to hear you.'

'In justice for us. Justice for us Negroes!'

'That right.'

He felt the fire in him and he could not be still. He wanted to sit up and speak in a loud voice—yet when he tried to raise himself he could not find the strength. The words in his heart grew big and they would not be silent But the old man had ceased to listen and there was no one to hear him.

'Git[②], Lee Jackson. Git, Honey. Pick up your feets and quit this here poking[③]. Us got a long way to go.'

---

① 参考译文：我相信所有亲人都应该团结在一起——血亲和姻亲。（kinfolk：亲属，亲人；kin：亲戚，家属）

② git：此处为语气词，指骑马的"驾"，正确完整说法应为 giddap 或 giddyap。

③ poke：闲逛，磨蹭

2

Afternoon

JAKE RAN at a violent, clumsy pace. He went through Weavers Lane and then cut into a side alley, climbed a fence, and hastened onward. Nausea rose in his belly so that there was the taste of vomit[1] in his throat. A barking dog chased beside him until he stopped long enough to threaten it with a rock. His eyes were wide with horror and he held his hand clapped to his open mouth.

Christ! So this was the finish. A brawl[2]. A riot. A fight with every man for himself. Bloody heads and eyes cut with broken bottles. Christ! And the wheezy music of the flying jinny above the noise. The dropped hamburgers and cotton candy and the screaming younguns. And him in it all. Fighting blind with the dust and sun. The sharp cut of teeth against his knuckles[3]. And laughing. Christ! And the feeling that he had let loose a wild, hard rhythm in him that wouldn't stop. And then looking close into the dead black face and not knowing. Not even knowing if he had killed or not. But wait. Christ! Nobody could have stopped it.

Jake slowed and jerked his head nervously to look behind him. The alley was empty. He vomited[4] and wiped his mouth and forehead

---

① vomit：呕吐物
② brawl：喧闹
③ knuckle：压关节，指关节
④ vomit：呕吐；喷出

with the sleeve of his shirt. Afterward he rested for a minute and felt better. He had run for about eight blocks and with short cuts there was about half a mile to go. The dizziness cleared in his head so that from all the wild feelings he could remember facts. He started off again, this time at a steady jog.

Nobody could have stopped it. All through the summer he had stamped[①] them out like sudden fires. All but this one. And this fight nobody could have stopped. It seemed to blaze up out of nothing.[②] He had been working on the machinery of the swings and had stopped to get a glass of water. As he passed across the grounds he saw a white boy and a Negro walking around each other. They were both drunk. Half the crowd was drunk that afternoon, for it was Saturday and the mills had run full time that week. The heat and the sun were sickening and there was a heavy stink in the air.

He saw the two fighters close in on each other. But he knew that this was not the beginning. He had felt a big fight coming for a long time. And the funny thing was he found time to think of all this. He stood watching for about five seconds before he pushed into the crowd. In that short time he thought of many things. He thought of Singer. He thought of the sullen summer afternoons and the black, hot nights, of all the fights he had broken up and the quarrels he had hushed.[③]

Then he saw the flash of a pocketknife[④] in the sun. He shouldered through a knot of people and jumped on the back of the Negro who held the knife. The man went down with him and they were on the ground together. The smell of sweat on the Negro was mixed with the heavy dust in his lungs. Someone trampled on his legs

---

① stamp：跺（脚），重踩，重踏

② 参考译文：它好像凭空便突然熊熊燃烧起来。（blaze up：突然燃起，指火焰从看似不燃烧的状态突然燃起。）

③ 参考译文：（他想到了辛格，）想到了那些苦闷夏日午后，想到了闷热的黑色，想到了他化解的所有斗争，想到了他消除的所有争吵。本句为多个并列的排比，使用名词并列及 of 重复的说法进行表达，译文则使用中文惯用的排比。

④ pocketknife：随身小折刀

and his head was kicked. By the time he got to his feet again the fight had become general. The Negroes were fighting the white men and the white men were fighting the Negroes. He saw clearly, second by second. The white boy who had picked the fight seemed a kind of leader. He was the leader of a gang that came often to the show. They were about sixteen years old and they wore white duck trousers and fancy rayon polo shirts. The Negroes fought back as best they could. Some had razors.

He began to yell out words: Order! Help! Police! But it was like yelling at a breaking dam. There was a terrible sound in his ear—terrible because it was human and yet without words. The sound rose to a roar that deafened him. He was hit on the head. He could not see what went on around him. He saw only eyes and mouths and fists—wild eyes and half-closed eyes, wet, loose mouths and clenched ones, black fists and white. He grabbed a knife from a hand and caught an upraised fist. Then the dust and the sun blinded him and the one thought in his mind was to get out and find a telephone to call for help.

But he was caught. And without knowing when it happened he piled into the fight himself. He hit out with his fists and felt the soft squish[①] of wet mouths. He fought with his eyes shut and his head lowered. A crazy sound came out of his throat. He hit with all his strength and charged with his head like a bull. Senseless words were in his mind and he was laughing. He did not see who he hit and did not know who hit him. But he knew that the line-up[②] of the fight had changed and now each man was for himself.

Then suddenly it was finished. He tripped and fell over backward. He was knocked out so that it may have been a minute or it may have been much longer before he opened his eyes. A few drunks were still fighting but two dicks were breaking it up fast. He saw what he

---

① squish：嘎吱声

② line-up：阵容，阵式

had tripped over. He lay half on and half beside the body of a young Negro boy. With only one look he knew that he was dead. There was a cut on the side of his neck but it was hard to see how he had died in such a hurry. He knew the face but could not place it. The boy's mouth was open and his eyes were open in surprise. The ground was littered with papers and broken bottles and trampled hamburgers. The head was broken off one of the jinny horses and a booth was destroyed. He was sitting up. He saw the dicks and in a panic① he started to run. By now they must have lost his track.

There were only four more blocks ahead, and then he would be safe for sure. Fear had shortened his breath so that he was winded. He clenched his fists and lowered his head. Then suddenly he slowed and halted. He was alone in an alley near the main street. On one side was the wall of a building and he slumped② against it, panting, the corded vein in his forehead inflamed. In his confusion he had run all the way across the town to reach the room of his friend. And Singer was dead. He began to cry. He sobbed aloud, and water dripped down③ from his nose and wet his mustache.

A wall, a flight of stairs, a road ahead. The burning sun was like a heavy weight on him. He started back the way he had come. This time he walked slowly, wiping his wet face with the greasy④ sleeve of his shirt. He could not stop the trembling of his lips and he bit them until he tasted blood.

At the corner of the next block he ran into Simms. The old codger⑤ was sitting on a box with his Bible on his knees. There was a tall board fence⑥ behind him, and on it a message was written with purple chalk.

---

① in a panic：惊慌地
② slump：（价格等）掉落，骤降；重重地坐下
③ drip down：滴下
④ greasy：油腻的；含脂肪多的
⑤ codger：怪人；有怪癖的人
⑥ fence：篱笆，栅栏

He Died to Save You
Hear the Story of His Love and Grace
Every Nite 7:15 P.M.

The street was empty. Jake tried to cross over to the other sidewalk, but Simms caught him by the arm.

'Come, all ye disconsolate① and sore of heart. Lay down your sins and troubles before the blessed feet of Him who died to save you. Wherefore goest thou, Brother Blount?'

'Home to hockey,' Jake said. 'I got to hockey. Does the Saviour have anything against that?'

'Sinner! The Lord remembers all your transgressions②. The Lord has a message for you this very night.'

'Does the Lord remember that dollar I gave you last week?'

'Jesus has a message for you at seven-fifteen tonight. You be here on time to hear His Word.'

Jake licked his mustache. 'You have such a crowd every night I can't get up close enough to hear.'

'There is a place for scoffers③. Besides, I have had a sign that soon the Saviour wants me to build a house for Him. On that lot at the corner of Eighteenth Avenue and Sixth Street. A tabernacle④ large enough to hold five hundred people. Then you scoffers will see. The Lord prepareth a table before me in the presence of mine enemies; he anoint-eth⑤ my head with oil. My cup runneth—'

'I can round you up a crowd tonight,' Jake said.

'How?'

'Give me your pretty colored chalk. I promise a big crowd.'

'I've seen your signs,' Simms said. ' "Workers! America Is the

① disconsolate：郁郁不乐的；忧郁的；孤独的
② transgression：犯罪；违反
③ scoffer：嘲笑者
④ tabernacle：临时房屋；帐篷
⑤ anoint-eth：给……涂油；用油擦（-eth 为古英语过去式写法）

Richest Country in the World Yet a Third of Us Are Starving. When Will We Unite and Demand Our Share?"—all that. Your signs are radical[1]. I wouldn't let you use my chalk.'

'But I don't plan to write signs.'

Simms fingered the pages of his Bible and waited suspiciously[2].

'I'll get you a fine crowd. On the pavements at each end of the block I'll draw you some good-looking naked floozies. All in color with arrows to point the way. Sweet, plump, bare-tailed—'

'Babylonian!' the old man screamed. 'Child of Sodom! God will remember this.'

Jake crossed over to the other sidewalk and started toward the house where he lived. 'So long, Brother.'

'Sinner[3],' the old man called. 'You come back here at seven-fifteen sharp. And hear the message from Jesus that will give you faith. Be saved.'

Singer was dead. And the way he had felt when he first heard that he had killed himself was not sad—it was angry. He was before a wall. He remembered all the innermost[4] thoughts that he had told to Singer, and with his death it seemed to him that they were lost. And why had Singer wanted to end his life? Maybe he had gone insane[5]. But anyway he was dead, dead, dead. He could not be seen or touched or spoken to, and the room where they had spent so many hours had been rented to a girl who worked as a typist. He could go there no longer. He was alone. A wall, a flight of stairs, an open road.

Jake locked the door of his room behind him. He was hungry and there was nothing to eat. He was thirsty and only a few drops of warm water were left in the pitcher by the table. The bed was unmade

---

① radical：激进的
② suspiciously：怀疑地；猜疑地
③ sinner：罪人
④ innermost：内心的
⑤ insane：疯狂的

and dusty fluff had accumulated[①] on the floor. Papers were scattered all about the room, because recently he had written many short notices and distributed them through the town. Moodily he glanced at one of the papers labeled 'The T.W.O.C. Is Your Best Friend.' Some of the notices consisted of only one sentence, others were longer. There was one full-page manifesto[②] entitled 'The Affinity Between Our Democracy and Fascism.'

For a month he had worked on these papers, scribbling[③] them during working hours, typing and making carbons on the typewriter at the New York Café, distributing them by hand. He had worked day and night. But who read them? What good had any of it done? A town this size was too big for any one man. And now he was leaving.

But where would it be this time? The names of cities called to him—Memphis, Wilmington, Gastonia, New Orleans. He would go somewhere. But not out of the South. The old restlessness and hunger were in him again. It was different this time. He did not long for open space and freedom—just the reverse. He remembered what the Negro, Copeland, had said to him, 'Do not attempt to stand alone.' There were times when that was best.

Jake moved the bed across the room. On the part of the floor the bed had hidden there were a suitcase and a pile of books and dirty clothes. Impatiently he began to pack. The old Negro's face was in his mind and some of the words they had said came back to him. Copeland was crazy. He was a fanatic[④], so that it was maddening to try to reason with him. Still the terrible anger that they had felt that night had been hard to understand. Copeland knew. And those who knew were like a handful of naked soldiers before an armed battalion[⑤]. And what had they done? They had turned to quarrel with each other.

---

① accumulate：积累
② manifesto：宣言；声明
③ scribble：涂鸦
④ fanatic：狂热入迷者；狂热分子
⑤ battalion：军队，部队

Copeland was wrong—yes—he was crazy. But on some points they might be able to work together after all. If they didn't talk too much. He would go and see him. A sudden urge to hurry came in him. Maybe that would be the best thing after all. Maybe that was the sign, the hand he had so long awaited.

Without pausing to wash the grime from his face and hands he strapped his suitcase and left the room.① Outside the air was sultry and there was a foul odor in the street. Clouds had formed in the sky. The atmosphere was so still that the smoke from a mill in the district went up in a straight, unbroken line. As Jake walked the suitcase bumped awkwardly against his knees, and often he jerked his head to look behind him. Copeland lived all the way across the town, so there was need to hurry. The clouds in the sky grew steadily denser, and foretold a heavy summer rain before nightfall.

When he reached the house where Copeland lived he saw that the shutters② were drawn. He walked to the back and peered through the window at the abandoned kitchen. A hollow, desperate disappointment made his hands feel sweaty and his heart lose the rhythm of its beat. He went to the house on the left but no one was at home. There was nothing to do except to go to the Kelly house and question Portia.

He hated to be near that house again. He couldn't stand to see the hatrack in the front hall and the long flight of stairs he had climbed so many times. He walked slowly back across the town and approached by way of the alley. He went in the rear door. Portia was in the kitchen and the little boy was with her.

'No, sir, Mr. Blount,' Portia said. 'I know you were a mighty good friend of Mr. Singer and you understand what Father thought of him. But we taken Father out in the country this morning and I know in my soul I got no business telling you exactly where he is. If you

---

① 参考译文：他没来得及洗净脸上和手上的污垢，便捆好箱子出了门。（pause to do：停下来去做某事；strap：用袋子系）

② shutter：百叶窗

don't mind I rather speak out and not minch the matter[①].'

'You don't have to minch anything,' Jake said. 'But why?'

'After the time you come to see us Father were so sick us expected him to die. It taken us along time to get him able to sit up. He doing right well now. He going to get a lot stronger where he is now. But whether you understand this or not he right bitter against white peoples just now and he very easy to upset. And besides, if you don't mind speaking out, what you want with Father, anyway?'

'Nothing,' Jake said. 'Nothing you would understand.'

'Us colored peoples have feelings just like anybody else. And I stand by what I said, Mr. Blount. Father just a sick old colored man and he had enough trouble already. Us got to look after him. And he not anxious to see you—I know that.'

Out in the street again he saw that the clouds had turned a deep, angry purple. In the stagnant[②] air there was a storm smell. The vivid green of the trees along the sidewalk seemed to steal into the atmosphere so that there was a strange greenish glow over the street. All was so hushed and still that Jake paused for a moment to sniff the air and look around him. Then he grasped his suitcase under his arm and began to run toward the awnings[③] of the main street. But he was not quick enough. There was one metallic[④] crash of thunder and the air chilled suddenly. Large silver drops of rain hissed on the pavement. An avalanche of water blinded him. When he reached the New York Café his clothes clung wet and shriveled to his body and his shoes squeaked[⑤] with water.

Brannon pushed aside his newspaper and leaned his elbows on the counter. 'Now, this is really curious. I had this intuition[⑥] you would

---

① minch the matter：应该是方言英语引起的语误，正确表达为：mince the matter，意为“拐弯抹角”。(下句对话中的 minch 同为 mince。)

② stagnant：污浊的

③ awning：遮阳篷；遮雨篷

④ metallic：金属的，含金属的

⑤ squeak：发出短而尖的声音

⑥ intuition：直觉

come here just after the rain broke. I knew in my bones you were coming and that you would make it just too late.' He mashed his nose with this thumb until it was white and flat. 'And a suitcase?'

'It looks like a suitcase,' Jake said. 'And it feels like a suitcase. So if you believe in the actuality of suitcases I reckon this is one, all right.'

'You ought not to stand around like this. Go on upstairs and throw me down your clothes. Louis will run over them with a hot iron.'

Jake sat at one of the back booth tables and rested his head in his hands. 'No, thanks. I just want to rest here and get my wind again.'

'But your lips are turning blue. You look all knocked up.'

'I'm all right. What I want is some supper.'

'Supper won't be ready for half an hour,' Brannon said patiently.

'Any old leftovers will do. Just put them on a plate. You don't even have to bother to heat them.'

The emptiness in him hurt. He wanted to look neither backward nor forward. He walked two of his short, chunky[①] fingers across the top of the table. It was more than a year now since he had sat at this table for the first time. And how much further was he now than then? No further. Nothing had happened except that he had made a friend and lost him. He had given Singer everything and then the man had killed himself. So he was left out on a limb[②]. And now it was up to him to get out of it by himself and make a new start again. At the thought of it panic came in him. He was tired. He leaned his head against the wall and put his feet on the seat beside him.

'Here you are,' Brannon said. 'This ought to help out.'

He put down a glass of some hot drink and a plate of chicken pie. The drink had a sweet, heavy smell. Jake inhaled the steam and closed his eyes. 'What's in it?'

---

① chunky：矮胖的；粗短的；厚实的

② out on a limb：孤立无援，例：When a worker is put out on a limb, he is inclined to quit. 当一名员工孤立无援时，很有可能会辞职。

'Lemon rind[1] rubbed on a lump of sugar and boiling water with rum. It's a good drink.'

'How much do I owe you?'

'I don't know offhand[2], but I'll figure it out before you leave.'

Jake took a deep draught of the toddy and washed it around in his mouth before swallowing.'You'll never get the money,' he said. 'I don't have it to pay you—and if I did I probably wouldn't anyway.'

'Well, have I been pressing you? Have I ever made you out a bill and asked you to pay up?'

'No,' Jake said. 'You been very reasonable. And since I think about it you're a right decent[3] guy—from the personal perspective, that is.'

Brannon sat across from him at the table. Something was on his mind. He slid the salt-shaker[4] back and forth and kept smoothing his hair. He smelled like perfume and his striped blue shirt was very fresh and clean. The sleeves were rolled and held in place by old-fashioned blue sleeve garters.

At last he cleared his throat in a hesitating[5] way and said: 'I was glancing through the afternoon paper just before you came. It seems you had a lot of trouble at your place today.'

'That's right. What did it say?'

'Wait. I'll get it.' Brannon fetched the paper from the counter and leaned against the partition of the booth. 'It says on the front page that at the Sunny Dixie Show, located so and so, there was a general disturbance[6]. Two Negroes were fatally[7] injured with wounds inflicted by knives. Three others suffered minor wounds and were taken for treatment to the city hospital. The dead were Jimmy Macy

---

① rind：壳；外皮
② offhand：即时地，未经核实地
③ decent：正派的；得体的；相当好的
④ salt-shaker：盐瓶
⑤ hesitating：犹豫的
⑥ disturbance：干扰；骚乱
⑦ fatally：致命地

and Lancy Davis. The wounded were John Hamlin, white, of Central Mill City, Various Wilson, Negro, and so forth and so on. Quote: 'A number of arrests were made. It is alleged that the disturbance was caused by labor agitation, as papers of a subversive nature were found on and about the site of disturbance.[①] Other arrests are expected shortly.' Brannon clicked his teeth together. 'The setup of this paper gets worse every day. Subversive spelled with a *u* in the second syllable and arrests with only one *r*.'

'They're smart, all right,' Jake said sneeringly. '"Caused by labor agitation[②]." That's remarkable[③].'

'Anyway, the whole thing is very unfortunate.'

Jake held his hand to his mouth and looked down at his empty plate.

'What do you mean to do now?'

'I'm leaving. I'm getting out of here this afternoon.'

Brannon polished his nails on the palm of his hand. 'Well, of course it's not necessary—but it might be a good thing. Why so headlong? No sense in starting out this time of day.'

'I just father.'

'I do not think it behooves[④] you to make a new start. At the same time why don't you take my advice on this? Myself—I'm a conservative and of course I think your opinions are radical. But at the same time I like to know all sides of a matter. Anyway, I want to see you straighten out. So why don't you go someplace where you can meet a few people more or less like yourself? And then settle down? '

Jake pushed his plate irritably[⑤] away from him. 'I don't know where I'm going. Leave me alone. I'm tired.'

---

① 参考译文：据称，这次骚乱是由劳工煽动而起，在骚乱地点及周围发现颠覆性内容的传单。（allege：宣称；agitation：煽动，搅动；subversive：破坏性的；nature：性质，本质）

② agitation：煽动，鼓动

③ remarkable：引人注目的，非凡的（此处为反语）

④ behoove：适宜

⑤ irritably：性急地；暴躁地

Brannon shrugged his shoulders and went back to the counter.

He was tired enough. The hot rum and the heavy sound of the rain made him drowsy. It felt good to be sitting safe in a booth and to have just eaten a good meal. If he wanted to he could lean over and take a nap—a short one. Already his head felt swollen and heavy and he was more comfortable with his eyes closed. But it would have to be a short sleep because soon he must get out of here.

'How long will this rain keep on?'

Brannon's voice had drowsy[①] overtones. 'You can't tell—a tropical cloudburst. Might clear up suddenly—or—might thin a little and set in for the night.'

Jake laid his head down on his arms. The sound of the rain was nice the swelling sound of the sea. He heard a clock tick and the far-off[②] rattle of dishes. Gradually his hands relaxed. They lay open, palm upward, on the table.

Then Brannon was shaking him by the shoulders and looking into his face. A terrible dream was in his mind. 'Wake up,' Brannon was saying. 'You've had a nightmare[③]. I looked over here and your mouth was open and you were groaning and shuffling your feet on the floor. I never saw anything to equal it.'

The dream was still heavy in his mind. He felt the old terror that always came as he awakened. He pushed Brannon away and stood up. 'You don't have to tell me I had a nightmare. I remember just how it was. And I've had the same dream for about fifteen times before.'

He did remember now. Every other time he had been unable to get the dream straight in his waking mind. He had been walking among a great crowd of people—like at the show. But there was also something Eastern about the people around him. There was a terrible bright sun and the people were half-naked[④]. They were silent and

---

① drowsy：昏昏欲睡的

② far-off：遥远的

③ nightmare：噩梦

④ half-naked：半裸的

slow and their faces had a look in them of starvation.[1] There was no sound, only the sun, and the silent crowd of people. He walked among them and he carried a huge covered basket. He was taking the basket somewhere but he could not find the place to leave it. And in the dream there was a peculiar horror in wandering on and on through the crowd and not knowing where to lay down the burden he had carried in his arms so long.

'What was it?' Brannon asked. 'Was the devil chasing you?'

Jake stood up and went to the mirror behind the counter. His face was dirty and sweaty. There were dark circles beneath his eyes. He wet his handkerchief under the fountain[2] faucet[3] and wiped off his face. Then he took out a pocket comb and neatly combed his mustache.

'The dream was nothing. You got to be asleep to understand why it was such a nightmare.'

The clock pointed to five-thirty. The rain had almost stopped. Jake picked up his suitcase and went to the front door. 'So long. I'll send you a postcard maybe.'

'Wait,' Brannon said. 'You can't go now. It's still raining a little.'

'Just dripping off the awning. I rather get out of town before dark.'

'But hold on. Do you have any money? Enough to keep going for a week?'

'I don't need money. I been broke before.'

Brannon had an envelope ready and in it were two twenty-dollar bills. Jake looked at them on both sides and put them in his pocket. 'God knows why you do it. You'll never smell them again. But thanks. I won't forget.'

---

① 参考译文：他们沉默无语，行动迟缓，脸上有种饥饿的表情。本句原文 had a look of starvation 中插入了 in them。

② fountain：喷泉

③ faucet：水龙头

'Good luck. And let me hear from you.'

'Adios!'

'Good-bye.'

The door closed behind him. When he looked back at the end of the block, Brannon was watching from the sidewalk. He walked until he reached the railroad tracks. On either side there were rows of dilapidated[①] two-room houses. In the cramped back yards were rotted privies and lines of torn, smoky rags hung out to dry. For two miles there was not one sight of comfort or space or cleanliness[②]. Even the earth itself seemed filthy and abandoned. Now and then there were signs that a vegetable row had been attempted, but only a few withered collards had survived. And a few fruitless, smutty[③] fig trees[④]. Little younguns swarmed in this filth, the smaller of them stark naked. The sight of this poverty was so cruel and hopeless that Jake snarled and clenched his fists.

He reached the edge of town and turned off on a highway. Cars passed him by. His shoulders were too wide and his arms too long. He was so strong and ugly that no one wanted to take him in. But maybe a truck would stop before long. The late afternoon sun was out again. Heat made the steam rise from the wet pavement. Jake walked steadily. As soon as the town was behind a new surge of energy came to him. But was this flight or was it onslaught[⑤]? Anyway, he was going. All this to begin another time. The road ahead lay to the north and slightly to the west. But he would not go too far away. He would not leave the South. That was one clear thing. There was hope in him, and soon perhaps the outline of his journey would take form[⑥].

---

① dilapidated：荒废的，破旧的

② cleanliness：清洁

③ smutty：弄脏的

④ fig tree：无花果树

⑤ onslaught：猛攻；突击

⑥ take form：成形，例：The artist's vision began to take form as she sketched out her ideas on paper. 艺术家的构想在她纸上勾勒出自己的想法时开始成形。

3

Evening

WHAT GOOD was it? That was the question she would like to know. What the hell good was it. All the plans she had made, and the music. When all that came of it was this trap—the store, then home to sleep, and back at the store again. The clock in front of the place where Mister Singer used to work pointed to seven. And she was just getting off. Whenever there was overtime the manager always told her to stay. Because she could stand longer on her feet and work harder before giving out than any other girl.

The heavy rain had left the sky a pale, quiet blue. Dark was coming. Already the lights were turned on. Automobile horns honked[①] in the street and the newsboys hollered out the headlines in the papers. She didn't want to go home. If she went home now she would lie down on the bed and bawl[②]. That was how tired she was. But if she went into the New York Café and ate some ice cream she might feel O.K. And smoke and be by herself a little while.

The front part of the café was crowded, so she went to the very last booth. It was the small of her back and her face that got so tired. Their motto was supposed to be 'Keep on your toes and smile.' Once she was out of the store she had to frown a long time to get her face

---

① honk：按汽车喇叭
② bawl：大叫

natural again. Even her ears were tired. She took off the dangling[1] green earrings and pinched the lobes of her ears. She had bought the earrings the week before—and also a silver bangle bracelet. At first she had worked in Pots and Pans, but now they had changed her to Costume Jewelry.

'Good evening, Mick,' Mister Brannon said. He wiped the bottom of a glass of water with a napkin and set it on the table.

'I want me a chocolate sundae[2] and a nickel glass of draw beer.'

'Together?' He put down a menu and pointed with his little finger that wore a lady's gold ring. 'See—here's some nice roast chicken or some veal[3] stew[4]. Why don't you have a little supper with me?'

'No, thanks. All I want is the sundae and the beer. Both plenty cold.'

Mick raked her hair from her forehead. Her mouth was open so that her cheeks seemed hollow. There were these two things she could never believe. That Mister Singer had killed himself and was dead. And that she was grown and had to work at Woolworth's.

She was the one who found him. They had thought the noise was a backfire[5] from a car, and it was not until the next day that they knew. She went in to play the radio. The blood was all over his neck and when her Dad came he pushed her out of the room. She had run into the dark and hit herself with her fists. And then the next night he was in a coffin in the living-room. The undertaker had put rouge and lipstick on his face to make him look natural. But he didn't look natural. He was very dead. And mixed with the smell of flowers there was this other smell so that she couldn't stay in the room. But through ail those days she held down the job. She wrapped packages and

---

① dangling：悬挂的；摇摆的
② sundae：圣代冰激凌
③ veal：小牛，小牛肉
④ stew：炖煮的菜肴
⑤ backfire：逆火，回火

handed them across the counter and rung the money in the till①. She walked when she was supposed to walk and ate when she sat down to the table. Only at first when she went to bed at night she couldn't sleep. But now she slept like she was supposed to, also.

Mick turned sideways in the seat so that she could cross her legs. There was a run in her stocking. It had started while she was walking to work and she had spit on it. Then later the run had gone farther and she had stuck a little piece of chewing-gum on the end. But even that didn't help. Now she would have to go home and sew. It was hard to know what she could do about stockings. She wore them out so fast. Unless she was the kind of common girl that would wear cotton stockings.

She oughtn't to have come in here. The bottoms of her shoes were clean worn out. She ought to have saved the twenty cents toward a new half-sole②. Because if she kept on standing on a shoe with a hole in it what would happen? A blister③ would come on her foot. And she would have to pick it with a burnt needle. She would have to stay home from work and be fired. And then what would happen?

'Here you are,' said Mister Brannon. 'But I never heard of such a combination④ before.'

He put the sundae and the beer on the table. She pretended to clean her fingernails because if she noticed him he would start talking. He didn't have this grudge⑤ against her anymore, so he must have forgotten about the pack of gum. Now he always wanted to talk to her. But she wanted to be quiet and by herself. The sundae was O.K., covered all over with chocolate and nuts and cherries. And the beer was relaxing. The beer had a nice bitter taste after the ice cream and it

---

① till：（现金出纳机的）放钱的抽屉
② half-sole：（鞋底的）前掌
③ blister：水泡
④ combination：结合；组合；联合
⑤ grudge：怨恨，嫌隙

made her drunk. Next to music beer was best.

But now no music was in her mind. That was a funny thing. It was like she was shut out from the inside room. Sometimes a quick little tune would come and go—but she never went into the inside room with music like she used to do. It was like she was too tense. Or maybe because it was like the store took all her energy and time. Woolworth's wasn't the same as school. When she used to come home from school she felt good and was ready to start working on the music. But now she was always tired. At home she just ate supper and slept and then ate breakfast and went off to the store again. A song she had started in her private notebook two months before was still not finished. And she wanted to stay in the inside room but she didn't know how. It was like the inside room was locked somewhere away from her. A very hard thing to understand.

Mick pushed her broken front tooth with her thumb. But she did have Mister Singer's radio. All the installments hadn't been paid and she took on the responsibility. It was good to have something that had belonged to him. And maybe one of these days she might be able to set aside[①] a little for a second-hand piano. Say two bucks a week. And she wouldn't let anybody touch this private piano but her—only she might teach George little pieces. She would keep it in the back room and play on it every night. And all day Sunday. But then suppose some week she couldn't make a payment[②]. So then would they come to take it away like the little red bicycle? And suppose like she wouldn't let them. Suppose she hid the piano under the house. Or else she would meet them at the front door. And fight. She would knock down[③] both the two men so they would have shiners[④] and broke noses and would be passed out on the hall floor.

Mick frowned and rubbed her fist hard across her forehead. That

---

① set aside：省出，抽出（时间或金钱）
② payment：付款，支付
③ knock down：击倒；拆卸
④ shiner：黑眼圈

was the way things were. It was like she was mad all the time. Not how a kid gets mad quick so that soon it is all over—but in another way.[1] Only there was nothing to be mad at. Unless the store. But the store hadn't asked her to take the job. So there was nothing to be mad at. It was like she was cheated. Only nobody had cheated her. So there was nobody to take it out on. However, just the same she had that feeling. Cheated.

But maybe it would be true about the piano and turn out[2] O.K. Maybe she would get a chance soon. Else what the hell good had it all been—the way she felt about music and the plans she had made in the inside room? It had to be some good if anything made sense. And it was too and it was too and it was too and it was too. It was some good.

All right!

O.K!

Some good.

---

① 参考译文：不是像孩子那样无端地生气然后又很快忘记——而是另外一种样子。

② turn out：最后是，结果是

4

Night

ALL WAS serene[①]. As Biff dried his face and hands a breeze tinkled[②] the glass pendants[③] of the little Japanese pagoda[④] on the table. He had just awakened from a nap and had smoked his night cigar. He thought of Blount and wondered if by now he had traveled far. A bottle of AguaFlorida was on the bathroom shelf and he touched the stopper to his temples. He whistled an old song, and as he descended[⑤] the narrow stairs the tune left a broken echo behind him.

Louis was supposed to be on duty behind the counter. But he had soldiered on the job and the place was deserted. The front door stood open to the empty street. The clock on the wall pointed to seventeen minutes before midnight. The radio was on and there was talk about the crisis[⑥] Hitler had cooked up over Danzig. He went back to the kitchen and found Louis asleep in a chair. The boy had taken off his shoes and unbuttoned his trousers. His head drooped on his chest. A long wet spot on his shirt showed that he had been sleeping a good while. His arms hung straight down at his sides and the wonder was

---

① serene：安详的；清澈的
② tinkle：发叮当（或清脆）声
③ pendant：悬挂物
④ pagoda：（南亚或东亚的）佛塔
⑤ descend：向下
⑥ crisis：危机

that he did not fall forward on his face. He slept soundly and there was no use to wake him. The night would be a quiet one.

Biff tiptoed[①] across the kitchen to a shelf which held a basket of tea olive and two water pitchers full of zinnias[②]. He carried the flowers up to the front of the restaurant and removed the cellophane-wrapped platters of the last special from the display window. He was sick of food. A window of fresh summer flowers—that would be good. His eyes were closed as he imagined how it could be arranged. A foundation of the tea olive strewn over the bottom, cool and green. The red pottery[③] tub filled with the brilliant zinnias. Nothing more. He began to arrange the window carefully. Among the flowers there was a freak plant, a zinnia with six bronze petals and two red. He examined this curio and laid it aside to save. Then the window was finished and he stood in the street to regard his handiwork[④]. The awkward stems of the flowers had been bent to just the right degree of restful looseness. The electric lights detracted[⑤], but when the sun rose the display would show at its best advantage. Downright artistic.

The black, starlit sky seemed close to the earth. He strolled along the sidewalk, pausing once to knock an orange peel into the gutter with the side of his foot. At the far end of the next block two men, small from the distance and motionless, stood arm in arm together. No one else could be seen. His place was the only store on all the street with an open door and lights inside.

And why? What was the reason for keeping the place open all through the night when every other café in the town was closed? He was often asked that question and could never speak the answer out in words. Not money. Sometimes a party would come for beer and scrambled eggs and spend five or ten dollars. But that was rare. Mostly

---

① tiptoe：踮着脚走，蹑手蹑脚地走
② zinnia：百日草属植物；百日菊
③ pottery：陶器
④ handiwork：手工艺
⑤ detract：贬低；减去，此处指降低了效果。

they came one at a time and ordered little and stayed long. And on some nights, between the hours of twelve and five o'clock, not a customer would enter. There was no profit in it—that was plain.

But he would never close up for the night—not as long as he stayed in the business. Night was the time. There were those he would never have seen otherwise. A few came regularly several times a week. Others had come into the place only once, had drunk a Coca-Cola, and never returned.

Biff folded his arms across his chest and walked more slowly. Inside the arc of the street light his shadow showed angular and black. The peaceful silence of the night settled in him. These were the hours for rest and meditation①. Maybe that was why he stayed downstairs and did not sleep. With a last quick glance he scanned the empty street and went inside.

The crisis voice still talked on the radio. The fans on the ceiling made a soothing whirl. From the kitchen came the sound of Louis snoring. He thought suddenly of poor Willie and decided to send him a quart of whiskey sometime soon. He turned to the crossword puzzle in the newspaper. There was a picture of a woman to identify in the center. He recognized her and wrote the name—Mona Lisa—across the first spaces. Number one down was a word for beggar, beginning with *m* and nine letters long. Mendicant②. Two horizontal was some word meaning to remove afar off. A six- letter word beginning with *e*. Elapse? He sounded trial③ combinations of letters④ aloud. Eloign. But he had lost interest There were puzzles enough without this kind. He folded and put away the paper. He would come back to it later.

He examined the zinnia he had intended to save. As he held it in the palm of his hand to the light the flower was not such a curious

---

① meditation：冥想；沉思

② mendicant：乞丐

③ trial：试验的

④ combinations of letters：字母组合

specimen[1] after all. Not worth saving. He plucked the soft, bright petals and the last one came out on love. But who? Who would he be loving now? No one person. Anybody decent who came in out of the street to sit for an hour and have a drink. But no one person. He had known his loves and they were over. Alice, Madeline and Gyp. Finished. Leaving him either better or worse. Which? However you looked at it.

And Mick. The one who in the last months had lived so strangely in his heart. Was that love done with too? Yes. It was finished. Early in the evenings Mick came in for a cold drink or a sundae. She had grown older. Her rough and childish ways were almost gone. And instead there was something ladylike and delicate about her that was hard to point out. The earrings, the dangle of her bracelets[2], and the new way she crossed her legs and pulled the hem of her skirt down past her knees. He watched her and felt only a sort of gentleness. In him the old feeling was gone. For a year this love had blossomed strangely. He had questioned it a hundred times and found no answer. And now, as a summer flower shatters in September, it was finished. There was no one.

Biff tapped[3] his nose with his forefinger. A foreign voice was now speaking over the radio. He could not decide for certain whether the voice was German, French, or Spanish. But it sounded like doom. It gave him the jitters to listen to it. When he turned it off the silence was deep and unbroken. He felt the night outside. Loneliness gripped[4] him so that his breath quickened. It was far too late to call Lucile on the telephone and speak to Baby. Nor could he expect a customer to enter at this hour. He went to the door and looked up and down the street. All was empty and dark.

'Louis!' he called. 'Are you awake, Louis?'

---

① specimen：样品，标本
② bracelet：手镯；手链
③ tap：轻敲
④ grip：对……产生强有力的影响

No answer. He put his elbows on the counter and held his head in his hands. He moved his dark bearded jaw from side to side and slowly his forehead lowered in a frown.

The riddle. The question that had taken root in him and would not let him rest. The puzzle of Singer and the rest of them. More than a year had gone by since it had started. More than a year since Blount had hung around the place on his first long drunk and seen the mute for the first time. Since Mick had begun to follow him in and out. And now for a month Singer had been dead and buried. And the riddle was still in him, so that he could not be tranquil. There was something not natural about it all—something like an ugly joke. When he thought of it he felt uneasy and in some unknown way afraid.

He had managed about the funeral. They had left all that to him. Singer's affairs were in a mess. There were installments due on everything he owned and the beneficiary of his life insurance was deceased.[1] There was just enough to bury him. The funeral was at noon. The sun burned down on them with savage heat as they stood around the open dank grave. The flowers curled and turned brown in the sun. Mick cried so hard that she choked herself and her father had to beat her on the back. Blount scowled down at the grave with his fist to his mouth. The town's Negro doctor, who was somehow related to poor Willie, stood on the edge of the crowd and moaned to himself. And there were strangers nobody had ever seen or heard of before. God knows where they came from or why they were there.

The silence in the room was deep as the night itself. Biff stood transfixed[2], lost in his meditations. Then suddenly he felt a quickening in him. His heart turned and he leaned his back against the counter for support. For in a swift radiance of illumination[3] he saw a glimpse of

① 参考译文：他所有的东西都有分期付款到期，而其人寿险的受益人已经过世。（due：到期的；beneficiary：受益人，受惠者）

② transfixed：（因吃惊、害怕、入迷等而）不能动弹的，惊呆的

③ illumination：光亮，照明；启迪，阐明

human struggle and of valor[①]. Of the endless fluid passage of humanity through endless time. And of those who labor and of those who—one word—love. His soul expanded[②]. But for a moment only. For in him he felt a warning, a shaft of terror. Between the two worlds he was suspended. He saw that he was looking at his own face in the counter glass before him. Sweat glistened on his temples and his face was contorted. One eye was opened wider than the other. The left eye delved narrowly into the past while the right gazed wide and affrighted into a future of blackness, error, and ruin.[③] And he was suspended between radiance and darkness. Between bitter irony and faith. Sharply he turned away.

'Louis!' he called. 'Louis! Louis!'

Again there was no answer. But, motherogod, was he a sensible man or was he not? And how could this terror throttle him nice this when he didn't even know what caused it? And would he just stand here like a jittery ninny or would he pull himself together and be reasonable? For after all was he a sensible man or was he not? Biff wet his handkerchief beneath the water tap and patted[④] his drawn, tense face. Somehow he remembered that the awning had not yet been raised. As he went to the door his walk gained steadiness. And when at last he was inside again he composed himself[⑤] soberly to await the morning sun.

---

① valor：英勇

② expand：扩大，增加；扩展

③ 参考译文：左眼眯着，深深地看着过去；而右眼圆睁，惊恐地凝视着黑暗、错误、毁灭的未来。本句是对比夫的升华，也是对辛格死后给人们带来的心理上影响的形象描述。（delve：钻研；探究）

④ pat：轻拍

⑤ compose oneself：使自己平静下来，控制自己的情绪或行为